THIS EMBODIED LIFE

A Three-Dimensional Holographic Virtual-Reality Game

Domonic Kay

This Embodied Life

A Three-Dimensional Holographic Virtual-Reality Game

Domonic Kay

ISBN-13: 978-0692850077
ISBN-10: 0692850074

Dedication

This book is dedicated to my beloved Masters—Param Sant Thakar Singh and his successor, Sant Baljit Singh. Through their immeasurable love, mercy and grace I was guided to the Path of the Masters also known as the Science of the Soul and connected with the inner Sound Current, the Audible Life Stream.

Contents

Introduction

THIS BOOK HAS been woven together with the intent and desire to awaken in you, the readers, a quickening, an expanding awareness and desire to aspire to cosmic consciousness and the ability to perceive the multiverse in all of its seemingly disparate parts as a unified whole bound together by love.

It is my fervent wish that you might come out on the other side of this reading aware of the contours of a deeper reality behind the multilayered kaleidoscope that appears as the world. May you begin a meditation practice so you can develop (if you haven't already done so) the ability to see through the inner spiritual eye and come to understand through a love-filled heart that we are all here on a sacred Soul journey. You are courageous ones indeed, for daring to venture into this holo-gram knowing you would be blinded, bound and squeezed in time's tight embrace for the duration of this embodied life.

In the nine years it has taken me to research and write this book, deep esoteric truths have seeped inward, settling and growing in the in-ner matrix of my being like osteoblasts forming the matrix of my bones. The life experiences I've had and the concepts developed form an inner scaffolding upon which I stand. From birth, I've led a bifurcated life of subtle inner Soul growth and expanding spiritual awareness paralleling an outer, egoically confined roller-coaster life of perpetual ups and downs.

The singular, most-defining event in my life described in Part II was my face-to-face inner meeting with a Living Master. This connection and the unerring inner guidance I've received have helped in the expan-sion of my consciousness beyond the limitations of the ego/mind and this matter-based world. The Saints and Masters continually refer to this world as "unreal," the ego as the "not self" and the world as an illusion, a holographic reflective "hall of mirrors." Following years of meditation practice as taught by the Sant Mat Masters, I've been able to establish within myself an experiential reference point verifying for me that the state of non-dual, transcendent, pure conscious awareness known as "sat-truth, chit-knowledge, ananda-bliss" is indeed real, does exist and is the Soul's true and eternal nature.

The premise upon which the book is based is that we, the humanoid species, have been unknowingly imprisoned within a multidimensional holographic virtual-reality world. A world intentionally, masterfully designed and constructed as a massive optical illusion, a delusion of consciousness, operative since this space/time matrix was created and set in motion. I further propose that the genetically designed "bio-suits" we wear have captured and confused our Souls into accepting this illusory, temporal thought-form-constructed world as an objective reality. Some of you reading this will recoil in disbelief at such an outlandish idea. That's perfectly okay and natural as I myself went through the very same disbelief and denial process during the writing of this book.

Part I explains three domains or ways of knowing, the linear domain being dualistic and polarized, locking the mind into limited, polarized views of our projected holographic reality. Humanity's collectively projected thought forms are enfolded into the morphogenetic information field, perpetuating our three-dimensional mind/brain-constructed hologram: the so-called objective world. Earth's entire world history is but a repeating time loop, and all the conceptualized beliefs about objective reality to which we so desperately cling are just illusive thought-form projections.

Part II encompasses my own life story, an account of events that generated the pressures necessary to launch me into a deep search for Truth. Each of us receives inspiration along infinite routes, and it's in the spirit of openness, especially about difficult moments as well as beautiful ones, and ultimately the extraordinary encounters with the Living Masters, that I share my journey.

In Part III, you'll be exposed to a number of belief systems embedded within twelve different worldviews—creation stories and the cultural structures that were engendered by them. The core beliefs underlying each worldview are teased out to reveal the underpinnings, the embedded beliefs in each of the creation stories. The intent in Part III is to facilitate and encourage an opening into new corridors of conscious understanding and awareness. To accomplish this probably impossible task, I'm sure you've heard the expression "Fools rush in where angels fear to tread." Well, I'm foolishly (or courageously, depending on your point of view) jumping in here with both feet, treading on humanity's sacred cows—their religious beliefs. As the philosopher Neil Kramer once said, "Truth destroys the world you used to live in." May it be so since the one we're currently living in is an insane asylum.

The chosen twelve creation stories have been retold in condensed form. Some of them make either veiled references or direct statements asserting that our naturally evolving humanoid species on Earth was "deviated via genetic engineering and cloning" by groups of techno-logically advanced intergalactic colonizers billions of years ago. Recent genetic research is proving this to be the case. There is also ample evidence supporting the conclusion that all the world's religions and their accompanying belief systems were intentionally designed mental constructs used to program humanity to be obedient to theistic authority figures. This result is understood in some scientific circles to have been partially accomplished by genetically altering the subconscious and unconscious layers of the brain/mind interface to make humanity easier to control and manipulate.

The stories have been presented in the order of their complexity, moving from the least complex to the more expansive, detailed and complex worldviews. Each story gives varying explanations as to how this multiverse was created, by whom and for what purpose. No definitive timelines were included simply because there are so many different worldviews of when things happened, depending on who is telling which story and whether the storyteller's perspective is being measured within Earth's three-dimensional space/time hologram—or beyond, where time doesn't exist as we perceive it. In fact time as we perceive it has no meaning or value in the higher dimensions where all information is perceived in the ever-present moment of "now." These two different experiential/perceptual dimensions—within time and outside it—will be in continual interplay throughout the book.

Part IV is written from a perspective inside time, inside the space/time hologram. The first chapter describes how this three-dimensional hologram is constructed to create the space/time illusion and how it is projected from the mind/brain bio-suit. The second chapter explains how human consciousness, from this perspective, is continually manipulated by hyperdimensional beings who move interdimensionally—between this three-dimensional world and the higher inner dimensions, unbeknownst to us and unseen by us.

Part V describes a basic plan for transcending the ego/mind by awakening the Soul essence to its higher-dimensional light or energy body through a meditative practice. The task is to go within, open the inner eye of spirit, so that we can begin to remember, to connect with the Soul Self and become conscious co-creators. As we learn to stand collectively together in cooperative unity consciousness, engaging in this two-fold outer/inner process, we'll succeed in dismantling this holographic, virtual-reality control game from the inside.

The Living Masters, Saints and Avatars, who come in every age to aid and guide humanity, embody their teachings as living, walking examples of love, compassion and the oneness of humanity. Their teachings are ever present as a universal map and guidebook for the way inward to Self-realization and ultimately to God-realization. I've attempted to distill their teachings and weave them throughout the book to provide a comparison of their teachings with the historical religions of the world—Earth's ancient mythologies and theologies—and yes, some of the so-called "fringe" concepts floating about in the world today. The Masters' books can by no means alone convey or embody the true essence of their teachings, as this level of Truth cannot be taught, verbalized or conveyed through any book or any mental thinking process. Such Truth can only be transmitted directly Soul to Soul, Essence to Essence while in the physical presence of a Living Master, a God-realized Soul, via the radiation of their Essence, their life force—called by Christians the bread and water of life or the Word, and, by the Living Masters, the Celestial Sound Current, Shabd, or Naam.

This book expresses my particular perspective gleaned from my unique life experiences and the inner and outer tutelage of two Living Masters. I am by no means a scholar, a scientist or a mystic. I've just had a lifelong burning desire to know Truth wherever it may be found. I've made analyses, comparisons and evaluations, and I've drawn conclusions about what I believe to be the ultimate purpose of this embodied life. It will be up to each of you to use your own discernment to decide which concepts resonate as Truth and which don't.

Each and every perspective has value along the way, for I would not be where I am today had it not been for those who have preceded me—questioning, studying, challenging, doubting, seeking, searching, writing, blogging, talking, telling, sharing and publishing what they've discovered by bringing their unique perspectives and their slice of truth to the plurific table of life. I honor each and every individual's efforts and appreciate their unique contributions to the collectively expanding knowledge base of humanity, as I hope you will mine. In some cases, you'll see that I've adopted some of the novel vocabulary they developed, new words that reflect inner understandings that haven't yet reached the mainstream vernacular. I hope you'll join me in appreciating these words that take us beyond the usual definitions.

The challenge in reading this book is that you will need to step away from your cherished beliefs and revered points of view long enough to be able to try on other possibilities and seemingly odd, foreign, far-fetched or outright unbelievable points of view. I propose that, contrary to popular belief, for example, we don't live in a singularly objective reality, living a single life, in one body with one singular male god deciding who goes to one heaven or to one hell. This is a quite limiting worldview. Many of us are maturing spiritually and waking up due to the exponential expansion of our collective consciousness and the activation of our dormant DNA strands, allowing for more inclusive, loving and empowering perspectives. Life is amazingly complex. So much so that it is truly beyond our capacity to understand intellectually through the mind/brain. Life is actually teeming with infinite possibilities and probability trajectories playing out simultaneously in multiple parallel realities in multiple dimensions in an infinity of ever-expanding galaxies—inhabited by a plethora of intelligent, sentient beings in every moment of Now.

It's up to each of us to choose our pathway forward, even while "flying blind," locked into this bio-suit, being challenged, churned and spurned at every turn. It has been my experience that whenever one has a sincere desire to know Truth, answers will be provided. The sincere Soul is always guided and shown the way to Truth in incremental stages. If we develop the inner "ears to hear" and the inner "eye to see," only then can we develop the capacity to discern truth from falsehood. This endeavor is actually beyond the capacity of the ego/mind but within the easy purview of the eternal Soul who perceives through the eye of spirit. The Soul already knows the Truth but this knowledge has been blocked from conscious awareness temporarily till we evolve in awareness and begin to see, to know, and to yearn for a return to the higher dimensions from whence we devolved.

Please take the time to read, ponder and explore the concepts and thought-form ideas presented, even if for just a short time. Give yourself permission to compare and contrast the ideas, concepts, theories and conclusions presented. Even though some of them may be beyond your current capacity or inclination to wrap your head around, please allow yourselves to play with them as an exercise in imaginative, non-judgmental, playful possibilities.

I do believe that if you weren't questioning your beliefs and seeking answers to life's dilemmas and conundrums, you wouldn't be reading this book in the first place. So please enter this reading adventure with an open, flexible mind and most of all with an open heart honoring the complexities of this embodied life. All things are possible through the heart, which the mind thinks too difficult. For as Rumi said, "The soul has been given its own ears to hear the things the mind does not understand.... The work of love is to create a window in the heart." So this book is my offering to you, dear readers, my labor of love.

Domonic Kay
Sedona, Arizona

Reference Keys: Rumi (web-a).

PART I

Beliefs, Contexts and Domains of Knowing

How Do We Know What We Know?

That Depends on How You Know!

One who has true intelligence channeled through the faculty of the higher mind has a keen ability to know the difference between the real and the unreal.

Tiara Kumara

Introduction to Part I

HAVING HAD MANY powerful spiritual experiences off and on throughout my life, I'm well aware that, even after having had such extraordinary experiences of being out-of-body, out-of-mind, in timeless blissful states of pure consciousness, I must confess I'm still unable to consistently live in the eternal present moment of Now. Nor am I able to consistently live as a loving, compassionate, inclusive spiritual being in this three-dimensional hologram of deception. I have to work at it daily. Often I fail and all too frequently, the distractions and demands of life sidetrack me and deter me from stepping out of time, out of mind, through meditation, into these non-temporal, non-spatial realms within: the subtle and transcendent domains.

This is the work of a meditation practice: to cultivate in the nonlinear domains a stable, enduring and clear presence—a link or inner connection to the higher or True Self. The interim goal is to achieve Self-realization, then unity consciousness by merging with the Oversoul, and ultimately God-realization by merging with Source—the Supreme Creator.

This journey can be framed through three different modes or methods of knowing, as addressed in Part I: the linear mode, the nonlinear mode, and the transcendent mode.

Identifying domains of knowing can help us begin to perceive the difference between the lower ego/mind, the higher self, and the transcendent Self—the Soul—which operates beyond the mind and perceives by direct conscious awareness. This process offers a conceptual understanding of just how our core beliefs are unconsciously formed, adhered to and maintained through our holographically constructed societal structures (paradigms).

Thus, it's important to understand what beliefs are, and what "paradigm blindness" is. Our beliefs create powerful albeit unconscious limits to our individual and collective embodied experience. What exactly is a belief? It's a statement, opinion or conviction accepted to be true; a state or habit of mind in which trust or confidence is placed in some person, thing, concept or ideal. What about the definition of a delusion? It's a fixed belief that is resistant to change by reason, logic or confrontation with actual verifiable facts. You could call it a "delusion of consciousness." In this context, we're all delusional, living, as it were, inside a hologram, believing it to be real. Sometimes a person will hold such a strongly fixed core belief, that even when presented with evidence to the contrary, they will deny the evidence because they are so attached to the belief, it has become part of their personal ego identity.

So it follows that a statement of "truth" made by one person, holding one particular set of core beliefs within a linear point of view, could be perceived to be totally false by another person holding a different set of core beliefs from their linear point of view. From the linear left-brain perspective it could be said that all statements of "truth" in the linear domain of content are actually only partial or interim truths. The nonlinear or right-brain perceptual domain is more inclusive as it encompasses more information and has a broader, higher or more-expansive perspective that can hold two or more opposing or complementary linear concepts or points of view in consciousness without judging any point of view as an absolute statement of truth or falsehood.

All concepts in the linear domain are relative or in juxtaposition to one another, collected into "paradigms." A paradigm is a set of beliefs that preselects a limited range of possible responses to situations encountered in daily life. In other words, we experience that which we believe to be true, that which is already held in the subconscious and unconscious mind. In some sense it could be considered to be a form of self-fulfilling prophecy.

What if everything you thought you knew about your life and your personal worldview up to this point in time was not necessarily true? In general, we don't voluntarily examine our beliefs. More often than not, we spend an inordinate amount of time fiercely defending them sometimes even unto death. However, life in this hologram has a way of bringing us experiences that challenge, disrupt or totally upend our long-held but unexamined beliefs. These experiences force us to pause, re-evaluate and revise our beliefs and our accompanying behaviors based on new information brought to us by unfamiliar or odd events, unusual circumstances, even traumas and tragedies.

For clarity of comparison, I'll note again the difference between the paradigmatic world and the transcendent: in the highest transcendent domains of pure conscious awareness there are no conceptualizations, no desires, no mental thought projections; there is only perfect stillness and perfect awareness in the infinite eternal present moment of NOW.

In Part I, understanding the modes of knowing conceptually as three distinct levels of consciousness provides the groundwork for deconstructing the chosen creation stories in Part III. Each ontological construct identifies the underlying paradigm sets and the interlocking core beliefs of each worldview. This way, we can begin to understand how each paradigm and accompanying belief set confines our individual and collective lives.

What is an ontological construct? It is a point of view or a theory about the organization of the universe and about the nature of being or existence. Humanity actually enacts or lives through whichever ontological construct or creation story it believes. We all do this both collectively and individually but mostly unconsciously and automatically. These constructed concepts can be divided into religious, racial, national, political, educational, artistic, environmental, relational, familial and spiritual scripts or schemas which structure and limit our life experiences.

Based on whichever specific belief sets we hold, we then experience the consequences of holding those specific beliefs. We just swim in them like fish swimming in water. We make meaning of our lives and experiences through these paradigm sets, which are powerful conveyors of ideas, values and moral imperatives upon which have been built the world's civilizations, its religions, cultural institutions, governmental and military structures, morals, ethics and laws. These are rendered even more powerful because the beliefs encoded within each of the creation-story paradigms, imprinted in childhood, are rarely, if ever, held up to scrutiny unless we encounter a life experience that challenges our beliefs. Then we either choose to expand our consciousness to include a larger more expansive and inclusive world view or paradigm—or we may instead disbelieve, block, negate and demean experiences that don't fit with our current beliefs, thereby generating psychological denial and "paradigm blindness."

As Boris Mouravieff wrote in *Gnosis* Vol I:

> In Western civilization the interior life of the individual, with all its richness, finds itself relegated to a minor role in existence. Man is so caught up in the toils of mechanical life that he has neither time to stop or the power of attention needed to turn his mental vision upon himself. Man thus passes his days absorbed by external circumstances. The great machine that drags him along turns without stopping, and forbids him to stop under penalty of being crushed. Today like yesterday, and tomorrow like today, he quickly exhausts himself in the frantic race, impelled in a direction which in the end leads nowhere. Life passes away from him almost unseen, swift as a ray of light, and man falls engulfed and still absent from himself. (p. 15)

―――――――

Reference Keys: Kumara (2016). Mouravieff (2014).

Chapter One

The Linear Domain of Beliefs
(What You See Is What You Get)

I'VE PAINSTAKINGLY GATHERED quotes from various authors to help explain and conceptualize the ego/mind as a "constructed self," a "false self" and a "foreign installation." I invite you to seriously examine how our many core beliefs are formed and how desperately the ego/mind clings to them for a sense of certainty and safety.

Most of our beliefs are definitely false, unreal, and actually serve to block the embodied Soul, individually and collectively, from evolving into the nonlinear domains and ultimately into the transcendent realms.

Werner Erhard, the founder and designer of the est training (Erhard Seminar Trainings) said that knowing the anatomy of the mind and how it is constructed was a core aspect of the training. The following paragraph, excerpted from *The Book of est* by Luke Rhinehart, gives an apt description of the mind:

> The mind is a linear arrangement of multisensory total records of successive moments of now. Its purpose, its design function, is survival: the survival of the being and anything which the being considers itself to be. When the being identifies itself with the mind, we call this state of affairs the ego, and it means that the mind's purpose becomes the survival of the mind itself. For the mind to

survive, it tries to keep itself intact, it seeks agreement and tries to avoid disagreement. It wants to dominate and avoid domination. It wants to justify its points of view, conclusions, decisions and avoid invalidation. It wants to be right. (p. 174)

According to Michael Talbot in *The Holographic Universe*, our so-called objective reality, our everyday mundane world of experience, doesn't exist in the way we believe it exists. What is real is an infinite resonating symphonic flow of light and sound waves creating varying frequencies that form the various dimensions or planes of existence in the multiverse.

From the linear perspective, this holographic world we are living within, due to its many information technologies both on- and off-planet, acts in opposition to the humanoid species' desire to solve the pressing problems of its origins and the purpose of its physical existence: our governments operate within a self-serving, power-based, systemic interlocking set of belief structures that control and maintain this negative, low-frequency hologram. This holographic world is truly a chaotic, confused, and broken Humpty Dumpty world that represents the negative pole of creation. Humanity cannot be restored to wholeness and unity consciousness through the ego/mind/intellect because the ego/mind/intellect IS the instrument of our imprisonment. This hologram of duality/polarity entraps us through the thought projections of the bicameral or split brain/mind with its faulty linear logic and the perception of opposites. This polarity is achieved through the body's sensory neuronal system, which generates emotions, expressed through language as polarized concepts (core beliefs) and feelings—creating a limited, confined and conflictual level of conscious awareness.

The ego/mind, the transient personality self that we believe to be real, grows and develops through the embodied life of each individual in each lifetime, as referenced in many of the creation stories in Part III. In Part III, you'll see descriptions of the mind as the "agent of Kal," mind as the "false self" described by the Saints and Masters, as the "foreign installation" described by Don Juan Matus to his student Carlos Castaneda, and as the "phantom self" described by David Icke. This self-referencing, conditioned ego/personality believes the stories it constructs about itself, about who and what it believes itself to be, based solely upon its personal life experiences, thanks to the binary splintering of the originally whole brain into two hemispheres that perceive in oppositional modes of either/or constructs, creating confusion and misperception. This is an existential trap, a tangled hierarchy. It is pervasive, subtle and enduring until we learn how to transcend this limiting three-dimensional holographic construction of the mind.

As Amit Goswami states in *The Self-Aware Universe: How Consciousness Creates the Material World*:

> A tangled hierarchy is a self-referential system which creates a ... holographic delusion. The ego/mind moves to and fro in a ... dualistic oscillation that holds the attention of the observer to itself and the objects and events of its creation. (p. 186)

In this to and fro, the ego/mind's serial perception "analyzes," which means to break down or separate out. The left brain reasons using logical analysis through language in a linear mode. It functions on the false belief that it is separate from that which it perceives. Believing itself to be separate from the world "out there," the mind perceives all objects and all other beings through the lens of the pairs of opposites, creating the illusion of separation, judgment and comparison. This is due to the brain's bicameral structure, which produces perceptual patterns of similarities or differences. The ego/mind cannot know wholeness or oneness except as a mental concept. Ego/mind can never know the One True Reality described in Chapter Three.

Dr. David Hawkins, in his audio lecture series *Transcending the Mind*, comments, "Our gift at each birth is the body/mind/intellect which locks us into the worst kind of slavery." Meaning the Soul has been enslaved within a system of life, death, rebirth (the reincarnational cycle) and has been given an indefinite prison sentence within this deceptive hologram of space/time. Adding to the burden, beyond the individual mind exists the collective or universal mind, a quantum energetic mind-field that records and maintains humanity's collective abstract thoughts and ideals in this field, which subordinates each individual mind to these vast unconsciously shared, conceptualized thought forms.

To put the linear consciousness into a developmental context—for an expanding comprehension—it would be helpful to engage in the process of evolving beyond this elementary evolutionary status. As an individual moves up the scale of consciousness from lifetime to lifetime, the thoughts, feelings, emotions, actions, beliefs and values of the individual evolve ever so slowly through the accumulated actions and choices made during each lifetime. Gradually moving up the scale of consciousness, the individual evolves to ever-larger, more-inclusive, altruistic, abstract ideals, more-compassionate behaviors and actions that reorder the meaning, significance, and purpose of individual lifetimes. This is a grindingly slow evolutionary process whereby we gradually make progress and awaken. Using Ken Wilber's terminology (*Integral Psychology*, p. 197), we progress from being ego-centric—I, me and mine— to ethno- or socio-centric—me, my family, tribe or like-minded group— to world-centric—all of us—to theo- or cosmo-centric—inclusive of all sentient beings everywhere.

To explain it yet another way, imagine these evolutionary growth stages as the movement of embodied Soul through multidimensional realms of ever-increasing subtlety and ever-widening inclusivity and unity, beginning with the form of consciousness we are most familiar with: cognitive consciousness in the gross physical/material domain. Here our attention is limited to and focused on concrete information about the world of things (the particle world) and the relationship between things. Here our attention is limited to thinking, feeling, reasoning, learning, understanding, organizing, remembering, storing, creating and making meaning of information and experiences we encounter in our day-to-day material/physical life. This is where we experience the constructed ego/ self and our self-constructed world, where we witness the manifestation of our thought patterns in the material world in slow motion—while being totally identified with and immersed in our seemingly separate egoic selves and the objects of our experience. All of which we transform from wave forms of pure conscious energy into the invisible particles of thought-form projections, which then collapse into the visible particles of material matter—the "form life" in the hologram.

The linear ego does not cease from operating even when higher evolutionary states are achieved. As Dr. Hawkins said in *Dissolving the Ego, Realizing the Self*:

> In contrast to the innate arrogance of the ego, true intelligence is a quality of conscious awareness and is not subject to attack because its essence is nonlinear. It is, however, utilized by the ego in its expression as mind, which then becomes and subserves the ego's drive for survival. (p. 18)

In light of our slow evolutionary evolvement, Dr. Hawkins tells us in *Transcending the Mind:*

> [T]the ego's capacity for effecting its own release [from this hologram of deception] is "nil" due to the ego's delusional subservience to the false self, the mind and its multifarious creations. This unreal ego/self mistakenly believes Itself to be real and has elevated Itself to the status of a god, placing it upon an altar, vowing death to anyone who dares to dethrone it by exposing its falsity, its cunning and its self-delusion.... To protect itself, the ego/mind, blind to its own limitations, thinks that accumulating information, status and power will secure its continuity. The mind is incapable of discerning truth, as knowledge of truth, is beyond the reach of mind.

This collective conundrum, this invisible trap or net, reigns supreme in the lower dimensions. Rarely do we discern our true predicament. Once in a great while, we may inadvertently become conscious of our dilemma, but the mind will quickly dismiss this idea as an odd anomaly. It is in the ego's best interest NOT to let the eternal Self, the Soul, see through this multilayered hologram of deception/illusion. If we were able to easily achieve this, it would be a death knell for the ego/mind. Removing this impediment would greatly accelerate our individual and collective ascension through the subtle, causal and supercausal domains or dimensions of consciousness and facilitate our return to Source.

The process—the goal and the starting point—is addressed by Dr. Hawkins in *Discovery of the Presence of God*:

> The core of spiritual work is to undo this identification of the ego self.... Identification presumes ownership and authorship; thus the ego sees and believes itself to be a personal, separate causal agent and the inferred source of its own existence. (p. 112)

Indeed the ego self is a "causal agent" in the sense that we think and in our thinking we create. Essentially we are blindly creating nothing but more and more illusions that perpetuate our self-created imprisonment.

Here is a quote from *The Yoga-Sutras of Patanjali* (translation with commentary by Chip Hartranft):

> While awareness easily accommodates all mental experience, the mind is too small a container for the contents of awareness.... It is therefore impossible for the mind to swallow. This would seem to be one of the factors that prevent the mind from accepting the knowable fact that awareness requires no experiencer or recipient. (p. 80)

And from Dr. Hawkins's *Dissolving the Ego, Realizing the Self*:

> All thinking from a spiritual viewpoint is merely vanity, illusion and pomposity. The less one thinks, the more delightful life becomes. Thinkingness eventually becomes replaced by knowingness.... It is helpful, therefore, to make a decision to stop mental conversation and useless babbling. (p. 69)

And another view of thinking: in his wonderfully humorous book, *The Geography of Bliss*, Eric Weiner, a former foreign correspondent for National Public Radio, traveled the globe in search of the world's happiest places. In his travels he spent time in Thailand, and while there interviewing various personages, he noticed that "Thais are deeply suspicious of thinking. They advocate 'not thinking too much' as a way to achieve happiness." After pondering introspectively on this idea, Eric writes:

> I've spent most of my life trying to think my way to happiness and my failure to achieve that goal only proves in my mind that I'm not a good enough thinker. It never occurred to me that the source of my unhappiness is not flawed thinking, but thinking itself. (p. 225)

A strikingly profound insight, but as the essence of the ego/mind is "thinkingness," he quickly dismisses that deep insight, reverting immediately back into the directional mental flow of his thoughts, which sweep him back into the concepts he is writing about in his book and back into his globe-circling travels—attempting to ferret out happiness in some geographical location in the holographic illusion that is the world.

To move out of subject-object left-brain deception, such as the illusion of geographical location in space/time, we have to evolve beyond it, into integration with the right brain. The left-brain-dominated ego/mind reasons, but it is blocked from passing through the dividing line between the linear and the nonlinear domains. The nonlinear domain of right-brain perception has different rules and exists in a different perceptual paradigm. It is not understandable, describable or logically explicable as it is holistic, diffuse, interior, contextual, subjective, non-temporal, non-spatial, and purely experiential.

The "veil"—the state of ignorance, unknowingness (avidya)—that has been placed upon humanity's consciousness isn't just a physical illusion we all see. It's an invisible illusion superimposed on our consciousness—the body/mind/intellect. (An exquisite description of it appears in Chapter Twelve, The Elohim/Ra group's version of the creation story.) To undo the deception, we first must become consciously aware of its existence, then realize that the undoing process lies NOT IN THE MIND but in the transcendental, non-dual domains beyond the ego/mind's blindness.

The veil itself, and its effects in the lower, linear domains of consciousness, cover and confine the consciousness even before birth into the body. Impressions (samskaras) from past incarnations begin to be imprinted genetically through DNA transfer during gestation. And additional new imprints begin immediately after birth during interactions with the external environment and within the familial circle surrounding us as infants and toddlers. Then we are further imprinted by early childhood experiences through the social, educational, cultural, scientific and religious structures of the culture and nation we are born into. These beliefs are programmed and held unexamined in our individual subconscious and in the collective unconscious mind. Additionally, we've all been indoctrinated and infected with mental viruses, "memes," which are concepts implanted through mass media, religious and educational systems, and governments that control and confine us with decrees, definitions, and rules we are collectively, unconsciously entrained to adhere to.

This conflicted state creates an emotional tension that is extremely uncomfortable, as if two minds with opposite points of view are at war with each other inside one's head. In psychological terms, this state is called "cognitive dissonance." Due to the intense emotional need of the ego to protect its core beliefs, the person will rationalize, ignore and even deny any evidence, fact, logic or concept that doesn't fit with its fixed belief no matter how insane, illogical or dysfunctional it may appear. This is the proverbial anathema encountered by psychotherapists treating clients and attempting to divest them of their so-called "presenting problems" and diagnoses. Most of which are, more often than not, attributable to unconsciously held and heretofore unexamined beliefs that some life event has disrupted, or blown out of the water, the mental/emotional scaffolding holding the ego's perceived world in place. In other words, the end of certainty caused by some unexpected life event, followed by an overwhelming feeling of insecurity and fear manifesting as intense avoidance patterns, panic, anxiety, insomnia and depression.

To help us move from the static dualistic limitations of polarized content, and into the flow of the domain of context, here are some helpful quotes from Dr. Hawkins's book *Dissolving the Ego, Realizing the Self*:

> The design of the human mind is comparable to that of
> a computer in which the brain is the hardware capable of

playing any software programs fed into it. The hardware is, by design, incapable of protecting itself from false information; therefore the mind will believe any software program with which society has programmed it, for it is innocently without any safeguard or protection…. All seeming separation is an artifact of thought. It is essential to see that the mind is at all times experiencing a point of view … and because of dualistic perception, the mind cannot discern the abstract symbol from (constructed) reality…. The ego really uses the mind as camouflage and becomes hidden in its clever constructions. This recognition clarifies why the ego's [beliefs] … have been central to its domination of large cultures for extended periods of time and the deaths of millions. (pp. 5, 18)

Knowing exactly how the ego/mind operates, and knowing that it is not the True Self but simply a temporary tool for navigating through this embodied life, supports us in learning of the necessity of detaching from the ego/mind and the mental gyrations it engages in whenever its survival is threatened. Loosening the grip of the ego and letting go of some of our most cherished but all too often unexamined core beliefs can serve to expand our conscious awareness and facilitate our transcendence beyond the ego/mind's game, allowing us to move more deeply into the nonlinear realms—as described in Chapter Two.

Reference Keys: Goswami (1993). Hawkins (2004, 2006a, 2011). Patanjali (2003). Rhinehart (1976). Talbot (1991). Weiner (2008). Wilber (2000).

Chapter Two

The Nonlinear Domain of Context

(Seeing Through)

IN THE DOMAINS beyond this material realm exist ascending dimensions of consciousness that interpenetrate and overlap the dimensions or realms below it. These are the subtle, nonlinear dimensions or domains of knowing. They are more inclusive than the material domain: in the subtle dimensions, the body/mind/intellect or egoic self becomes aware of and attuned to its inner sensory world of emotions, feelings, impulses, memories, ideals, dreams, daydreams, desires, fantasies, fears, nightmares, etc. through its right-brain perceptual field.

It's especially helpful to understand this process of inner ascension, and expansion into higher subtle realms, within a broader context. Quantum physicists tell us that in the quantum ether or morphogenetic field, tiny particles of intelligent energy, seemingly solid matter, exist in an indeterminate state as waves of vibrating energy. Matter and energy constantly fluctuate between the particle state and the wave state. Observation by a single or collective human mind collapses the wave state into the particle state, producing the illusion of objective physical reality. The reverse can also happen as in my case (explained in Part II) where a portion of physical reality dissolved back into its wave state, resulting in the disappearance of so-called "objective reality." This is not a common occurrence. It is so uncommon that many individuals living within the confines of "consensus reality" will deny that such a thing could happen and will explain it away as a hallucination.

Feelings, thoughts, ideas, beliefs and concepts all exist within the quantum energetic thought-field in multiple possibility states simultaneously, called superpositions. However, once an embodied Soul possessing a conscious ego/mind using its three-dimensional visual projector produces a holographically projected physical object outside of itself, or gives attention to and holds an idea or object in consciousness, the wave state collapses into the particle state. Thus, any time the ego/mind projects a series of thought forms about some object or idea, it attaches to it as an aspect or extension of the egoic self as "me" or "mine."

Take a belief, for instance: the quantum wave function collapses once the mentally conceived/projected concept becomes particalized and thereby morphs from a possibility wave into its mentally observed/projected particle state. That belief or concept then becomes seemingly real or objective in the mind of the creator who holds the concept in consciousness. Contrary to our false belief systems, we are *not separate* from the projected outer/inner worlds we construct, observe, define, symbolize and conceptualize for ourselves. Each embodied human being literally projects, creates and maintains its inner/outer thought-projected personal holographic world.

The individual mind's inner/outer-constructed world is also projected through the collective thought forms of the collective consciousness of humanity. Our perceptions, unconsciously projected, create the world that shapes, limits and confines us within the hologram.

Think of the CONTENT of one's mind as individual, invisible, coalesced particles of thought-form representations: visual symbols, conceptual constructs of meanings, explanations, feelings, beliefs, memories, etc. These are the "form of thoughts as things." Now think of the CONTEXT as the unlimited quantum field of possibility waves, within which thoughts and ideas form, dissolve and flow freely as superpositions or waves of possibilities. These unfixed, mobile waves of energy expand, morphing into and out of various shapes, swirling among and through larger and more expansive lofty concepts and ideals: this is the phenomenon of intelligent energy moving freely, unimpeded in constant wavelike motion from the smaller to the larger, from the contracted to the ever-wider, more-inclusive, light-love-infused, directly perceived ways of knowing and understanding the multiverse through the expansive higher mind.

CONTENT = particles = thoughts. The contracted static form of thoughts as things, including paradigm sets and beliefs = the lower ego/mind.

CONTEXT = Quantum energy waves of possibility = unimpeded free-flowing energy, ideas, expansion, inclusive direct knowing and comprehension = the higher intuitive mind.

To deepen our awareness of the movement from content to context, Sri Aurobindo presents us with a useful concept of the ego, early on in the evolutionary progression, as being a helper or adjunct through which humanity expresses its individuated body/mind/intellect, the ego self. But then much later on in the evolutionary trajectory of humanity it becomes a bar or block to transcendence out of the illusion known in the East as Maya and in some scientific circles as the three-dimensional hologram of deception. Here is a quote from his book *The Synthesis of Yoga*, Chapter IX, "The Release From the Ego":

> The formation of a mental and vital ego tied to the body-sense was the first great labor of the cosmic life in its progressive evolution; for this was the means it found for creating out of matter a conscious individual. The dissolution of this limiting ego is the one condition, the necessary means for this very cosmic life to arrive at its divine fruition: for only so can the conscious individual find either his transcendent Self or his True Self. This double movement is usually represented as a fall and a redemption or a creation and a destruction—the kindling of a light and its extinction or the formation first of a smaller temporary and unreal self and a release from it into our true self's eternal largeness.

Spiritual traditions and advanced esoteric science are beginning to converge on this topic. A huge body of scientific research was compiled into the book *Radiant Minds: Scientists Explore the Dimensions of Consciousness*. This 600-page anthology documents twenty-five years of research projects conducted by a remarkable group of leading-edge doctors from the fields of physics, biochemistry, anthropology, psychology, philosophy, parapsychology, computer sciences and engineering. The findings of the members of this paranormal research group (PRG) investigating the structures of consciousness present valid challenges to mainstream science's outdated theories about the nature of reality.

Their combined efforts implanted the concept of the multidimensionality of consciousness into twenty-first-century science. Their research results have proven through focused inner practices that the limited lower ego/mind can be trained to allow the higher mind to reach into the nonlinear domains of knowing. The general consensus reached by the PRG studying the dimensions of consciousness is that there is no unbridgeable division between the world of matter and the vast multidimensional levels of the energetic frequencies of creation permeating the cosmos.

Their research validates and supports our efforts at expanding our consciousness into the nonlinear domains. Knowing and understanding we are self-individuating aspects of multidimensional consciousness allows us to move beyond the constricted linear thinking of the ego/mind and opens the way for the exploration of non-local fields of consciousness. This in turn opens new possibilities for being, doing and co-creating together using the powerful inner collective consciousness of humanity existing in the nonlinear and transcendent domains.

As Nikola Tesla is quoted as saying: "The day science begins to study non-physical phenomena, it will make more progress in one decade than in all the previous centuries of existence."

This kind of research can help us, through specific practices, expand into more subtle dimensions. The ability to see ourselves as self-individuating aspects of multidimensional consciousness allows us to move beyond the constrictions of the linear thinking of the ego/mind and be open to exploring nonlocal fields of consciousness, exploring new possibilities for being, doing and co-creating through the inner collective consciousness of humanity existing in the nonlinear dimensions.

Please consider the following commentary by Werner Erhard, excerpted from the pamphlet *The End of Starvation: Creating an Idea Whose Time Has Come*. It accurately depicts the inner struggle we all face and the resistance we encounter in trying to discern the truth of our predicament:

If you and I were caterpillars talking about flight, can you imagine what the talk would sound like? "We don't have the power to fly. Caterpillars don't fly. They wiggle. We're too bulky and fat and we don't have wings. We can't do it. To which someone might reply: "But if a caterpillar could fly, by what method do you suppose it would happen?" Don't you see that you can't answer that with a caterpillar mentality? Whatever answer you figure out comes from the limited condition; it is deduced from what already exists, that is, the form of the caterpillar. The creation of a context (a nonlinear domain) alters conditions; it transforms the condition of unworkability and creates an opportunity for solutions to occur. (pp. 28–29)

To create anew, we cannot draw from our past references. As Buckminster Fuller once said, "You never change things by fighting the existing reality. To change something, build a new model that makes the existing model obsolete." Rudolf Steiner stated a similar concept in his own phraseology: "The task of understanding is not to replicate in conceptual form something that already exists but rather to create a wholly new realm."

Here is another quote from Dr. Hawkins (*Transcending the Levels of Consciousness*) describing the difference between the lower, false, linear ego/mind versus the higher mind. Linear thinking could be conceptualized as horizontal thinking—the perceived cause creating an effect—whereas nonlinear thinking could be conceptualized as multidirectional, inclusive of many perspectives and points of view simultaneously:

The world is experienced and viewed quite differently from Higher Mind ... in contrast to Lower Mind.... The degree of difference is almost equivalent to describing two different, contrasting civilizations with different levels of the quality of interpersonal relationships, pleasure, happiness in life, worldly success, philosophies, politics, and most importantly, the level of spiritual awareness and alignment.... Lower Mind focuses on the linear specifics of a situation and sees them in terms of self-interest. In contrast Higher Mind includes the overall context and is thereby aware of the abstract nonlinear meaning, including spiritual significance. (p. 171)

An additional quote from Dr. Hawkins (*I: Reality and Subjectivity*) expresses the same concept as Aurobindo on the need for humanity to learn to transcend the ego:

The ego has to be first accepted as though it is a reality in order to be dealt with before it can be transcended. At the higher levels, the ego is seen to be an illusion, without any innate reality.... Spiritual progress is possible because the mind, through understanding, is able to recontextualize the contents of the ego and discern its very mechanism. Once this occurs, one is no longer blindly at the mercy of the ego.... In this sequence, first, the ego is like a wild animal ... then it is tamed and controlled. Next the ego is transcended and ... at last ... it disappears. (p. 118)

Reference Keys: Aurobindo (1990). Erhard (1982). Fuller (web). Hawkins (2003, 2006b, 2011). Millay (2010). Steiner (web-d). Tesla (web).

Chapter Three

The Transcendent Domains

(Being Beyond)

NEXT IN ORDER of evolvement or expanded perception is the quantum field of consciousness called by the Saints and Masters the causal domain or dimension: This is one level within the transcendent domains. In this domain or sphere, thoughts, ideas, ideals, themes, values, concepts and contexts exist within a field of infinite consciousness as possibility waves. The awareness in this dimension is a vastly more extensive quantum plasmic energy field than the thought field of the collective unconscious.

Included in the transcendent dimensions is cosmic consciousness, a state of pure conscious awareness without identification with an individual ego self or identification with any thought-form projections. It encompasses and includes in the field of awareness all the contents of the gross and subtle domains of consciousness, but this domain of consciousness itself is non-local, beyond all thought, non-temporal, non-spatial, pure, blissfully aware and in resonance with the Supreme Self. For example, the Middle Way of the Buddhists describes it as an empty void-state, free, beyond all conceptualization. Other teachings have described this state as the ground of all being, the perfect immovable void of the potentiality of All That Is, through which the Soul passed in its descent into the lower dimensions. This is where we now exist—confined within the body/mind/intellect as the egoic self, the ego complex, believing ourselves to be separate individual personalities in this hologram.

This imprisoned eternal Soul will eventually wake up, become aware of its predicament, and begin searching for the exit, the means to ending its reincarnational cycles of suffering.

For the Soul to become conscious of itself and reach the awareness of unity consciousness, a primary direct knowing, we must engage in an inner process. Beginning with ego-based self-consciousness, we must turn our attention inward through a daily meditative process, thereby allowing us to enter into the nonlinear domains so we can begin decrystallizing and deconstructing the holographic world we create and maintain through the thought forms that we continually project into manifested form-life.

David Hawkins and Sri Aurobindo have expressed in different words very similar conceptualizations: that we must first come to know ourselves as the individually constructed personality ego/self, the "I," in order to be able to eventually evolve beyond the clutches of this false construction. This "not self" must be transcended to arrive at a place of knowing ourselves as the universal "we," the awakened collective unity consciousness of humanity. Then we will know the truth of our essential Oneness beyond duality and the split-brain/mind's constructed illusion of separateness.

This understanding has been expressed in thousands of ways for thousands of years. Here is a quote from the *Brihadaranyaka Upanishad*, I.iv.10:

> And to this day those who know the Self as I am ...
> Oneness, even the gods cannot prevent his becoming
> this, for he has become their Self.... [I]f a man worships
> another deity thinking: He is one and I am another, he
> does not know. He who does not know is like a sacrificial
> animal to the gods. As many animals serve a man so does
> each man serve the gods. Even if one animal is taken
> away, it causes anguish to the owner; how much more so
> when many are taken away! Therefore it is not pleasing
> to the gods that men should know this; that they are the
> Oneness.

I do believe the above quote is in need of some interpretation as it can be confusing to those whose core beliefs are embedded within a paradigm set that believes in a singular transcendent god, a singular universe, a singular lifetime followed by entry into a singular eternal heaven or hell where one must wait for a Savior to redeem him or save him. The statement "those who know the Self as I am ... Oneness" is heresy to those religions who believe in a singular, transcendent God attainable only after death or through resurrection. Within that belief system, for "sinful" humans to even aspire to oneness with God is unthinkable heresy. Within that belief system, one is forever relegated to worshipping God or some other divine being, believing himself to be separate from that which he worships.

Again, in the language from the Upanishad: "Even the gods cannot prevent his becoming this, for he has become their Self." Indeed, once we enter into the transcendent domains, we do become One in consciousness and One in awareness with All That Is. In the transcendent domains we know and embrace in love all sentient life forms, who perform a necessary function in the evolution of the multiverse. This includes all the lesser creator gods who, in the worldviews to be described in Part III, operate as Prime Creator's servants. This would include the creator/sustainer/destroyer gods of the Hindus (Brahma, Vishnu and Shiva); Kal, the negative pole of creation described by the Sant Mat Masters; William Bramly's Custodial Gods of Eden; the Elohim/Ra group's description of the guardians; and Morning Sky's, Sitchin's and Parks's descriptions of the extraterrestrial colonizing empire-building Anunnaki gods. These lesser creator gods include even the Old Testament biblical God Yahweh along with Lucifer and his fallen angels, the Nephilim, Yaldabaoth and the Archons, and even the Buddhist demon Mara, the Asuras and Devas, and the AIs (artificial intelligences). All these creator gods are simply thought-form projections that capture, manipulate and direct the collective thought-form projections of humanity.

Returning to the Upanishad quote—"If a man worships another deity thinking: he is one and I am another, he does not know"—"thinking" is the key word here because within the linear thinking domain, one cannot BUT conceive of the ego/self as a separate and distinct being separate from all other selves and separate from the sub-creator gods and the Supreme Creator. In these realms—thought-form projections—the lesser gods or lesser beings exist in the energetic quantum field of the higher dimensions. In these dimensions or realms reside disembodied and never-embodied beings, angels, Devas, Asuras, sub-logoi creator gods and hyperdimensional entities.

A faction of thought-form projections that present as the various sub-creator gods act to manipulate humanity within the hologram. They behave like prison wardens. They don't want us to escape from their "constructed holographic worlds." They want to keep us as their servants and underlings because we maintain and perpetuate the dimensional holograms that the sub-creator gods created: the physical, astral and causal realms. If too many of us escape all at once, then their dimensional holographically constructed worlds would begin to dissolve away.

"Therefore it is not pleasing to the gods that men should know this … that they are the Oneness." If we were to transcend the three lower planes of existence, we would be able to see and know, through the divine inner spiritual eye of direct perception, the truth of our divinity in eternity. We would know ourselves as pure conscious awareness itself, which is what we truly are. On the fifth plane, known by the Saints and Masters as Sant Lok, is the plane of the One True Reality. Here the Soul knows that ALL of the creator, sustainer and destroyer gods are All of Us, "pluriforms" of the Supreme Creator.

Now with those concepts elaborated, we can summarize, using a conceptual or representational map of these domains of knowing. There are diffractions, gradations and differences of perspective within each domain of knowing. This allows for endless varieties of creative perceptual constructs for the perceiver within each domain of knowing.

LINEAR DOMAIN OF CAUSE/EFFECT THINKING

Includes Chakras 1–3

Material universe—the three-dimensional hologram
Waking Consciousness—spatial orientation in space/time
Electromagnetic frequencies of physicality
Intellectual world of content and linear causality
Outward-focused awareness—doing

Biological sensing neuronal system projecting feelings/emotions
Brain/mind split perception creating self-other dichotomy
Left-brain serial perception of paired opposites creating...
Thought-form projections of judgment, separation, opposition

SUBTLE ENERGETIC NONLINEAR DOMAIN OF CONTEXT

Includes Chakras 4–6

The dreaming/meditating self
Inner non-temporal, non-spatial frequency dimensions
Extraordinary states of consciousness
Interdimensional awareness
Witnessing self—inward subjective focused awareness
Right-brain perception—intuitive knowing by direct perception
Conscious awareness of energies moving within the
subtle electromagnetic fields
Sensing, Feeling, Knowing, Being

SUBTLE ENERGETIC TRANSCENDENT DOMAIN

Includes 7th or Crown chakra and above

Beyond the phenomenal worlds
The eternal NOW
Interdimensional pure conscious awareness
Beyond the binary brain perception
Knower/knowledge/known become One
Pure conscious awareness
Infinite awareness of All That Is
Radiant all-pervasive conscious awareness
Light/sound plasma frequency planes
Consciousness without an object
Sat (Truth) – Chit (Knowledge) – Ananda (Bliss) planes

These fields, and the ways we move between and among them, are
masterfully expressed by Dr. Hawkins in his audio series *The Way to God:
Radical Subjectivity, Perception and Illusion: The I of Self*.

Consciousness is the field which supports the phenomenon called "mind." Consciousness itself is without form. Just before you think a thought, what you're experiencing is awareness, which is radiating out of ... is an aspect of consciousness.... It's said that the entryway into enlightenment is in the instant of now. That "now" is always present. It only takes a curiosity.... So to become enlightened is to see that one is the field and not the content of the field. You're the field in which the thought presents itself.... [T]he minute you get curious about what is there prior to thought, prior to mind ... that fires off the quantum potential for that to present itself. To merely be interested in it, curious about it, to hold that in mind, tends to increase the potentiality and the likelihood of it manifesting as an experiential reality.

The expression of this movement was the center of Jalaluddin Rumi's life and work. He said:

This place is a dream. Only a sleeper considers it real.... Humankind is being led along an evolving course, through this migration of intelligences, and though we seem to be sleeping, there is an inner wakefulness that directs the dream, and that will eventually startle us back to the truth of who we are.

And from *The Prophet* by Khalil Gibran:

And a poet said, Speak to us of Beauty. And he answered ... beauty is not a need but an ecstasy. It is not a mouth thirsting nor an empty hand stretched forth. But rather a heart enflamed and a Soul enchanted. It is not the image you would see nor the song you would hear, But rather an image you see though you close your eyes and a song you hear though you shut your ears. It is not the sap within the furrowed bark, nor a wing attached to a claw, But rather a garden forever in bloom and a flock of angels forever in flight. People of Orphalese ... beauty is life when life unveils her holy face. But you are life and you are the veil. Beauty is eternity gazing at itself in a mirror.... [Y]ou are eternity and you are the mirror. (p. 83)

Reference Keys: Aurobindo (1990/web). *Brihadaranyaka* (web). Gibran (1986). Hawkins (2002). Joye (2012). Rumi (web-b).

PART II

Entering the Hologram

Who Am I?

Awakening most often occurs when there is something revealed that was not known before which rocks the foundation that people based their lives upon. This shakes the template that has been in place around the earth and around each inhabitant and opens up the contemplation of other possibilities that were not considered before.

Marlene Swetlishoff

Introduction to Part II

Entering the Hologram

When did I agree to participate in this seething insanity called life?

Oh no, not again, I protest ... in vain.
But here I go, into the hologram where time and space reign.

Wrapped in sinew, bones and skin,
The illusion of separation sealing me in.

The parameters of my being contained,
Sentenced to a life ... prearranged.

From the pool of the infinite I am plucked,
And into finitude I am tucked. Snug in the folds of my mother's womb,
I await the formation of my bodily tomb.

Down, down, down, I descend once more,
Entering the Wheel of Eighty-Four. *

Consciousness confined to form.
To another body I am born,
I feel ... I move ... I know ... I mourn.

Domonic Kay

*The ever-revolving wheel of karmic law under which all Souls are bound, moving through thousands of bodies of species of gross and subtle life forms, eventually passing through all eight million, four hundred thousand different species of life over eons of time. This includes gaseous, metal, rock and plant forms; insect, bird, reptile, animal and finally human forms. Then advancing beyond physical forms including all classes of angelic beings (Devas), demonic beings (Asuras), archangels and divine beings in subtle light bodies which inhabit the subtle, causal and supercausal planes.

Reference Keys: Swetlishoff (web)

Chapter Four

My Story

"There is but one history and that is the soul's."

Harald Goddard

I WAS BORN into this body and this life at Mount Carmel Hospital in the town of Pittsburg in the state of Kansas on the Ides of March (the 15th) near the tail end of World War II. My parents were young, in love, and very pleased with my birth. I was their firstborn and they welcomed me into the world with the utmost love and tenderness.

I was a curious, inquisitive child with an insatiable desire to know the whats and wherefores of all things. My mother was an avid reader. She began reading me bedtime stories early on, passing to me her love of reading and of books. My favorites were the lavishly illustrated fairy-tale books. She was a wonderful storyteller, embellishing the fairy-tale characters with voices, facial expressions, attitudes and body gestures that brought them to vivid life in my child's imagination. She once told me that even when I was a toddler she could sit me down on the floor beside a stack of old magazines and I would entertain myself for hours, carefully turning the pages, absorbed in looking at the color photos, appearing to read the pages. She also mentioned that as a child I often drove her to distraction with my inquisitiveness, asking her endless questions, especially the question "why?" hundreds of times daily.

All my life I've had a burning desire to know the truth—the real truth about life, answers to the big questions like: Who am I? Why am I here? What is the purpose of life? Why do we die? And where do we go after death? I have never been satisfied with half-truths or partial explanations. I always wanted the whole truth and nothing but the truth about life.

My mother told me about a funny incident that happened when I was around two-and-a-half years old. Of course, I have no recollection of it except for an abiding fear of lightning. As my mother told it, she was in the kitchen cooking one summer day during a Kansas thunderstorm. It was pouring rain, thunder was rumbling and lightning was flashing in crackly white zigzags across the sky. I ran terrified and sobbing into her arms. She picked me up, held me close, rocking me while rubbing my back to calm me. A few minutes later just as I lifted my head, a huge lightning bolt flashed through the open kitchen window and hit the top of the metal stove emitting a loud crackling sound, spewing out a blinding flash of light.

My wailing resumed doubly loud, to which my mother soothingly replied, "There's nothing to be afraid of, darling, God is with us." Peeking all around the room and seeing no one, I said, "Where is God, Mommy?" To which she serenely replied, "He's in our hearts, honey." Without a moment's hesitation, I replied, "Well … I don't want him in there. I want him out where I can see him!" Little did I know that my desire would be fulfilled some thirty-eight years later.

My parents moved to California a few years after World War II ended following my father's release from the US Army Air Corp when I was about three. My grandmother—my father's mother—and two of his sisters had already moved to Hollywood from Missouri so we stayed with them for several months while getting settled in.

Then when I was about six, to my delight, our family moved to San Diego and rented a beautiful house right on the water in the small beach community of Mission Bay. Just on the other side of our white-picket-fenced yard was a wide expanse of sand stretching about three hundred yards down to the waters of the bay. I spent many carefree happy days roaming the shoreline, swimming, collecting shells, sea urchins, sand dollars, crabs, starfish and an occasional dead shark. I relished discovering and examining nature's many wondrous creatures. I even kept a pet horny toad and a large pet lizard in my room in big shoe boxes and faithfully fed them insects daily.

I loved being in the water—ocean, bay or bathtub it didn't matter. My mother frequently had to order me out of the water, in spite of my chattering teeth, shivering, blue lips and shriveled skin. It was the same story with bath time. I never wanted to get out of the water. Perhaps it was due to the influence of my birth sign, Pisces the fish, ruled by Neptune, God of the Sea.

My parents weren't very religious. Their church attendance was at best sporadic, usually only in observance of a holiday like Christmas or Easter. At seven, after having attended a small local church a few times with my parents, I asked and was allowed to walk down the boardwalk a few blocks on my own to attend the church Sunday school classes. I was fascinated by the Bible stories read in Sunday school and I loved looking at the lavishly illustrated pictures, especially those depicting Jesus and his disciples. I enjoyed the hymns and sang each of them earnestly at the top of my lungs with the rest of my Sunday school class. It was here, at the tender age of seven, that I encountered my first conflict with church doctrine.

One Sunday there was a lot of hullabaloo about some church missionaries returning from a trip to Africa. Our class was allowed to join in with the main congregation to listen to the missionaries tell of their experiences and show slides. The Sunday school lesson that day was all about missionaries and "saving Souls" by teaching the gospel of Jesus Christ to the "unsaved" peoples of the world.

Our teacher showed us several colored slides of Africans dressed in their native clothing entering a church to be baptized by a white preacher. With my customary curiosity and inquisitiveness, and with some concern, I asked the teacher, "But what will happen to those Africans who couldn't get to the church or who didn't know about the preacher being there to baptize them?" With my seven-year-old's perception, I believed God to be all powerful, all loving and competent to handle any situation. I wanted to know how He would handle this minor "problem." The Sunday school teacher replied very matter-of-factly, "If a person is not baptized and doesn't accept Jesus as their Lord and savior, that person will go straight to hell when they die."

Well, I was totally shocked and dismayed by this pronouncement. I felt desolate and heartbroken about this terrible news and it really bothered me for weeks. This statement was in direct conflict with the concept I had been taught in Sunday school that Jesus is our savior and that he died for our sins so all the world would be redeemed and find salvation. How could this be? How could God provide us with a savior, his own son, and yet condemn people to eternal hell because they had not had the good fortune to hear about Jesus or get baptized during their lifetime. Something was terribly wrong with this view. No, worse than that, it was a cruel lie and most unfair according to my seven-year-old's understanding. After much fretting, worrying and praying, I finally came to the conclusion that an all-loving, merciful God would not do such a thing and the Sunday school teacher must be telling a big giant fib. I had already in my short life span seen firsthand evidence of adults telling fibs. My own father and grandmother were masterful fibbers. My mother used to say by way of explanation when I would catch one of them in a fib and question her about it, "Oh, they're just embroidering on their stories." From that day forward I mistrusted the church and its teachings.

My church attendance was sporadic at best so that by the time I entered my teens I had developed a serious aversion to churches in general and an intense aversion to the fiery sermons of the fundamentalist Christian preachers railing against "us sinners" and putting the fear of God into us by describing in gruesome detail the terrible fate that awaited us in hell if we did not "repent our sins" or failed to "accept Jesus as our savior through baptism." For most of my adulthood I inwardly cringed whenever I heard that singsong tone of voice used by the preachers when admonishing their congregations. It made my skin crawl and the hairs on the back of my neck stand up. Only much later in life was I able to understand my aversion to this false depiction of God as an angry, vengeful, punishing God. I knew intuitively this primitive, mythic, fear-based God as expressed through the Old Testament stories in the Bible was false and not the One True God of Eternal Love, Mercy and Grace.

My family saw to it that I was "saved" by arranging to have me baptized along with my two cousins and my uncle when I was about twelve. The event was scheduled for a Saturday morning. We kids got new outfits for the occasion as well as a lecture, on the way to the church, about how special and holy baptism is. I tried my best to be in the appropriate "holy" mood, but try as I might, I didn't feel very holy, just curious, confused, and a little nervous about venturing into this heretofore unknown domain of "the holy." Upon entering the church, I looked around for the baptismal bowl at the front of the church but found none. Instead, I spied a square white, tiled, water-filled pool six by seven feet long, about five feet deep with steps at one corner. It then dawned on me that my baptism was not to be a gentle sprinkling of holy water on the forehead, but a full-body dunking akin to the biblical baptism of Jesus in the river Jordan and I'd be dunked not once, but thrice, in the name of the Father, the Son and the Holy Spirit. It was so cold in the unheated church that my teeth started chattering, though as much from anxiety as from the cold.

We were led to the back of the church to a small cramped dressing room where we exchanged our new clothes for simple white cotton gowns that looked like hospital gowns but were happily lacking the open backs. So attired, we were led back to the front of the church which was still, cold and empty except for my aunt, my mother and the minister. The minister began the ceremony, his voice echoing off the empty pews and barren walls. My shivering increased as the sound of my chattering teeth ricocheted around and through his words. I was shortly thereafter led into the icy pool and dunked unceremoniously under the water three times by the minister. Icy water went up my nose and took my breath away. I gasped for air and at this point my teeth-chattering so intensified, I became so intently focused on keeping my tongue out of the way of my teeth, that I completely missed the remainder of the dreary ceremony.

My baptism was thoroughly disappointing. I felt no different after it than before and did not feel saved, holy or altered in any way. I, in truth, felt hostile toward the minister who had so impersonally shoved me under the ice-cold water, making me feel more like a prop in a play than a "holy child of God" receiving the sacraments of baptism.

These feelings of intense disappointment and frustration, which have reoccurred regularly throughout my life, eventually began to be mixed in with bouts of elation bubbling up—generating a heartwarming feeling accompanied by the thought that at last I've found that "indefinable something" I'm so yearning for.

In hindsight, I came to see that as these high and low states alternated over time, ever so gradually, unconsciously, automatically, I was inculcated and acculturated into this physical body, this uniquely torqued egoic personality self, my physical surroundings, the rhythms of daily life, the peculiarities of my physical life experiences and those of my family, the teachings of the churches and schools I attended, the influences of the communities I lived in and the culture and country into which I was born.

Speaking of physical life experiences, I come from a family genetic line that just happens to be highly sensitive and violently allergic to any number of natural and chemical substances. My aunt almost died from a Novocain shot at the dentist's office and my cousin almost died from an over-the-counter cold remedy by going into anaphylactic shock. I, and many of my close relatives, were cursed with eczema, migraines and various other severe and unpredictable allergic reactions. I developed severe allergic reactions to milk products, pet dander and grasses and also began to have recurrent bouts of strep throat and tonsillitis starting around age eight that would lay me low, causing me to sometimes miss weeks of school. I'd be pumped full of antibiotics till the infection abated only to have it flare up all over again. During these bouts I developed a severe allergic reaction to penicillin and had to be switched to other alternative drugs.

My mother finally, with the persistent urging of the family doctor, scheduled me for a tonsillectomy at twelve. Being adamantly against it, I sulked and pouted all the way through my hospital stay of three miserable days and rebelled by telling the nursing staff I'd rather pee on the floor than use that icky bed pan. My tonsils, according to the doctor, were the size of golf balls, so big he said he had to stitch up the gaping holes they left after their removal. He gleefully wanted to show them to me but I firmly refused his offer (I didn't know it at the time or maybe that particular quirk in me hadn't yet developed, but I do have a tendency to faint at the sight of blood, my own or anyone's.) Well yes, I knew he'd done something nasty to my throat because besides the pain and swelling, he left a miniscule surgical thread hanging over my epiglottis, perpetually tickling it for a week, causing me to develop an uncontrollable swallowing reflex and a persistent feeling of choking, along with feelings of panic and the avoidance of any solid foods.

There is a reason for my giving this detailed history. As you'll see, this seemingly minor medical event in my childhood, along with some family history, led to the subsequent behavioral patterns I developed. All of which culminates in explaining how I developed obsessive compulsive disorder (OCD) which has plagued me for most of my life. First of all I had no awareness of my budding OCD behaviors as a teen other than the fact that both my mother and my closest aunt both had OCD which I behaviorally mimicked growing up (fear of germs, excessive cleaning compulsions and compulsive organizing of objects in my immediate surroundings). It wasn't until I was well into my forties working as a licensed mental health therapist and doing some online research that I discovered the deeper implications for the origins of these OCD behavior patterns. I happened to come across some studies on the International OCD Foundation's website. There I discovered that I had developed something called PANDAS (Pediatric Autoimmune Neuropsychiatric Disorder Associated with Strep), which was not even recognized, studied or defined until the late 1990s. Per the research, this syndrome usually begins between three and fourteen years of age, correlated with a diagnosis of strep throat (and/or other specific bacteria-borne infections) involving subclinical symptoms that gradually get more severe over time and can include obsessional fears, obsessive repetitive behaviors and anxiety attacks. Auto-antibodies have been implicated in causing the problem by mistakenly attacking the basal ganglia in the brain rather than the strep or other causative bacteria.

My aunt contracted typhoid fever when she was about five or six years old and almost died of it, and my mother contracted severe rheumatic fever as a small child. Both of these illnesses are included as possible indicators for the later development of OCD, which they both had. In my adulthood and with the help of an education in psychological disorders, I've been able to consciously control and severely reduce the intensity and frequency of these compulsive thoughts and behaviors. I'm elated to no longer be imprisoned within those compulsive cleaning cycles.

As I entered my teen years, my search for the deeper truths of life waxed and waned like the moon's cycles. My search was mostly held in abeyance throughout my high school years as most of my attention and energy went into academic studies, sports, dancing, primping, shopping, partying and dating. I fumbled forward, sporadically reading, studying, questioning and wondering about the hidden side of things, seeking answers to the conundrums of life as my day-to-day life flowed irreversibly onward.

My parents, after a few short-lived reconciliations, divorced when I was about twelve or so. About three years later, my mother got promoted to a new job in Torrance, California, which meant we had to move from the San Fernando Valley to this new area just as I was about to enter high school. I was sad to be leaving all my friends but elated to be living just three blocks from the Pacific Ocean where we settled into an apartment in Redondo Beach. There I had a very brief foray into Catholicism at the gentle urging of a Catholic schoolmate. I accompanied her to one of her catechism classes and afterward she took me to have a talk with her parish priest. During our brief conversation he emphasized the need for us to "confess our sins regularly at confession." When I asked what those sins might be and how did he know we were all sinners, he gave me a most depreciating, disdainful look and launched into the usual religious dogma of humans being "born in sin," etc., etc. Then I asked him how come we can't we just talk to God directly. And why do the priests have to be the intermediaries? Well ... so much for my foray into Catholicism.

In high school I met and dated a boyfriend for the last two years and we decided to marry just after graduation. My mother was devastated as she didn't want me to marry so young and definitely not "him" whom she deemed "not of my intellectual or social caliber." Sadly she was right as our marriage lasted only three short years. I began feeling unhappy, bored and intellectually and emotionally stifled shortly after the honeymoon phase wore off. I stuck it out for three years during which time I graduated from cosmetology school, became a licensed hairdresser and also became a mother. I didn't want to have a child right away, but my husband insisted on it, which caused much dissension between us. When I became pregnant, at first I was irate but then as I came to accept the inevitable and immersed myself in approaching motherhood along with adjusting to all the alterations my body was going through, I tuned in to the new life growing within my womb and knew that I was going to have a girl. I only picked girls' names to choose from during my pregnancy.

My husband thought I was nuts and didn't believe me, so he picked out a few boys' names in spite of my telling him I was going to have a girl. Sure enough she was a sweet delightful baby girl and I named her Valerie Rochelle. After doing a lot of Soul searching and questioning myself about who I was and what I desired to accomplish in my life, I explained to my husband that I was miserably unhappy and wanted a divorce. He was understandably shocked and irate and tried every which way to get me to change my mind but I was determined. I divided our belongings, left half with him, took my half and moved back home with my mother and sister for about eight months along with our delightful toddler who was about eighteen months old by then and a chubby, sweet-dispositioned, but mischievous little explorer, getting into everything within arm's reach.

I spent the following eight months working as a hairdresser, saving money so I could get my own place. I was immediately shoved into the realm of the workaday world earning a living to support myself and my daughter. With my focus turned now toward fulfilling the financial necessities of life, the desires of my Soul to know the Truth and pursue my deepest spiritual yearnings were yet again put in abeyance, submerged in the subconscious nether regions of my mind.

On occasion, these yearnings would bubble to the surface of my conscious awareness, camouflaged and entangled in the consuming circumstances and events of daily life. Sometimes subtle and sometimes glaring tracers would shoot up out of my unconscious, shedding momentary light on some hidden, deeper, realm lying just under the surface of my lived life. It would spark a momentary flash of desire, a yearning for something I could not grasp or define. This desire would be quickly extinguished, sinking back into the mire of minutia that totally occupied my mind, engaged my emotions and held my mental focus entirely on physical and financial needs—wholly immersing me in the three-dimensional material world of the daily necessities of survival.

For me to garner the necessary life experiences that would provide me with the requisite growth of consciousness and allow me to eventually recognize the illusory-ego-bound futility of embodied life with all its ego-driven cravings and desires, I had to play out my pre-patterned role in the theater of the world, this three-dimensional hologram. Each and every seemingly mundane life experience offered me multiple opportunities to look beneath the surface of events to begin to discern the underlying spiritual concepts and principles I needed to learn. I slowly began to see intuitively and to be able to discern the real from the unreal, the truth from the lies. Lies I told myself and the lies others told to me. The only way this growth of consciousness occurred was by walking through the "fires of karma": my samskaras (impressions left on the Soul as memories from former lives which determine one's desires and actions in the present life), delivered in this lifetime as my unique life experiences—pre-packaged, pre-ordained and imprinted into my DNA at conception, signaling a new cycle of embodied life playing itself out.

After several years of on-and-off dating, while working to support myself and my daughter, I eventually met, dated and fell in love with a an older man, fourteen years older than me. We dated for about five years and then married in New York City with his best friend and his wife as our witnesses. As husband number two, he was the polar opposite of my first husband. He had been born and raised in an Arabic country, immigrated to the US and become a naturalized citizen in his early twenties. He came from a wealthy family and lived a very sophisticated, affluent lifestyle as a realtor/broker/property owner. You might erroneously be thinking that after dating for five years, we loved and knew each other well enough to believe that we would be compatible partners. Wrong! We were in love yes, but incompatible in every conceivable way and our differences were exacerbated and highlighted by our marriage and living together in a single household. But I, who still believed in fairy tales and that love could conquer all problems, was, against all odds, convinced we could make it work. To say that our marriage was tumultuous would be a gross understatement. I felt I had climbed into a Mr. Toad's wild ride car at Disneyland and couldn't find a way to stop the ride or find the exit. Our diametrically opposed life experiences fueled endless familial, cultural, political, sexual, financial and relational clashes which were intense and ongoing. It was a perennial emotional roller coaster, an intense love-hate relationship, highly emotional, volatile and passionate. We were locked in a major power struggle over clashing cultural values and belief systems. He appointed himself my teacher but the things he tried to teach me were opposed to my innate character and nature and not the things I learned from him. I failed his curriculum utterly for it was a curriculum of domination, manipulation, lies, control and deceitfulness. The lessons I learned in the relationship were of a wholly different order than the lessons he had intended to teach me. One of the most important lessons I learned is that you can't love another person into being honest or loyal and you most certainly can't force them to change through any form of ego manipulation or cohesion.

Disillusionment hit me hard as all the idyllic dreams forged in my youth, fed by childhood cultural memes, fairy tales and romantic movie myths of women being fulfilled and completed by a perfect complementary male mate lay in tatters, trampled and torn by the emotional scars inflicted by one failed marriage and an impending possible second failure. I loved him deeply but abhorred his materialistic, money-mongering value system, his jealousy and his persistent attempts to dominate and control.

Shortly after being hit by a deep disillusionment, I fell into a metaphorical black hole. I was home alone cleaning out the refrigerator one day and this horrific empty feeling welled up inside of me and settled in the pit of my stomach. I became so nauseated I had to sit down. I thought to myself, "What in the world is happening here?" I mentally ran through various possible medical causes for the nausea in the pit of my stomach, then I realized in backtracking through my thoughts that just before the nausea hit me I'd been thinking to myself, "Is this all there is to life? If so, I can't bear it. This life is empty and meaningless and I don't want to be here anymore." The emptiness and deep despair weighed me down and pushed me into a depression such that I could hardly get out of bed or function for several days and I became physically immobilized. After several days, I gradually recovered and determined that I would begin in earnest a search for I knew not what but some indefinable thing or experience to fill this yawning emptiness and this ache inside of me which neither my husbands nor even I could fathom.

I would like to interrupt the story at this point to quote the words of Meher Baba from the book *Discourses*:

> [M]an does not usually turn to a real search for God as a matter of voluntary and joyous enterprise. He has to be driven to this search by disillusionment.... [T]here often arises some occasion when he begins to ask

himself, "What is the point of all this?"... [I]f a deep craving happens to meet an impasse so that there is not the slightest chance of it ever being fulfilled, the psyche receives such a shock that it can no longer accept the type of life that may have been accepted hitherto without question.... Divine desperateness is the beginning of spiritual awakening because it gives rise to the aspiration for God-realization. (pp. 125–26)

Here is another quote from Shankara's book *The Crest Jewel of Discrimination:*

The longing for liberation is the will to be free from the fetters forged by ignorance—beginning with the ego-sense and so on, down to the physical body itself—through the realization of one's true nature. (p. 36)

Many spiritual teachers have stated that when we were originally separated from the One Source/God, He knew of the seeming pain and suffering we would experience during embodied life, so He placed within each of us an inextinguishable flame (His divine essence) to light our way home once we finally recognize and admit to the intolerability of the ego-driven life.

For the next few years I invested much of my free time reading spiritual books, trying out various forms of spiritual practices, taking self-help classes, visiting local meditation centers and attending various consciousness-raising workshops while maintaining our household in the San Fernando Valley, an outlying area of Los Angeles. A friend invited me one day to accompany her to the Self-Realization Fellowship Center in Pacific Palisades. I was enchanted with the magnificent lushly landscaped grounds, which were flush with exotic flowers and plants artfully arranged on the hillsides surrounding a beautiful natural lake with a lake shrine on the far shore. The shrine holds some of the ashes of Mahatma Gandhi, whom the founder Yogananda had personally met and whom he greatly admired. The grounds were only a few long blocks from the ocean, which could be seen from the parking lot entryway to the center.

I spent about nine months attending meditation services at the center. I read Yogananda's famous book, *Autobiography of a Yogi*, and was mesmerized by the amazing tales of his many meetings with various saints in India and his meetings with his own Master, Sri Yukteswar. Reading that book awakened some deep, dormant yearning in me and a sense of sadness that I would never be privy to such lofty spiritual experiences. I was in awe of the guru/disciple relationship so exquisitely described by Yogananda. My conceptualization of such a divine/eternal relationship was severely cramped by my limited orthodox Christian upbringing. The biblical descriptions of Jesus's relationship with his disciples seemed rather diluted compared to the love-imbued miraculous stories Yogananda told of his many divine interdimensional, otherworldly astral encounters with his own Master and various masters and saints of his era. The depth of love present in the guru/disciple relationship he had with his Master Sri Yukteswar seemed unfathomable to me at this juncture of my life.

I ordered the SRF meditation manual and tried to follow the instructions, which urged switching to a vegetarian diet and doing daily kriya yoga meditation practices. My husband, being a totally materialistic skeptic, raised such a fuss at my desire to avoid preparing and eating meat products, that after several weeks I gave it up. It was too hard making double meals, a vegetarian one for me and a meat-laden one for the rest of the family. He also ridiculed my desire to meditate and took every opportunity to tease me and to interrupt my silent meditations by talking to me and making numerous noisy entrances and exits from the room where I would be trying to meditate. This game lasted a few months, after which I gave up that practice too.

Another girlfriend around this time introduced me to est (Erhard Seminar Training). She was totally involved in their graduate seminar programs. Est was a training which took place over two long-weekend sessions lasting over sixty hours. It consisted of various psychotherapeutic group processes designed to break through the mind games the ego plays. The essence of est, you might say, was that of a living, participatory encounter theater. My girlfriend eventually convinced me to take the training, which happened to be one of the largest trainings ever held. It took place at the Roosevelt Hotel in Hollywood in a huge chandelier-lit ballroom filled with five hundred people. For me it was an amazing event and opened up a plethora of self-empowering experiences and new concepts that engendered in me a heady sense of exhilaration and realization of the exponential possibilities inherent in this embodied life. I gained entrée to a stimulating network of new friends through the ongoing graduate workshops, which I plunged into with both feet. This marked a turning point in my life and sparked anew my search for Truth—which had been repeatedly sidelined.

My husband was quite disapproving of my forays into the est world and ridiculed my workshop activities as costly and utterly useless. But due to expanding new business opportunities and partnerships, he became otherwise occupied and began spending more and more time traveling out of state and out of the country, putting together business deals with individuals and some corporate groups. He began traveling extensively internationally and probably spent as much time in the air as on the ground, which provided me with an added influx of free time with which to pursue my own interests and develop my est-related friendships and social networks.

Then, inconceivably and unbelievably in the middle of the night on a February predawn in 1981, I was awakened by the sound of my own sobbing. Apparently I had been crying for quite a while before I woke up because I was shocked to notice the entire front of my gown was sopping wet with my tears. My heart felt it had been shattered into a million pieces. I felt so bereft and grief-stricken, I thought for a moment I might be dying because there was such a heavy pain and pressure in my heart I could hardly breathe. It was such a deep aching pain that I clutched my chest, rocking back and forth in bed. I turned on the bedside light and looked at the clock, it was 3:30 a.m. Then as the pain in my heart receded, in its place the most beautiful feeling of peace and calm enveloped me. A divine presence of love so intense, so soothing and so blissful filled me to the degree that I felt as light as a feather, like I was being lifted out of my body. I opened my eyes and looking up I noticed a soft golden light suffusing the room, hovering and concentrated at the top far corner of the ceiling. This gold-tinged pink orb of light enveloped me in a feeling of absolute safety, love and peace. I felt physically held by this presence, this energy of pure divine love. It lasted several minutes then gradually faded. As my sobs subsided, I became still and quiet inside. Then slowly this blissful state dissipated and I was left wondering what in the world had just happened and what it meant.

I found out at 6:00 p.m. that evening. I received a phone call notifying me that my husband had been murdered in a park outside his Tel Aviv hotel. As the shock and disbelief gradually wore off, it dawned on me I had foreseen this loss in a prophetic dream I'd had two years previously that had greatly disturbed me. That dream had been partially responsible for precipitating my immobility and severe bout of depression. At some unconscious level I had been preparing myself emotionally and mentally to proceed with my life solo, unbeknownst to my conscious self, by fortifying my life with a wonderful network of loving and supportive friends.

Many months later after all the necessary burial arrangements, the legal, financial, familial and physical details accompanying my husband's death, had been attended to, I received a copy of his death certificate in the mail. Checking the time of his death Tel Aviv time, I was amazed to see that it coincided with the exact time I'd had my strange experience on the other side of the world. I sensed that a long chapter of my life karma was completed. It felt as if some huge invisible curtain had dropped down over the theater of my life, ending that intensely painful and entangled relationship irrevocably—a scene that had lasted close to fourteen years.

I processed and expressed my grief and temporary loss of identity through the encircling and embracing arms of the est community and my very close and loving est graduate friends over the next two years of my life. During this time period my search for Truth resumed with ferocious intensity. I was as crazed as a secret agent on a covert mission-impossible assignment. I dove head-first into the spiritual marketplace of LA, sampling every offering I could find. I probably read more books, took more courses and attended more workshops in the three years after my husband's death than the average person might complete in an entire lifetime. The est training itself was only the beginning of many graduate seminar series I completed. These were subsequently followed by my immersion in the est Train the Trainer course, the est Impact Training and, for two weeks in New York, the est Mastery of Psychotherapy Course. All these took place from 1981 to 1983.

I enrolled in a Master's degree program in counseling psychology toward the end of 1983. I began attending college full time and working part time with the full support and encouragement of my est friends. Other trainings I took included the Insight Training and the Tony Robbins Fire Walk in Santa Monica, where I did indeed walk on hot burning coals without getting burned. There are just too many others to enumerate here. I resumed attending, for several months, Paramahansa Yogananda's Self-Realization Fellowship Center's weekly meditation services in Pacific Palisades. I then began attending a Buddhist temple in Los Angeles, began chanting, and dropped that. I studied Vedantism for a while and dropped that too. Next I attended lectures at the Theosophical Society in LA and read H.P. Blavatsky's writings and most of Alice Bailey's book series. I briefly tried Transcendental Meditation with Maharishi Mahesh Yogi, a Vedic sage. I read *A Course in Miracles*, joined a Course in Miracles study group, attended for a while, then dropped that. I also attended, for a period of time, The Church of Religious Science, during which time I read all of Ernest Holmes's books on the Science of Mind. Next, I explored Eckankar, read almost all of Paul Twitchell's books and attended briefly an Eckankar meditation group. In addition to all this searching and sampling, I attended lectures by various gurus passing through the LA spiritual community of the day, including Da Free John, Osho and a few others whose names I can't recall.

Basically, I was ingesting and regurgitating spiritual paradigms like a binging/purging bulimic. While engaged in this intense three-year search for Truth, I began having an increasing number of random paranormal experiences of which I will describe just a few. One experience occurred as I was in the process of reading the entire series of books by Jane Roberts. This particular book, *The Nature of Personal Reality*, I happened to be reading when I was called to jury duty. I showed up at the appointed location with this book in hand to pass the time while waiting for the jury selection process. As I was sitting in the courtroom waiting my turn to be interviewed, the walls of the courtroom suddenly began to morph into a mass of rapidly vibrating light molecules, and then the walls became all sparkly and then just faded away into nothingness. One minute they were solid, the next they dissolved into a vibrating mass of transparent sparkling molecules, then they disappeared altogether. I blinked a few times thinking my eyes were playing tricks on me. I looked around again but the solid walls were still gone. I looked around the room to see if anyone else was noticing this phenomenon. I even asked the person sitting next to me if he noticed anything odd going on the courtroom and he replied, "Nope, I don't see anything unusual going on." No one seemed concerned that anything out of the ordinary was happening. I became so distracted by this strange visual phenomenon that I failed to coherently answer the attorney's qualifying questions and probably sounded like a blithering idiot. Gratefully, I was dismissed from the jury selection process.

It was as if the concepts I had been so engrossed in reading about in *The Nature of Physical Reality* were being literally demonstrated to me in the courtroom. This randomly occurring visual phenomenon of watching solid matter dissolve and then reconstitute itself, at various intervals in my life, eventually ceased to unnerve me. Here is a quote from Yogananda's book *Autobiography of a Yogi* describing a similar experience he had with this visual alteration:

> I felt a floating sensation.... I looked around the room; the furniture and walls were as usual, but the little mass of light had so multiplied that the ceiling was invisible.... "This is the cosmic motion-picture mechanism." A Voice spoke... "[Y]our form is nothing but light!" I gazed at my arms and moved them back and forth, yet could not feel their weight.... The cosmic stem of light, blossoming as my body, seemed a divine reproduction of the light beams that stream out of the projection booth in a cinema house.... As the illusion of a solid body was completely dissipated ... my realization deepened that the essence of all objects is light.... (pp. 320–21)

Bernhard Haisch, a physicist, states in his article "*Brilliant Disguise: Light, Matter and the Zero-Point Field*": "The solid stable world of matter appears to be sustained at every instant by an underlying sea of quantum light."

I've since learned, over the years, how to shift my visual focus and attention so as to allow matter to reconstitute itself back into its usual "illusion of solidity." Quantum physicists have proved this reality to be nothing but a persistent illusion and tell us that in reality there is no such thing as solid, static or stationary matter, that everything, no matter how solid and inanimate it appears to be, is a mass of vibrating light photons alive and in constant motion. Um.... Yes, I've really had several first-hand demonstrations of that physics lesson in my life.

Another curious incident happened around this same time period. It happened while I was taking a self-hypnosis class, learning relaxation and visualization techniques. One evening during class, while sitting in a large recliner in the classroom, I went into a deep self-induced trance state while engaged in visualizing the different parts of my body and directing attention to each part to relax it. I somehow shrank down to microscopic size and "fell into the inside of my body." I didn't realize initially that this was what had happened, though. From this microscopic perspective, I looked all around me amazed, feeling like a wide-eyed child inside an amusement park ride. I looked up and directly in front of my line of vision was a gigantic red pulsating shining wet object with multiple blue and red cordlike things wrapped around it, running through it and disappearing out into an immense space. This object appeared to my microscopic cellular self as large as a giant three-story-tall locomotive. It was emitting huge pulsating energy surges that were flowing in and out and swirling like the ebb and flow of some gigantic tidal wave. These pulsing energy surges were pushing me back and forth with great force like some kind of tidal wave. For a moment I was mesmerized and awestruck till it dawned on me I was actually on the inside of my own body watching my own heart beating. At that point I panicked, which caused me to be immediately catapulted back into full waking conscious awareness back in the recliner, whereupon I gasped, sat upright in the chair and tried to coax my pounding heart to slow down while taking multiple deep breaths. The teacher saw my extreme alarm reaction and asked if I was okay. I just said, "Ah, um, yeah I'm fine, no problem."

During this same time frame, I would on occasion wake up in the middle of the night feeling energy surging through my body, flowing down and out through my feet and up and out through the top of my head. It was not an unpleasant sensation but it would wake me up and sometimes keep me up the rest of the night. It felt like I was being plugged into some massive electrical energy source with a portion of it being diverted through my body. This happened randomly with no seeming pattern to it. I would store up tremendous amounts of energy whenever this flow happened and would often sleep very little for days at a time. I later discovered while reading numerous spiritual books on yoga and meditation that this was a manifestation of awakened Kundalini energy flowing randomly and spontaneously.

As I continued to embrace then discard one supposed "pathway to Truth" after another, through some serendipitous coincidence while taking a class in biofeedback for a college requirement, I happened to hear from a classmate, during a casual conversation, about a two-week spiritual retreat scheduled to start within a week or two at the Joshua Tree Retreat Center in the desert near Palm Springs. This is the same retreat center where UFO enthusiasts now gather yearly to attend the well publicized Contact in the Desert UFO Conferences. Back then the center was small, rustic and out in the middle of nowhere. It has since been renovated, remodeled, landscaped and expanded considerably into the popular gathering place it is today. The retreat was to be facilitated there by Brugh Joy, an MD, alternative healer and spiritual teacher. I decided on the spur of the moment to attend at the recommendation of a classmate and another colleague from college who'd heard good things about his retreats. I booked a room at the center, packed, bought a map of the area and drove myself to this center in the middle of nowhere, tucked into a valley dotted with giant Joshua Trees at the foot of a barren mountain range. This would be the first time I'd ever engaged in a group retreat with daily meditations, days of silence and days of fasting.

Thus began another amazing process of expanding awareness, connecting me to new depths of inner knowledge, feelings of deep love and compassion wrapped in a growing awareness and recognition of the sacred connectedness of all sentient life. During the retreat, in the silence of the desert, I began hearing a faint hum inside my right ear, an odd high-pitched subtle sound. At the time I thought I was developing some medical condition and thought I'd have to have my ears checked when I got back home. More about the sound current in the coming chapters.

I had many enlightening inner and outer experiences at the retreat, just one of which I'll share here. Toward the end of the retreat, Brugh Joy scheduled each participant, on the next-to-last day, to receive a personal healing session with him that included the laying on of hands during a sacred meditative process—for which we had all been prepared through the numerous daily group exercises, emotional processes, fasting and meditations. On the day of the healing event I entered the main hall in an altered state of consciousness, having prepared myself through meditation for my turn to receive the healing session. Everyone was gathered in the main hall quietly meditating while awaiting their turns.

When my turn came, I climbed up onto the massage table, lying face up, and closed my eyes. Everything around me receded into the background and I became wholly enveloped in a whirling energy vortex of bliss and love. My body became light as a feather and literally lifted off the table an inch or so where I remained for a period of time. Gradually my body settled back onto the massage table but I was not conscious of anything that was happening on the outside of me as I was in a timeless blissful dimension for the duration of the healing session. Someone in the group observing my session told me afterward that he had observed my body levitating. As a matter of fact I didn't want to come back into this reality at all so when Dr. Joy began gently calling to me, coaxing me back into my body, I resisted leaving that place of peace and bliss and began crying and sobbing uncontrollably as I slowly, reluctantly, returned to my body in the meditation hall.

I felt so disconnected from this reality after the session that I wasn't able to function in the normal waking state for the rest of that day, so I sequestered myself in my room and avoided contact with the other participants since I was unable to carry on a normal conversation anyway due to being in a "mindless" altered state of consciousness. I meditated and rested in my room until my normal mental functioning gradually returned.

I learned several years later while reading a book on yoga that levitating is very common among siddha yogis and that siddhi powers are intentionally developed by some sects of Siddha Yoga practitioners in India—including the ability to become very large, very small, very heavy or very light at will, to become invisible, to bi-locate, to exhibit clairvoyance, clairaudience, clairsentience and claircognizance.

Through these many inner and outer experiences, I slowly began to comprehend that the ego/mind is not the true self and that there exists an inner being or Soul that can know truth by direct perception. Cause/effect, linear analysis and five-sense experience is what traps us in this three-dimensional hologram of deception. Once the restless mind is stilled through meditative practices, the higher mind can enter a space of conscious awareness where Truth can be directly perceived and higher knowledge is unfolded. The meditation practices gradually engender an expansion of conscious awareness beyond the phenomenal world of duality (the hologram) and the mind/body split-consciousness state and into the transcendent realms, the quantum field of unity consciousness.

Reference Keys: Goddard (web). Haisch (web). Meher (1995). PANDAS (web). Rhinehart (1976). Roberts (1982). Shankara (1970). Yogananda (2003).

Chapter Five

Meetings with the Living Master

ABOUT SIX MONTHS after the October desert retreat experience in 1983, I met a multi-talented woman, an already licensed therapist, at a fundraising party in Beverly Hills. We developed a friendship over several months' time and spent many hours together talking about psychotherapy in general, about spirituality and various spiritual paths and practices. She invited me to come to her house for tea one day in July of 1984. Upon my arrival, while passing through her living room, I noticed a strikingly large life-sized framed color photo of a bearded man in a white turban. I was immediately drawn to his face and eyes. "Who is this?" I asked as I paused in front of his picture, staring at his beautiful countenance, which was radiating some sort of spiritual energy that I could sense. She said he was her spiritual teacher, a Living Master by the name of Sant Thakar Singh, currently living in India. She explained how she had met him, how it had changed her life and how rare it is to find and be initiated by a Living Master. She handed me a brochure and a newsletter about the Master and the Sant Mat Path to take home and read. I went on my way. Later at home that night, I read the materials, and after reading through everything I set them aside and went to sleep.

The date was July 7, 1984. At 4:00 a.m. I was brought to full waking consciousness by a bright luminous light filling my inner vision. There, before me, behind my closed eyes, appeared the shining, radiant form of the Master, Sant Thakar Singh. He was elevated about four feet off the floor, surrounded by a glowing, golden-white light, dressed in a flowing white garment and wearing a white turban.

His eyes were piercing me with such an intensely loving embrace, I felt an energy of the most beautiful joy and bliss surging through me like a sonic wave. Its intensity brought tears of yearning to my closed eyes. I gasped inaudibly as this blissful love energy expanded and pulsated through my heart chakra and set every cell of my body to vibrating. I have no recollection of the amount of time that passed while immersed in this divine blissful, loving state. If ecstasy means the sudden intrusion of the sacred into ordinary life, that is what I experienced. My entire being was bathed in ecstatic bliss and my heart was "pierced" through and through with this emanation of divine love. After a time, I returned to some semblance of bodily awareness and waking consciousness as the inner vision faded. The utter shock of having had this "out of this world" divine experience energized me to the point that I felt lit up like a thousand-watt light bulb. I sat up and slowly reoriented myself to my room, at which point the blissful feelings slowly dissipated and I became conscious of the wetness of tears on my face. Since sleep was out of the question I got up and read and reread the brochure and materials about the Sant Mat Path of the Masters while waiting for morning to come. My mind couldn't quite comprehend the significance of this experience so I wrestled with it and analyzed it, trying to make some rational sense of the meaning of this extraordinary happening.

I called my friend as early as I dared that morning to tell her about my experience, feeling awkward and hesitant, fully expecting her to think me some kind of a nut case. But much to my surprise, she became happily elated upon hearing of my experience and told me I should definitely get "initiated" as soon as possible. I had a vague conceptual idea at that time of what "initiation" meant due to my having recently read Elizabeth Haight's book, *Initiation*. The full realization of what this event represented in my life, though, was only to dawn on me many years later. Though I was not fully cognizant of it at the time, this event had been the answer to all my unspoken prayers, my lifetimes of yearning, of seeking and searching for Truth. From that moment forward my life's trajectory was forever altered as my intense longing for Truth had finally been fulfilled. I began my searching without any conscious intention of seeking out a personal guru or Master. I was simply searching for the Truth about life, its purpose and why I was in this body on this planet at this time.

In the sacred teachings of the Masters it is said that a Living Master is "TRUTH PERSONIFIED," the living embodiment of all the qualities of the Creator, a living fountain out of which the audible life stream proceeds. This audible life stream is also known as Shabd or Nam or simply the sound current.

Below are quotes from a few different sources that emphasize the importance of such an event in a seeker's life.

Sri Aurobindo said in *The Life Divine*:

> A single decisive spiritual experience may undo a whole edifice of reasonings and conclusions erected by logical intelligence. (p. 487)

Dr. David Hawkins's view appears in *The Eye of the I from Which Nothing is Hidden*:

> In the end, faith is replaced by certainty, and therefore it is said that God is found by those who seek Him. (p. 228)

Meher Baba's understanding is clear in *Discourses*:

> An aspirant is usually helped by a Perfect Master through ordinary means and the Master prefers to take him veiled along the spiritual path. But when there are specific indications, he may also use occult techniques to help the aspirant.... Very often, when the aspirant is undergoing psychic unfoldment, he has occasional mystic experiences of the subtle world in the form of significant visions. (pp. 180–81)

And Dr. Hawkins highlights in *Reality, Spirituality and Modern Man*:

> Events that may serve the High Self do not always co-
> incide with the wishes of the ego/self but serve the un-
> seen higher purpose of the real Self. (pp. 68–69)

Specifically attuned to *The Path of The Masters*, its author, Julian Johnson, focuses directly on the experience:

> Anyone who has had that experience will tell you that
> there is no joy in this world as great as that which the
> disciple experiences when he first beholds the radiant
> Master. It is the culmination of ages of struggle. It is the
> signal of victory in his long battle with mind and matter.
> He is then halfway to the end of all his labors for spiritu-
> al liberation. (p. 121)

My friend invited me to attend her meditation group with her that
very next Sunday and I happily agreed. We drove to a private home in
the La Canada hills. I later learned that I was not supposed to sit with
the other initiates in meditation until I was formally initiated. However,
not knowing this, I walked in, quietly sat down, closed my eyes and immediately went into a deep meditative state such that no one disturbed
me. During this hour's meditation time I had another very unusual inner
experience. It felt like a visual viewing of some past-life experience as
the scene was crystal clear, quite detailed and accompanied by intense
emotional feelings and a sense of "déja vu."

I saw myself inside a large gray stone tower on the top of a very
high craggy mountain range. I could see the silhouette of the surrounding steep, barren mountain ranges through one of the small high windows. It seemed to be some sort of large stone monastery, this room
being at the very topmost level. Inside I was gathered with a group of
about fifty or sixty other men and women. We were all dressed alike in
white flowing robes with tall cloth head coverings. We were all engaged
in a synchronized dance, repeating certain phrases, locked arm in arm in
a starburst formation. A group of musicians were playing Middle Eastern music. Everyone else was moving in perfect unison and we appeared
to be in some ecstatic trance state. The feelings accompanying the scene

were of deep devotion, love, yearning and a sense of being melded or united with the group in this form of worship.

Later on, I happened onto the following quote about the dance ceremonies of the Mevlevi Sufis of Celaladin Rumi that exactly described the experience I had in my vision that day. In David Leeming's *Myth, A Biography of Belief*:

> "[I]n the "whirling" dance ceremonies of the Mevlevi Sufis … we find a perfect balance of the communal act and the personal. In this ceremony pashas, shoemakers, plumbers, professors and jewelers, nobles, professionals and menials alike dance in planetary togetherness in trance-like personal ecstasy circumambulating love. (p. 138)

After the meditation, I was given an application form for initiation to fill out. The requirements for initiation are (1) to become a vegetarian, giving up all meat, fowl, fish, eggs and any byproducts thereof, (2) to give up the use of all intoxicating substances, (3) to meditate three hours per day according to the instructions of the Master as given during the initiation, (4) to give up all forms of psychic healing activity including hypnosis, tarot card readings, psychic readings, channeled readings, Reiki, crystal healing, laying on of hands, etc., (5) to strive to apply in my daily life the principles and practices of truthfulness, universal love and selfless service, and (6) to attend regular weekly Sant Mat group meditations and participate in scheduled meditation retreats.

I completed the form and mailed it to the Master, Sant Thakar Singh, in India who would then need to approve the application prior to my initiation. The three-month waiting period was to allow me time to adjust to the new dietary and meditation requirements and do some reading about the theory of Sant Mat to gain some understanding about the Path of the Masters and a specific form of meditation which I would be taught on the day of my initiation. My application was approved and I was initiated three months later on October 21, 1984, by a local representative approved by the Master to convey the initiation instructions. The girlfriend who had introduced me to this path and I became very close friends. We attended the weekly local meditation groups together and I later helped the local Sat Sang (meditation group) set up numerous free public education programs about Sant Mat in the LA area. We met personally with the Master on many occasions during retreats and during Master's world tours each time he passed through the greater Los Angeles area.

My first physical meeting with the Master happened in the spring of 1985 when he came to the US on tour. This ten-day retreat had been planned for the LA area and took place in Griffith Park in a Boy Scout campground area. I arrived on the first day of the retreat not knowing what to expect and found there were hundreds of people staying at the campgrounds. Everyone I met and talked with was thrilled to be there in the physical presence of the Master. All of us attended the morning and evening discourses (spiritual talks given by the Master) and all initiated attendees were able to sign up for brief personal interviews with the Master. Group initiations were also offered freely by the Master to all who attended the various planned free public talks and were willing to commit to following the meditation and lifestyle guidelines.

I was scheduled for a personal meeting during the retreat and waited anxiously till the appointed day. The day of the meeting turned out to be a beautiful warm sunny spring day. I stood in a long winding line on the sidewalk outside the meeting room for about two hours waiting my turn. As the time finally came near, my mind went splintering off in a million directions and I couldn't decide what I should ask or say to the Master. I became so mentally muddled I finally just gave up, saying to myself, "I guess I won't know what I'm going to say till it comes out of my mouth."

Then my turn came. As I sat down face-to-face with the Master, my attention became riveted on his eyes. Gazing deeply into his eyes, tears welled up and I was not able to speak as my throat closed up. My heart expanded and with that an intense pulsating love energy drew me inward through his eyes and I expanded out into the depths of the universe. It all happened in less than five seconds. The Master then asked me to close my eyes as he placed his thumb on my third-eye center. He asked me what I was seeing. With closed eyes, I said, "I see the color purple, Master." He said, "Ah, yes my dear Soul, this is the color of love and devotion." Then I blurted out, "Master, I want to go home faster." He remained silent while continuing to look at me with an amused, slight smile. He then leaned forward, literally looking down into my third-eye center and, rubbing it firmly with his thumb, said, "Hmmm, you are a very old Soul my dear and if you go along with the meditations and follow the instructions of the Master you will surely achieve it." He then stood up indicating the interview was ended. I asked him for a hug at this point, not wanting to leave Him and casting about for any way to prolong our meeting. I learned later to my chagrin, after reading some printed guidelines and protocols handed out during the public talks, that initiates are instructed not to touch the Master, to be respectful of him and honor his personal space. He paused, hugged me to him, then stood back and said to me very emphatically and forcefully while pointing his finger at my heart, "Remember, you are always in my heart and I am always in your heart and we are never separate." I then said, in parting, "I love you, Master" at which point he wrinkled up his nose in an expression of distaste but said nothing more to me. His expression puzzled me, but quickly passed out of my awareness as I was so God-intoxicated I couldn't hold onto a single thought.

After leaving the meeting room, I wandered around aimlessly in some altered state that transcended and suspended all my thinking processes. My entire body was so suffused with His divine light and love energy, all I could do was cry. Tears poured out faster than I could wipe them away so eventually I gave up trying. I walked over to a quiet grassy area and lay down under a tree where I remained for I know not how many hours as I completely left my body. I have included two more quotes here explaining what happens during this most special and sacred meeting between the Soul and the Master.

Quoted from *The Secret of Life,* which contains excerpts of talks given by Sant Thakar Singh:

> God has to come in the garb of a human being so that He looks like you and so that you can talk to him, you can love him, you can have something in common with him, you can listen to him, you can eat with him, you can walk with him and that brings you near to him. But when you are near to him, then you are also near to God ...

when you come into contact with that body, which looks like other human beings, but there is God in it, awakened and working, then at once a great change is there.... [G]reat wide vistas are opened in you ... and will remain with you forever, for eternity because you have touched a human body which has God in it. (p. 301)

And from *Spiritual Elixir* by Sant Kirpal Singh:

The Master ignites the great love on the first day of initiation by granting the gift of holy Nam in celestial Light and Sound Divine. The extent of this gift depends greatly on the capacity and receptivity of each one. This loving fire grows in intensity and volume and gives bliss, serenity and calmness.... This should be kept within like the fire in a kiln ... so that all other desires short of Him are slowly and slowly burned away and eradicated from one's heart. (p. 225)

Several hours later, I finally became conscious of my surroundings, sat up, wiped my tears and looked around. It was late afternoon and a small group of people were gathering together laying out blankets in front of a raised white-cloth-covered dais that had been set up under a large tree. I walked over and sat down, and shortly thereafter the Master arrived. He sat down upon the dais and gave those of us gathered (about twenty-five or so) a spiritual discourse. The topic of the talk was an explanation of the difference between human love and Divine love. He looked directly at me several times during the talk so eventually I intuited that he was communicating some very important ideal or concept to me related to what had transpired between us at the very end of our meeting when he had wrinkled his nose up at me after I had said "I love you" to the Master in parting.

Thus began my first teaching lesson from the Master and it was a potent lesson. In essence the Master explained to us during this talk that human love is born of the mind and as such is limited and imperfect and leads to endless complications and entanglements, as do all things in this illusory, dualistic world. He said, "All human love is an incomplete and conditional expression, a dim shadow reflection of True Love, which is Divine." He further explained that Divine Love, which is complete, whole and unconditional, is inexpressible in any spoken language form as it exists in a form beyond words. This unspoken form of language is called "dhunatmak" in Sanskrit. It is the primal essence of God, the Living Word of God, the audible sound current, which is the essence of Divine Love Itself vibrating throughout interstellar space emanating from the Creator and sustaining all creation on all planes of existence.

Now, some thirty-odd years later, since my initiation in 1984, I've spent these intervening years listening to the audible sound current in meditation, to the discourses of the Masters in person, at many retreats, on CDs and on DVDs. I've studied the teachings of the Sant Mat Masters also known as "The Science of the Soul" and read the hundreds of books available on this subject while practicing the Sant Mat meditation methods and I can through my own personal experiences vouch for its veracity.

Reference Keys: Aurobindo (2010). Hawkins (2001, 2008). Johnson (1997). Leeming (2002). Meher (1995). Singh-SK (1988). Singh-ST (2005).

PART III

Twelve Creation Stories

How Did We Get Here?

That Depends on What You Believe

And God created every living creature that now moveth, and one was man. Mud as man alone could speak. God leaned close as Mud man sat up, looked around and spoke. Man blinked. "What is the purpose of all this?" he asked politely.

"Everything must have a purpose?" asked God.

"Certainly," said man.

"Then I leave it to you to think of one for all this," said God. And he went away.

Kurt Vonnegut

Introduction to Part III

SINCE OUR BELIEFS about ourselves, who we are, how the world around us was created and how it functions determine what kinds of experiences we will have in this embodied life, it is important for us to be conscious of what we believe. It isn't my purpose in this book to tell any of you what to believe, but rather to provide you with some new information representing various points of view from a myriad of perspectives on how our world came into existence.

I hope you will be curious as you read this section because curiosity draws us into exploration and growth into broader deeper concepts and the desire to understand them and benefit from them. I must warn you, though, that just like every other thinking being on the planet, I too have a particular perspective about how the world works and some very specific experiences, sets of theories and beliefs about how we were created and how we came to be here on this planetary body in this particular corner of the multiverse—evolved in part from the experiences I shared with you in Part II. More on those topics in succeeding chapters.

Before you read the creation stories in Part III, a brief overview might enhance your experience:

All ancient cosmologies were created as a means of constructing the worldview of a particular culture. A mythic story or epic poem constructs a paradigm to give the seemingly chaotic world a structure through which to make meaning of life and give it purpose. Each culture has its own set of sacred texts or narratives that condition the collective mind of its people to look at the world in a particular way, and every culture distinguishes itself from all others by creating its own unique mythic story or operating paradigm. Two of the most common forms of mythic stories are those that reflect a linear worldview and those that reflect a cyclical worldview. In the linear stories, found in Judaism, Christianity and Islam, there is only one life and an eternal afterlife. In the cyclical stories, found in the cultures of India, China, Tibet and Japan, life follows death endlessly in a continuous series of spiraling or repeating cycles.

There is a thread of truth that runs through every world religion but it is so subtle and faint a thread that great discernment is needed to tease out the deeper spiritual meanings hidden within each creation story. The creation myths and stories of every religion on Earth reflect the narrative power of stories and the power of imagination to convey meaning embedded in these stories, legends and myths which have had and continue to have profound effects on our resulting cultures; on our moral and ethical attitudes, social mores and laws; and on the political structures that proceed from the beliefs embedded in each creation story.

As you grow and expand your own horizons—especially through embracing the multidimensional perspectives presented in Part I—you are benefiting the collective consciousness of humanity. According to David Hawkins (quoted from his audio book *The Highest Level of Enlightenment*), "That which you are doing is affecting everyone. The whole world benefits from your growth and consciousness expansion." I wholly subscribe to this concept, which prompted my writing this book.

Once you explore the sampling of various creation stories about the origin and evolution of our species, you can then gain some clarity about what you actually do believe about how the world was created, who created it and why from your unique perspective. Hopefully you'll also be able to include and incorporate some of the more comprehensive paradigms that include Earth-bound concepts and multidimensional concepts and perspectives.

There is an accumulating but as yet anomalous (not accepted by mainstream science) body of information and research being presented by numerous authors, scientists, archaeologists, cosmologists, philologists, scholars, astrobiologists, astrophysicists, geneticists and plasma physicists the world over, who are providing valid evidence for "alternative paradigms" explaining the origin of our species and the purpose of life.

In this section of the book we'll be examining twelve creation stories and their embedded belief sets, which I'll identify and parse out for you.

Reference Keys: Hawkins (2004). Vonnegut (1998).

Chapter Six

Scientific Materialism Worldview

MATERIALISM IS THE philosophical belief that matter is the only reality and everything in the world can be explained only in terms of matter. Matter being a substance that occupies physical space and has elements and parts that can be perceived by the senses and be scientifically measured. Beginning in the nineteenth century, scientific materialism was born and experimentation methods were developed that were confined to what could be touched, weighed, seen, heard and observed. The experiments served to study, detect, describe and formulate theories, laws and principles confined to the linear domain of knowing; that is, the three-dimensional space/time world (three dimensions of space—width, length, depth—and a single dimension of time). Then with the advent of nuclear science and quantum physics in the twentieth century, there was a change in the scientific materialism paradigm. It was discovered that at the quantum level the very act of observation itself affects that which is observed. Science, up till that discovery, had believed in an objective reality "out there" existing separately from the person observing it.

With the advent of quantum physics, a new paradigm evolved. Scientists came to understand that, at the quantum level, our perceived reality is not objective at all but is actually subjective. Objective generally means existing outside of the mind; existing in the "real world," whereas subjective refers to the way a person experiences things in his or her own mind, based on feelings, beliefs and opinions rather than "objective facts." Studies began focusing on trying to understand the subject, the observer, the one doing the experimentations, and how the observer's beliefs affect the outcomes of scientific and social experiments. Quantum physicists have since discovered that each person is a focal point of intention and attention and that the observer will always affect the outcome of any experiment. The observer is both the observed and the act of observing. It is a loop of intention and attention playing out in space/time, our three-dimensional experience.

The most commonly accepted cosmological model of how the universe was created—looking through the lens of scientific materialism—is the Big Bang theory. This theory was originally proposed by a Belgian Catholic priest, Georges Lemaître, professor of physics at the Catholic University of Leuven. In a 1925 paper that he wrote, he theorized that the universe began from a single primordial atom—a static-universe model. This concept of an expanding universe was later extended and supported by Edwin Hubble's observations in 1929 that galaxies are constantly speeding away from our planet in all directions. According to this theory, the Big Bang occurred about 13.82 billion years ago. At that time the entire universe was believed to be in an extremely hot, molten, dense and rapidly expanding state. After an initial explosion, the universe began to cool and over eons of time was eventually able to support the formation of subatomic particles including protons, neutrons and electrons. Giant clouds of these primordial elements then coalesced through gravity to form the stars and the galaxies. The Big Bang theory describes and explains one understanding of how our universe evolved from the point of the Big Bang event forward. This event was believed to be a cosmic starting point for space and time and was described by Lemaître as "the day without a yesterday." This theoretical framework was further bolstered several years later by Albert Einstein's theory of general relativity which held sway until the advent of quantum theory and quantum physics.

Modern-day physicists and other scientists have argued that recent discoveries in physics such as quantum mechanics and chaos theory have disproven the theory of scientific materialism—replacing it with quantum theory, which has totally transformed our collective conceptualization of matter. Quantum theory or quantum optics deals with phenomena at nanoscopic scales where the actions operate primarily at the quantum level of superluminal neutrinos, or tachyons, that travel faster than light. This theory provides descriptions and theoretical explanations of the dual particle-like and wave-like behavior of the interactions of energy and matter, described as quantum optical effects by Raymond Chiao, professor of physics at the University of California–Berkeley (quoted below).

In *The Matter Myth*, Chapter One, "The Death of Materialism" by Paul Davies and John Gribbin, they state:

> The old assumption that the microscopic world of atoms was simply a scaled-down version of the everyday world had to be abandoned. Newton's deterministic machine has been replaced by a shadowy and paradoxical conjunction of waves and particles, governed by a very different set of operating principles compared to the rigid rules of causality. An extension of the quantum theory goes beyond even this; it paints a picture in which solid matter dissolves away, to be replaced by ... excitations and vibrations of wave forms, invisible photonic light energy, known as the fifth element—ether. Quantum physics undermines materialism because it reveals that matter has far less "substance" than previously believed.

Some very recent developments in physics have further undermined old Newtonian concepts of determinism and causality. Dr. Michio Kaku, a theoretical physicist and co-founder of String Field Theory, is quoted on the CNS News website:

> [T]he Big Bang theory wasn't very big.... [T]here was no bang.... Big Bang theory doesn't tell you what banged, when it banged, how it banged ... it just said it did bang. So the Big Bang theory in some sense is a total misnomer.... [S]cientists have cracked the mystery behind quantum mechanics ... by the discovery of particles known as "primitive semi-radius tachyons"....

After analyzing the behavior of these subatomic particles—which can move faster than the speed of light and have the ability to "unstick" space and matter, using technology created in 2005 that allows observation of these particles—Kaku concludes:

> [T]he universe is a "Matrix" governed by laws and principles that could only have been designed by an intelligent being. The mind of God, we believe, is cosmic music, the music of strings resonating through an 11-dimensional hyperspace.

Raymond Chiao's *Scientific American* article, in which he designates the superluminal phenomena as tachyons, includes the following:

> [T]achyons are theoretically postulated particles that travel faster than light and have "imaginary" masses.... Quantum optical effects can produce a different kind of "faster-than-light" effect [called] quasi-particles moving through laser-like media. There are actually two different kinds of "faster-than-light" effects that we have found in quantum optics experiments. The tachyon-like quasi-particle in inverted media described above is yet a third kind of faster-than-light effect.

An additional scientific development called chaos theory has further disproven the materialistic view of matter as inert. Chaos theory is the idea that a minor difference measured at the start of a process can result in a major change in a system over time and distance. Take for example weather predictions: since a single butterfly can make enough wind with its wings to make a small perturbation in the air, the end effect over time and distance may be a shift in a weather pattern thousands of miles away. This is why chaos theory is sometimes called the "butterfly effect" since no weather computer system knows enough to be able to predict how this single small wind movement in one part of the world may change the weather over time in another part of the world.

In *The Biology of Belief*, Bruce Lipton refers to the New Physics as

...planting both feet firmly on thin air ... because quantum physicists discovered that physical atoms are made up of vortices of energy that are constantly spinning and vibrating; each atom is like a wobbly spinning top that radiates energy. Because each atom has its own specific energy signature (wobble), assemblies of atoms (molecules) collectively radiate their own identifying energy patterns. So every material structure in the universe, including you and me, radiates a unique energy signature. (p. 100)

Since materialistic science generally denies the existence of God, deities, life after life or the existence of eternal Souls, it is incompatible with most world religions. Materialists believe that all that exists is the physical universe and there is only one substance in the universe, which is physical, empirical and material—including kinetic energy. They hold a unidimensional view of the universe, meaning everything is part of and limited to the material realm. John Horgan, in *The End of Science,* states that science has reached its limits and describes some major scientific theories, still currently held, as "modern creation myths" that are in the process of imploding.

He lists the following as modern myths: (1) the Big Bang theory, (2) the four forces: the strong force and the weak force (explaining the behavior of fundamental particles), the electromagnetic force and the gravitational force, (3) the chance evolution of life, and (4) the biological determinism of behavior—all of which, in light of recent advancements in the field of quantum physics, have been shown to be inadequate and inaccurate explanations of experienced reality.

The materialistic explanation of the universe is that everything is matter and kinetic energy and there is nothing else. Anything invisible, insensible, untouchable is dismissed as unreal. Spiritual realms are believed to be an illusion or delusion and not real. Consciousness is believed to be secondary to reality and explained as an emergent phenomenon or epiphenomena of the physical brain. There can therefore be no such thing as superconsciousness, paranormal phenomena, post-mortem existence or paranormal phenomena such as ghosts, poltergeists, angels or aliens as these are believed to be either delusions or reducible to physical forces. Materialists are not necessarily atheists but atheism is often a corollary of materialism, especially in the sense of a disbelief in the possibility of a metaphysical reality, transcendent realms of consciousness, deities or a transcendent God or a Soul or any sort of higher creative power or pervasive consciousness. Intangible qualities such as love, justice, beauty or goodness, being subjective, are not well explained through the so-called "objective" scientific materialism lens, and so such concepts were relegated to the realm of philosophy by the nineteenth-century academics.

Mainstream science supported this paradigm for a century and a half, presenting a view of all matter as inert and of all life as exterior, existing in things out there, a clockwork world. With emphasis on the primacy of matter it naturally followed that societies such as ours in America would have focused primarily on the matter/material world and be directed to developing materialistic lifestyles. It follows that if we believe we have only one life and there is no afterlife, then it is important to accumulate as much as possible and engage in pleasure-seeking and self-gratification by going places, doing things and buying things that make us feel good and look good and bring us financial, social, personal, professional and political status and power. The more one has, the more the individual's perceived value/worth. If you believe there is only one life and no afterlife, then what happens in this single life span matters a lot and what happens after death matters not at all, since the materialist does not believe that one has a Soul, an eternal Self that survives the death of the body. Therefore, the materialist believes that at death they will cease to exist for all eternity.

Deconstructing the Scientific Materialism Paradigm

This paradigm is the simplest explanation of the creation story.

Belief in a one-dimensional view of the universe.

Belief that the universe began with a big bang, a primordial explosion.

Belief that all that exists is matter and/or kinetic energy that can be seen and measured through the five senses and man-made scientific instruments.

Belief that consciousness is an emergent phenomenon of the physical brain and has no separate existence.

Belief that there is no life after death; when you die you cease to exist.

Belief that there is no immanent or transcendent supernatural creative power or God that created the universe.

Belief that all life is formed by a random evolutionary process, an accident of nature.

Belief that there is no eternal Soul; nothing exists beyond this space/time dimension.

Belief that there is no such thing as metaphysical, supernatural or paranormal phenomena, no such thing as ghosts, interdimensional beings or multidimensional universes.

Belief that there is only one life lived in an exterior world of matter (things out there that can be seen and touched).

Chiao (web). Davies (2007). Horgan (1996). Kaku (web). Lipton (2005). Materialism (web). National (web).

Chapter Seven

The Abrahamic Worldview

THE ABRAHAMIC RELIGIONS in the chronological order of their founding are Judaism, Christianity and Islam. All came from a single source in that they all claim a direct lineage to Abraham (Ibrahim), the biblical patriarch to whom God revealed himself. From a singular creation story proceeded three religious ideologies that evolved into three sets of religious beliefs.

The shared meaning of this singular creation story becomes more vivid after exploring the different ideologies that flowed from it. All three conceptualize God as a transcendent creator God, the source of moral law and the bestower of salvation on the faithful. The Abrahamic religions are called "revealed religions," meaning their respective holy scriptures are considered divine revelations transmitted to humanity through specially revered prophets such as Abraham and Moses, Jesus and his apostles, and Mohammad. These three religions also have commandments—moral laws—which were formulated by Yahweh/God/Allah and delivered to the people through his prophets to regulate, order and control the details of daily life of the faithful believers.

The original Hebrew/Judaic laws or commandments were delivered to the people by Moses in approximately 1400 BCE, as told in the Old Testament, Exodus 20:1-17. These laws now called the Aseret ha-D'vareem (The Ten Things) are believed to have been written during the tenth century BCE. Here is a brief version of the how the laws were lowered to Earth: after God brought the Hebrews out of Egypt they camped at the foot of Mount Sinai. Moses went to the top of the mountain to pray. There God appeared to him and talked with him, telling him he had rescued the Hebrews from Egypt because the Hebrews were his "chosen people" to be made into a holy nation of priests for God, his "treasured possessions." God then gave Moses a simple system of laws for his people to follow, called the Ten Commandments, which God wrote with his own finger on stone tablets that outlined the basic spiritual and moral laws for living a religious, righteous life.

Modern Judaism was founded on these and a succession of oral laws expressed in the ancient Talmud and the Mishna. Beginning around 200 BCE it was agreed among the rabbis that a written record of their laws was needed, and so began a lengthy process of codifying into a written transcript the orally transmitted laws for living. These laws were collected and codified in the Torah, which contains 613 commandments, and later became canonized and incorporated into the first five books of the Hebrew Bible: Genesis, Exodus, Leviticus, Numbers and Deuteronomy, also known as the Pentateuch. The Ten Commandments of the Christian Bible listed below are a greatly condensed version of the earlier 613 commandments in the Torah. Many Protestant Christians follow various readings of the Catholic translation, taken from the Hebrew Exodus version:

> I am the Lord thy God.... Thou shalt have no other gods before me.
> Thou shalt not make unto thee any graven images.
> Thou shalt not take the name of the Lord thy God in vain.
> Remember the Sabbath day, to keep it holy.
> Honor thy father and thy mother, that thy days may be long.
> Thou shalt not kill.
> Thou shalt not commit adultery.
> Thou shalt not steal.
> Thou shalt not bear false witness against thy neighbor.
> Thou shalt not covet thy neighbor's house.

Commandments appear in the Qur'an of the Islamic faith as well. The Qur'an is the holy book revealed by God through the Archangel Gabriel to Prophet Mohammad over a period of twenty-three years. Historical accounts of the life of Muhammed, written by different people who knew him and documented the spoken words of the Prophet, are contained in the Hadith. The divine Sharia Laws that faithful Muslins are taught to obey are established upon the teachings extracted from the Qur'an and the Hadith.

All three Abrahamic religions share a similar creation story that took place over six or seven "days." (The meaning of the word "days" has been variously interpreted by religious scholars. The Bible alone, beginning with the Hebrew scriptures, was translated into Aramaic, then later into a Greek version called the Septuagint (because the translation was done by seventy Latin religious scholars: sept = seven). Later versions include the Apocrypha, and then more translations appeared in Syriac, Coptic and Latin. A Latin translation of the Bible called the "Vulgate or common Bible" was used for hundreds of years in Protestant and Catholic European churches (Roman Catholics maintained that the Vulgate was the only authoritative version). Then came the Protestant/Catholic split in doctrines and the eventual development of the King James Version of the Bible printed originally in 1611 CE.

I've judiciously avoided delving into the voluminous interpretations of religious scripture, of which the above much-abbreviated versions are only a few. Interpretations are ubiquitous, and cornucopias of information can be found on the internet, in videos, in books and through various Judaic, Christian and Islamic websites ad infinitum. The material included here is admittedly quite brief. For scholarly dissertations, I refer you to you to rabbis, preachers, priests, bishops and imams from every sect and sector of the worldwide religious community who make their living dissecting their religious canons. The purpose here is to simply provide condensed versions to make for a more efficient comparison from among the many creation stories included in this book.

The following creation story, very similar to accounts in Islamic sources, was excerpted from a King James Version of the Old Testament, from the First Book of Moses called Genesis, Chapters One and Two.

Chapter One

1 In the beginning God created the heaven and the earth.

2 And the earth was without form, and void; and darkness was upon the face of the deep. And the Spirit of God moved upon the face of the waters.

3 And God said, Let there be light: and there was light.

4 And God saw the light, that it was good: and God divided the light from the darkness.

5 And God called the light Day, and the darkness he called Night. And the evening and the morning were the first day.

6 And God said, Let there be a firmament in the midst of the waters, and let it divide the waters from the waters.

7 And God made the firmament, and divided the waters which were under the firmament from the waters which were above the firmament: and it was so.

8 And God called the firmament Heaven. And the evening and the morning were the second day.

9 And God said, Let the waters under the heaven be gathered together unto one place, and let the dry land appear: and it was so.

10 And God called the dry land Earth; and the gathering together of the waters called the Seas: and God saw that it was good.

11 And God said, Let the earth bring forth grass, the herb yielding seed, and the fruit tree yielding fruit after his kind, whose seed is in itself, upon the earth: and it was so.

12 And the earth brought forth grass, and herb yielding seed after his kind, and the tree yielding fruit, whose seed was in itself, after his kind: and God saw that it was good.

13 And the evening and the morning were the third day.

14 And God said, Let there be lights in the firmament of the heaven to divide the day from the night; and let them be for signs, and for seasons, and for days, and years;

15 and let them be for lights in the firmament of the heaven to give light upon the earth: and it was so.

16 And God made two great lights; the greater light to rule the day, and the lesser light to rule the night: he made the stars also.

17 And God set them in the firmament of the heaven to give light upon the earth,

18 and to rule over the day and over the night, and to divide the light from the darkness: and God saw that it was good.

19 And the evening and the morning were the fourth day.

20 And God said, Let the waters bring forth abundantly the moving creature that hath life, and fowl that may fly above the earth in the open firmament of heaven.

21 And God created great whales, and every living creature that moveth, which the waters brought forth abundantly, after their kind, and every winged fowl after his kind: and God saw that it was good.

22 And God blessed them, saying, Be fruitful, and multiply, and fill the waters in the seas, and let fowl multiply in the earth.

23 And the evening and the morning were the fifth day.

24 And God said, Let the earth bring forth the living creature after his kind, cattle, and creeping thing, and beast of the earth after his kind: and it was so.

25 And God made the beast of the earth after his kind, and cattle after their kind, and everything that creepeth upon the earth after his kind: and God saw that it was good.

26 And God said, Let us make man in our image, after our likeness: and let them have dominion over the fish of the sea, and over the fowl of the air, and over the cattle, and over all the earth, and over every creeping thing that creepeth upon the earth.

27 So God created man in his own image, in the image of God created he him; male and female created he them.

28 And God blessed them, and God said unto them, Be fruitful, and multiply, and replenish the earth, and subdue it: and have dominion over the fish of the sea, and over the fowl of the air, and over every living thing that moveth upon the earth.

29 And God said, Behold, I have given you every herb bearing seed, which is upon the face of all the earth, and every tree, in the which is the fruit of a tree yielding seed; to you it shall be for meat.

30 And to every beast of the earth, and to every fowl of the air, and to everything that creepeth upon the earth, wherein there is life, I have given every green herb for meat: and it was so.

31 And God saw everything that he had made, and, behold, it was very good. And the evening and the morning were the sixth day.

Chapter Two

1 Thus the heavens and the earth were finished, and all the host of them.

2 And on the seventh day God ended his work which he had made; and he rested on the seventh day.

3 And God blessed the seventh day and sanctified it: because that in it he had rested from all his work which God created and made.

Deconstructing the Abrahamic Paradigm

From their respective creation stories, the three Abrahamic religions have adapted multiple variations of core belief systems briefly enumerated below:

Belief that the universe was created by one God alone (Yahweh/Allah) assisted in its later differentiation by divine beings or angels.

Belief that God is omnipotent and transcendent standing outside and above or beyond direct access by mortal men, thus requiring the need of ordained intermediaries to mediate between God and humanity, interpret religious scriptures, uphold laws and perform rites and rituals.

Belief in one single life with one eternal afterlife consisting of a heaven and a hell.

Belief in the concept of "original sin" which is a Judeo-Christian concept that one is born in sin and is in need of redemption/salvation to overcome the unworthiness of humanity and to make man worthy of God's acceptance, love, mercy and grace. Unless one seeks redemption/salvation through acceptance of specific tenets of faith, purification rites and rituals during this lifetime one will be condemned to hell in the afterlife. The Qur'an tells the same Genesis story of the fall of man but in the Islamic version Adam and Eve sinned, begged forgiveness of Allah and were forgiven by Allah. Thus returning them to their "original sinless state" due to their "true repentance from sin." From the Islamic perspective, pride is the cardinal sin and the cardinal virtue is submission to Allah's will or "Islam."

Belief that questioning of or disobedience to religious laws will incur God's punishment enacted by ordained religious authorities through punitive measures and/or threats of exclusion from the religious community and from attaining heaven in the afterlife, causing the transgressor to suffer in eternal hell after death.

Belief that adherents must undergo baptism, pilgrimages and in some instances circumcision as these represent forms of purification, cleansing and sanctification.

Belief in the need for making sacrifices, doing penances and tithing as part of the doctrine of faith accompanied by the belief that genuine repentance will save one from hell and earn one's acceptance into heaven after death.

Belief in divine miracles, superhuman intervention by God and divine retribution by God for injustices inflicted on the true believers and followers of the "One True Religion."

Belief that unbelievers are wrong, lost and in need of conversion through missionary outreach and sometimes through harsh actions used to threaten or force unbelievers to convert to the "One True Religion."

Belief in the need of a savior, messiah or mahdi—one having lived in the past or one to return or arrive in the future—who will save the faithful believers and bring eternal damnation on the unbelievers in a final apocalyptic judgment day.

Belief in the need of the faithful to be bound to the community of the temple church or mosque through shared religious practices, ritual acts of worship, celebration of specific holy days and abiding by religious laws.

Belief in the need for daily prayer and worship rituals in remembrance of God to earn God's mercy, grace and forgiveness.

Belief that God has the power to redeem believers, to protect them from harm by releasing them from the consequences of actions taken against unbelievers in the name of their God; resulting in sorrowful and destructive consequences due to the acting out of this belief, observable in the ongoing chaos of worldwide religious wars and killings.

Reference Keys: "Abrahamic" (web). "Ancient" (web). Bartlett's (web). "Bible Version" (web). "Biblical Canon" (web) "Biblical Cosmology" (web). "Bible Version" (web). English Bible (web). Genesis (web). "Genesis" (web). "Genesis Creation" (web). Holy Bible (1940). "Islamic" (web). Oral Law (web). "Talmud" (web). "Ten Commandments" (web).

Chapter Eight

The Sumerian/Babylonian Worldview

THERE ARE VOLUMES upon volumes of interpretations of the Sumerian/Babylonian creation story, with each version providing sometimes similar and sometimes divergent worldviews depending on which philologist was doing the translations on the voluminous cache of cuneiform tablets recovered from various archaeological digs. Most translations have been published only recently—in the past few hundred years. In this chapter only a few summarized versions are provided. From my perspective, this creation story, strange and unusual as it may seem, forms the underpinnings of the Judeo-Christian and Islamic religions. Each of the Abrahamic religions evolved from the Hebrew biblical version of the creation story, which has been called into question by the excavation and translation of the much older Sumerian/Babylonian creation story. This fact highlights, in retrospect, the many distortions and discontinuities found in the Hebrew Bible.

According to a recent historical biography of the Patriarch Abraham (David Rosenberg's *Abraham, The First Historical Biography*), he was called Abram before a covenant was made by him with Yahweh, God of the Old Testament: "Abram was born in the Sumerian city of Ur in 1433 BCE. His father, Terah, was a priest in the local temple and he had two brothers, Nahor and Haran, who also lived in Ur, a Sumerian city." This is an important piece of historical information since many recovered Sumerian clay tablets were found in and around the ruins of the ancient city of Ur, Abram's birthplace.

Over 20,000 clay tablets, some intact, many broken and fragmented, were found among the ruins of the palace and library of Ashurbanipal (668–626 BCE) at Nineveh (modern-day Iraq) between 1866 and 1870. A small number of the retrieved tablets tell the story of the creation in what is known as the Babylonian Enuma Elish: The Seven Tablets of Creation. Some translations of this creation story present a poetic, cosmic, mythological version of the creation story while others present a more concrete, literal interpretation. The worldviews included in this chapter provide crucial puzzle pieces for comprehending the ancient history of planet Earth, how humanity originated and how civilizations and religions evolved on this planet.

The Sumerian tablets provide the earliest written record of a creation story in the history of mankind, which is why the famous Sumerologist Samuel Noah Kramer titled his 1956 bestselling book *History Begins in Sumer*. Earlier translations of the tablets were edited and published by George Smith in 1872. Another version was translated and privately published by L. W. King, an assistant in the British Museum's Department of Egyptian and Assyrian Antiquities, in 1902. A later extrapolation titled *The Babylonian Legend of Creation* was published by E. A. Wallis Budge in 1921. Budge was an English Egyptologist, Orientalist and philologist who also worked for the British Museum and published numerous works on the ancient Near East.

In 1915 Stephen Langdon published *The Sumerian Epic of Paradise, the Flood and the Fall of Man* through the University of Pennsylvania, based on the Sumerian text known today as "Enki and Ninhursag." In 1945 Samuel Noah Kramer, expert in cuneiform writing, continued Langdon's work by further studying "Enki and Ninhursag" and published "A Sumerian Paradise Myth" in the *Bulletin of the American Schools of Oriental Research*. He also published with John Maier a more recent version of this material: *Myths of Enki, The Crafty God*, published by Oxford University Press in 1989. As you can see, in these two centuries several philologists, scholars, Assyriologists and Sumerologists have translated and published various interpretations of the Enuma Elish, The Seven Tablets of Creation and other Sumerian, Akkadian and Babylonian tablets.

Some of the most valuable recovered Sumerian cuneiform tablets found in Ur, Nippur, Eridu, Ubaid, Girsu and other nearby ruins along the Tigris and Euphrates rivers include the following:

(1) The Atrahasis. The name Atra-Hasis also appears on one of the Sumerian king lists as king of Shuruppak. The oldest known copy of the epic concerning the Atrahasis can be dated by colophon— scribal identification—to the reign of Hammurabi's great-grandson, Ammi-Saduqa (1646–1626 BCE), but various Old Babylonian fragments exist and it continued to be copied into the first millennium BCE.

(2) The Enuma Elish, the Seven Tablets of Creation. This is the Babylonian creation story recovered by Austen Henry Layard in 1849, in fragmentary form, in the ruined Library of Ashurbanipal at Nineveh (Mosul, Iraq), and published by George Smith in 1876.

(3) The Epic of Gilgamesh. Gilgamesh is the central character in the Epic of Gilgamesh, the greatest surviving work of early Mesopotamian literature. He was the fifth king of Uruk (modern-day Iraq) in early Dynastic II, first dynasty of Uruk, placing his reign ca. 2500 BCE. According to the Sumerian King List he reigned for 126 years.

These written histories predate the first Hebrew Bible by more than a thousand years. It was well known by many renowned archaeologists that for hundreds of years archaeological dig sites were closely controlled and monitored by Roman Catholic church authorities. The very same authorities that protected and perpetuated the altered stories presented in the canonical Bible established by the First Council of Nicea in 325 CE convened by the Roman Emperor Constantine. In modern times, numerous ancient artifacts, codices, cylinder seals and tablet fragments have been excavated and pieced together by biblical scholars, linguists, philologists and archaeologists. Their combined efforts have revealed a much expanded, detailed version of the truncated, incomplete and fragmented version preserved in the ancient Hebrew Bible.

In Zecharia Sitchin's book *Genesis Revisited*, he states:

> Texts found in the library of the Assyrian king Ashur-
> banipal in Nineveh ... recorded the tale of creation that
> matches, in some parts word for word, the Tale of Gen-
> esis. The Chaldean Genesis ... conclusively established
> that there indeed existed an Akkadian text of the Genesis
> tale, written in the Old Babylonian dialect, that preceded
> the biblical text by at least a thousand years. Excavations
> between 1902 and 1914 uncovered tablets with the As-
> syrian version of the creation epic. (pp. 41–42)

Sitchin was well known for producing a series of sensationally popular books, fifteen or so, on the Sumerian/Anunnaki. He claimed his
translations came from direct translations of various Sumerian tablets.
However, many Sumerian scholars and translators have since called into
question the translations and conclusions presented in his books, claiming that he never provided clear or exact textual references, such as tablet
catalog numbers, museum locations, etc. for the tablets from which he
claimed his information was extracted. While his books do provide many
well researched facts and missing puzzle pieces, they are mixed in with
his speculations to such a degree that a number of his conclusions have
since been called into question.

Joseph P. Farrell also authored several books on the Sumerian/
Anunnaki. Many of his books focus more on describing their interplanetary cosmic wars and how they constructed global electromagnetic power grids around Earth, which they used as energetic power sources and a
means of controlling Earth's humanoid inhabitants.

Maximillien de Lafayette, another scholar, linguist and writer, has
also authored several books on the Anunnaki. Scott Alan Roberts, Gerald Clark, Michael Tellinger, Chris Hardy and many others have written
books focusing on different aspects of the history of the Sumerian/
Anunnaki colonizers of Earth.

Below is a summarized condensed cosmic version of The Seven
Tablets of Creation story taken from *The Babylonian Legends of Creation* by
E. A. Wallis Budge, excerpted from sacred-texts.com:

In the beginning nothing existed except a boundless, confused and disordered mass of watery cosmic substance, the void. Out of this cosmic substance evolved two orders of beings: demons and deities or gods. They originally had no matter-based forms but over eons of time developed etheric light bodies and then eventually physical humanoid forms. The demonic beings took on hideous-looking etheric forms and later physical forms that were part animal, part bird, part reptile and part humanoid. The gods developed transparent golden glowing etheric light bodies, sometimes with wing-like appendages and they too eventually took on physical humanoid forms. Subtle and physical-matter worlds were represented as three layers of the comprehensible world—the underworld comprising the Earth, the atmosphere, and the sky or heavens. The first two "gods" were represented as two conceptualized forces of pre-matter: the masculine or chaotic and the feminine or ordering creative principles. The ANSHAR represented the hosts of Heaven (the gods or deities), and the KISHAR represented the hosts of Earth (the demons).

When the ANSHAR (the gods) first appeared in the void of the watery cosmic substance of pre-matter, "order" came into being. The KISHAR (the demons, chaotic forces), also existed in the void of the watery cosmic substance of pre-matter. They observed this initial ordering of the cosmos by the ANSHAR. They perceived this action as a threat to their domain: the confused darkness and disorder of the void of the primeval formless watery cosmos. The KISHAR conspired to destroy this "ordering" of the unformed primeval cosmic substance. Thus began the battle between the demonic forces of chaos and the creative life-bringing, organizing forces of the gods/deities. The powers of darkness and chaos, intent on destroying the powers of light and order, thus brought into manifestation the earliest formation of the dualistic polarized forces of creation/destruction or attraction/repulsion cycles in the cosmos.

This ongoing war between the creative forces (positive pole) and the destructive forces (negative pole) of the cosmos was waged over possession of the "Tablets of Destinies." The wars of the gods over these creation templates or formulas for creating universes and living life forms comprise a central theme in the Enuma Elish. The gods, the hosts of Heaven, the ordering forces, were initially represented as the "deified bodies" of various galaxies and solar systems formed out of the formless void of primeval matter. These galactic formations were considered superconscious intelligent light beings existing before any planetary solar systems or life forms came into existence. As the creation evolved, the gods/hosts of Heaven were deified, personified and named as the constellations in our solar system. Over eons they came to be represented by the archetypal twelve signs of the zodiac, and after another indefinitely long time period, they became personified as living gods in humanoid forms. These living gods were worshipped as a deified trinity in the Sumerian/Babylonian temple complexes as An (Anu), Ea (Enki) and Bel or Baal (Enlil). Anu was represented as the sky god of the heavens. Enlil was represented as god of the region under the sky—the atmosphere. And Enki was represented as god of the Earth—the underworld.

The next two versions of the Sumerian/Babylonian creation story are two of the most fascinatingly detailed, in-depth stories of Earth's hidden intergalactic history and the history of the Sumerian/Anunnaki I've come across. One story is presented in *The Terra Papers: The Hidden History of Planet Earth* by Robert Morning Sky, and the other came from Anton Parks's book *Eden, The Truth about Our Origins*. Robert is an Apache/Hopi Indian ceremonial spirit dancer, a storyteller, author and researcher. There are a limited number of videos posted on Youtube of Robert animatedly telling the story of the hidden history of planet Earth to audiences during the one-year period from February 1995 to February 1996. He did this to keep a promise he'd made to his Hopi Elder grandfather to tell the story of this hidden history when he reached adulthood. There are no documented scholarly works, archaeological artifacts or recovered alien spacecraft remnants to verify this story. It's simply an amazingly detailed story told to Robert Morning Sky's grandfather and his five Hopi Indian companions by an extraterrestrial who crashed his spacecraft on Hopi land in the Four Corners area of Arizona in 1945:

The Hopis were camping out in the hills when they observed a fiery crash from their campsite. They hiked to the site of the crash and pulled a lone survivor from the spacecraft. This downed interplanetary space traveler was named Bek'Ti and he told this amazing story to the Hopis who rescued him from the crash site and saved his life. What follows is a very condensed version of Robert's *Terra Papers*. The original written version by Robert Morning Sky is some 80–100 pages long and can be found on the Scribd.com website.

According to Bek'Ti, an intergalactic cosmic war has been raging above our heads for billions of years. He was engaged in this war when his craft was downed. His story provides a detailed history of the race we've come to know as the Sumerian/Anunnaki, who Bek'Ti said came from the star system of Sirius. He described their colonization of our solar system and gave a detailed account of how Earth's planetary body was formed.

Many details of Bek'Ti's story match the stories told of the ancient history of Earth by many African tribes, especially the Dogon tribe. Credo Mutwa, a well-known African shaman, has told a similar story of Earth's ancient history. There are a number of videos of David Icke interviewing Credo Mutwa on this very topic on Youtube. There are also ancient stories recorded in the Vedas and other sacred Hindu texts that tell a similar story of intergalactic wars that destroyed many advanced civilizations on Earth.

According to Bek'Ti, Eridanus began as a primitive star system, with Earth located in one small part of this vast galaxy. As planetary bodies, stars and suns formed, numerous humanoid and other species of beings also evolved on the stars and planets in this galaxy. These primitive beings eventually evolved into civilized races who then founded various galactic civilizations and empires. As civilizations rose and fell, a continuous series of wars and chaos engulfed the entire star system of Eridanus. Constant warring and aggression among the various technologically advanced races resulted in their creating cloned warrior races, genetically engineered to operate as killing machines. One race from the Orion star system became known as the ARI-AN, the "supreme masters of war." They evolved from a race of cold-blooded dragon-faced reptilians feared all over the galaxy, ruled by a group of ruthless reptilian queens. They commanded a fierce military force and controlled the entire Ninth Sector/Star Passageway of the Eridanus star system. Their society was based on an autocratic system of kingship with total domination and control of their subjects and aggression and domination toward other races through perpetual war.

Within the Sirius star system another reptilian race from Orion, the ASA-RRR, evolved as a race of ruthless, aggressive, warrior killers known as the "warlords." They commanded a fleet of deadly starships with which they would attack and decimate any and all military installations of the other civilizations in their galaxy. They genetically engineered a race of fierce warriors known as the IKU, cloned from a dog race who would attack, kill and then eat the flesh of their conquered enemies. A perpetual galactic war developed between these two different engineered cyborg species, created by the Sirians and the Orions, over control of the Ninth Sector/Star Passageway, a major starship lane used for intergalactic space travel and the transport of raw materials from one star system to another.

Both factions had developed plasma-beam and sonic weapons and used planetoid-sized starships that could disintegrate entire planets. They could move planets from one location to another and even alter planetary orbits. Both civilizations were highly technologically advanced with knowledge and skills in planetary terraforming technologies, energy production, monolith building, metallurgy, complex advanced computer technology, and genetic engineering of plant, animal and humanoid species, as well as intergalactic and interdimensional space travel and telepathic communication. After countless wars over millions of years, the Orion reptilian empire discovered that by executing their war captives they deprived themselves of an able-bodied slave workforce, so they devised methods of electromagnetic mind control and the means for reprogramming the brains of their captives to erase memories and thereby any resistance, turning their captives into docile slave workers.

Alliances were forged and quickly broken between these two major warring races due to the constant treachery, lies, assassination plots, alien invasions and infighting that abounded in their respective royal courts. This constant fighting culminated in the Galactic Great Wars, during which time a royal family heir to the Sirian kingship was captured and sent into exile—which set off a series of counter-plots of revenge, assassinations and more wars. A young prince of the exiled royal family named Anu was determined to become king of Sirius. He devised a plan to claim the kingship for himself from his uncle who had stolen the kingship from Anu's father. While these events were occurring, in the outer arms of the Eridanus galaxy new planets and solar systems were forming, promising a steady new supply of precious mineral ores and an income stream for the Sirian and Orion empires. A new planet was accreting near the Ninth Passageway's trade route, and the Sirian king wanted to be first to colonize this new planet to capture its riches for himself. He sent an administrator to establish colonies on the planet and to build a palace for himself there, allowing him to claim ownership of this budding, beautiful new planet called Tiamat.

This move upset the Orion reptilian queens who also wanted to have access to the precious ores of the new planet and to the tariff fees charged for passage through the Ninth Passageway Star Lanes. Aware of the infighting between the Sirian king and his nephew, Prince Anu, the Orion queens were wary of civil war erupting on Sirius over Tiamat that could disrupt supply lines and their lucrative income streams. An uneasy alliance was arranged between the Sirians and the Orions. However, Prince Anu and his military forces attacked Tiamat, destroyed the Sirian king's palace and deposed the king. Prince Anu, now King Anu, forged a new alliance between himself and the Orion queens and placed his two sons, Enlil and Enki, in charge of affairs on Tiamat.

Another conflict broke out between King Anu and his grandson, Prince Iku-Mar-Beh, who had been raised among an elite IKIKI warrior caste. Iku-Mar-Beh conspired with his loyal IKIKI warriors to overthrow his grandfather, King Anu, and take the kingship for himself. A fierce galactic battle ensued between the two warring forces that resulted in the destruction of the planet known as Tiamat, which was literally blown apart, killing millions.

One portion of this planet disintegrated into the debris field now known as the asteroid belt orbiting between Mars and Jupiter. The larger chunk of the exploded planet was catapulted towards the Sun but on the way was captured into the outer gravitational field of Mars. That chunk of Tiamet became what is now called Earth, which gradually settled into its new orbit between Venus and Mars.

Iku-Mar-Beh retreated with his elite force to his military base on Mars. King Anu, enraged by the attempted coup and the desecration of Tiamat, descended with his star fleet onto Mars, executed Iku-Mar-Beh, annihilated his entire military force, and in the process destroyed all life on Mars by vaporizing the entire planet, turning it into a barren, red-sanded wasteland. Billions perished in this great solar-system-wide war.

King Anu then appointed his eldest son, Prince Ea (Enki), Lord of the Airways, to orbit and police the intergalactic star lanes and to survey the newly accreting planet Earth. King Anu wanted to colonize this planet so he sent Prince Ea to Earth to begin rebuilding the planet and terraforming it.

Commander Enki landed on Earth within a narrow strip of land around the equator with a small team of Anunnaki who were promised titles, property and monetary rewards in return for their toils in rebuilding the planet. They initially built a large stone compound but encountered major problems due to the highly unstable and fluctuating gravity of Earth, a result of the great collision splitting apart Tiamat. They had to build energy houses (pyramids) as focusing centers to extract energy from the planetary core, utilizing crystals to run their construction equipment and their "re-animation centers" where the bodies of injured technicians were taken to be healed and repaired.

The rebuilding work was strenuous and dangerous. The Anunnaki master stone masons (much later becoming known as the free masons) had difficulty using their highly technical cutting equipment due to power anomalies forcing them to resort to alternative methods involving hard physical labor. The mining operations they set up encountered similar technical problems and power issues that interfered with the transport of the gold and mineral ores from Earth mines to space transport stations, where the materials were loaded onto starships for transport to interplanetary metallurgical refineries. Enki and his team built an Agricultural-Biological Center near the Tigris River. In this center, Enki, being a master geneticist, bioengineered new animal and plant life forms that could thrive in Earth's harsh atmosphere. He set up atmospheric conditioning units to filter the air and make it breathable and warmer over time. He produced hybrid seedlings and hybrid creatures which he seeded around the globe. The center became Enki's pride and joy, a garden of life on the "Edin," the Mesopotamian plains (later to become known as the Garden of Eden in the Bible).

Enki's skills and rebuilding efforts allowed his father, King Anu, to retain control over Earth's solar system and keep control of the Ninth Passageway Star Lanes. Tiamat had been reborn as Earth, and Enki was given the title of Lord of Eridanus (Earth) for his efforts. In the meantime his half-brother, Prince Enlil, was unhappy and complained, wanting another higher post. King Anu appeased him by appointing him to the post of administrative controller of the planet and of the now-established agricultural center of Eridu/Sumer. This enraged Enki who felt his powers had been stripped away by his father's actions, leading to an escalating hatred between the half-brothers.

Enki left the city of Eridu/Sumer and relocated to South Africa where he built another Agricultural-Biological Center, the remnants of which still exist in modern-day Zimbabwe. There he developed gold-mining operations. His half-sister, Princess Ninhursag, also a master geneticist, joined him and they continued their genetic work of creating new life forms for the planet. Due to the shortage of laborers, Ninhursag eventually succeeded in cloning a new hybrid ape-beast, a "LuLu," which meant a mixed breed or "earthling" that would forever change the destiny of Earth and its reptilian Sumerian/Anunnaki overlords.

This hybridized beast of burden was presented to King Anu as a remedy for their manpower problems, and he approved of this cloned earthling. Enlil hated the beasts from the beginning and was opposed to their creation but, once created, he used them mercilessly for the most dangerous jobs and let them die where they fell of exhaustion or injuries as he considered them expendable beasts of burden. This horrified Enki who vowed to make Enlil pay for his cruelty. Enki took a trip back to the original Agricultural-Biological Center in Eridu/Sumer. While there, he searched out the hybrid beasts in the garden area where they were fed and kept. He and his half-sister had developed the structured breeding program which was strictly controlled by Enlil. The hybrids' reproductive functions were tightly monitored to keep the genetic lines pure. Males and females were kept separate and had no knowledge of mating. As a retaliatory act against Enlil, Enki, wearing the master geneticist's emblem of two intertwined strands of DNA on his uniform, secretly entered the garden center and took a male and a female hybrid earthling aside, and showed them how to mate.

Shortly thereafter, Enlil observed this more-recently developed genetic line, the "adamu," mating in the Agri-Bio Center and became enraged, certain that Enki was somehow behind this criminal act, this sacrilege. To prevent further transgressions and the destruction of the controlled hybrid genetic breeding programs, he threw the offending adamu beasts out of the agricultural center and decreed a strict set of new commands that the remaining lines of hybrid beasts in the Agri-Bio Life Center must all obey. They were commanded to give complete and total obedience to Enlil only. They were forbidden any contact with or remembrance of Enki or of making any "angry sounds" toward Enlil. All hybrid beasts were required to take an obedience lesson every seventh day and all mating was undertaken only under the strict supervision of Enlil. He further threatened the adamu beasts, saying any who disobeyed him would be cast out into the wilderness and the female beasts would be denied access to the birthing chambers in the Life Center and would then suffer pain in childbirth.

Enlil divided the genetic lines into two categories: the adapa and the adamu. The adapa, the faithful and the obedient, were allowed to stay in the Life Center, their genetic line developed and controlled by Enlil. The adamu, the disobedient and rebellious ones, he continued to cast out into the wilderness, forcing them to survive outside the controlled environment of the walled Agri-Bio Center. Enki continued his experiments with the cast-out adamus and helped them to survive by teaching them survival skills. He believed the adamus would now have an opportunity to grow in intelligence, to evolve, and to develop survival skills, emotional connections, family communities, and language skills. Most importantly they would be freed from the master control system imposed upon the hybrids by his authoritarian, dominating, cruel half-brother Enlil. The granting of "free will" to the adamus had been part of Enki's original intention in setting up the genetic experiments. Over generations of time both the adamus and the adapas interbred and became intelligent, self-sufficient, responsible contributing members of society—fully capable of building, administering and running the civilizations and social systems established on Earth by the Sumerian/Anunnaki overlords.

The Sumerian/Anunnaki empire continued on Earth as civilization evolved, as did the deceit, betrayals, coups and wars between the royal family members down through the centuries. Both the adapa and adamu hybrid species were eventually fully incorporated into the Sumerian/Anunnaki-built civilizations all over Earth, but they continued to be used as slaves and as expendable soldiers to fight their endless empire-induced wars on Earth.

Also continuing on Earth were ongoing wars, conflicts and competition between the Orion empire and the Sirian empire. One rebellious troublemaker, Marduk, a son of Enki's and grandson of king Anu, was sent to live in Egypt where he plotted and planned to make himself King of Earth. He initiated a secret revolution using Enlil's own cloned loyal priest ranks. He eventually succeeded in ousting both his father Enki and his uncle Enlil, forcing both half-brothers and their royal offspring to flee Earth for other star systems. Enlil returned to Sirius while Enki, with many of his faithful adamu hybrids, fled to the star system of the Pleiades, called by the hybrids Baal-Ea-Daus, the Place of the Creator.

Marduk seized the Empire of Earth and appointed himself Lord God and Creator of the Universe of Eridu. During his reign in Egypt he ordered the destruction of all previous records of Earth's history before his reign and began using the same mind-control technologies on the populace of Earth that had been developed and used on the enslaved populaces in the empires of Sirius and Orion. He became known as the only god of record. He employed the huge stone monoliths erected all over Earth which emitted EMFs (electromagnetic frequencies) to create an electromagnetic grid transmitting clouds of electronic signals designed to keep all the subjugated earthling hybrids in a mental fog and in a docile state so they could be easily controlled and programmed by the loyal lizard-cloned priesthood taken over by Marduk.

This planet-wide electronic grid also served to prevent intergalactic communication with the population of Earth and to block starships from other galaxies from reaching Earth. Actually there was an interesting article recently published online at Nanowerk News (www.nanowerk.com) verifying that such an electronic barrier exists around Earth: "NASA's Van Allen Probes Spot an Impenetrable Barrier in Space" was posted November 26, 2014. It states that two donuts of seething radiation surround Earth. The Van Allen radiation belts have been found to contain a nearly impenetrable torus-like barrier that prevents the fastest most energetic photons from reaching Earth. The discovery of this barrier was made using NASA's Van Allen probes launched in 2012. A cloud of cold charged gas around Earth called the plasmasphere interacts with the particles in Earth's radiation belts, creating an impenetrable barrier that blocks high-frequency photons from entering Earth's atmosphere.

To further control the humanoid slaves, all "Houses of Obedience" previously erected by Enlil were taken over by Marduk and turned into temples of worship, used to teach the same doctrine and dogma of the Sumerian empire under the guise of various "religions" as another form of mind control. The ways of Enki, still remembered and revered by some earthling hybrids, were demonized by Enlil and later by Enki's son Marduk. Using indoctrination and propaganda, Enlil intentionally transformed the memory of Enki into the image of "the evil one," the diabolic one, the serpent one in the minds of the earthlings, representing him in symbolic imagery as the "serpent in the garden." This story was specifically designed to blame the "fall of humanity into sin" on Enki, the serpent one, the master geneticist. This demonization was intentionally introduced by Enlil to erase all memories of Enki, the genetic engineer of humanity, and any memory of his efforts to help humanity escape from the cruelty of Enlil who wanted to destroy the entire hybrid humanoid population he despised.

The dictatorial, punishing biblical god written about in the Old Testament, named Yahweh, was the personification of Enlil. Likewise Enki became the personification of the serpent, the evil one, for causing the adamus to "sin through the act of mating." According to Anton Parks, author of *Eden, the Truth about Our Origins*, "sin" is a pre-Sumerian word meaning "genetic defect." The continuing uncontrolled mating, against Enlil's commands, caused a defect in the genetic line. Enlil has also been referred to as the personification of Satan, the deceiver and destroyer. In the Sumerian language, the word "Satam" means administrator. Enlil was named in the ancient texts the administrator and lord of the Empire of Earth.

Enki's son Marduk, enforcing the Sirian empire's program of control and indoctrination, extensively employed the cloned hive-minded ant-like race of cyborgs originally genetically engineered from the combined genetic materials of the Sirian and the Orion races. These faithful cyborg-cloned priests of Enlil were secretly infiltrated, enticed and manipulated by Marduk and his forces into overthrowing Enlil. Marduk then used these hybrid clone priests to control the humanoid populace by placing them into positions of power as administrators of his Earth empire. This cloned race Bek'Ti called the SHET-I and, according to Bek'Ti, this species is known today as the "Gray ETs" who live in underground facilities all over the world. They are a highly intelligent but dying hybrid cloned species skilled at using mind-control techniques, physical paralysis, memory erasure, mental telepathy and implantation of screen memories. A mummy of one of these hybrids was recently excavated from a small tomb near the larger Egyptian tomb of Senusret II in Lahun, Egypt. A photo of this mummy was posted on the internet along with an article about its discovery.

Beyond Bek'Ti's version, there are dizzying numbers of Sumerian creation stories recounted in books and in videos on the internet. For example, Wes Penre and other authors such as Barbara Marciniak, author of *Earth: The Pleiadian Keys to the Living Library*, assert that before the Sumerian/Anunnaki ever arrived on Earth to colonize it, other intergalactic races of divine beings had already been present, monitoring Earth and watching the progress of their "Living Library" on Earth. These intergalactic progenitors—life planners or Elohim—had been involved in the terraforming of life forms on planet Earth and include the Lyran, Pleiadian, Arcturian and Andromedan races. This Living Library contained their most precious experiment: the twelve-strand DNA humanoid template, the humanoid species in evolvement in the form of the then-present ape-man species. Their master plan had been to allow the twelve helices of DNA inherent in this ape species to evolve naturally into Homo Sapiens and eventually into the fully functioning, enlightened twelve-stranded God-conscious divine being Homo Luminous—conscious beings of light.

However, their original plan was thwarted due to the invading, colonizing reptilian races who usurped the then-present ape species for their own ends. They genetically altered this evolving species by deactivating ten of the original twelve strands of DNA to reduce the conscious awareness and the intellectual capacity of the ape species to make them into obedient, unknowing and unaware slaves. This is when the Anunnaki blocked all outside intergalactic species from communication with the humanoid species by intentionally creating an electromagnetic frequency grid around Earth and blocking the intergalactic portals and star gates on Earth. This frequency grid also served to block the energetic photonic "light" naturally emanating from the galactic center, connecting the galaxies. star systems and planetary bodies energetically, thus preventing these energetic emanations of light from activating the dormant ten DNA strands in the humanoid species.

The intergalactic races who had initiated the Living Library on Earth were blocked from entering Earth's solar system during a series of intergalactic wars initiated by the Anunnaki in the process of their colonization of Earth. No matter which worldview you favor, one thing is certain: the Sumerian/Anunnaki reptilian creator gods, "those who from heaven to Earth came" depicted in the Enuma Elish Seven Tablets of Creation, the Divine Genealogy of the Firm Ground tablets, and later in the distilled biblical creation story, were not by any conceivable stretch of the imagination divine loving creator gods. They are a psychotic, paranoid, domineering, warlike, reptilian race of vicious, sexually promiscuous, self-serving destroyers, deceivers and liars descended from a reptilian cold-blooded genotype from another star system. They altered the original divine plan for humanity's evolvement and rewrote Earth's history in their favor, setting themselves up to be worshipped as gods by the hybrid humanoids they genetically manipulated, reproduced and controlled to serve as their slaves.

Conquest and war were a way of life for the Sumerian Anunnaki. According to translations of the Sumerian lamentation texts, there were a series of major battles on Earth that included the use of powerful nuclear and scalar plasma-beam weapons. Here is just one account taken from a tablet titled "the lament for Urim: c.2.2.2":

> Enlil brought Gibil [the divine fire weapon of Baal] as his aide. He called the great storm of heaven—the people groan. The great storm howls above—the people groan. The storm that annihilates the Land roars below—the people groan. The evil wind, like a rushing torrent, cannot be restrained. The weapons in the city smash heads

and consume indiscriminately. The storm whirled gloom around the base of the horizon—the people groan. In front of the storm, heat blazes—the people groan. A fiery glow burns with the raging storm. (web)

King Anu authorized the use of scalar weapons to settle the ongoing series of endless battles between the Anunnaki kings of various city-states. According to Sitchin's calculations, one of these battles happened around 2024 BCE and is described in the Bible as the "upheaving of Sodom and Gomorrah." Actually the entire populace and many cities in the area were vaporized. The southern end of the Dead Sea was blasted open and many of the natural water springs around the Dead Sea are still contaminated with radioactive waste. The scorched barren desert terrain of the Sinai area, the result of another such war, is still visible. Sumer, Ur, Nippur and many other Sumerian cities were destroyed in various wars and holocausts and then in later centuries rebuilt on top of the ruins. Many buried humanoid skeletal bones recovered from these ancient archaeological sites are still radioactive today.

In the Galactic Great Wars described by Bek'Ti, during which time he said Mars was destroyed, recent evidence has been discovered verifying his story. A plasma physicist, Dr. John Brandenburg, an expert in propulsion technologies and directed-energy weapons, has discovered evidence that an ancient civilization on Mars was wiped out by two massive thermonuclear explosions. Recent analysis of isotopic, gamma-ray and imaging data from Mars supports his hypothesis. New images taken from Odyssey, MRO and Mars Express orbiters show strong evidence of eroded archaeological objects on the surface of the planet and evidence that two planet-wide nuclear catastrophes occurred. NASA spacecraft, using gamma-ray spectrometry, detected fallout from these past nuclear explosions, including uranium and thorium, on the surface of the red planet. Dr. Brandenburg is the author of two books, *Dead Mars, Dying Earth* and *Life and Death on Mars: The New Mars Synthesis*. Both books present evidence that Mars was once a thriving living biosphere, a sister planet to Earth that was decimated by a massive nuclear catastrophe.

When the original Anunnaki "creator gods" withdrew their physical presence from Earth after being driven off the planet by Marduk, he remained to rule over the Earth's civilizations and peoples. After a millennium he too withdrew physically from Earth but continued his rule from permanent space orbit around Earth, utilizing his genetically engineered SHETI servants, the cloned Gray ETs, and the previously built electromagnetic energy grids around Earth to control and monitor Earth's population from his satellite, our Moon, and from the interdimensional planes. According to David Icke and the authors of *Who Built the Moon?*—Christopher Knight and Alan Butler—the Moon is an artificially constructed hollowed-out planetoid towed into orbit around Earth eons ago by the conquering Anunnaki race who use it as a spaceport fort for their spaceships and as an Earth-monitoring satellite.

These Earth-colonizing Anunnaki have been referred to as the "Nine Worms of Amenti" visually depicted in the form of serpents and mentioned in the *Egyptian Book of the Dead*. Recent re-interpretations of the term "nine worms" and the visual images on temple walls have determined these wormholes to be interdimensional portals through which the Anunnaki traveled between star systems and galaxies. All the kingships depicted throughout Earth's long archaeological history are actually one and the same unbroken line of god/king rulers, interdimensional reptilian overlords who continue to rule Earth today through their DNA bloodline lineages. A detailed tracing of these originally intergalactic DNA bloodlines down through history can be found in Alan Alford's book *Gods of the New Millennium: Scientific Proof of Flesh and Blood Gods*, R. A. Boulay's book *Flying Serpents and Dragons: The Story of Mankind's Reptilian Past* and Anton Parks's books *Adam Genesis* and *Eden: The Truth About Our Origins*.

I've spent an inordinate amount of extra time and research on the Sumerian/Babylonian creation story because it represents the beginnings of Earth's recorded history. The biblical Genesis creation story is a very fragmented version of the excavated Babylonian creation tablets previously mentioned, known as The Divine Genealogy of the Firm Ground (British Museum catalog number BM 74329).

In doing research for this book I stumbled upon an interview of Anton Parks discussing his books. I had to wait about a year for some of his books to be translated from French into English and made available for English-speaking readers. Parks's history of our galaxy and of our origins closely parallels Bek'Ti's story of the galactic history of Eridanus, and his books are well researched and definitively detailed in their depth and breadth. His explanation of how he came to study, research and decipher the ancient Sumerian/Babylonian texts leading to the authorship of his several books is quite an amazing story and one well worth telling here.

It all began when Anton, at fourteen years of age, began having regular and vivid flashbacks of a previous incarnation of himself as a being called Sa'am, a member of a reptilian race known as the Gina'Abul (a Sumerian word meaning "lizards filled with splendor"). The same race written about in the Enuma Elish Tablets of Creation. Parks experienced these flashbacks for ten years from age fourteen to twenty-four. At first he was alarmed by the vividness of the flashbacks which were like living motion pictures in which he was reliving a life through the eyes, mind and body of a reptilian being called Sa'am. At first he feared he might be losing his mind and told no one of his visions. Eventually, though, he told his mother of his visions, and she was very supportive of him and non-judgmental of his unique experiences.

After almost ten years of daily flashbacks, some of which lasted up to ten minutes each, Parks decided to end the visions and began intentionally blocking them out of conscious awareness, which he succeeded in doing around 1991. His interest was piqued, though, causing him to begin a serious study of the ancient Sumerian texts.

He was shocked to discover that the visions he relived were practically identical to the history of the reptilian race written of in the Sumerian texts. He studied the Sumerian language and began gathering all the information he studied into written notes beginning in 2000. He eventually wrote several fiction and nonfiction books. A fictionalized version titled *The Secret of the Dark Stars* chronicled Sa'am's life experiences. He discovered Sa'am was none other than the famous Enki, the genetic cloner and creator of the hybrid humanoid race.

Parks started his career as a graphic artist, but later became a specialist in the study of the proto-Sumerian language. He studied Sumerian with the Assyriologist Don Moore (1929–2010). In time, Parks turned his attention to the Texts of Kharsag excavated from Nippur, originally translated by Christian O'Brien in a publication titled *The Genius of the Few.* Parks's nonfiction book *Eden: The Truth about Our Origins* refers frequently to the Texts of Kharsag and to the text called The Divine Genealogy of the Firm Ground. Both of these tablets delineate a cosmic timeline of the colonization of Earth paralleling in many instances Bek'Ti's story of Earth's galactic history and the colonization of Earth by the Sumerian/Anunnaki reptilian race. Thus, you'll encounter similarities in this next story.

According to Parks, the Anunna (Anunnaki) were a reptilian warrior race genetically engineered by Lord Anu to defend his empire in a great cosmic war against his foe, the reptilian queens. Anu and his forces were defeated in a galactic battle and forced to leave their home constellation of Draco. The Draco constellation, in the northern sky, is one of the largest constellations and its name means "the dragon" in Latin. This great cosmic war split the Gina'Abul (the reptilian races) apart and they scattered throughout many star systems before one faction or subspecies immigrated to Earth. They traveled in chariots (spaceships) and landed in the mountains of Turkey near a tributary of the Tigris River. The chief administrator of the colony was a son of Anu, Enlil. Enki, his older half-brother, also arrived with his troops known as the "Igigi" in the Akkadian language. The Igigi were a genetically engineered observer-messenger race as opposed to the Anunna who were a reptilian warrior race. All factions joined together and erected a command post and settlement on the "Edin"—the Mesopotamian plains.

Key recovered tablets document these developments, including the Divine Genealogy of the Firm Ground tablets and the Enuma Elish tablets, both essential because they elaborate fragments of episodes written of the in the first chapter of Genesis about the Elohim creator gods. In his book *Eden*, Parks makes a startling comparison between the words written on the clay tablets of the Enuma Elish tablets (lines 81–86) and the altered translations as written in the New American Standard Bible Genesis 1:21 and Genesis 1:26-27. The Enuma Elish tablets state:

> [T]he mother of the Haber (the deep) who created all things ... gave birth to giant serpents with sharp teeth, ruthless jaws.... [I]nstead of blood, she filled their body with venom.... She clad with horror the furious dragons,

charged them with splendor and made them as the gods.
(p. 54)

The Genesis version states in Genesis 1:21:

[Elohim] created the great sea monsters and every living creature that moves with which the waters swarmed after their kind and the [Elohim] saw that it was good.... Then [Elohim] said, "Let us make man in our image according to our likeness." [Elohim] created man in His own image.

This is an extraordinary discovery as it verifies that the Elohim of the Genesis story, the celestial Life Planners, originally created man in their image as the species Homo Erectus, carrying in their genetic DNA all the divine qualities of the Elohim sub-creator gods. The "dragons filled with splendor," the Anunnaki reptilian race who colonized Earth, usurped this already-existing species created by the Elohim and genetically altered their DNA to become the species Homo Sapiens, altering their brain and body structure and severing the DNA link holding the direct knowledge of their divine origins, awareness of the higher dimensions, and full conscious remembrance of their eternal, higher-frequency, light-bodied Soul selves.

In Parks's further translations of the tablets, he tells us that after altering the early ape species, the Anunnaki cloned the "black ape-beasts" and reproduced them en masse as slaves to feed, clothe and serve the reptilian god-kings who colonized Earth. Enki, the master geneticist/cloner, at a later date upgraded the original adamic genetic line to an improved mixed-blood race of ape-men, known as the LuLu or the "mixed earthlings." The genetically improved version, the Homo Sapiens species, carried the superior genes of the Kingu-Babbar royal dragon race in them. According to Parks, the Sumerian word Gina'Abul means "real ancestors of splendor" and the Sumerian word "a-dam" traces back to the Sumerian word nam-mas-Su, literally meaning "the half portion to charge" or "the cattle." This is how the first series of cloned ape-beasts were categorized by their reptilian overlords. Parks's book *Adam Genesis* contains charts showing the genetic evolvement of ape Primates into

Hominins and the genetic evolvement of the Adamic genetic lines into Homo Erectus and later into the Homo Sapiens species.

The Divine Genealogy of the Firm Ground text is the only surviving example of Mesopotamian cosmology apart from the Enuma Elish tablets that tell of the presence of these "deities" the Life Planners, called in Sumerian the "Kadistu." The Elohim formed a cosmic family of divine creator deities eons before the creation of the planet Earth or the establishment of the Sumerian civilization on Earth. These tablets tell of a slow, cyclic, step-by-step creation process seven cosmic cycles long; whereby the prime elements of nature were used by the Elohim or the Life Planners to create planetary bodies, star systems and galaxies, to receive animal and plant life and various other species of higher life forms, all originally created by the Elohim, the original sub-logoi creator gods.

Through his years of studying the Sumerian language and his translations of the preserved Texts of Kharsag, Parks provides excellent insight into the major problems encountered over the past few centuries of archaeological excavations. He states that numerous incorrect translations of tens of thousands of clay tablets were published at different times by different authors over the past few hundred years. He points out in his book *Eden* that many of the archaeological excavations were undertaken by major American universities who were in turn funded by the private donations of wealthy American Christians who "interpret the Bible literally." Therefore any researchers whose translations differed from the official biblical account were suppressed and access was restricted to a limited number of persons. Accurate translations can be found, according to Parks, in university publications, but they were intentionally withheld from release to the general public because it would have called into question the roots of the Abrahamic religions, the veracity of the Bible and the foundations of Western society. In his estimation the number of translators able to accurately decipher the Sumerian language amounts to about one hundred or so individuals. And those who are familiar with the collections held by the University Museum in Philadelphia (texts collected within the last one hundred years) total not more than thirty individuals. He concludes by saying that not more than fifteen philologists worldwide know of the true content of these texts.

Parks's retelling of the story of the colonization of Earth was primarily extracted from the Texts of Kharsag excavated from Nippur. His version differs somewhat from Sitchin's version in that the battalions of Anunna troops who built the first command post on Earth were also responsible for planting and growing crops to feed not only themselves but additional troops arriving periodically from outer space. In the texts, the Anunna troops complain about being overrun by the already-existing ape species on Earth. They described the beasts as "a stream of locusts" trespassing on their settlement and making off with their fruits, plants and grain reserves. The apes drank from the water canals the Anunna had built to water their crops. At one point, described in the Texts of Kharsag, the ape beasts contaminated the Anunna troops' water supply with some kind of virus that infected the entire settlement and almost wiped them out.

They eventually recovered, at which point Enki the master geneticist and his half-sister Ninhursag were called upon to genetically engineer this species into a more intelligent, androgynous and sterile hybrid species, which they could then clone and use to till their fields and raise their crops for them. They later upgraded this hybrid species and created a male and female who could then reproduce themselves, eliminating the need for artificial cloning matrices. These hybrids multiplied and filled the region of the plains of Edin. According to Parks's translations of the Kharsag texts, Enki taught the hybrid beasts the secrets of "the casting of metal" so that they could make tools to aid them in their agricultural work. Enki was later condemned for revealing this tightly guarded metallurgical knowledge to the beasts as it resulted in the herds of beasts using their metal farming implements to fight back against the cruel treatment they received at the hands of the Anunna conquerors. The Anunna treated their cloned slaves cruelly, locking them up in pens like cattle and forcing them to eat grasses and drink from specifically designated agricultural water canals.

These hybrids who were taught the use of flint implements came to be called in the Kharsag texts "the people of the flint." Enlil vowed to get revenge on the beasts for their acts of rebellion and for using their metal farming implements against the colonizers. Taking up his "storm weapon" (the Gibil), Enlil in his chariot (spaceship), attacked and burned all the beasts living on the plains around the settlement for rebelling against the gods and for "stealing the food of the gods." Enlil, cursing the beasts, then unfolded "a divine net"—an electromagnetic weapon of the gods—over the "enemy of clay" to control them.

Unraveling the threads of the many fragmented pieces of the original story of the happenings on the Edin—the Mesopotamian plains—it is understandable how it became so convoluted and misinterpreted by the Hebrew temple priests several generations later. Then, compounding the confusion, the biblical scholars of the Old Testament added their misinterpretations to an already-altered version of the story of the creation. The so-called "original sin" or "fall of man" was not man's doing but the blaming, shaming and retaliatory punishments perpetrated upon the hybrid species by the Anunna colonizers. The Texts of Kharsag contain the true history of our planet's colonization, including the true story of the happenings in the compound on the Edin. These preserved tablets tell us who the serpent of the Bible truly was (Enlil aka Yahweh) and what the so-called original sin truly was about and how it was later misrepresented and deviated by the scholars, with of course the guidance of the Anunnaki overlords who created the falsehoods embedded into the worlds' earliest religions. We can now begin to see and understand from whence the sociocultural ideals and beliefs of modern civilization came, as well as the origins of dogmas embedded into the three great monotheistic religions.

The importance of acknowledging the Sumerian/Babylonian role in the developmental creation of world culture can't be overstated. The Sumerians were a masterfully technologically skilled and powerful intergalactic race of conquerors, colonizers and planetary enslavers who employed advanced scalar and plasma-physics weapons in their intergalactic conquests. Joseph P. Farrell, in his books *The Cosmic War: Interplanetary Warfare, Modern Physics and Ancient Texts* and *The Giza Death Star Destroyed,* among other authors, pieced together a loosely temporal ordering of the numerous cosmic wars fought among warring intergalactic factions, including the Sumerian colonizers, over possession of the Tablets of Destinies. It's important to expand the basic understanding of what the Tablets of Destinies were because they played a central role in fueling the *interplanetary* conflicts that were extant prior to historically recorded

Earth-bound wars fought among factions of early Sumerian colonizers—over the possession of these tablets.

Preserved Sumerian texts document multiple cosmic wars among these colonizers eons of time before our particular planetary solar system was ever terraformed. The Tablets of Destinies, according to Farrell's interpretations of a number of ancient texts, represented a sort of computerized tablet containing sets of formulas utilizing a form of hyperdimensional physics. This included complex applications for the use of scalar physics and the use of holographic geometry and advanced mathematics through which entire planetary systems, stars, suns and moons could be physically formed, moved about the galaxy and their massive core energies harnessed. The Tablets conferred the supreme power of creation/destruction to the possessor and allowed the possessor to "challenge the divine order." By using the complex physics formulas, the holder could create, control or destroy planetary bodies, life forms and civilizations. The tablets also contained formulas for establishing the laws of rulership/kingship over the created civilizations in the galaxies.

These specialized tablets were discussed in many ancient tablets, and stories were told of wars fought over their possession by the Anunnaki overlords. In Sumerian the word *me* means stone or tablet and is pronounced like "may." These tablets were small computerized information devices containing radiant light beams that allowed the holder to tap into the energy of the universe, possibly through the use of scalar-wave technology. Their possession conferred kingship/rulership and godlike power with the ability to create, control or destroy anything in the creation. This universal energetic force, of torsion-wave technology, could be wielded to transmute the vacuum or ether of space, the prima materia, through the manipulation of scalar waves. Whatever the holder of the tablet "imagined" was instantly manifested through the consciousness of the holder of the tablet. The possessor of such a tablet could even manifest or create the concept of space/time itself, using their mind to manifest a holographic projection laid out in the ether of interstellar space, creating entire moving galaxies filled with constellations and rotating planetary bodies.

The Sumerian word *me* also means "a decree of the gods": a template for laying out the foundational concepts for structuring civilizations, monetary systems, social institutions, religious institutions and worship practices; ordering and placing god/ruler/kings in various city-states around the planet along with their accompanying military forces; and creating rules and laws for managing and controlling the lives and behavior of the humanoid/slave species under the crown and scepter of their "divine kingship." These "decrees of the gods" are fundamental to understanding how the Sumerian colonizers intentionally wielded their godlike powers and structured their systems of rulership, which they used to control their genetically engineered humanoid species to keep them enslaved.

Only sixty fragmentary tablets (containing the decrees) were ever recovered and deciphered from a poem entitled "Enki and the World Order." The first translation of these tablets was accomplished by Samuel Noah Kramer in *Sumerian Mythology*. The tablets contain a long list of *me* decrees, also called sacred measures, that were used by the Anunnaki/Sumerians to maintain sovereign rulership over their humanoid subjects. The decrees, described and explained in the tablets, not only were concerned with implementing laws but directed and organized all human activities—from how their subjects should behave, to how and when they should mate, whom they should worship and how, what they should eat and how they should live their lives in service to their god/king/rulers. This royal reptilian bloodline conferred upon themselves the divine right to rule not only planet Earth and its inhabitants but Heaven too. They demanded undying loyalty, obedience, and worship through gift-giving and later blood sacrifices. They made their subjects indentured servants for life through their system of divine kingship and eternal serfdom through debt slavery.

These "decrees" provide a chillingly clear view of Earth's inherited systems of laws and the origins of civilization's social structures, still in place today. Structures that humanity is still unwittingly subjected to and entangled within—a worldwide holographic system of deception and enslavement. This mind matrix contains false mental conceptualizations or paradigms explaining how humanity came to be, the purpose of life and the many accompanying subsets of core beliefs carefully laid down by the Sumerian god/king colonizers. All these decrees or sets of structured belief systems were "imported" from their own civilization, originating (depending on whose version you are following) from Sirius, Orion or the Draco (Dragon) star system. From whichever constellation they came, they imported their values and beliefs when they colonized Earth. They duplicated their laws in every ancient civilization they built on every continent on Earth for the purpose of control and domination. These imported concepts were cleverly obfuscated by being deeply embedded through the use of symbolic visual imagery and rituals representing deep archetypal mental constructs obscuring their imposed paradigms. These invisible embedded sets of core beliefs generate, direct and control every aspect of human life and are still operant today.

In the Sumerian/Babylonian context, the Abrahamic Ten Commandments are a paltry remnant of the original Sumerian *me* decrees of the creator gods: rules for living and rules for worshipping Enlil (the Abrahamic God—Yahweh).

Deconstructing the Sumerian/Babylonian Paradigm

Belief that this intergalactic race of reptilians were forced from their home constellation due to a great galactic war which they lost, forcing them to migrate into Earth's solar system 500,000 years ago.

Belief in "the divine right of kingship" through a matrilineal royal bloodline succession established to maintain power and control within a civilization/empire.

Belief in themselves as the "triune Gods," represented by Anu, Enki and Enlil standing over and above their creation.

Belief in themselves as an unconquerable superior royal reptilian race, the supreme rulers of the universe with no concept of any creator god above or beyond themselves.

Belief in the use of war, destruction, deceit and murder as desirable and acceptable means of conquest.

Belief that they are flesh-and-blood beings, exceptionally tall, strong, and immortal, a reptilian race able to move about interdimensionally, to shapeshift, to read minds and communicate telepathically.

Belief that they terraformed Earth, genetically engineered Earth's weather, manipulated its core energy grids and genetically engineered all native plant, animal and humanoid life forms on Earth.

Belief that they own planet Earth and all of its mineral wealth and natural resources, including their slaves, the humanoid populace.

Belief that they built the pyramid structures all over Earth and established every early civilization on Earth, setting themselves up as "divine immortal creator gods" demanding to be worshiped by all humanoids.

Belief that they genetically engineered and evolved the adamu/adapa humanoid species, later known as Homo Sapiens, who originated from an already-existing native ape species who were genetically altered and bred as beasts of burden, slaves in service to themselves and their ruling dynasties on Earth.

Belief that the humanoid species owes a debt of gratitude to their Sumerian creator gods for genetically engineering them and mixing their own royal/divine genes with human genes thereby granting them a higher or enhanced intelligence, a gift from the DNA of the gods. This "debt" is eternal and must be paid off through worship, sacrifice, obedience and servitude to the creator gods.

Belief that all power resides with the gods, and humans may rarely, if obedient and faithful, be elevated in status or favored by the gods if the gods so will it.

Belief that the humanoid species are essentially lesser beings, "genetic defects," weak, ignorant, short-lived, unworthy and guilty of "sinning" against their creator gods, for which they must be punished and controlled through eternal servitude and toil by earning their daily bread from the sweat of their brows.

Belief that humanity must make pilgrimages, do daily ritual worship, pray to and make ongoing ritual sacrifices to the gods to appease them so that they might grant redemption/salvation after death.

Belief that humanity must not be allowed, at any cost, to escape from the control of the creator gods ruling the physical, astral and causal planes.

Belief that the humanoid species must be maintained as perpetual slaves and be prevented from awakening to their true divine nature as immortal sovereign Souls.

Belief that it is humanity's inheritance to live under an enslaving set of *me* decrees instituted and enshrined by the Anunnaki/Sumerian gods … "those who from heaven to Earth came"… and took control over planet Earth.

Reference Keys: Alford (1999, 2000). Alien (web-a–d). Babylonian (web-a–b). Boulay (2003). Brandenburg (1999, 2011). Budge (1921). Clark (2013). Dalley (2000). Farrell (2005, 2007, 2011a, 2011b). Gateways (web). Gibil (web). Hardy (2014). King (web). Knight (2006). Kramer (1945, 1956, 1961, 1971, 1989). Langdon (1915). Marciniak (1994). "Me" (web). Morning Sky (1996). Mummy (web). Mutwa (2003). O'Brien (1999). Parks (2007, 2013a, 2013b, web-a–e). Penre (web). Project Gutenberg (web). Rosenberg (2006). Scranton (2010). Sitchin (1990, 1998, 2001). Smith (web). Stephany (2013). Tellinger (2012).

Chapter Nine

The Hindu Worldview

THE VEDAS ARE some of the oldest sacred texts of Hinduism. Calculations as to the age of these hymns vary but in general they are said to have been composed sometime between 1500 to 1000 BCE in the northwestern region of the subcontinent. Many of these texts were found in the region of the Indus Valley at the sites of the ancient buried cities of Harappa and Mohenjo-Daro bordering Western India and Pakistan. The Rig Veda consists of about 1,028 series of hymns depicting stories of the creator gods of the multiverse and how the creation came to be. The texts are divided into two groups: *sruti* are works that are the product of divine revelation, considered to have been transmitted directly to earthly sages by divinities, and *smriti* are hymns remembered and transmitted orally over many generations. It was centuries before these sacred texts were written down, which makes it very difficult to determine their exact age.

The four basic collections of these sacred texts include the Rig Veda, Yajur Veda, Sama Veda and Atharva Veda, handed down through the centuries primarily by the Brahmin priests and written in Sanskrit. The Vedas contain numerous esoteric word symbols in the form of ritualistic hymns and poems. According to Sri Aurobindo in *Secret of the Vedas*:

> One of the leading principles of the mystics was the
> sacredness and secrecy of self-knowledge and the true
> knowledge of the Gods. This wisdom, they thought un-

fit, perhaps even dangerous to the ordinary human mind or in any case liable to perversion and misuse and loss of virtue if revealed to vulgar and unpurified spirits. Hence they favored the existence of an outer worship, effective but imperfect for the profane, an inner discipline for the initiate and clothed their language in words and images which had equally a spiritual sense for the elect, a concrete sense for the mass of ordinary worshippers. The Vedic hymns were conceived and constructed on this principle. (p. 8)

Hinduism is basically an umbrella term referring to a conglomerate of different religious practices sharing many similar essential characteristics. It is a mystical religion with its main aim of guiding the adherent to personally experience the Truth within, finally reaching the pinnacle of consciousness where man and God become one. In spite of its complex diversity in terms of sects and practices, Hinduism can be considered as an integral whole, embracing and guiding religious, social, economic, literary, philosophic and artistic aspects of Hindu life. It comprises three main traditions or sects: Saivism, Vaishnavism, and Shaktism, whose adherents consider, respectively, Shiva, Vishnu and Shakti to be the supreme deities. There are multitudinous deities or demigods honored in this religion, related to various incarnations of the different deities, making it a seemingly polytheistic religion with monotheistic aspects as well. All these sects generally agree that Brahman is the highest principle in the universe and pervades all of existence, a monotheistic God.

The ancient texts are not easy to read or translate as the esoteric and allegorical word symbols of the Vedic period are very difficult to translate into the familiar word symbols of modern-day Hindu communication styles. Like the biblical scriptures, the Vedas have been interpreted through many lenses over many centuries. In each epoch, scholars have studied and interpreted these sacred texts through the lens of their particular worldview and level of cultural and intellectual development.

There are so many Hindu/Vedic versions of the creation story that it made it difficult to settle on a single version. Please keep in mind the following versions are just two of many, which have been condensed and simplified for easier reading. The following version was extracted from scholar W. Norman Brown's interpretation of the Vedic creation myth, published by the *Journal of the American Oriental Society* in 1942.

The authors of the Rig Veda describe the massive creational forces present in the early formation of the multiverse at large as opposing forces of contraction and expansion, positive and negative, bondage and freedom. They are personified as Adityas and Asuras, described below.

The Rig Veda speaks of thirty-three gods called the Tridasha, consisting of twelve Adityas (sun gods), eight Vasus (elemental gods), eleven Rudras (deities of wind and storm) and two Ashvins (twin chariot warriors or deities). Indra, also called Sakra, is the first of the thirty-three gods and is known as Lord of the gods. The Hindu scriptures claim there are 330 million gods (also known as Devas or angels) generally classified as deities of heaven, air and earth; celestial gods and goddesses; and atmospheric and terrestrial deities. These lineages are very complex and difficult to clearly sort from among the numerous hymns, poems and mythological stories. The version below tells the tale of Tvastar, the firstborn God of Creation, also known as "the Artificer" who is an Aditya, a divine solar deity.

In the beginning there were the inanimate, passive cosmic waters and the god Tvastar, "the one born at the beginning." Tvastar represents the first active or dynamic force in the universe emanating from within the Cosmic Waters. Tvastar created the Sky and the Earth, and endowed them with the principle or essence of life, and they begot the Devas, divine light beings, who then proceeded with all else needed to construct the multiverse. It was Tvastar who created all creatures adorned with forms and their parents, the Sky and the Earth. He was named "the great fashioner, the universal impregnator or vivifier"; combining both male and female qualities within himself, he placed the element of life, the essence, in creatures, making them multiply. Sky and Earth then birthed the Suras, the first class of divine beings, as their children. A second class of divine beings came into being out of the first class of divine Devas. This second class of divine beings over time developed bad qualities and metamorphosed into a negative force opposing the creation, a race of superhuman beings called Asuras. They wielded great power and became power-seeking and power-hungry such that in mythological language they came to be referred to as "demons" who had no father, only a mother.

These two classes of Devas or demigods became known as the Adityas (Suras or solar deities) and the Danavas (Asuras or demonic deities). The Danavas are beings of negative power, wielding the superhuman, magical powers of "maya or illusion." They are space aggressors, gigantic in appearance, and can appear in human form or in the form of serpents or dragons. They bind, restrain, hold in check, cover over and enclose the Cosmic Waters and the Sun. The Adityas are in appearance like men or men-birds. They are divine beings of light, of unbinding, of freedom and liberation, and in primordial times their goal or task was the creation itself. The Danavas in contrast are antagonists, propagators of inertia and destruction. They dwell in the realms of darkness and chaos under the Earth, where neither the Sun nor cosmic order reaches. The Danavas were opposed to the creation in the beginning.

The Adityas and humans live on the Earth's broad surface, in the vault of the sky overhead and in the atmosphere in between. This realm is called the Sat, "the existent." Below the Earth, reached by a great chasm, is a place of horror, inhabited by the Danavas, called the Asat, "the nonexistent." These demigods, the Suras and Asuras of the upper and lower regions of creation, are in a constant state of enmity with each other, and the two regions are antithetical. In the Sat is light, warmth, moisture, all the requisites for life. These qualities and all the phenomena of nature concerned with their appearance and use are subject to universal cosmic law. To make the Sat operate properly, every being has its duty and function, and in living by these laws one is upholding universal cosmic law. The result is life, growth and prosperity. In the Asat there is cold, darkness and inertia causing decay and death. This place is without cosmic law and is therefore chaotic, with the demons in the Asat looking for every opportunity to injure the beings born of the Sat, the Earth and Sky. Varuna is the chief of the Adityas, Suras or solar deities, and Vritra, a serpent dragon/arch-demon, is chief of the Danavas, Asuras or demons.

The existence of these opposing forces is present at all levels or dimensions of the creation, until a certain level of conscious evolvement or enlightenment is reached, at which time these opposing forces come into balance and are then transcended in the achievement of *moksha* or liberation from the pairs of opposites and the cycle of rebirth.

Here is a second version of the Hindu creation story summarized from the *Srimad-Bhagavatam*, Canto Two, Chapter Ten, translated by A. C. Bhaktivedanata Swami Prabhupada, founder of the International Society for Krishna Consciousness, which will give you a slightly different interpretation of the creation story using different language to express similar concepts.

The Supreme Godhead manifests his energies of transcendental Light and divides Himself into three called the controlling deities: Brahma, Vishnu and Shiva. These deities created the controlling entities, the conditioned Souls and the material creation. The first created purusha or god is Maha Vishnu who goes into a mystic sleep as innumerable universes are created from the potency of his transcendental body. This internal potency reacts when it contacts the external potency, and all the living entities, including all the deities, are created. This secondary creation is a reactive result of the original ingredients made by Brahma, and the activities of the universe are put into motion by Vishnu, who maintains the creation generated by Brahma through his ceaseless mercy. Shiva, the god of destruction, annihilates the creation. Thus are they known as the Creator, Sustainer, and Destroyer gods of Hinduism.

All conditioned Souls take life in this material world. Through the five senses the Soul gets trapped in the illusion created by the external energy of Vishnu and becomes subject to the laws of material creation and destruction. In this worldview, for example, all planets in the universe are destructible. Also, conditioned Souls may travel in space by good or bad works or by modern spacecraft, but all will die—although the duration of life on different planets and planes is different.

The only means of attaining eternal life is to go back to the Godhead, thus ending rebirth on one of the material or astral planets in the universe. Conditioned Souls, forgetting their relationship with the Lord, try to live a permanent life in the material world. In illusion they become attached to the world and fully engaged in religious, social and economic activities, forgetting they are meant to return to the Godhead. This forgetfulness is induced by the illusion of form life.

Thus through sense enjoyment, conditioned Souls become trapped in the cycle of rebirth. The purpose of the sacred scriptures is to pass on the teachings and divine knowledge of the Manus (Saints, Avatars and Masters) of all ages to show the conditioned Souls how to successfully exit the temporary and illusive material creation. These teachings form the right way of living and include duties, called Sad-dharma, performed for going back to the Godhead. For accomplishing this, the Manus advise the conditioned Souls to give up all religious activities (rituals) and engage in devotional service also known as meditation on the Godhead.

The material universe is created for the liberation of the conditioned Souls. During the cosmic manifestation, the chronology of history is created and the activities of all living entities is recorded. The merciful Lord descends to various planets in the material and astral worlds (as embodied Masters, Saints and Avatars) and shows the conditioned Souls how to achieve liberation, which is the permanent solution for their suffering in illusion. Conditioned Souls must eventually give up their changeable (impermanent) gross and subtle material bodies.

There are two types of living entities. Most of them are ever-liberated and some of them are ever-conditioned. The ever-conditioned entities have two kinds of choices: one is a tendency is to attempt to control or "lord it over" cosmic creation, and the other is to develop devotion and a desire to return to the Godhead. Those who take the devotional path and heed the teachings of the Manus coming in different incarnations or lineages are taught to follow the transcendental sound current in meditation. By doing this they are able to develop spiritual light bodies, leaving their conditioned gross and subtle material bodies behind.

All Vedic texts aim at teaching devotional service to the Godhead. As soon as the conditioned Soul is fixed on devotional service to the Lord, he becomes eligible to be freed from the conditioned state. The *Srimad-Bhagavatam* explains that the representation of the Godhead is a "sound" incarnation of Lord Krishna.

Lord Krishna is described as the ultimate source of all energies, and the word "Krishna" means the sound current or Word, the source of all energies and all creation in all dimensions of the creation. All controlling deities—Brahma, Vishnu and Shiva—are different manifestations of the Supreme Personality of the Godhead, who exhibits himself by entering into each and every being and universe generated from him in the form of sound. Every being the in the material and astral worlds is controlled by the higher demigods and sub-creator gods, and all of the five senses are controlled by these planetary deities. For instance, conditioned Souls in bodies cannot see without light. The Sun is a planetary deity and the controller of light. The sun god resides in the Sun as a living entity having a gigantic body, but it is, in essence, spirit, as is the conditioned Soul.

Both are part and parcel of the Supreme Godhead. The Sun is the controller and the conditioned Soul is the controlled. Without the medium of perception, no one can know who is the controlled and who is the controller. All living entities (the deities and the conditioned Soul) are interdependent. The individual Soul is dependent on the Oversoul for achieving Self-realization in order to be liberated from the illusion of materiality. The conditioned Soul is under the illusion of materiality and identifies himself with matter. To get out of this illusion, the conditioned Soul has to realize itself as the Oversoul and become one with It. The conditioned Souls cannot know of the reality of the Godhead in his eternal form of truth, knowledge, bliss or Sat, Chit, Ananda because the conditioned Souls cannot comprehend the infinite power of the Godhead. They mistakenly think he is something like they are.

The most perfect divine manifestation of the Lord's mercy and power is exhibited when the infinite Lord becomes "visible to our eyes as one of us" in the form of the Godman or Living Master. When conditioned Souls listen to the messages of the Lord through the lineages of Living Masters, Avatars and Saints, such conditioned Souls become devotees of the Lord by the grace of his pure devotees, the Masters, Saints and Avatars. All living entities are dependent on the total energy of the Supreme Godhead. Just as an electric lamp has no independent effulgence, all beings, all creation depends on the Supreme Godhead who is the cause of all causes.

Deconstructing the Hindu Paradigm

The following list represents only the most basic core beliefs of Hinduism. This list is in no way complete as there are so many sects and denominations of Hinduism, each having its own variegated beliefs and practices.

Belief in a cyclic view of life, believing that the universe goes through endless repeating cycles of creation, preservation and dissolution over eons of time in repeating cycles known as "yugas" or ages: the Satya yuga, Treta yuga, Dvapara yuga, and the Kali yuga, the last of which is the time cycle we are currently living in, which began in 3102 BCE.

Belief in one all-pervasive Supreme Godhead who is both immanent and transcendent: the Creator, the created and the Unmanifest Infinite Totality. Hinduism can appear to be a polytheistic religion due to their belief in and worship of many deities, gods and goddesses; but since all these deities are the creations of the Supreme Godhead, in that sense it could be considered polytheistic—but ultimately is monotheistic.

Belief in karma (the law of cause and effect); the transmigration of the Soul whereby one evolves through various species of life until one is born into a human body where one's words, actions and thoughts in each individual life create one's future karmic circumstances in each succeeding life cycle.

Belief in reincarnation whereby the Soul lives many lives and evolves through many rebirths until the Soul achieves *moksha* or liberation from the karmic cycle and is no longer obligated to reincarnate into a physical form.

Belief that the four main Vedic scriptures are the divinely given word of the Supreme Being in the form of hymns representing Dharma—the divine principle or cosmic law that orders the universe and is tantamount to the "eternal way."

Belief in the sacredness of all life such that every living being is to be loved and revered.

Belief in the practice of meditation as the means of transcending mind and all form-life to reach the higher realms of non-being, of transcendent infinite consciousness.

Belief in the practice of *ahimsa* or non-injury to other life forms.

Belief in divine beings (deities) existing in unseen worlds, such that temple worship, rituals, sacraments and personal devotional pujas (prayers and offerings) create a connection or communication with these Devas, or lords of the higher regions.

Belief that no single world religion is the sole or singular way to salvation but that all genuine spiritual paths are ways and means of expressing different methods of achieving the same ideal of *moksha* or liberation; and are to be understood and accepted with tolerance and respect.

Belief that an enlightened Master or Satguru is essential on the spiritual path to help one achieve knowledge of the Transcendent Absolute Reality and a return to the Source of all creation.

———

Reference Keys: Aurobindo (1995). Prabhupada (2011). Bishop (1988). Brown (1942). Chatterji (1992). Hinduism (web-a–b). "Hinduism" (web). Meredith (2010). Pattanaik (2003).

Chapter Ten

The Buddhist Worldview

THE MAN NAMED Siddhartha Gautama who later became known as the Buddha or the Enlightened One was born in Northeast India or what is present-day Nepal in the sixth century BCE. He became known as the Buddha or the Enlightened One once he achieved enlightenment after many years of meditation. He first renounced family life to engage in years of ascetic practices. Then he gave these practices up and began meditating. Through his years of meditations he became enlightened and arrived at the great Truth, the core of which was expressed as the Four Noble Truths: that all suffering is rooted in desire, in the will to live and in possessive attachment to this world and to the ego identity. His realization was that to be released from suffering one had to completely destroy desire. The doctrine he proclaimed and taught became known as *dharma*—the body of teachings of the Buddha. This doctrine includes the concept of *samskaras*—mental impressions causing the cycles of rebirth.

The way to overcome them is to follow the eightfold path, also known as the Middle Way, consisting of right viewpoint, right intention, right speech, right action, right work, right effort, right mindfulness, and right meditation.

All activities and understandings listed above are undertaken to liberate the mind from its bonds. This liberation is known as *nirvana* leading to enlightenment, and these concepts form the pillars of Buddhism.

Buddhist cosmology was extracted from the discourses or sermons of the Buddha called *sutras* which later developed into Theravada, Mahayana, and Vajrayana Buddhist traditions, as described here briefly. The Buddha died about 483 BCE, and shortly thereafter a council of five hundred monks met to discuss how to preserve the Buddha's teachings, which had till then been preserved only through memorized oral chanting. There were subsequently two more council meetings; then at the Fourth Buddhist Council meeting, in Sri Lanka in the first century BCE, the Tripitaku or Pali Canon as it has come to be named was written down on palm leaves and became the first written text of the Buddhist scriptures. These became the foundation of Theravada Buddhism.

Around this same period a schism developed among the practitioners about conflicting ideas of how Buddhism should be practiced and taught. The older school of Theravada Buddhists were committed to the ideas of monastic discipline, lengthy meditations, scholarly endeavors and strict adherence to the scriptures. Others saw these practices as being too difficult for the average person to adopt. There began attempts to reformulate Buddha's teachings to accommodate the common people from all walks of life, which eventually evolved into the new Buddhism—which came to be known as Mahayana Buddhism. Buddhism is widely practiced in the Asian countries of China, Japan, Korea, Vietnam, Thailand, Cambodia, Tibet, Nepal, Bhutan and Mongolia—with a continuing presence in India. In Tibet, Buddhism blended with indigenous traditions and evolved into Vajrayana Buddhism, in which the role of lamas is central. When Tibet was overrun by invaders in the 1950s, lamas and practitioners escaped to all parts of the world; thus the Vajrayana tradition is widely practiced in the West as well as the East, alongside worldwide expansion of Zen Buddhism, which also emphasizes meditative insight in interaction with an accomplished teacher.

The Buddha perpetually challenged his followers to seek the Truth within themselves. He stressed that his followers should accept no idea on faith but by analysis and practice of precepts conducive to the good, and to the welfare of all beings. The body of his teachings became the sutras or discourses of the Buddha that provide direction and guidance for seekers after Truth. As such, Buddhism is not a revealed, linearly constructed religion with rules decreed by a transcendent god as are the Abrahamic religions. Rather Buddhism represents a philosophy or way of life consisting of sets of precepts to follow for achieving liberation from the cycle of rebirths on the wheel of karma. Since Buddhism developed within an older Hindu civilization, it shares a cyclical worldview with continual cycles of rebirth or transmigration as in Hindu cosmology. The intellectual discourses and teachings of Buddhism understandably contain some beliefs similar to those found in Hinduism.

In the Buddhist sutras, the world is described as illusion, as nothing but *samsara*, the ocean of cycles of repeated births, deaths and rebirths in an impermanent phenomenal universe, consisting of the physical form, sensations, perceptions, mental formations and volitional activities of consciousness. In his discourses, the Buddha describes the universe as a "conditioned existence" that holds individuals within a field of consciousness creating samskaras (impressions generated from the cycle of rebirths) until individuals can achieve their own liberation out of the phenomenal universe. The Buddha described the cosmos or levels of creation as he saw them through his "divine or inner eye," whereby he was able to perceive the many non-physical worlds and all the beings inhabiting them.

According to the Buddhist cosmology, the beginning and the ending of the universe are inconceivable because in their view when one portion disappears, another portion reappears or evolves out of the dispersed matter of the previous universe in an endless cyclic process. According to the Buddha, no amount of study of the origins of the phenomenal universe can effect a release from it. For this reason the Buddha did not give any attention to this issue in his sutras. In scientific materialism, knowledge of the material world is highly valued and it is believed that by studying the separate components of physical matter in the world one can master it, gain from it material wealth, personal comfort, and personal safety. Buddhism teaches that any analysis or study of the origin of the world is useless; therefore no time or attention is given to this topic. Adepts are instructed to strive diligently inwardly through meditation, for until one arrives at an understanding of his own true nature and of the impermanent and changing nature of the physical universe, they are lost in samsara. Meditation is a mainstay of Buddhist practice as it enables the individual to realize the inner workings of the mind, to transcend its limitations and to move into radically different dimensions of conscious awareness beyond the normal contents of our Earth-bound mental perceptions. In Buddhism there is no concept of an external savior coming to "save" individuals who adhere to a particular set of laws or religion. The Buddha taught that each individual is responsible for achieving their own enlightenment and for securing their release from the cycle of rebirths.

There is no specific Buddhist creation story. Buddhists believe the universe is in eternal movement through vast cycles of time; periods of increase and decrease called *kalpas*. These kalpas represent cycles of nothingness, creation, duration and dissolution similar to the Hindu conceptualization of the yugas. Buddhists understand the universe to contain multilayered levels of created worlds similar to the Hindu beliefs and describe these worlds as being inhabited by diverse types of beings, all in the process of transmigration through the variegated realms of illusion.

The goal of Buddhism is liberation from the cycle of rebirths. This liberation process begins with the control of the physical sense organs through meditation, an inward-turning focus of attention allowing the meditator to become aware of the inner worlds—eventually reaching the inner awareness of the infinity of consciousness; a state called nirvana leading to pure enlightenment; consciousness existing beyond all form and beyond all thought, arriving at the abode of nothingness or nothing-ness, the great void.

Buddhist cosmology is quite complex, intricate and multilayered. For my purposes, I am again taking the liberty of greatly condensing this vast body of teachings into a much-abbreviated version of their cosmology. Buddhism teaches that there are thirty-one distinct planes or realms of existence within the multiverse, into which beings can be reborn during their entanglement with their samskaras. These realms range from the extraordinarily horrific and frightful hell realms all the way up to the most exquisitely beatific and blissful heavenly realms. Existence in any of these realms is temporary and due to an individual's karmic earnings: wholesome actions bringing about a favorable birth and unwholesome actions leading to an unfavorable incarnation. These thirty-one planes of existence are further divided into three distinct worlds also known as *lokas* which are listed below in descending order of refinement of frequency vibration:

The Immaterial World (*arupa loka*), also known as the Formless Realm, consists of four realms that are accessible to those who pass away while meditating on the formless *jhanas*—a series of cultivated states of mind that lead to a state of perfect equanimity and awareness. Beings here have neither shape nor form nor location and exist within the sphere of infinite consciousness, infinite intelligence, dwelling in the *akasha* (the first primary element, also known as sound or *shabd* in Sanskrit). The other four elements being air, fire, water and earth. The akasha or sound element is infinitely pervasive as infinite consciousness.

The Fine-Material World *(rupa loka),* also known as the Subtle Realms, consists of sixteen realms whose inhabitants (Devas) experience extremely refined degrees of mental pleasure. These realms are accessible to those who have gained some level of equanimity and awareness and have been able to eliminate all thought forms of hatred or ill will. In these realms the Devas or divine beings possess extremely refined bodies of pure limitless light which emit flashing rays of light like lightening. These Devas are known as Devas of splendor.

The highest of these realms called the Pure Abodes are accessible only to those who have attained to "non-returning," the third stage of awakening, where one is on the path to perfection and has attained nirvana (liberation from the cycles of rebirth) but not full Buddhahood. This world and the immaterial worlds together comprise the "heavens."

The Sensuous World (the Desire Realm) *(kama-loka),* also known as the Form Realm, consists of eleven realms which are all ruled by Mahesvara, ruler of the three realms of samsara, the illusory worlds where all beings are subject to cycles of rebirth. All beings here are under the domination of the "*devaputra* demons," a supernatural race of negative beings who use passions to tempt, snare and delude humanity, blocking their spiritual development. A particularly powerful demon, Mara, tried to prevent Gautama Buddha from attaining liberation by employing all manner of temptations to deceive and deter him. This world is dominated by the five senses. Seven of these eleven form realms are favorable destinations and include the human realm as well as several realms occupied by benevolent divine beings. The four lowest realms are negative or painful destinations as they include existence as animals, ghosts, subhuman beings or Asuras (demons) in the hell realms. The devaputra demons endeavor to keep all beings in the desire realm and under the grip of sensual desires.

Buddhist cosmology describes a "spatial" arrangement of the various physical and non-physical worlds within the universe and a "temporal" arrangement which describes how those worlds come into existence and then pass away over massive time cycles (the kalpas). I'm avoiding going into the details of these concepts as they are quite complex and beyond the scope of this book. Below is one small condensed, summarized version of how the universe is arranged according to Buddhist belief:

The world of Mt. Meru—known as the World Mountain—is an immense peak that arises in the center of our universe, around which the Sun and Moon revolve. Its base rests in a vast ocean and it is surrounded by many rings of lesser mountain ranges and oceans. Three worlds are located on or around Mt. Meru. Different types of Devas (divine beings) live on its peak and on its slopes. Devas who guide the Sun and Moon are considered part of this upper world, as are the dragons, ghosts, goblins, fairies and elementals. At its base, in the ocean around the base, live the Asuras (the demons).

The Asuras who devolved or fell from the higher worlds are always trying to regain their lost kingdom at the top of Mt. Meru. The Asuras are divided into many groups and are divided among themselves as they have no single ruler. In the earthly realm live human and human-like beings, subject to death and rebirth, on four main continents.

Lastly are the hell realms or *Narakas*. These worlds are where the greatest suffering is endured by beings born into one of these realms as a result of their negative karma. Beings reside here for a finite length of time after which they are reborn again into one of the higher worlds. The mentality of beings in hell corresponds to states of extreme fear, despair, anguish and helplessness. It is said that the entire infinite universe is Lord Buddha's, so he is able to traverse to any realm and can spread light to any living being who lives anyplace in any of these universes.

A Mahayana text encapsulates Buddhist doctrine by stating:

> The body of the perfect Buddha irradiates everything;
> its suchness is undifferentiated and the road to Buddha-
> hood is open to all. At all times have all beings the seed
> of Buddhahood in them. (web)

Another quote states:

> Whatever exists is an emanation from the inexhaustible storehouse of Buddha consciousness which holds all things effortlessly. (web)

Buddhists do not believe in a transcendental or supreme creator god from whom they seek salvation. Rather they conceive of infinite consciousness itself as the Source from which all forms of life emanate and to which all will eventually return within eternal repeating cycles of nothingness, creation, duration and dissolution.

Deconstructing the Buddhist Paradigm

Many of the Buddhist core beliefs overlap some of the Hindu core beliefs even though different terminology is used to describe similar concepts. As with Hinduism, Buddhism has numerous sects and branches, each having its own variations and forms of devotion.

Belief in existence without a unitary deity, but many forms of deities, gods and demons as emanations of divine energy.

Belief in the sacredness of all life.

Belief in a cyclic view of the creation, meaning that the universe undergoes endless cycles of creation, duration and dissolution over eons of time in repeating cycles known as kalpas.

Belief in the transmigration of the Soul through many lives, moving up or down the karmic wheel depending on one's positive or negative actions in each life.

Belief that the purpose of life is to escape from the cycle of rebirths through enlightenment (liberation through nirvana leading to enlightenment allowing one liberation from all form life).

Belief that all embodied Souls must earn their liberation by their own efforts.

Belief in the practice of meditation as the means to transcend mind and all form life to reach the higher realms of non-being, of transcendent infinite consciousness.

Belief in the Four Noble Truths and Eightfold Path.

Belief in following the sutras or teachings of the Buddha, which include moral rules for living such as (1) do no harm to any living being, (2) do not take what does not belong to one, (3) refrain from sexual misconduct, (4) do not tell falsehoods, and (5) avoid intoxicants.

Belief in the value of paying tribute to and venerating past physically embodied beings who achieved enlightenment during their lifetimes.

Belief in the value of honoring and venerating relics—the remains, hair, nails, bones or mummified bodies—of once-living enlightened beings and the erection of shrines and temples as places to worship these divine beings. Relics and statues are housed in stupas or temples and sometimes bathed, dressed and adorned with flowers and offerings in ritual celebrations.

Reference Keys: Bishop (1988). Bodhi (2005). Buddha (web-a–b). Buddhism (web-a–f). Edmunds (1904). Gunasekara (web). Nanamoli (web). "Pali" (web). Robinson (1997). Sadakata (1997). Walshe (1987). "Zen" (web).

Chapter Eleven

The Gnostic Worldview

IN 1945 A treasure trove of Gnostic scriptures was discovered in the Nag Hammadi valley in Upper Egypt. In ancient times this location was called Sheniset (the acacias of Seth), pointing to the possibility that this geographical region had long ago been the sanctuary of a Gnostic sect calling themselves "Sethians," the children of Seth who was the third son of the biblical Adam and Eve. The Gnostics of the first century CE considered themselves to be initiates of a spiritual lineage of illumined Masters of the Mysteries who preserved and taught the sacred transmission of Gnosis: Truth, or divine knowledge. Their masters were called "phosters" (light bearers) and were the equivalent of the Indian *vidyaharas* (the knowledge holders) of the Vedas and the "illumined or awakened one" known as the Buddha.

About fifty years before the Nag Hammadi find, there had been scholars working on other codices. One of these scholars was Jean Doresse, a Catholic archaeologist, who published in 1958 the book *The Secret Books of the Egyptian Gnostics: An Introduction to the Gnostic Coptic Manuscripts*, describing documents discovered at Chenoboskion, a town just east of the larger town of Nag-Hammadi. These documents dated from 400 CE and were derived from far older origins. About one-fifth of the Coptic Gnostic texts concern the origin, motive and methods of the Archons (inorganic alien beings), including precise instructions by the "phosters" on how to detect and overcome their influence. Doresse states in the book: "Here we find legends anterior to Gnosticism—those for instance which attributed a sacred character to Mount Hermon, the supposed residence of the Children of Seth" (p. 255). The Children of Seth are described in the Bible as the children of God and were called the Bene Ha-Elohim. Seth was described in Judaism, Christianity, Mandaeism and Islam as the third son of Adam and Eve and the brother of Cain and Abel. The beginnings of the Gnostic movement according to Doresse originated on the border of northwestern Iran, near a high plateau before Mount Hermon, fed by Lake Urmia. The Urmian Plateau was a center of the ancient cultures of Mesopotamia.

Gnosticism and its tenets were carried forward from the original Magian Order in ancient Iran, but the Gnostics later split off from this order due to ideological differences. The Gnostics embraced the concept of dualism: a two-world system where the problem facing humanity was not evil but "error," rather than the conceptualization of a split-source world system where good and evil were believed to have originated from the same source—God. This latter ideology gradually became the basis of the teachings of the Zoroastrian religion as taught by the Magian Order priesthood.

The Gnostic phosters' (light-bearing Masters') function was to maintain the lineage of the revealers, to preserve the sacred methods of instruction by divine light for teaching and transmitting gnosis to their followers. They were consecrated to this sacred aim. The "Children of Seth," "Sons of God" or "Bene-Ha-Elohim" are the original names given to this sacred lineage of phosters or revealers, who worked within a spiritual complex that emerged in prehistoric Iran. Later in historical texts, they came to be known as the Magian Order, according to the translated Coptic codices. The Magi were originally regarded as dedicated servants of God, illumined Masters, teaching the cosmological sciences to their initiates.

The Nag Hammadi Library is a recovered body of over fifty texts found in the town of Nag Hammadi in Egypt in 1947. The texts were not fully translated until the 1970s. The codices contain six major categories of cosmological writings: (1) Gnostic versions of the creation story, (2) methods of achieving liberation, (3) the nature of the Soul and the relationship of the Soul to the world, (4) liturgical and initiatory texts, (5) the divine feminine force of creation—Sophia, and (6) the lives and experiences of some of the Christian apostles and some of the Christian scriptures which contain the sayings of Jesus. About one-fifth of the surviving Gnostic texts describe the cosmic origins of the creation of planet Earth and the origins of the creation of a predatory species of inorganic alien beings called Archons (from the Greek root word "archai" which means primordial), who arose within the solar system before Earth's terrestrial biosphere was formed.

Before I delve into the creation story of the Gnostics, I would like to take a small side trip to review some historical events that were occurring during the time of the pervasive presence of the Gnostic religion, around 100 BCE, that led to its being intentionally erased almost entirely from the cadre of ancient world religions. That is, until the discovery of the Gnostic Coptic texts and the Nag Hammadi texts.

The Gnostics were highly educated mystics and had amassed a vast collection of sacred scrolls and manuscripts housed at the Royal Library in Alexandria. When a fire destroyed over 40,000 of these precious manuscripts, this storehouse of knowledge was virtually erased from history. For centuries Roman, Christian and Judaic religious and political leaders aggressively endeavored to eradicate and destroy all evidence of the Gnostics and their mystical religious teachings, in essence erasing them from the face of the ancient world. The Gnostics were diametrically opposed to the newly forming Christian and co-developing Catholic religion. They tried to expose the lies being disseminated among the masses through the re-interpretation and rewriting of the Old Testament Genesis creation story (originally told on the Sumerian clay tablets) by Hebrew rabbis and scholars. Almost all of the Gnostics' writings were burned. They were hunted, persecuted and murdered by the thousands as heretics to Christianity, and had it not been for the discovery of the Gnostic Coptic texts and the codices preserved on papyrus, bound in leather and hidden in clay pots in a cave in Nag Hammadi, Egypt, their version of the creation story might never have been told.

The Gnostics were mystics who proclaimed that gnosis, or knowledge of Truth, was the way to liberation and believed that we could know the One True God directly if guided by the phosters, the illumined Masters who taught this mystical method of discerning gnosis or Truth. They didn't believe that individuals needed the intercession of rabbis, bishops, priests, imams or other religious officials. They drew knowledge from many different sources and found Truth and insight through the directed, focused practice of meditation on inner awareness. Thus they referenced no single sacred canon, book or text. Many of their teachings were hidden or secret and only disclosed orally to their inner circle of initiates or disciples. The word "canon" originally meant a measuring stick but the term later came to be applied to any standard used to determine if a person's thoughts and actions measured up to the "standard of correctness" according to a written canon or religious text such as the Bible, Torah or Qur'an.

The Gnostics who authored the Nag Hammadi texts knew that the Genesis story, written in the Old Testament biblical canon, was not a true history. They said in their recovered written codices that it was a "deviated twisted story" with intentionally altered meanings designed to install false religious beliefs as a "theocratic control paradigm" into the ancient world's societies. This assertion had earlier become the cause of the split between the Gnostics and the Magian Order because the Zoroastrian Magi were co-opted into a system of state-sponsored priests. Their administrative powers were used to implement the state's agenda of military invasion, domination and control of the populace.

In the Gnostic teachings, the Adam and Eve of the biblical story were not the literal first physical male and female Earth beings but were representative of two intrapsychic principles or aspects of the etheric Anthropos, the conceptual model for the eventually developing physical humanoids. Adam represented the embodiment of the psyche (the emotional, mental and thinking functions of the personality self) and Eve represented embodiment of the pneuma or spirit (the light of consciousness of the higher Soul Self—the divine essence). They did not believe in the concept of original sin or the "fall of man," nor of the need for a messiah to "die for man's sins." All these ideas embedded into the Old Testament biblical story of creation they openly challenged, calling them lies and heresies, which was why they were persecuted and silenced and their teachings destroyed.

The following version of the Gnostic creation story was excerpted and condensed from a variety of sources but primarily from John Lamb Lash's book *Not in His Image* and from the website www.metahistory.

org. Additional material was extracted from a lengthy text called *Against Heresies* by Irenaeus of Lyons, a bishop of Lyon, France, born in Smyrna in Asia Minor, who studied under Bishop Polycarp, a disciple of the Apostle John. His writings, composed between 175 and 185 CE, are contained in five books and numerous volumes, all of which were directed at attacking and refuting each of the beliefs and teachings of the second-century BCE Gnostics. Essentially, scholars were able to extract from Irenaeus's preserved written attacks on the Gnostic beliefs just what their beliefs were and thereby reconstruct the Gnostic cosmology or story of how the world was created and for what purpose.

I've again greatly condensed and reduced these voluminous writings for simplicity of reading and comparison with the other creation stories in this book. Their creation story is quite complex, like the creation stories of the Hindus and Buddhists.

The One, greater than a god, doesn't exist within anything as everything exists within IT which is ALL THAT IS. Within the One or All That Is exist the Aeons, the creator gods, who reside in the galactic center in the eternal fullness of the Pleroma. These divine energetic emanations remain within the Pleroma and do not enter the Kenoma (the galactic vortices of the outer cosmos), where finite bounded potential develops. From out of the Kenoma (the spiral arms of the galaxies into which the Aeons direct their dreaming) comes the Dema (dense elementary-matter arrays moving as massive fields of inorganic elementary particles circulating in the galactic limbs).

The eternal realm of Truth has no shadow in it because the immeasurable light is everywhere within it. The power that came into being in a portion of the infinite realm is called the shadow realm, the limitless chaos of the Dema, which is in the finite realm. From this darkness every kind of deity was brought forth and they appeared in the abyss, the limitless chaos of the darkness of the finite realm.

The joy of the Aeons (the creator gods) is to behold the spontaneous arising and dissolving of myriad ideas or conceptual forms for worlds which they energetically create out of themselves as infinite organic light forms (quantum plasma currents). There are thirty Aeons—immense energetic plasma currents—that are alive, self-aware and intelligent, of which Sophia was the last or youngest. Sophia means "wisdom," the living light of divine intelligence or "nous." In her delight of dreaming her creation into being, she neglected to stay with her paired creator Aeon, Christos. She followed her dream creation alone, watching its amorphous forming from outside the Pleroma. Her fascination with her creation caused her to accidentally fall or descend from the Pleroma (the galactic center) into the Kenoma (galactic vortices) and then further down into the Dema (the realm of inorganic elementary particles) where she became captured and metamorphosed over eons of time into the living sentient Earth of our solar system, located in the third arm of the Milky Way spiral galaxy, called the Orion Arm.

In her desire to create the Anthropos (the template for humanoid life forms) she inadvertently created an anomaly in the Kenoma (galactic vortices): an inorganic species called the "Archons" and another species called the "Reptilians." The Archons and Reptilians appeared in the Kenoma long before Earth's solar system ever existed and long before Sophia metamorphosed from an etheric planet into the material planet Earth in the Dema (realm of elementary particles). According to the Gnostics, the Archons are inorganic predators, cybernetic intelligences, fractal amoebic forms (looking like aborted fetuses) that inhabit the solar system at large. They excel in the "psycho-technology of replication" and of "virtual-reality creation." They intrude into the minds of humanity and so have been called "mind parasites" by the Gnostics and "messengers of deception." The Archons, according to the Gnostics, were instrumental in the formation of the inorganic planets of our solar system with the exception of the Earth, the Sun and the Moon.

Sophia, while dreaming the Anthropos (template for humanoids) into existence within a molecular cloud located in the third spiral arm of the Milky Way galaxy, became trapped inside the Dema (realm of inorganic particles) and within the boundaries of Earth's solar system. She metamorphosed into the planet Earth, Gaia/Sophia, source of all consciousness, wisdom, light and life on planet Earth. The Gnostic texts' emphasis on "the descent of the redeemer goddess" Sophia accounts for the very strong matriarchal emphasis of most Gnostic texts about the sacred cosmological story of the goddess Sophia and how she came to be embodied as the living sentient planet Earth.

Sophia, in the process of dreaming the Anthropos template into existence, directed her attention into the Kenoma, where her reflected image appeared to Yaldabaoth and the Archons, intelligent beings existing in the cosmic waters of the Dema.

Yaldabaoth and the Archons became enamored of her reflected dream-creation of the Anthropos and desired to replicate it through the creation of a model of their own, made of elemental particles in the Dema. However, because Sophia carried the organic light (the essence of spirit) within her, she was able to imbue all her creations with it, including the human-genome species template, the Anthropos. When Yaldabaoth and the Archons tried to create an "Adam," a being, as a trap to ensnare the image that had appeared to them in the cosmic waters, they failed as they could only create a substitute, a dead form, the body of an Adamic being that had no spirit or life essence in it.

According to the Gnostic seers and mystics, the Archons cannot fully access our innate fully divine genetic makeup, so they make fake copies through the alteration and replication of physical and mental templates of the human mind/body. They create mental simulations of virtual realities, thus allowing their intrusion into our intrapsychic mental and emotional worlds. The Gnostic phosters or Masters, having full paranormal, interdimensional vision, knew of Yaldabaoth and the Archons' enmeshment with humanity and of their malicious intentions. The phosters explained to their initiates that Yaldabaoth and the Archons envy humans and feed upon their fear energy. Their aim is to prevent human beings from awakening and evolving their inner Soul light, the gift from the Aeon Sophia that all humanoid species carry—the divine essence, the organic light within—coiled up and hidden inside the human body as the kundalini energy stored in the energetic chakra centers.

Gnostic texts clearly state that the "Jehovah/Yaldabaoth" of the Old Testament Bible is a reptilian type of alien predator that presides over the smaller fractal, hive-like, embryonic, inorganic and more passive Archontic forces. Jehovah/Yaldabaoth, say the Gnostics, is a fallen angel, a demiurge, whom they refer to in their sacred texts as a "demented extraterrestrial reptilian" with superhuman, deific powers whose realm is our entire solar system. Jehovah/Yaldabaoth commanded the Archons, inorganic predators in the Dema, to serve him, and they help him govern this solar system and rule over the seven heavens: the seven visible planets of the "hebdomad" which is the sevenfold planetary system in our solar system excluding the Earth, Sun and Moon.

The Gnostic scriptures say that the Garden of Eden was not a paradise but a prison laboratory where the reptilians led by Jehovah/Yaldabaoth conducted a series of experiments in an attempt to reproduce a compliant strain of primate slaves called "Adamus." Jehovah/Yaldabaoth boasted to his Archons that he was the supreme being and that there were no other gods before him and demanded that the Archons worship him alone. Sophia, knowing of this blemish on her creation—who Yaldabaoth had become—warned him, saying:

> You are mistaken Samael [Samael means blind god]. An enlightened immortal man exists before you and he will appear within your molded bodies and he will trample upon you as potter's clay is trampled. And you will go with those who are yours down to the shadowy abyss. (web)

In referring to Jehovah as a blind god, the Aeon Sophia is reminding him that he is only a local god and is blind to the infinite One True Creator God who is the infinite and eternal light of creation that he, Jehovah/Yahweh/Yaldabaoth, is contained within.

After Jehovah/Yaldabaoth was told of this primal cosmic immortal man who came before him and was above him, he became angry and devised a cunning scheme. Asking for the help of the Archons he said, "Let us create a man from the Earth according to the image of our body so he may serve us and we shall make those who are begotten from the light essence our servants." Thus the powers of darkness, the Archons, dragged immortal man down to the Earth where they fragmented, overpowered and trapped his light essence in these organic bodies, intending that immortal man would lose his true identity, lose his higher spiritual knowledge, lose remembrance of his divinity, and thereby become confused and lost. Sophia then sent a spirit, a divine messenger known as the "instructor," to the lost humans in the Garden of Eden. This spirit, this divine essence, took up residence inside the human bodies as the inner serpent, the coiled kundalini, which when aroused climbs up the chakra energy channels to the dome of the skull, opens the third eye, re-connecting the human to the hidden world of the divine "nous," the realms of Truth, thereby providing spiritual liberation to humans, so that they can again become the knowers of the truth of their being.

Gnosticism shares the Hindu and Buddhist perspective of a cyclic view of creation; a repetitive process of moving through life cycles and bodies, developing the divine spirit within until the perfected Soul is liberated and no longer needs to return to embodied life forms in the lower dimensions of the Dema, the material realm of matter. This creation story has some elements similar to the Sumerian creation story about the colonization of Earth by the Anunnaki reptilians and their accompanying minions, the cloned Grays. Looking at the chronology of the development of various world religions set down in history books, it becomes apparent that sects of Gnostics along with their teachings spread throughout the ancient Mediterranean lands including areas of Iran, Iraq, Syria, Babylonia, Palestine, Judea, and Egypt. Gnostics living in these areas formed into small communities, spread their sacred teachings and preserved them on papyrus scrolls.

The Hebrew priests around the same general time period were in the process of compiling their "deviated version" of the creation story, which they constructed in the Old Testament Bible. The Gnostics could see the heresy and the misinformation presented by the Hebrew leaders, so they openly protested the establishment of this patriarchal, punishing religion. This conflict of beliefs fueled a great conflagration which resulted in the reigning powers at the time—the Christians, Romans and Hebrews—vowing to eradicate the Gnostics and their teachings, which they almost succeeded in doing. Their story contains many detailed points, so the deconstruction of this paradigm is correspondingly detailed. The Gnostics dedicated volumes of written texts to refuting the doctrines and beliefs presented in the Old Testament. Their main refutations are listed below their core beliefs.

Deconstructing the Gnostic Paradigm

Belief that all that exists within the universe exists within the One—All That Is—as the eternal and infinite One True God without beginning or end (monotheism).

Belief that the Source of All is eternal and immutable but the created universe is in perpetual change—a cyclic view of life.

Belief in many universes of which the Originator is a single unitary essence pervading all creation.

Belief that the galaxies—massive spiraling plasma vortices—are formed by Aeons: creator gods residing in the Pleroma (the galactic center), emanating from the One True God.

Belief that the Aeons autonomously manifest/create each separate galaxy through plasma physics.

Belief in the emanation theory of the cosmos: that all that emerges in the cosmos is self-ordering and each thing that lives is fractally interconnected with all that lives—the holographic concept.

Belief that a veil exists between the world above—the Pleroma, the galactic center—and the exterior realms below, emanating from the galactic limbs of the Kenoma, creating the outer realms of chaos and darkness.

Belief that a "shadow world" came into existence, the veiled world of the Dema, where atomic matter was projected into elementary particles and eventually formed the inorganic planets of the solar system.

Belief that this Dema or "shadow world" is an imperfect creation filled with suffering because all created life forms in this solar system consume each other in order to nourish themselves.

Belief that Sophia, one of thirty paired creator Aeons, accidentally emanated from her creation a flawed deviated consciousness known as the demiurge—Yaldabaoth.

Belief that our solar system is flawed because it was created by a false, flawed demiurgic creator god called Yaldabaoth/Yahweh—a reptilian creator god assisted by his minions, the Archons.

Belief that the demiurge/reptilian creator god (desiring to replace God and have no other above himself so as to rule over others) created the material and astral worlds, duplicating his original flaw.

Belief that the Archons are an anomalous species of inorganic cybernetic intelligences living in the realm of the Dema, the fields of inorganic elementary particles circulating in the cosmos and in solar systems at large.

Belief that the Archons are an aberration, an amoebic form of insectoid mind parasites, virtual-reality creators and deceivers who attached themselves to the Aeon Sophia's creation, the Anthropos.

Belief that the Archons are interdimensional inorganic intelligences who guard the interface between the Dema and the Kenoma, between the planetary biosphere and the spiral galaxy in which Earth and humanity are captured.

Belief that the flaw of the demiurge is reflected in the design of the human ego/mind, causing it to believe itself to be the sole creator of its world and the controller of its life.

Belief that all organic matter-forms or creations in this world contain the divine essence encased in a perishable physical-matter body and in subtle-energy bodies.

Belief that the earthly creations in the Dema were designed to keep humanity enslaved through attachment to the form life of the body and through enmeshment in false religious doctrines that present the demiurge, Yaldabaoth/Yahweh, as the One True God to intentionally deceive humanity and thereby prevent humans from knowing the truth of their divine origins.

Belief that the Soul, trapped in the body/mind, ignorant of its origins, mistakenly believes in the concept of the existence of evil external to itself.

Belief that the root of evil is not due to human sinfulness but due to the ignorance of the mind, inhabited by the Archons, which acts as a barrier to Truth.

Belief that there has been an alien intrusion of mind parasites (the Archons) into the human mind, creating a web of deception through the mind itself that keeps humanity in ignorance/unawareness.

Belief that the Aeon Sophia became captured within the Dema (the realm of elementary particles) and metamorphosed into planet Earth.

Belief that the phosters or Masters knowing of this enmeshment and intrusion warned their initiates of their presence and gave specific instructions on how to transcend the mind in order to achieve liberation/enlightenment from this system of control.

Belief that the Archons feed upon negative human emotions, especially the emotion of fear which they use to deceive and prevent humans from evolving and returning to Source.

Belief that humans were intentionally designed by Sophia with full conscious awareness of their origins and of the divine essence within them, but this knowledge was intentionally veiled by the false creator god and his Archons.

Belief that the earthly creation allows for the evolution of consciousness whereby humans will eventually learn how to liberate themselves from physical existence and the karmic cycles of rebirth.

Belief that liberation can be achieved through the help and guidance of living phosters, messengers of light, the illumined ones, the Masters such as Mani, Seth, Jesus, Buddha, Krishna, Kabir, et al., who show their followers how to use specific inner practices to regain the original knowledge of the spiritual realms.

Belief that the Soul on its return journey to the Pleroma has to pass through Yaldabaoth's created worlds, guarded by the Seven Rulers (his Archontic forces or deities) who guard the seven inner gates leading to the higher dimensions which the Soul must pass through in its evolutionary journey back to Source.

Belief in the value and necessity of specific meditative disciplines to activate the chakras so the Soul can rise above the veil of the body-mind that creates the phenomenal false world of duality in the Dema.

Belief that gnosis or direct knowledge is the way to perfection and liberation, gnosis meaning to know the ineffable divine reality from whence the Anthropos originally came (transcendental knowledge that must be realized while embodied on Earth).

Belief in the practice of attuning to the Aeonic forces, which have acoustic (sound) and luminal (light) signatures. Telesti or illumined Masters teach their initiates how to attune to the light and sound frequencies of the Aeons and of the Godhead.

Refutations of the Christian Bible

Rejection of the biblical story about the Garden of Eden, believing it to be a prison laboratory where the reptilians and Archons genetically engineered the primate humanoids to be their slaves and instilled in them false beliefs to control and enslave them.

Rejection of the biblical "salvationist" paradigm that arose after 150 BCE.

Rejection of the idea of the redemptive value of suffering, calling it irrational and false.

Rejection of the Old Testament biblical story of the Hebrews as the "chosen people of God" and the concept of a divine plan ending in an apocalyptic day of retribution.

Rejection of the ideas put forth in the biblical creation story such as sin, the fall of man, the right of divine rulership, judgment, retribution, salvation and the crucifixion of Jesus to atone for man's sins.

Rejection of these concepts as false, claiming they were intentionally designed and introduced to the populace to institute a worldwide theocracy—a rulership of kings and priestly administrators who claimed authority from a divine source.

Rejection of the Nicene Creed which teaches of a physical resurrection of all believers.

Rejection of the Jewish god Yaldabaoth/Yahweh of the Old Testament Bible, believing him to be a false god, a demented, psychopathic reptilian god.

Rejection of all religious doctrines, commandments and rules of conduct which lead not to liberation but to continued enslavement.

Rejection of the idea that death automatically brings about liberation of the Soul from bondage. This false belief they say causes the Soul to stay entrapped indefinitely in the karmic cycle of rebirth.

Rejection of the concept of the "fall of man" as a false, deviated concept designed to trap embodied souls through the false belief in their sinfulness.

Rejection of the belief in the second coming of a single messiah who will save all believers.

Rejection of the belief in "judgment day" when the people will be judged in an apocalyptic day of retribution where the believers (the chosen people) will be saved and the non-believers will be sent to damnation or hell.

Reference Keys: Barnstone (2003). Behr (2015). Doresse (1970). Hoeller (web). Irenaeus (web). Lash (2006, web). Layton (web). *Nag Hammadi* (web). Reimer (2013).

Chapter Twelve

The Ra Group/Elohim Worldview

─────────────────

THE LAW OF One books are a body of teachings channeled and compiled into four original books through L/L Research, published by Schiffer Books in 1984. Carla Rueckert was the trance channel, Jim McCarty the scribe, and Don Elkins, PhD, physicist and university professor, was the questioner. The messenger delivering the information described himself as an intergalactic non-physical "social memory complex" known as the Ra group. This group, according to Ra, their messenger, operate from the sixth dimension and originated from the planet Venus.

Combined in this chapter with the Ra group creation story is that of the Elohim-channeled material described below. Their cosmologies (explanations of the origin, evolution and structure of the universe) are closely intertwined. The Elohim-channeled material was tape-recorded by Wynne Free beginning in 2002 and compiled several years later into a book titled *The Creator Gods of the Physical Universe Want to Talk to You*, which is available on his website, listed in the References. The original channeler for this material was Daphne Karandanis, and later Terry Brown. Carla Rueckert, now deceased, the channel for the Ra group, was a personal longtime friend of Wynne, Daphne and Terry, and she frequently joined them in online discussions about the Ra/Elohim materials. Sometimes the Ra group consciousness also spoke through the Elohim group channelers.

In the *Law of One* books, the Ra group refers to itself as a "social memory complex or group consciousness" that is three evolutionary cycles ahead of humans and is from the sixth dimension. Ra states they are members of the Confederation of Planets in the Service of the One Infinite Creator. The Confederation, per the Ra group, is governed by the Council of Saturn, which maintains a constant watch over planet Earth. This Confederation is sometimes referred to as the "Guardians," of which there are nine main members and twenty-four backup members available as needed. The Confederation and Council of Saturn operate via telepathic contact. Their function, they said, is to guard the free will of the mind/body/spirit complexes (human beings) of third density. A group of fifty-three different galactic civilizations and approximately five hundred planetary consciousness complexes make up this particular Confederation.

Ra states in *The Law of One*, Book I:

> All contacts with humans are made for one purpose and that is to enunciate the laws of creation known as The Law of One.... In an infinite creator there is only unity. All distortions are a lack of understanding. Thought binds all things. Life in this space/time dimension is used as a medium for the development of freely chosen experience within finity, for a period of time. You are everything, every being, every emotion, every event, every situation. You are all One. This is The Law of One. (p. 67)

This entire body of channeled teachings form an epistemology, an in-depth study of the nature, sources and limits of human knowledge. The Ra group materials represent a cyclic view of the multiverse, which is both the origin and the completion of all sentient beings.

According to the Ra group, the Law of One governs the reincarnational cycles, the forgetting process that occurs at each birth, the struggle to remember, to move beyond the individualized conscious of the mind/body/spirit complex in order to see beyond the illusion that is this holographic multiverse. The Ra group tells us we return again and again until we learn the Law of One, which is the Law of Love, and learn that all beings within the finite creation have free will and choose in each lifetime a path of either "service to self" or "service to others."

To choose to operate in service to others, consciously loving and honoring all beings, eventually leads to the completion of all reincarnational cycles and a return to Intelligent Infinity/the Supreme Creator. The Ra group uses the terms "service to self versus service to others" as a way of explaining the dualistic concept of how this three-dimensional world functions as a teaching tool for humanity, so that as humans evolve they will eventually be able to transcend the dualistic world, moving into the higher spiritual realms and eventually back into unity consciousness.

Before narrating the Ra group/Elohim's creation story, I'm going to sidestep here and provide a brief timeline of intergalactic events that occurred in Earth's ancient and obscured pre-history according to the Ra group. Beginning with the oldest events, approximately 705,000 years ago, the Ra group states there was a highly advanced technological civilization living on the planet Maldek. The inhabitants abused their power, began warring among themselves and eventually destroyed their biosphere. Then through nuclear war their entire planet was blown up and large areas of Earth were also destroyed. When Maldek exploded, its fragments became the Asteroid Belt. The disincarnate beings from blown-up Maldek were confined to the lower astral planes for a lengthy period of time. They eventually reincarnated into early ape bodies on planet Earth some 500,000 years ago. The explosion that blew up Maldek also destroyed all of the then-existing space ports on Earth, stopping all travel to Earth by other races from other galaxies.

A second race of extraterrestrial beings arrived on Earth from Mars approximately 75,000 years ago, their planet having become inhospitable due to the loss of their oxygen layer. These beings were genetically manipulated by non-reproductive means by the Guardian race present on Earth at that time: their genes were mingled with those of the Guardian race. There were also two other bipedal ape beings on Earth that had evolved from second-density life forms natural to planet Earth. Next to arrive was the Lemurian race, who came from a planet in the galaxy of Deneb. They colonized Earth around 53,000 years ago. They built a peaceful civilization. Their island civilization was destroyed when the Earth was inundated by the Pacific Ocean due to the movement of Earth's tectonic plates that caused major upheavals in the area.

A fourth civilization, the Atlantean, formed on the planet about 31,000 years ago. The Ra group give no geographical location for Atlantis. Ra states that the Atlanteans were a highly advanced technological society engaging in intergalactic space travel and utilizing quantum energy manipulation with stones and crystals. They were master geneticists adept at creating life forms. Their society eventually turned to negative, service-to-self, controlling, dominating actions, and approximately 11,000 years ago they started a war, which destroyed 40 percent of their population. Then in 10,821 BCE they started another war that completely destroyed their civilization, causing it to sink beneath the ocean. Three small Atlantean groups, having foreknowledge of the coming devastation, left prior to the end and migrated to Tibet, Peru and Turkey, where they began new civilizations.

Ra states that his race, a very old race functioning from the sixth dimension, originated from Venus. He describes them as being very tall, delicate of form with an outer body covering or shell of golden light, rather than a dense physical body like humans. Eleven thousand years ago his race came to Earth interdimensionally and established two planetary civilizations, one in Egypt and one in South America, with the intention of teaching the human populace by direct contact a series of technical methods to heal mental and physical illnesses/distortions through the use of crystals. They constructed many pyramids on Earth and created megalithic energy grids with their technologies, and their knowledge was freely given. However, those in power at that time kept the knowledge for their own exclusive use and used the technologies to dominate and enslave the populace. The Ra group contacted Ikhnaton, ruler of the Eighteenth Dynasty of Egypt, and attempted to introduce the Law of One teachings to the populace through him: Ikhnaton tried to establish a religion of the Law of One.

This became known at that time as the worship of the Sun God Ra, but his efforts were eventually thwarted by the reigning priesthood who worshipped many gods and refused to accept monotheism. According to the Ra group, they withdrew from the planet around that time and now operate from beyond the sixth dimension via interdimensional telepathic contact.

Ra's explanation of the creation story is more like a dissertation on the cosmology of the multiverse given in Book I of the *Law of One* series in response to Don Elkins's question "How was the universe created?" Here is his response. Following the direct quote is a summarized version of the Ra group/Elohim's version of how the universe was created.

> The first known thing in creation is infinity. Infinity is creation. Infinity became aware. The primal paradox or distortion of the Law of One is the concept of freedom of will of awareness. This concept is "finity, limitation or boundedness." The One Intelligent Infinity invested itself in an exploration of many-ness. Due to the infinite possibilities of intelligent infinity there is no ending to many-ness. The exploration is free to continue infinitely in an eternal present. Awareness led to the focus of infinity into infinite energy/Logos/ Love. The Creator focusing infinity as a "conscious principle" is called "intelligent infinity." Next came an infinite reaction to the creative principle in one of its primal distortions, freedom of will.... [E]nergy moves from intelligent infinity ... due first to the outpouring of randomized creative force, this then is creating patterns which in holographic style appear as the entire creation no matter which direction or energy is explored. These patterns of energy begin then to regularize into their own local ... rhythms and fields of energy, thus creating dimensions and universes.... [T]he energies move in increasingly intelligent patterns until the individualization of various energies emanating from the creative principle of intelligent infinity ... become energetic co-creators of universes. (pp. 129–31)

Thus the so-called illusion of physical matter came into being. The concept of light is instrumental in grasping this great leap of thought as this vibrational distortion of infinity is the building block of that which is known as matter:

The light, being intelligent and full of energy, thus being the first distortion of intelligent infinity which is called "the creative principle." This light of love is made to have ... certain characteristics, among them the infinite whole paradoxically described by the straight line.... This paradox is responsible for the shape of various holographic illusions ... you call solar systems, galaxies and revolving planets ... tending toward the lenticular [shaped like a bi-convex lens]. (p. 130)

The galaxies and all other illusory or so-called "material" things are products of individualized portions of intelligent infinity. Each energetic co-creator created the universes and, allowing the rhythms of free choice to flow, playing with the infinite spectrum of possibilities using intelligent energy, created the natural laws of each particular universe. These natural laws appear in the vibrational patterns of each solar system. Thus each solar system has its own local system of illusory natural laws. Any portion, no matter how small, of any density or illusory pattern, contains within it a holograph of the One Creator which is infinity. The solar system you inhabit has patterns, rhythms and natural laws unique to itself. The creation progresses from the spiraling galactic energy to the spiraling solar energy, to the spiraling planetary energy, to the experiential circumstances of spiraling energy—which begins the first-density awareness of consciousness, which is the density of the mineral and water life upon the planet. Movement is the characteristic of second density plant and animal life, the striving towards light and growth. The third density is the density of self-consciousness or self-awareness and is the beginning density of consciousness of being and consciousness of spirit. The fourth through seventh densities freely chose not to be visible. (pp. 129–33)

The densities can be described as dimensions or planes, depicting different levels of consciousness and different phenomenological ways of being in creation that is formed of various different frequencies of light. Each succeeding density is more light-filled, and there are seven densities in each octave. The eighth density of the present creation equals the first density of the next octave or cycle of evolution in the creation. For instance, once a being evolves and takes on a mind/body/spirit complex in third density, they continue to evolve by spiritually progressing through higher and higher densities using non-physical, energetic light bodies beyond the third density; eventually reuniting or merging with the One Supreme Creator after traversing through all the densities till the eighth density is achieved.

First density is the density of the elements: solids, liquids, gases and plasmas. Second density is the density of organic life: plants and animals. Third density is a visible physical density of conscious self- awareness whereby the mind/spirit is veiled in duality and the being must choose the polarity of service to self (STS) or service to others (STO) through life experiences. Fourth density and all above it are invisible. This is the density of love and understanding. Fifth density is the density of light or wisdom inhabited by non-physical beings in light bodies (deities or angels) of a higher level of spiritual evolution than humans. Sixth density is the density of unity consciousness, where love and wisdom are united without any illusion of polarity or duality. Seventh density is the gateway density, the last density before the merging back with the One Supreme Creator of all that is.

The creation story of the Elohim is also a channeled body of work and has been excerpted from the book *The Creator Gods of the Physical Universe Want to Talk to You*, by Wynne Free. Their creation story is quite similar to Ra's and this group complex operates in a manner very similar to the Ra group. They are fully aware of each other and work cooperatively, each in their own sphere of influence. Their functions often overlap. They are fully aware of all other intergalactic groups, councils and confederations of which there are many, some of whom operate in service-to-self and others in service-to-others orientation.

The Elohim state they speak on behalf of the Solar Logos. The Elohim differentiate themselves from the Ra group, stating they are a more feminine group-energy complex, residing in the tenth dimension, whose purpose is to bring life and life forms to third-dimensional planets such as Earth. They describe the Ra group as a more masculine group-energy complex with a broader more general scope of function of sustaining and loving all life forms. The Elohim state that

> ...billions of years ago some of their group evolved from physical bodies in Andromeda to their present position.... [T]here is an overseeing force that has not incarnated into bodies and intends specifically not to, to maintain the purity of intention that is needed to guide and direct creation. (p. 115)

The Elohim say they represent a collective of the galactic star-seeding system of the local Andromedan "star-gate" system that oversees the belt of Orion. (The Andromedan Galaxy is the closest one to our Milky Way Galaxy.) They further say that they entered our solar system four million years ago and originated as an intergalactic, non-physical species from the star system of Alcyon. (Alcyon is in the constellation of Taurus and is the brightest star in the Pleiades star cluster.)

The Elohim describe themselves as "a division of the Creator Gods of the physical universe from tenth density." They state their function in this solar system is to protect the fledgling humanoid species, which they state were both bred on Earth and also brought here from other planetary civilizations and hybridized via genetic manipulation.

Their life span is many thousands of years beyond the normal human life span. They interface with Earth's energy body and coordinate energies between suns and star systems. They work with life forms, transmuting third-dimensional experiences so that the lessons of love may be learned and entities may be brought forward or evolved into the non-physical fourth- through seventh-dimensional light bodies.

They are recipients of the light rays of the sixth-dimensional ray of service and are a "collective Oversoul" of sixth through tenth density. The densities represent levels of consciousness and levels of fineness of vibrational frequencies as described above in the *Law of One* materials. The densities, according to the Elohim, are organized just as described by the Ra group, with first density representing the cycle of awareness; second density, growth and movement; third density, self-awareness; fourth density, love and understanding; fifth density, light and wisdom; sixth density, light/love or unity; and seventh density, the gateway cycle where one fully perceives and merges into the sacred unity and oneness of All That Is. An individual being or an entire planetary body can move from one density to the next. This occurs naturally as planetary systems traverse different areas of energy density within a galaxy, thus creating dimensional shifts in precise measureable cosmic cycles of time.

The Elohim form an amalgamation of energetic light intensities within sixth- through tenth-density frequencies. They create by projecting into this realm sacred geometric and mathematical forms, using the higher octaves of light frequencies. By formulating and introducing geometric anchor points through intention, they create loose holographic structures that are not initially physical or visible. Etheric energy holds these structures in place and binds energy into these loose holographic structures, resulting in etheric forms that are precursors to three-dimensional holographic-matter structures.

The Elohim state that the basic building blocks for life forms are tetrahedrons and octagons, which originate and secure a location within a density. Thus sacred geometry and mathematics provide an avenue for life to express itself through a multiplicity of forms and provides etheric blueprints or patterns that are precursors to life forms in the matter worlds. Mathematical formulas express an exact language of relationships between dimension, speed, light, frequency and intention. These precise formulas are mathematically activated to create spinningness (torsion waves) in proximity to each other, which at their intersections create frequency wave forms.

The Elohim state they created the initial templates in space by the projection of thought forms as anchor points or nodes in the akasha/ether; then, spinning energy through them, they created rudimentary holograms throughout the cosmos as the galaxies. The Elohim, as Logoi or galactic creator gods, delighted in spinning out projections that created the galaxies. These vast spinning plasma energies of congealed light created light photons appearing and disappearing, flickering on and off, spiraling into galaxies. As forms increased in density, they became solidified as particle structures. For forms to solidify, interlocking holograms were required. The Logos, a creator god of a single galaxy, created many sub-Logoi (sub-creator gods of star systems and planets) which in turn contributed to the creation of sub-sub-Logoi (humanoid life forms) with each being a microcosm of the One Supreme Creator God.

These geometric structures, having different spin velocities, different densities and different proximities to each other, form varying constructs which eventually solidify into matter structures resulting in the formation of independent, conscious, thinking entities who could exist in physical forms or in non-physical forms. During this creational process, multiple entities can get infused into the same geometric structures. Confusion arises as the structure (body) that houses or binds an entity becomes shared with other entities who make this same structure their home. As the mind develops, the thinking within such a bound entity may generate thoughts not its own over which it has no direct control (the ego/mind). Thoughts can be triggered by the circumstances of life and the structure (body) the entity occupies, which is connected with other entities occupying the same structure (body). The ego/mind can therefore be a deviation from the entity's experience of who it really is, although the mind can also serve and solve problems for the entity. Thus, the ego/mind becomes an aspect of the "veil" that can hinder or block the entity's connection with the realms from which it came (pp. 82–83).

According to the Elohim's version of the creation story, they evolved billions of years ago from physical bodies created in Andromeda to their present position as light beings. A portion of their Soul group never have incarnated in order to maintain the purity of energetic intent needed to guide and direct the creational process (p. 115).

At some point in the creational process, after having created the third dimension, some of the sub-Logoi (sub-creator gods), delighting in all their creations, desired to possess their created forms. This was the initial hook that attracted the sub-creator-gods into this three-dimensional matter-based physical realm. They desired to solidify their forms and to live in love by glorifying themselves through life, to gain proof of their existence through extending themselves into matter and taking on an exterior form that solidified as part of the physical creation. Sexual functioning played a part in their devolvement as it increased their capacity to feel love and enhanced the existence of one with another by merging. This original creation of the third dimension was such a delight to the sub-Logoi that many began disappearing into the lower realms, which caused great concern among the other sub-Logoi remaining in the higher realms.

There developed a division of intention among the many groups of sub-creator-gods, as some were opposed to the concept of free will (choice-polarity) being extended into the lower dimensions and affecting, in unknown ways, fledgling humanity. Many of the sub-creator-gods were concerned about the contingent of sub-creator-gods who were merging into and intermingling with their creations. However, the experimentation continued. The larger portion of the sub-creator-gods continued evolving their creations in the unpolarized worlds of love/light and unity consciousness, founding the sixth–twelfth densities of "service to other light beings" that maintained the paradisiacal conditions of constant contentment, peace, love, unity and bliss (pp. 83–86).

Those sub-creator gods desiring to introduce the concept of free will set up their creations in the lower densities incorporating free will, generating the choice of a service-to-self or service-to-others orientation, thereby creating a polarized/dualistic holographic world which, from their perspective, would enable humanity to evolve more rapidly beyond third density. The Elohim's version of the creation story matches somewhat the Abrahamic biblical story of Lucifer, an archangel, known as the "morning star or light bearer" who was instrumental in bringing into the world the concept of polarity (knowledge of good and evil). Lucifer was referred to as the "covering angel." Isaiah 14 reveals the fall of Lucifer from the heights of heaven: "How you are fallen from heaven, O Lucifer, son of the morning.... For you have said in your heart: 'I will ascend into heaven, I will exalt my throne above the stars of God; I will also sit on the mount. I will ascend above the heights of the clouds, I will be like the Most High.'" This sounds very much like the same demiurgic desire to possess, rule over and control that drove Yaldabaoth's actions in the Gnostic creation story and Enlil's actions in the Sumerian creation story.

The Elohim stated that the original intention of these sub-creator gods was to provide an opportunity for "accelerated spiritual evolution" of the mind/body/spirit complexes (humanoid entities) of this planetary system. It was believed, by those sub-creator gods who originally created this hologram, that through unknowing or ignorant discontent, seeking through movement and learning from experience the lessons of love, that humans might achieve more rapid evolution beyond third density. In order to create this illusion of duality (confusion) in third density, primary knowledge that had been naturally present in the human species was "veiled."

The Ra group explained the veiling process to Don Elkins in Book IV of the *Law of One* Series. Ra states:

> The primary veiling was of such significance that it may be seen to be analogous to the mantling of the Earth over all the jewels within the Earth's crust; whereas previously all facets of the Creator were consciously known. After the veiling, almost no facets of the Creator were known to the mind. Almost all was buried beneath the veil. (p. 94)

The Ra group describes how this original knowledge was intentionally "veiled" or blocked through DNA manipulation. It included blocking the ability (1) to envision or have far sight, clairvoyance, clairaudience and clairsentience, (2) to remember dreams, having precognition, (3) to know the body/mind as a single unit instead of the illusory belief in the separation of body from mind, (4) to experience the full potency of pure will or pure desire, (5) to experience complete perceptual memory, (6) to move consciously and freely between the conscious, subconscious and unconscious minds, and (7) to perceive beyond the illusion of space/time. This DNA manipulation caused humanity to become trapped in this three-dimensional illusion. This "veil of unknowing" was pulled down over humanity, causing the illusion of separation and a forgetting or amnestic state of forgetfulness of humanity's Oneness with the Supreme Creator.

Through the great experimental split in the creational process, polarity/duality was created and the mind was blocked from all higher knowledge which had been previously available. Consequently, the eternal, divine Soul essence became trapped within the body/mind/spirit complex of this third-dimensional hologram, with all memory of our divinity and connectedness to the One True Creator God erased.

According to the Ra group and the Elohim, as long as our attention continues to be focused on the physical body, the mind and the temporal cause/effect world of materiality, we remain trapped in this illusory hologram. The aim of life is for humanity to become more aware and more conscious, which takes many lifetimes of learning how to move consciousness out of time, out of duality, out of judgment and into the eternal now of unconditional acceptance of self and others and ultimately moving into the transcendental realms of unconditional love and unity consciousness. Thus by moving from linearity to nonlinearity, from the horizontal to the vertical inner or higher-dimensional planes, we move beyond the duality/polarity illusion into the higher dimensions of existence and eventually evolve till we merge back into Source/unity consciousness with the One Infinite Creator.

Deconstructing the Ra Group/Elohim Paradigm

This cosmology is dense, complex, multilayered and multidimensional. I've tried to parse out the basic core tenets from among the volumes both groups have narrated as to how the multiverse was formed, by whom and for what purpose:

Belief that the Law of One is the Law of Love.

Belief that All That Is is Intelligent Infinity, the Infinite Creator.

Belief that the Infinite Creator is the origin and completion of all sentient life.

Belief that the Law of One also encompasses the Law of Confusion, which is introduced through the duality/illusion of the space/time hologram.

Belief that within the Infinite Creator there is only Unity/Oneness/Love.

Belief that within finity there is boundedness, limitation and distortion.

Belief that the finite creations are cyclic and never-ending.

Belief that the Ra group/Elohim sub-creator gods govern the cause/effect karmic and reincarnational cycles of life forms in the lower dimensions.

Belief that the Logos is a creator god of a galaxy.

Belief that a portion of the Ra group/Elohim are light beings, creator gods of galaxies, while the rest function as sub-logoi or creator gods of planetary systems, stars and all life forms on various planetary bodies.

Belief that the Elohim evolved their creations in the unpolarized or unified sixth through twelfth densities as service-to-others light beings.

Belief that a division of intention occurred among the sub-logoi creator gods, and that a small contingent of them, exercising their free will, chose to experiment with the first- through fifth-density holograms in our solar system.

Belief that the thought projection of the concept of choice/free-will into the creation caused a confusion and a splitting of the originally harmonious, unified light and sound frequencies into positive and negative poles, thereby creating duality/illusion/choice/free-will in the lower dimensions of the creation.

Belief that this small contingent of sub-creator gods then entered into their created matter-based physical forms to enjoy, experience and possess their holographic creations.

Belief that the original intent in of the sub-creator gods in creating the third density was to provide an opportunity for "accelerated growth" of the humanoid species on this and other holograms in this and other solar systems.

Belief that this duality/polarity experiment creating free will and choice in third-density holograms might affect "in unknown ways" (producing unintended consequences in) the developing humanoids within the matter-based holograms.

Belief that this experimental split in the brain/mind consciousness of humanity via DNA manipulation caused confusion and misperception through the veiling of the human mind and senses, causing humanity to believe the illusive three-dimensional hologram to be real, thereby trapping humanity within the dualistic illusion of the third dimension.

Belief that this split in conscious awareness and the veil or block placed over the body/mind/spirit complex has retarded humanity's spiritual evolution rather than accelerated it.

Belief that the remedy for healing this block/split/illusion in humanity's consciousness is to move individual/collective awareness beyond the space/time illusion into the higher-frequency dimensions of unified consciousness through meditation and inner awareness so that unity consciousness and unconditional love can become once more operative in humanity.

Belief that a service-to-self orientation is a self-centered egoistic view of self/other causing one to take from others, to possess, to have control over and use others for self-gratification (the epitome of the behaviors of the demiurge living in us as the lower mind in its lower-vibrational, veiled state).

Belief that a free-will choice to adopt a service-to-others orientation is the movement of the body/mind/spirit complex into an inclusive attitude, reawakening unity consciousness through acts of kindness, compassion, love and caring while incarnated.

A Cautionary Note

Please be aware and use discernment when reading any channeled materials, including those presented in this book, as all are subject to intentional misdirection, omissions of information, abrupt changes in the flow of thoughts and ideas, avoidance of answering certain questions, time lapses, incomplete and obscure idea constructions and other subtle anomalies that can mislead and confuse. Don't forget that one of the primal distortions of the Law of One is "The Law of Confusion." Remember that the best place to hide a lie is between two truths. And remember that the mind itself has been DNA-altered so as to create confusion in the split/brain mind itself. Remember the Ra group/Elohim both said the mind was blocked or veiled so that all knowledge of our divinity and our telepathic abilities were intentionally blocked and shut down.

Reference Keys: Free (2004, web). L/L (1984, web).

Chapter Thirteen

The Anthroposophic Worldview

RUDOLF STEINER (1861–1925) was the founder of a spiritual philosophy which he named Anthroposophy, meaning "wisdom of the human being." He was born in Austria and devoted his adult life to building up a complete body of work called a "science of the spirit," a study of the evolution of man at work throughout the cosmos. He was a scholar, historian, scientist, writer and philosopher. He wrote thirty books and delivered over six thousand lectures across Europe on the topics of agriculture, medicine, economics, architecture, science, religion, metaphysics and the arts. He founded the Waldorf Schools and the Anthroposophical Society, both of which have branches throughout the world. In an account of his life and work by A. P. Shepherd, Steiner was aptly called "a scientist of the invisible," the title of Shepherd's book.

Cosmic Memory, published in 1959, contains a series of Steiner's lectures in which he describes in vivid detail the insoluble link between man and the cosmos, stating that this link is the fundamental basis of human evolution. Steiner had extreme extrasensory capabilities from early childhood and only began sharing this information with the world in the latter portion of his life via his lectures and books. In *Cosmic Memory*, he gives a comprehensive overview of the cosmology of the universe and, particularly in chapters twelve through seventeen, describes the origins of the Earth. He shows us that ordinary human consciousness is just a single form of consciousness and that there are both higher and lower forms of consciousness in and out of bodily form. He describes multiple levels and dimensions of consciousness and states there are beings who are conscious in other dimensions and reach into the physical universe but not through any physical form. What follows is an excerpted, albeit miniscule and condensed, version of Steiner's creation story, the full version of which fills volumes.

Steiner states that before the life of man developed on Earth, there were previous formative stages of development that took place on the early planetary bodies, first on Saturn, secondly on Mars, then on the Sun followed by life on the Moon and then culminating with life on planet Earth. Man is now in his Earth stage and will eventually pass through several more developmental stages of evolution in order to arrive at the highest, most evolved states of being. Life and the evolution of consciousness go through long waking or active cycles and long dormant or sleeping cycles of growth over eons of cosmic time. Man formed his current level of consciousness—sensory awareness, perception, proprioception, emotional responses, mental logic, intellectual reasoning and comprehension which can be defined as "higher" states of consciousness—on Earth.

Steiner continues, saying the most basic or lowest state of consciousness, mostly dull and dim, the consciousness of "immediate sensation," developed on Saturn. This level of consciousness can, however, perceive everything that takes place in the universe, even down to the last detail, and can observe objects and beings on other planetary bodies. It can exercise influence on other objects and beings. As man's consciousness was developing on Saturn, concurrently other superior and subordinate entities and consciousnesses were also developing on other planetary bodies.

Consciousness then slowly developed at the next level on the planet Mars, then on the Sun, where man developed consciousness of a different kind, clearer and more focused but limited to the sphere of the Sun and the planets most closely connected to it. Man's next existence took place on the Moon where it was more like a sleep state filled with dreamlike images, amorphous and shifting, filled with colors, tones and feelings, dim sensations totally within the being and not spatially outside of its being. This dim, dreamlike consciousness consisted of constant shifting and moving images, tones and feelings which ebbed and flowed.

The next development of man formed on Earth with sounds, colors and forms beginning to appear externally and spatially in formed objects outside of his consciousness. This change in perception from internal to external gradually formed the "objective" world and "objective" consciousness. Physical sense organs slowly developed from a germinal state to a fully functioning state. As the physical body of man formed and evolved so did the planetary body of Earth, evolving more and more complex forms. Thus, the colored, sounding, feeling world that had developed within consciousness began developing outside of consciousness in external space through physical forms and also through the world of ideas, concepts and thought forms about external objects. This development constituted the basis for the development of memory and self-conscious awareness through conceptualization. Thinking allowed conscious man to differentiate himself from his surrounding environment as an independent aware being recognizable as an "I." This fourth stage of development encompassed not only consciousness but "self-consciousness" and only with these capacities could man develop a memory of what he was perceiving and experiencing so he could differentiate himself from the surrounding environment as a separate and individuated "I."

According to Steiner, the next stage of human development will occur on Jupiter, and it will be the development of a suprapsychic consciousness through which man will be able to consciously, intelligently, knowingly create images, objects and beings. He will be able to communicate with beings that are currently hidden from sensory perception. Birth and death as experienced on Earth will no longer occur as man will no longer depend on the external world or his bodily senses to perceive external objects in the environment. He will receive influences through images the Soul creates out of itself and life will not be interrupted against his will. This extrasensory, clairvoyant and clairsentient consciousness will allow man to transcend the need for birth and death and he will become knowingly immortal. Man will become a conscious co-creator at this point in his evolvement. But first he has to develop the higher organs of conscious awareness whereby he will be able to see into the spiritual worlds and see nonphysical beings, auras and subtle thought forms. He as yet needs to develop the capacity to perceive highly advanced mathematical and geometric conceptualizations and spiritual ideals, which will be seen and known through the development of the higher mind. As this is happening within man on Earth, other planetary bodies will be developing concurrently as well. In all, man will pass through twelve stages of consciousness over eons of cosmic time.

As Steiner says in *Cosmic Memory*, "Everything which comes into being in time has its origin in the eternal. But the eternal is not accessible to sensory perception" (p. 38). On planet Earth, where the beginning of human consciousness was developed, it was aided in its unfoldment. The earliest form of consciousness, the dullest form akin to a "deep trance" state, developed concurrently with the formation of the first rudimentary physical bodies. The developmental stages pass through seven phases which, he states, are guided and facilitated by a hierarchy of higher spiritual beings who each have specific functions to perform in aiding the development of the fledgling human being. The first cycle is guided by the Spirits of Will (Thrones), the second cycle by the Spirits of Wisdom (Dominions), the third cycle by the Spirits of Motion (Principalities), the fourth by the Spirits of Form (Powers), the fifth by the Spirits of Personality (Primal Beings or Archai) and the Spirits of Love (Seraphim), the sixth by the Spirits of Fire (Cherubim/Archangels) and the seventh cycle by the Spirits of Twilight (Lunar Pitris/Angels).

Beginning with the fifth cycle, as man develops his inner sight, the Spirits of Personality (Archai or Asuras) and the Spirits of Love (Seraphim) will reveal themselves to man. Steiner states, "Now the Spirits of Personality seize upon this higher astral body and implant in it ... independence ... and therewith also selfishness" (p. 212). He continues, saying that from the sixth cycle onward, the Cherubim will reveal themselves, and from the seventh cycle onward the Thrones, the true creators of men, will reveal themselves. It is during the seventh cycle on Earth that the spiritual man, the "Atma" or Soul, will be fully developed. Through the human body, imbued with a fully evolved and developed Soul, will blossom a true and full understanding in man of his own Self as an eternal divine Soul. Steiner explains that man must first develop his powers from below in order that the enlightenment from above can occur. He continues, saying that as this understanding pours out over the planet among humanity, the Spirits of Will (Thrones) will be revealed and known to man as the original creators of the human body which they radiated out of their own nature.

Thus the states and stages of development of planetary bodies, human bodies, and the consciousness of both, evolve in tandem. In the beginning all was formless, then an etheric stage developed, followed by an astral stage with the development of astral forms culminating in physical forms imbued with consciousness. Steiner makes a point in his lectures of stating that all of his conceptualizations about the formation of the universe are described by way of similes or word symbols that can only approximate the depiction of very vast and complex processes of development that happen ever so slowly over eons of cycles of time through the transformation of consciousness. He states in *How to Know the Higher Worlds* that

> the most insignificant experience, which offers itself to humanity stands in connection with cosmic beings and cosmic events. When once this connection is revealed to him in his moments of contemplation, he comes to his daily activities with a new, fuller power. For now he knows that his labor and his suffering are given and endured for the sake of a great, spiritual cosmic whole. (web)

Deconstructing the Anthroposophic Paradigm

Belief that anthroposophy is the study of the science of spirit and the cosmic evolution of man.

Belief that human consciousness is only one kind of consciousness in the multiverse.

Belief that there are higher and lower forms of conscious beings both in and out of physical form.

Belief in multiple dimensions of consciousness.

Belief that formative stages of development took place on other planets before man evolved on Earth and these formative states took place first on Saturn, then on Mars, then on the Sun, then on the Moon before man began incarnating on Earth in physical form.

Belief that man evolved over eons of long active and dormant cosmic cycles.

Belief that higher states of consciousness such as sensory awareness, self-consciousness, reasoning and comprehension occurred on Earth, where perception changed from an internal to an external form of attention, with the mental development of man expressing and manifesting a world of ideas and thought forms external to the self.

Belief that the next level of development will occur on Jupiter and will be a suprapsychic consciousness where man will be able to see and communicate with interdimensional beings of the higher and lower dimensions and will no longer experience birth and death in a physical body but will be immortal, living in a spiritual or light body.

Belief that man passes through seven developmental phases, all of which are guided and facilitated by a hierarchy of spiritual beings: the first cycle guided by the Thrones, the second cycle by the Dominions, the third cycle by the Principalities, the fourth by the Powers, the fifth by the Archai and Seraphim, the sixth by the Cherubim and the seventh by Lunar-Pitris Angels.

Belief that planetary bodies and human bodies and the consciousness of both develop in tandem, moving from the etheric to the astral to the physical, to a suprapsychic or telepathic interdimensional consciousness.

Belief that the Spirits of Will (the Thrones) will eventually reveal themselves to man as the original creator gods of the human form which they radiated out of their own natures.

_____

Reference Keys: Shepherd (1954). Steiner (1959, 1994, 2008, 2015, web-a–b).

Chapter Fourteen

The Sant Mat Masters Worldview

THE MASTERS PROVIDE a cosmology that is eternal and cyclic and has many similarities to the Hindu creation story, except that the Masters' version is somewhat less complex and more explicit in the details of how the multiverse was created, by whom and for what purpose. Their creation story covers vast cosmic time cycles similar to those described in the Hindu texts. A brief explanation is again repeated here to provide an overview of the cycles of creation and dissolution described by the Masters.

Yugas are vast cosmic time cycles repeating slowly over eons of time. The Sat Yuga, Golden Age or Age of Truth, is the longest cycle of time, lasting 1,728,000 years, where humans lived an average lifespan of 100,000 years. During this yuga, life was so easy, carefree and secure that humans didn't realize the nature of the space/time trap, the illusory world they were in. The Treta Yuga, the Silver Age, lasts 1,296,000 years, and humans lived up to ten thousand years in each lifetime. According to Hindu records, Vishnu incarnated during this yuga as Lord Rama and the events of his life were recorded in the Ramayana. The Dwapar Yuga or Copper Age lasts 864,000 years and it was during this yuga that the biblical records were written down in keeping with the life spans of humans as described in Genesis. For example, the Old Testament biblical prophets lived up to a thousand years, then as time passed, life spans gradually declined down to 120 years where it more or less generally remains today. The current yuga, the Kali Yuga also known as the Iron Age, began in 3200 BCE and lasts 432,000 years.

This version of the creation story was taken from an epic poem written by Saint Kabir during his lifetime. He lived from approximately 1398 to 1518 CE. Kabir is one of the original Masters in this Kali Yuga who descended directly from God and incarnated to bring Sat or Truth to humanity. He was born in Benares (then called Kashi), the holiest of all Hindu cities in his time, and grew up in a Muslim family of the weaver caste. Kabir founded a line of forty-two Masters which continues uninterrupted into the present era. The Masters incarnate in each yuga to maintain a continuous line of Masters in the world. The Sant Mat teachings are also called the Science of God-Realization or the Science of the Soul. The teachings of the Masters have remained virtually the same throughout recorded history.

Before I get into Kabir's creation story, I'm going to provide you with a summary of the teachings of the Masters so you may better understand and follow Kabir's creation story.

Terminologies referring to the Masters may change slightly from epoch to epoch depending on the culture and country into which the Masters are born. The largest number of Masters have been born on the Indian continent. India carries an ancient spiritual tradition of venerating the many lineages of Masters who've lived in India, as evidenced by the numerous temples built to honor them and their lives over the centuries. Due to this, there are many confusing definitions of what constitutes a Master, and many distinctions are made between different types of spiritual teachers, Masters, saints and gurus, especially among the Hindu spiritual traditions. In ancient Persia, Masters were called the Magi; Islamic Sufi Masters are called murshid; Gnostics called them phosters, light bearers or oracles; Muslims call them mahatmas; Buddhists call them buddhas or illumined ones; and Christians referred to Jesus as a Master, a messiah or "the anointed one." In India a guru is known as a "dispeller of darkness" (darkness meaning humans in spiritual ignorance). A sadh guru is a holy man who has risen above the causal plane. Fakirs, sadhus and yogeshwaras are also holy men who have risen to various inner planes. Param sant gurus are known as great Masters who have become one with the Supreme Creator and have been given the task of incarnating to gather, initiate and guide Souls through the inner planes back to Source.

Another distinction is made between the types of Masters who in-carnate on Earth. The first type gets an order from the Supreme Creator to go into the world as a Master and then takes birth, having his full powers with him from birth. The second type of Master receives his orders to act as a Master after he has been born. Both have equal and full spiritual powers. One comes in with these powers and the other has this power bestowed upon him during his lifetime by an already incar-nate Master. This God-power residing in the body of the Master, who is sometimes called a Godman, emanates the sound-current, the Essence of life, from their bodies. They are highly venerated and honored as the literal bearers of the divine light and sound current from which all the creation is made, from the highest to the lowest. Masters can see the in-ner planes as clearly as we see outwardly. They can see clearly the astral, casual and supercausal or light bodies of all beings whether in physical incarnation or existing in any higher or lower dimension.

According to the Masters, every embodied human Soul born into the material world (the third dimension) is under the control of the mind and the senses, causing the Soul's Essence to be dispersed downward throughout the bodily senses and outward as "attention" to the objects and events of the material world; all of which confuse and entrap the Soul in maya/illusion. The remedy for this malady, per the Masters, is to draw the Soul's Essence, the spirit current, inward and upward to the third-eye center (the eye of spirit) which is the gateway to the inner planes. All the chakra centers—invisible spiraling energy vortices—are connect-ed through the nerve ganglia (the nadis) to the three upward-flowing spiritual currents. Two currents (called the ida and pingala) twirl or curl around the main column of spiritual energy called the sushumna. These two currents curl in what visually looks like the DNA spiral around the main spirit current that flows through the cerebrospinal fluid in the spi-nal column. This threefold column of energy is how the spirit current passes up and out of the body into the inner/higher spiritual dimensions or planes.

There are five gross and five subtle senses that keep humans focused on, attached to and enmeshed within the illusory hologram: sight, sound, taste/smell, touch and speech. Through these sensory organs, the body/mind/spirit is constantly engaged in receiving impressions as feelings and thoughts and in expressing these impressions through speech, all of which drain the Soul-energy Essence of the mind/body/spirit into the astral or quantum energy field surrounding Earth. Through this setup the Soul, enmeshed in the body/mind, becomes attached to the illusory world outside itself, misperceiving it as an objective world external to itself. This is the epitome of the "externalized being," the personalized self, the false ego-self created through sensory and mental impressions garnered through "embodied life" in the three-dimensional hologram called "objective reality."

The process of meditation taught by the Masters is designed specifically to reverse the entrapment of the Soul in this delusional system. The constructed personalized ego-self, reinforced through impressions (samskaras) received and retained over many incarnations, needs to be removed or erased through the inversion of the attention. It is necessary to deconstruct or disassemble the ego-self with its false sense of "I-ness" and "my-ness" (called *ahankar* by the Hindus, meaning "I do"), along with all its attachments to things and to its thought forms retained as memories, ideas, concepts and beliefs. Three main methods of restraining the outpouring of the Essence are taught by the Masters as a means of retraining the body/mind/spirit's outgoing faculties to work inwardly, thereby strengthening the Soul Essence and building an "internalized awareness" of the true Self; in other words, "being in the world but not of it."

The first restraint is the restraining of outward speech, a practice that consists of constant repetition of a mantra with the "tongue of thought" (mentally). The second restraint is the restraint of outward sight which consists of inward-turning attention toward the development of inner spiritual sight that reveals the inner planes of existence, planes that can eventually be seen once the attention is held at the third-eye center (behind and between the eyebrows). The third restraint is the restraint of outer hearing by turning the attention inward and listening to the inner spiritual sound currents of which there are five kinds, again corresponding to the five inner spiritual planes.

These three spiritual practices and the guidance and protection of the Masters are the means by which the Soul transcends the bodily senses and the mind—the "Earth-bound" intellectual and rational reasoning capacities that produce thought forms. These projected thought forms create and maintain the physical, astral and causal worlds of illusion. According to the teachings of the Masters, Truth is found in the silence of the heart, not through any thought or verbal expression of the mind, as mind is mired in confusion. The "veil of the mind" is the barrier that was placed between the Soul and the Supreme Creator by the negative power at the negative pole of creation.

The Sant Mat teachings follow disciplines similar to many of the Hindu and Buddhist teachings, such as the practice of non-violence, tolerance and forgiveness; abstinence from indulgence in sense pleasures; the practice of compassion, discrimination, detachment and humility; following a vegetarian diet; avoidance of any form of intoxicants; and daily practice of meditation.

The creation story that comes to us through the Sant Mat Masters is elaborated in the *Anurag Sagar* (the Ocean of Love) of Kabir, one of the least-known esoteric poems but the most valued in all the literature of the Masters. It was written by Kabir in a little-known pre-Hindi dialect called Braj, a difficult dialect to read as the language is quite antiquated compared to modern-day Hindi. It was translated and edited from Braj into English by Raj Kumar Bagga, Partap Singh and Kent Bicknell under the direction of Sant Ajaib Singh and published in book form by Sant Bani Ashram. The poem is a lengthy dialogue between Kabir and his disciple and eventual successor named Dharam Das. Kabir is answering Dharam Das's questions and explaining in great detail how all the universes were created and how all the Souls have been deceived and trapped in time/illusion. What follows is a much-condensed and summarized version of the Master Kabir's story of the creation which in its entirety fills a whole book.

Originally the Supreme Creator existed in latent form as the infinite absolute unmanifested Essence without form. Out of his will/desire he created the Souls (his Essence) and from the first emanation of Shabd, the sound current, he created all the heavens, all the worlds of eighty thousand universes and the thrones or pillars of the four worlds: the physical, astral, causal and supercausal planes. (The emanation means the origination of the world by a series of hierarchically descending radiations from the Godhead through intermediate stages of creation into matter.) This happened within vast developmental cosmic time cycles through which the absolute Essence slowly manifested into various levels of existence. With the second emanation of the sound current he created Kurma, that aspect of God that holds all lower creation in latency. With the third emanation of the sound current, Gyan, the quality of intelligence/knowledge was born. These Knowers of Truth from the fifth, pure spiritual plane called Sat Lok incarnate into the world in each yuga as living Masters. When the fourth emanation of the sound current sounded, Vivek manifested, which was the quality of discernment. Each divine aspect of the Supreme Creator manifested separately in order for creation to take place as God separated himself into many qualities and parts. Since the ultimate reality is Oneness, the Essence, the many manifesting in the eighty thousand universes, as separate entities, are illusory.

The Absolute Godhead projects itself into varying forms and qualities, which are the variegated expressions of its power. With the fifth utterance or emanation of the sound current, a brilliant light came into existence known as Kal, who later came to be known as the "Negative Power." (This power is known in biblical terms as Lucifer the fallen light bearer, and by the Gnostics as Yahweh or Yaldabaoth, the demiurge who deceives Souls by preventing them from leaving the confines of his three realms.) With the sixth emanation, effortlessness was born; with the seventh, contentment; with the eighth, attention was set into the world. With the ninth, infinite happiness manifested; the tenth manifestation created the quality of forgiveness; the eleventh, selflessness; the twelfth, devotion; the thirteenth, worrylessness; the fourteenth, love; the fifteenth, mercy; and the sixteenth, patience. In this way sixteen "sons" were born and they all meditated on God, existing together in unity, love, peace and happiness. Please interpret the sixteen "sons" as qualities or emanations of light and sound frequencies to reduce any confusion between an embodied human and the higher energies of divine light and sound emanating as an ideal or quality.

As all the sons/emanations did the devotion to God, Kal did also but he exceeded all others by doing the devotion for seventy yugas, more than fifteen times as long as the period of the creation which took four yugas to complete. This devotion pleased God very much. Then Kal asked God for a gift. He asked for a place to live that he could call his own. God loved his son very much as an emanation of himself and so agreed to his request. He gave Kal ownership of the three lower worlds and the void plane and told him he was free to create his own universes. Kal didn't know how to create a universe and so asked God to help him. God told him to go and ask for the assistance of his brother Kurma, who held all ideas or templates for lower creation in latency. Kal, becoming swollen with pride, anger and impatience, went to Kurma but instead of asking respectfully for his assistance, attacked him and took what he needed from the latent forms of creation held by Kurma to make his own creations from within the void plane.

Kal then created from out of this void plane the lower causal, astral and matter-based planes in "latent form" (conceptualized but not manifest) along with the five elements (earth, air, fire, water and ether) and the Moon, Sun, stars and planets floating in the cosmic sea. Kal's creations are confined to shaping or developing various forms that come from the "root seed" or "Essence of life" which comes only from the Supreme Creator. Kal in his greed and desire then asked God for this root seed/ Soul Essence so he could "create" the subtle and matter-based life forms for all his three worlds.

Kal's method of "creation" requires some understanding of the nature of the dimensions he was working within. Above the causal plane there is no duality, no division of the sexes, but for lower creation to come into being there has to be a splitting of the One aspect into two, the masculine and the feminine aspects of the One, the positive and the negative poles, the yin and yang energies. To develop the lower worlds, Kal emanated a crystallization of his feminine aspect and projected it outside of himself into a separate energetic feminine emanation called Kali or Adhya. Even though Kal had asked for the root seed, God denied Kal the root seed Essence and instead gave it to this female emanation Kali/Adhya, Kal's consort, whose original role is mother/nourisher and creator of all subtle energy that forms the lower worlds, including all matter-based life forms. When Kal saw this female emanation containing the root seed within her, he became angry, jealous and impatient and devoured her cosmic form in an attempt to reincorporate what had been his own projected feminine aspect back into himself. Kali, going into the stomach of Kal, called out to the Supreme Creator in protest of Kal's violence toward her, a form of cosmic rape. God saw Kal's actions and realized his son's bad character, and even though he loved him, cursed him saying, "You will not have the root seed, it will be carried by Kali/Adhya, and if you devour one lakh (one hundred thousand) Souls daily, one and one quarter lakh Souls will be created by me." By these actions Kal became the Negative Power who fell from grace through demanding sovereignty over the three lower worlds and desiring to possess the root seed/the Essence of life of the eternal Souls.

Kal then joined with his consort Kali/Adhya in the process of co-creating all the lower worlds, and out of their merging or union "desire" was born. From Kal and Kali's creation came the dynasty of the creator gods Brahma, Vishnu and Shiva, the sons of Kal and Kali. Kal was expelled from the pure spiritual realms of eternity by the Supreme Creator causing him to sink into the lower realms of creation/illusion where he became Lord and ruler over these lower realms. The Negative Power rules by encapsulating the lower regions in the illusion of space/time. As "finity and limitation" he stands opposite to infinity and Oneness. As the creator of sins and virtues, good and bad, duality/polarity, he and his sons became the Lords of Law, the Lords of Judgment, the Lords of Karma who locked the Souls into his realms and onto the wheel of karma, transmigration and the endless cycles of death and rebirth. Karma is the law of action and reaction in thought, word or deed. Desire's actions are what keeps the Soul in perpetual bondage on the Wheel of Karma extending upward from the physical through the astral to the top of the causal plane.

Kal's work was necessary in the overall creation but he demanded to be worshipped as the Supreme Creator which he is not, and therefore the Masters see him as a foe, an adversary, because he stands to block the ascension of the Souls out of the lower planes. Kabir told his initiate Dharam Das that the Head of Kal is the "individualized mind in each embodied Soul" and that the mind is the "instrument of Kal" (the thousand-headed serpent) just as the Soul Essence is the instrument of God, the immortal love/light eternally shining as Truth. The higher law of God prevails in the higher realms, which is the law of love, mercy and grace taught by all the Masters. It is the way of return to the higher realms and the means of exiting the revolving wheel of karma, the way back to unity consciousness and eventual reunion with the Supreme Creator.

In contrast, through Kal's churning of the cosmic sea, the three lower realms from the causal to the astral to the physical plane were conceived in violence as were his three sons, Brahma, Vishnu and Shiva. After all of Kal's creations came into existence, he withdrew into the void plane saying to Kali, "Tell no one of my existence, not even my sons. If no one knows of my existence then all of creation will be ascribed to me 'as the One True God, the Supreme Creator' and in this way I will prevent the worship of the True Supreme Creator in my worlds." By this action, Kal preempts all creation for himself, deceiving the Souls in his created worlds into believing he is the Supreme Creator. Kal even deceived his own sons with the help of Kali and made them believe he is the Supreme Creator: he sent them into the three lower worlds, setting them up as Gods to be worshipped by the deceived Souls. His sons perpetuate more traps as they give out false information by making the Souls worship temples, gods, stone idols; perform fasts and rituals, make sacrifices, go on pilgrimages and follow religious laws of daily conduct, all designed to mislead and entrap. He also created the Hindu vedas, smritis, shastras and puranas and every other sacred religious text in the world designed to mislead the Souls. Kabir told his initiate Dharam Das, "Know that the mind IS Kal and when one defeats the mind, one will get the knowledge of the One True God, the Supreme Creator, and he will manifest himself in such a person."

The Sant Mat Masters all teach the same message, which is that the written scriptures and sacred texts of all the world's religions are representations and encapsulations of the idea of religion as an expression of moral law. As such, all of these laws originated with Kal and are therefore to be ignored and transcended as they bind, mislead and keep the Souls in the cycles of death and rebirth. Kabir says, "This is the trick of Kal, the Negative Power, perpetuated in this fallen illusory world." Kabir continues his creation story, telling Dharam Das that the Masters incarnate and enter into Kal's world as direct emissaries of the Supreme Creator for the sole purpose of liberating the Souls. Kal knows whenever an incarnation, a Master, enters his realm, and he tries to block the Masters from reaching the Souls but he is powerless to stop the incarnations. The incarnations come in every age to liberate the Souls by making them understand the Truth. These "Knowers of the Truth" come from the fifth spiritual plane called Sat Lok.

Kabir told Dharam Das that this lineage will become the liberators of the world and eighty-eight crore (ten million) prisons will be opened at the end of the Kali Yuga. The Masters will keep their foot on Kal's head and humble his arrogance by exposing the illusions created by him, cutting them away and releasing the Souls by giving them Sat (Truth) and Naam (the sound current)—the means of liberation. Kal will not be able to touch or come near these Souls and they will be freed from his worlds. This is the promise of the Masters who have been incarnating into the multiverse, including the astral and physical universes inhabited by Souls throughout the starry depths of the cosmos since the beginning of the creation of the lower dimensions by Kal.

Deconstructing the Sant Mat Masters Paradigm

Belief that the Supreme Creator created eighty thousand universes including the pillars of the four worlds—the physical, astral, causal and supercausal planes—through the emanation of his primal energies of light and sound.

Belief that the Masters incarnate from the fifth or pure spiritual plane, called the plane of Truth or Sat Lok, into the lower dimensions to liberate and awaken the Souls and teach them how to transcend the lower dimensions and escape from the prison of the body/mind.

Belief that sixteen qualities or ideals were emanated from the Supreme Creator and manifested as cosmic creator gods or angelic light beings embodying each of the qualities.

Belief that one of these creator gods or cosmic light beings named Kal rebelled against the Supreme Creator and through his desire and willful actions the negative pole of creation came into being, standing in opposition to the positive pole of creation and manifesting as the dualistic lower worlds of attraction/repulsion.

Belief that the creator god Kal was denied access to the Essence of life or "root seed atom" which was given to his consort or feminine counterpart Kali-Adhya-Maya, who became the creator, the mother-goddess, of all matter-based life forms and subtle-energy life forms.

Belief that the Supreme Creator recognized the bad character of Kal who fell from grace due to his selfish demands for a Kingdom of his own separate from the Supreme Creator and for the desire to have power over his creations, resulting in his becoming a demiurge.

Belief that Kal was expelled from the pure spiritual realms of eternity/ infinity and was relegated to creating and ruling over only the three lowest dimensions of the creation.

Belief that Kal and his sons rule by encapsulating the lower dimensions in a space/time/illusion representing finity and therefore limitation and boundedness, which veils or blocks the Soul's awareness of its origins via the creation of the mind/body container and the dimensional realms of illusion.

Belief that Kal is a false god, a usurper and a foe of the seed Essence (the Souls), whose aim is to imprison Souls within his kingdom (the lower dimensions) and to block their ascension and keep them revolving on the wheel of reincarnation.

Belief that Kal, creator of duality/separation, placed into each created humanoid form (the body/mind/spirit complex) an aspect of his self as "the individuated mind"—the egoistic personality self which mimics the demiurge.

Belief that Kal sent his three sons, the creator/sustainer/destroyer gods, to create the lower dimensions—physical, astral and causal—which they rule over as the Lords of Karma: Brahma, Vishnu and Shiva, whom the Souls worship, falsely believing them to be the highest gods in the creation.

Belief that Kal set up innumerable mental traps to deceive the Souls through the creation of the world's religious ideologies, laws and religious practices, which falsely promise salvation for the Souls after death.

Belief that Truth can be perceived only by the Soul, and that the means of discovering this Truth is achieved by transcending the mind, awakening the Soul at the third-eye center "while living" because after the death of the body, the Soul is again cast into the cycles of rebirth.

Belief that the Science of the Soul/the Sant Mat teachings provide a specific set of practices that can free the Soul from its bonds and these can only be gotten from a Master (a God-Realized) Soul who, having come from the pure spiritual planes of non-duality, knows the way and can guide and protect the Soul on its inner journey as it ascends back to Source.

Belief that Truth cannot be discerned through any thought form or verbal expression of the mind because the veil placed between the Soul and God, "the mind," will deflect, doubt, block and confuse through the ego-self all attempts by the Soul to escape its bondage.

Belief in the necessity of the practice of non-violence, tolerance and forgiveness; abstinence from indulgence in sense pleasures; compassion, discrimination, detachment and humility; following a vegetarian diet; avoidance of any form of intoxicants; and daily practice of the Sant Mat meditation methods—all of which practices enable the Soul to become purified, enabling it to begin its inner journey in its light body through the inner worlds back to Source.

Reference Keys: Kabir (1982). Philosophy (1967). Sar (1955). Singh-MS (1963). Singh-SK (1967, 1976).

Chapter Fifteen

The Wingmakers Worldview

THIS WORLDVIEW COMES from the Wingmakers, who call themselves "The Central Race." The originator of the Wingmakers materials, James Mahu, is the creator, author, artist, translator and presenter of this massive body of work. His works include several novels, poetry, music, artwork, a large body of philosophical/spiritual discourses and a blog site—all of which were created to convey the mythology, cosmology, teachings and philosophy of the Wingmakers to humanity.

Having compiled the material for this chapter in 2012, I rechecked the websites for the Wingmakers materials for accuracy in 2017. After I re-accessed the sites five years later, it's become clear that the materials and sites have been in a perpetual state of evolvement since their inception and they continue to change shape and form as new materials are created, sites are updated, and new Lyricus discourses and new book releases are added. There are five websites total now, each of which can be accessed through the main Wingmakers website.

The original website, http://www.Wingmakers.com, was activated in the fall of 1998. The webmaster responsible for developing and managing the site is Mark Hempel. In 2001 the site was redesigned. Paintings, artwork, music, poetry and Mahu's first novel were added, all of which became available to the public. The second site, http://www.Lyricus. org, appeared in late 2003 and a third site, http://www.EventTemples. com, appeared in July 2007. Two additional sites have since come online: http://www.SpiritState.com and http://www.SovereignIntegral.

blogspot.com, which are teaching sites containing esoteric and spiritual discourses on the liminal cosmology and philosophy of the Wingmakers.

The Wingmakers state they are interdimensional time travelers who were instrumental in creating and seeding the seven super-universes, including our own universe, each of which revolves around a central sun. Just as the Sumerian texts are some of the oldest recovered cuneiform writings in the world to date, this material is some of the newest. It provides an intergalactic understanding of how vast universes, beyond Earth's space/time three-dimensional holographic universe, were and continue to be created by groups of these highly evolved, technologically and spiritually advanced beings. Members of this Central Race called by the Wingmakers the "Teachers of Lyricus" have sometimes been referred to as the Elohim or the Shining Ones in other books and texts.

According to Mahu, a small number of this race of beings have quietly incarnated on our planet at this time to assist humanity in awakening to the realization of our infinite and eternal Sovereign Integral Selves, which exist eternally as the life-force/essence, fragments of the Supreme Creator. The Wingmakers, says Mahu, have time-traveled into our space/time dimension stating they are our future selves reaching backward in time to us from seven hundred fifty years in our future. They desire to help Earth's human race (their collective past selves) transcend the three-dimensional virtual-reality world within which humanity has been trapped for hundreds of thousands of years. Their intention is to help humanity move into a liberation pathway over the next eighty to one hundred years of Earth time. They state they are culture bearers, bringing the seeds of new art forms, science and cosmology to humanity.

In Mahu's first book, a novel called *The Ancient Arrow Project*, this Central Race is described as having implanted or left behind for humanity a total of seven time capsules, one on each of Earth's seven continents. These time capsules will eventually be found and deciphered, revealing a predetermined and orchestrated plan for the evolvement of humanity as conceived and implemented by the Wingmakers. The first of these time capsules, its discovery and decoding, is what Mahu's first novel is all about. The story tells of the finding of the first time capsule, an encoded hieroglyphic disc, by a group of hikers who also discover multiple cave artworks—after which the caves are cordoned off from public access and NASA scientists take over the site, located in a series of twenty-three carved rock chambers near Chaco Canyon in New Mexico. You can get the full ebook on the Wingmakers website.

In his archived interviews, Mahu explains why he publishes his books as fiction rather than nonfiction. A quite extensive in-depth interview, called on the Wingmakers site "The Fifth Interview," was given to a journalist, Sarah De Rosnay (probably a pseudonym), in 1998. In this interview a Dr. Jamisson Neruda tells the Wingmakers' version of the ancient history of humanity's creation and their explanation of our universe as a constructed hologram that functions to enslave humanity. It turns out this interview was actually given by James Mahu, operating under the pseudonym of Dr. Jamisson Neruda. This Fifth Interview covers some very deep and controversial information about the holographic construct of our universe which, per Mahu, is in reality a computer-programmed false matrix. Even though this interview was given in 1998, it wasn't released to the public through the Wingmakers website until March 2014. Mahu did give a couple of public interviews as himself, one with Project Camelot in November 2008 and another in November 2009 to the Conscious Media Network, both of which are available on the main Wingmakers website under "Interviews."

The following version of the Wingmakers creation story was excerpted and markedly condensed from the original eighty pages of the Fifth Interview. It is highly recommend that readers of this book take the time to read the full interview. It is extraordinary in its depth and breadth. When I first read it I was shocked, reeling in disbelief, deeply dismayed and in a head-spinning state for days.

What follows is the intergalactic history of planet Earth and of humanity according to the Wingmakers. They tell us that Earth is a unique planet. It was originally made entirely of water with the core having gravitational force that allowed the planet to traverse from an interdimensional planet of sound frequencies to a planet of physical matter over eons of time. When Earth was still in its fluid-like etheric water state, a race called Atlanteans lived within the planet as energetic interdimensional beings of higher dimensional frequencies. The Sumerian Anunnaki, from another star system, also interdimensional beings, came to planet Earth and met with the Atlanteans to negotiate an agreement to be allowed to mine semi-transparent gold from near the semi-fluid core of the planet. They needed this substance for their planet's and their own survival. Eventually Earth and everything on it began solidifying and gold mining became impossible to continue as the Anunnaki's bodies were etheric at that time. They needed solidified bodies that could operate in Earth's density to continue their mining operation, which occurred over a period of tens of thousands of years of Earth time.

The Anunnaki tried numerous genetic experiments in an attempt to create a physical vessel or bodily form that could function in Earth's solidifying atmosphere to continue doing their mining work for them. They succeeded in designing, through genetic manipulation, a biological form that was ape-like, partly physical and partly etheric, which they synchronized with the evolving densification of Earth. The Anunnaki were aided in their genetic experimentation by the Sirians, a race from another star system, and a race called the Serpents from yet another star system. These three races, all master geneticists, highly intelligent and technologically skilled, were interested in colonizing planetary bodies and in learning how to inhabit physical planets and create physical life forms.

According to the Wingmakers, this group of three extraterrestrial races conspired together to use the evolving Atlantean race without their knowledge for their experiments. They tricked the Atlanteans into inhabiting these genetically engineered, semi-physical, pre-human, ape-like biological forms. The geneticists needed an energy source for powering these biological forms they had created, as they were not operable without some "power" source (the life essence). Thus, the Atlanteans, having the life-force/Soul essence within them, were used as the power generators for the newly designed ape-like etheric/biological body forms. Once the Atlanteans were lured into inhabiting these forms, they were locked inside by computerized interfaces installed within the body suits that erased the Atlanteans' memories of their true being as eternal, infinite Soul essences. The locked-in Soul essences of the Atlanteans were then programmed through a mind/brain/body computer interface to focus their consciousness one hundred percent on physical survival and functional performance within the solidifying Earth hologram—as miner slaves for the Anunnaki, Sirian and Serpent races.

They were turned into ape-like worker drones by these three inter-dimensional, conquering, dominating races whose mathematically structured algorithms in the mind/brain/body implants created a three-dimensional holographic world, within which the automated genetically engineered bodily forms operated. These three races were then able to clone the biological ape-humanoid forms. Then after some additional genetic manipulations and refinement, reproduction cycles were added to the created ape-humanoid forms so they could reproduce themselves without the need of cloning. This addition was implemented so that when the bodily forms expired or were killed in mining or other kinds of accidents, the Atlantean beings' power source (their life essence) could be transferred to an interdimensional "holding plane" (the astral plane) until the Soul essence/life-force could be recycled (reincarnated) by being placed into a newly formed body/brain/mind container. The Soul essences contained in these bodily containers were moved interdimensionally from the holding planes by their creators/manipulators back into new biological forms on Earth. Thus the mind/brain/body-encased Souls could continue as and where needed to perform the physical tasks needed to maintain the holographic world ruled by these creator races, who set themselves up as humanity's creator gods.

The Atlanteans were duped as they never conceived of the possibility that they, as infinite beings, could be enslaved by being locked into ape-like humanoid forms. They were totally trusting and naïve as they had no concept or understanding of deceit and no understanding of the cunning attack made on them by the Anunnaki, Sirian and Serpent races. Part of what allowed these races to develop and capture this "work force" was the system interface of the designed physical body and the computerized mind, creating an electromagnetic matrix that produced a three-dimensional holographic false reality. So seemingly real was this false matrix, this illusory hologram, that it suppressed the consciousness and blocked any awareness of humanity's true infinite and eternal life-force/Soul essence. Very effectively, humanity was locked into believing themselves to be solely the mind/brain/body, the humanoid bodily vessel, with no awareness whatsoever of their infinite, divine sovereign Soul essences.

The Wingmakers state they have traveled back in time to reach out to humanity, to us as descendants of the Atlantean race, to teach us the truth they discovered in their past: that all humanity has been trapped within this vast multilevel hologram of deception. Our universe, the Wingmakers explain, was created with soundwave frequencies. Our universe is basically sound vibrations holographically organized to look and feel real to the collectively embodied humanoid population.

Our three-dimensional space/time world, they assert, is a prison of illusion where humanity has been programmed to believe we are separate from the Supreme Creator and have consequently lost contact with our life-force/Soul essence, and therefore need to strive to regain awareness of it. The Wingmakers say that one component of the many intentionally designed false-mental-construct/false-paradigm "implants" placed in the mind of humanity at the time of its creation is the religious belief that if humans strive, try hard, are good, have faith in god (the gods) and learn our spiritual lessons, we will be rewarded, emancipated and ascended to the higher planes of bliss and joy at death. This belief system was designed to keep humans eternally striving, searching and seeking outside of ourselves to deter humanity from ever finding out the truth of our imprisonment. This "conceptual mind implant" has been reinforced through the establishment of every religion in the world that functions to keep humanity enslaved in various sets of false beliefs, in constant fear, hope, self-sacrifice and striving mode for eternity in a continual state of recycling or reincarnation. This ensures a steady supply of energy and humans to "serve" these advanced races and "inhabit" their interdimensionally created and controlled holographic virtual-reality worlds.

The remedy, according to the Wingmakers and Dr. Neruda's explanation in his lengthy Fifth Interview, is to step out of this constructed universe, this virtual-reality hologram, by living in each moment of NOW as the self-expression of the I AM/WE ARE, the Sovereign Integral Self that is our true eternal Soul essence and is present within us NOW and always has been. Within a programmed finite holographic false-reality construct, we cannot possibly conceive of ourselves as the infinite beings that we truly are. The "Sovereign Integral," states Dr. Neruda, IS the life-force/Soul essence that powers human consciousness within our biological body-suits and mind-brain interfaces within the electromagnetically maintained hologram. When we are stripped of all illusion, all deception, all limitation, all veils, all false-paradigm mind implants, including the repository of lifetimes of memories retained in the Soul, then we can live as Sovereign Integral Selves, knowing we are imbued with Supreme Creator's infinite intelligence, and express ourselves knowingly by living through the heart center and expressing the virtues of love, appreciation, gratitude, compassion, humility, forgiveness, understanding and courage in the NOW.

Dr. Neruda states that each human being is responsible for accomplishing this transformation within themselves because no spiritual being, ascended Master, angel or heavenly hierarchical creator god is going to save us from ourselves. The Wingmakers want us to know that "we are the saviors we have been waiting for." They tell us the unconscious mind is the doorway or connector between all beings embodied or otherwise. When humanity is able to collectively synchronize all consciousnesses to this truth, to this one realization, humanity will begin to be freed from this hologram of deception by becoming consciously able to transcend it.

Deconstructing the Wingmakers Worldview

The belief that the Wingmakers are a "central race" of interdimensional time travelers who have traveled back in time to our current space/time dimension.

The belief that they are our "future selves" who have traveled backward in time to meet and instruct us from seven hundred fifty years in our future.

The belief that twelve to fifteen of them have quietly incarnated on Earth to assist the humanoid species in awakening to our infinite eternal selves and our eternal unity with the Supreme Creator.

The belief that the human race are their "collective past selves" trapped in a hologram whom they've come back to assist in transcending/ escaping the three-dimensional holographic trap.

The belief that they have come to seed new ideas and open the eyes of humanity to Earth's ancient cosmology and its hidden intergalactic history, which they say has been hidden intentionally by the three races who colonized and captured Earth into their holographic net and altered the human DNA template.

The belief that Earth was originally etheric and evolved slowly into a physical matter-based planet over eons of time.

The belief that the Atlantean race lived within the Earth when it was an etheric planet as interdimensional light beings of higher frequencies.

The belief that the Sumerian-Anunnaki, the Sirians and a Serpent race all colluded to genetically manipulate the DNA of the Atlanteans to create a biologically altered ape-humanoid life form (partly etheric and partly physical) to do the physical labor of mining the Earth for these races and to serve as their servants.

The belief that the Atlanteans (having the Soul essence/life-force within them) were used as "power generators" for these DNA-designed and engineered biological bodies.

The belief that this race was locked inside of these biological bodies through a mind/body computerized interface installed in the brains of this body-suit that erased awareness of their true essence as eternal Souls and caused them to be focused one hundred percent on external awareness, survival and performance of tasks on the solidifying Earth as worker drones.

The belief that that the Soul essences of the Atlanteans were moved from their bodily forms at death and placed in a holding place (the astral plane) until the Soul essences could be reincarnated or placed into a newly formed body-suit on Earth to continue as worker slaves for their creators.

The belief that a holographic electromagnetic matrix was constructed by these races to surround the planet in order to simulate a three-dimensional holographic reality that appears so real, from within the computerized mind/brain/body interface, that it blocks and veils any awareness or knowledge of the true eternal life-force/Soul essence within us, which is what powers our humanoid mind/brain/body-suits.

The belief that this hologram or virtual reality was created by using sound frequencies and electromagnetic energies organized to look and feel real to the embodied beings trapped inside.

The belief that intentionally designed false paradigms or mental constructs were placed into the mind/brain interfaces of humanity as religious beliefs to keep humanity imprisoned in the belief that they must strive, work hard, struggle and willingly sacrifice, be good and become worthy of being saved by a superhuman power at some point in the future or after death.

The belief that these mental memes or paradigms keep humanity enslaved, ensuring a steady supply of energy and recycled beings to inhabit this interdimensionally controlled hologram, which serves the three ruling races.

The belief that the remedy for humanity is to wake up and realize it is living in a constructed programmed holographic virtual-reality world.

The belief that humanity must break free of this illusion, including the false-mind implants such as past-life memories retained by the Soul, so that humans can live free as sovereign Souls aware of our unity consciousness with the Supreme Creator by living from the heart in the NOW.

The belief that "we are the saviors we have been waiting for" and that humanity must learn to synchronize its collective conscious awareness. For in this single realization and in subsequent actions humanity has the means to free itself from the hologram of deception and its perpetual slavery.

Reference Keys: Childress (2007). Mahu (1998, 2008, 2009). Neruda (1998). Wingmakers (web-a–e).

Chapter Sixteen

The Cassiopaean Worldview

THIS CREATION STORY closely resembles elements of the intergalactic history presented in the Ra group/Elohim worldview and echoes some of the concepts in the Wingmakers and Sumerian/Babylonian versions of the creation story. All the materials for this chapter have been extracted, quoted and condensed exclusively from Laura Knight-Jadczyk's many books and from the Cassiopaean Transcripts, which consist of a series of questions asked by Knight-Jadczyk and her inquiry group members to a group of entities existing in the sixth dimension called Corsas, from the planet Carcosa located in the Cassiopaea constellation near Orion. Her explorations began in 1994 as an experiment in superluminal communication (the ability to transmit and receive information faster than the speed of light between two or more entities no matter their distance from one another).

In some of their earliest transmissions, the Cassiopaeans (the Cs) communicated the following to Knight-Jadczyk (*The Secret History of the World*):

> We are you in the future; we transmit through the opening that is present in the locator that you represent as Cassiopaea, due to the strong radio pulses aligned from Cassiopaea which are due to a pulsar from a neutron star 300 light years behind it, as seen from your locator. This facilitates a clear channel transmission from sixth density to third density ... [in] zero time. (p. 623)

The inquiry group met at irregularly scheduled meetings from 1994 through 2000. Knight-Jadczyk's experiment began by using a traditional Ouija board and planchette, which she and the group would place their hands on after having formulated a question to ask. It took about two years for them to make clear and direct ongoing contact with the Cs. In the early transmissions, the group had trouble recording the Cs' spelled-out responses due to the rapidity of their transmissions, causing some early materials to be lost. What follows is an excerpt of a series of questions asked by Knight-Jadczyk and the Cs' responses (*High Strangeness*, pp. 122–23), from a transcript dated July 6, 1994, in the Cassiopaean Logs.

LK-J: Are you an alien from another planet?

The Cs: Alien from your perspective, yes.

LK-J: What is your group called?

The Cs: Corsas.

LK-J: Where are you from?

The Cs: Cassiopaea.

LK-J: Where is that?

The Cs: Near Orion.

LK-J: Where do you live specifically?

The Cs: Live in omnipresence.

LK-J: What does that mean?

The Cs: All realms.

LK-J: Do you serve self or other?

The Cs: Serve both, self through others.

LK-J: What planet are you from?

The Cs: Carcosa.

LK-J: Where is that? Is this in the constellation we know as Cassiopaea?

The Cs: Yes.

LK-J: What are you here for?

The Cs: Prophecy.

LK-J: Specifically what?

The Cs: Sinister plot ... experiment with human reproduction. Don't ignore!

LK-J: Plot by whom?

The Cs: Consortium.

LK-J: Who are members of the Consortium?

The Cs: Aliens, [your] government.

After doing some research on alien races, Knight-Jadczyk discovered, and the Cs later verified (in *High Strangeness,* appendix p. 372), that they are "an insectoid race of higher-dimensional beings existing in the sixth dimension within the Cassiopaean star system whose job is genetic research." The Cs also said (in *Debugging the Universe*, pp. 91–92) that they are "part of the original group of sub-creator gods from the sixth dimension."

Knight-Jadczyk took the completed Cassiopaean transcripts and eventually turned them into a series of eight books called "The Wave Series," each book having a different title. Her life story is woven into these books as well. In addition, she has meticulously researched and written several other books documenting events that occurred in Earth's ancient hidden past but which have been intentionally obscured and or misrepresented by historians.

She has in essence turned the world's official history upside down by presenting new evidence to the public of a disinformation agenda underlying Earth's intentionally hidden ancient past. Her book *The Secret History of the World and How to Get Out Alive* and its sequel, *Comets and the Horns of Moses*, are both extraordinary in their scope and depth.

The Cassiopaeans explained to Knight-Jadczyk (in *Debugging the Universe*, p. 276) that this three-dimensional holographic universe "is based on a nonlinear complex self-referencing and self-organizing cosmos ... constructed and maintained by consciousness." Per the Cassiopaeans' version of the creation story, our world—planet Earth and its dualistic, polarized phenomenal reality structure—"was projected from the higher consciousness of seventh density, which projected itself into consciousness units ... each vibrating at different frequencies into the [holographic] structure of [our three-dimensional] space/time."

The Cassiopaeans say in *Debugging the Universe:*

> What we perceive as reality is nothing more than the myriad oscillations of the primeval prismatically divided waveform of seventh density [causal plane].... The brain is an instrument devised to focus reality in mathematical constructs—interpreting waveforms as material objects. (p. 306)

And in *High Strangeness:*

> Our reality is projected onto a screen [our minds] looping over and over again in space/time in endless repeating patterns. The fact that history repeats itself lends credibility to the concept of repeating cycles of time. (p. 320)

Our three-dimensional worldview and our belief in reductionism and mechanism go hand in hand with the worlds' religious and scientific doctrines. Phenomena in our material world appear to be orderly and linear with everything supposedly being able to be explained through cause/effect thinking. However, with the advent of mathematical advances, advances in physics and the development of high-speed computing, scientists are able to explore the complex interior of nonlinear physics. In nonlinear physics a small change in one variable can have a disproportionate impact on other variables, which can be catastrophic, chaotic or beneficial as the case may be. It was discovered that in the nonlinear, higher-dimensional or hyperdimensional worlds, long-term prediction is theoretically and practically impossible because concepts such as scientific determinism and religious prophecy can't be accurately predicted within an open-ended, nonlinear world.

Knight-Jadczyk refers to this concept as "the hyperdimensional hypothesis" of creation. The hyperdimensional hypothesis goes a long way in explaining why human history is a long story of war, violence, famine, pestilence and natural disaster—in one word, "suffering." This suffering is the product sought for by our keepers in this higher realm:

> [H]yperdimensional tinkering with the timeline of human events [on Earth] ... opens the door to a scientific understanding of what ... the Cs have called the "ultimate secret;" that we are prisoners of an experiment [and] ... hyperdimensional physics puts the idea of such a conspiracy in a new context. (p. 323)

The Cs explained to Knight-Jadczyk and her group that

> A race of reptilians (the Cs call them "Lizzies"), the Grays and the Nordics have been interfering with [and manipulating events in] our world ... for approximately 74,000 years. And they have been doing so in a completely still state of space/time traveling backward and forward at will.... Humans have been intentionally genetically manipulated/engineered ... to be "body-cen-

tric" [through the lowering of a veil over consciousness].
Despite all efforts by fourth- through sixth-density STO
[service-to-others] beings, this "veil" remains unbroken.
(p. 325)

The Cassiopaean version of the creation story is rather grim, so
brace yourselves as we delve into their version of intergalactic history
and their understanding of how humanity came into existence, how our
ancestral species arrived on this planet and where humanity is headed.
The Cs caution Knight-Jadczyk over and over in their transmissions that
if humanity doesn't wake up, educate itself and rebel against the hidden,
destructive agendas of the hyperdimensional races controlling Earth, the
human race will be eventually eliminated. Their methods of subtle control have included instituting scientific and religious belief systems into
our Earth-bound civilizations that reinforce the reptilian hyperdimensional control system set in place eons ago. The humanoid species on
Earth has been manipulated and controlled, and human Souls have been
trapped in bodies and recycled within this three-dimensional space/time
hologram for thousands of years of Earth time.

Knight-Jadczyk lamented (*Debugging the Universe*) that the most for-
midable difficulty she encounters in sharing the Cassiopaean information in the public domain is

> the fact that many people are incapable of esoteric un-
> derstanding. There are many who say they would like
> very much to inquire into the nature of reality and being
> [ontology], but their curiosity is ephemeral ... and they
> find themselves too attached to their linear modes of
> thinking to enter the temple (of truth) so to speak. (p.
> 278)

Ontology is dealt with at some length in *Debugging the Universe*.
Knight-Jadczyk asks the Cs, "How did humankind come to be?" Here is
a summarized version of their lengthy response (pp. 166–67):

In the earliest stages of the development of the creation, there was
a plethora of experimentation going on with the creation of various life

forms by the creator gods. These various forms were created as "containers" for the consciousness of Prime Creator. As this great creative experiment proceeded, some of the creator gods became fascinated by their own thought-form creations. These creator gods wanted to better comprehend the multidimensional worlds they had manifested and the subtle and matter-congealed life forms inhabiting these lower-dimensional worlds. They desired to inhabit these variegated subtle, astral and physical life forms. Many of them entered into mineral, plant and animal forms for the sheer joy of the experience. When they did this they found that their life force became concentrated or contracted into these inhabited forms. This created a uniquely intense sensory experience such that it was sought after and repeated many times. This caused a reaction within the collective spiritual consciousness-energy fields of these creator gods, resulting in a crystallization or solidification of dimensions one, two and three.

This crystallization became a "veil" between pure Soul consciousness and the individual embodied Soul locked into a container, the physical form. Forgetting their Source, these creator gods created energy imbalances (duality/polarity) by acting in ways that completely disregarded the free will and choice of other Souls. By dividing and separating pure Soul consciousness from embodied life in physical forms, the free will and free choice of all embodied sentient beings in the lower dimensions was violated. This split in consciousness and intention then created a service-to-self (STS) negative pole of creation versus a service-to-others (STO) positive pole of creation. This split or duality of consciousness devolved into the self-perpetuating cycles of reincarnation, entrapping all sentient beings (living within the lower- or first- through third-dimensional realms) into the space/time holograms, causing the Souls of these sentient beings to be continually recycled.

Another group of creator gods, not engaged in this activity of embodied existence, sought to create a means to heighten the energies and perceptions of those creator gods who had become trapped in the reincarnational cycle. A physical form was created and directly manifested to accommodate this purpose, and this physical form was the humanoid species. In a further quote from *Debugging the Universe*, the Cs state:

This humanoid form [the divine blueprint for the Anthropos—the man/god—the upward-looking one] is the one that was taken over and altered by three different races ... the reptilian races through the Grays, the Nephilim and the Orion races. The Orions were the first to put souls into seeded Neanderthal bodies which were put there for an incubation process. (p. 167)

From this same book (pp. 118–19), the dialogue continues:

LK-J: The Orion beings entered into living creatures on this planet to experience three-dimensional reality and by entering in caused mutation?

The Cs: Yes. Very early on during the creation of galaxies and solar systems "numerous interdimensional races desired to experience physical existence. Their original forms were created or molecularized on the planet D'Ankhair in the constellation Scorpio. [Molecularization in chemistry means the conversion of a chemical substance into molecular form—molecules being the smallest component of chemical compounds.] Their original molecularized forms were then altered by three forces: the reptilians, their Gray slave clones and the Nephilim enforcers from Orion, Planet 3C, in the Orion Constellation. The Ankh is an ancient symbol representing the mother planet D'Ankhair which used to exist in the constellation Scorpio and is the source of all human mitochondrial DNA. This planet no longer exists as it was incinerated according to the Cs.

And from pp. 166–69:

LK-J: Where did the souls come from that entered into the bodies on planet Earth? Were they in bodies on other planets before they came here?

The Cs: Not this group.

LK-J: Were they in the universe somewhere?

The Cs: In union with the One. Have you heard of the super-ancient legend of Lucifer, the fallen angel?

LK-J: Who is Lucifer?

The Cs: You, the human race.... You are members of a fragmented soul unit.

LK-J: Prior to the fall in Eden, mankind lived in a fourth-dimensional state. Is that correct?

The Cs: Fourth density in another realm, such as time/space continuum [the astral realms].

LK-J: OK, so this [three-dimensional] realm changed as part of a cycle as various choices were made. The human race ... became aligned with [entrapped by] the reptilians.... [W]hat essential thing occurred?

The Cs: This resulted in a number of effects: the breaking up of the DNA, the burning off of the first ten factors of DNA, the separation of the hemispheres of the brain [by the reptilian, the Gray, the Nephilim and the Orion geneticists].

LK-J: You once said that it was "desire" that caused an imbalance. What was it a desire for?

The Cs: Increased physicality ... increased sensate [sensory experience].

LK-J: Was there any understanding or realization of any kind [in humanity] that increased physicality [being embodied in physical forms] could be like Osiris being lured into his own coffin by Set? That they would slam the lid shut and nail him in?

The Cs: Obviously such understanding was lacking.

LK-J: ...does the lack of this understanding reflect a lack of knowledge?

The Cs: Of course ... these events took place 309,000 years ago.... [T] his is when the first prototype of what you call "modern man" was created. The controllers had the bodies ready, they just needed the right soul matrix to jump in [agree to inhabit the bodies].

LK-J: Once they [the souls] "jumped" into the physical bodies, as you put it, what was their level of conceptualization [understanding of the nature of the trap of third dimension]?

The Cs: Kind of like the understanding one has after a severe head trauma; vis à vis your normal understanding in your current state [of amnesia].

LK-J: What was the first thing put together [they experienced] regarding the cosmos around them?

The Cs: Sex.

LK-J: What precisely are the mechanics of it? What energy is generated? What is the conceptualization of the misuse of this energy?

The Cs: It is simply the introduction of the concept of self-gratification of a physical sort.... [O]ne gives because of the pleasant sensation which results.... [P]ossession is the key.... [I]n STS [service-to-self beings] one possesses or ... desires to possess another in order to experience pleasure by drawing energy from another and having power over another. A STS [being] "eats" whatever it wants to, if it is able. ["Eats" in this context can mean to either consume the essence or life energy of another being or to consume the flesh-and-bone body of another being.]

LK-J: What makes STO (service-to-other beings) unavailable or inedible [energetically]?

The Cs: Frequency resonance not in sync…. [Vibrational rate is too high to resonate with the lower frequencies of STS beings who desire to take, own, possess, control and "eat" the energies and or bodies of other beings.]

LK-J: So, you seem to be suggesting that … [we] become non-attached to anything or anybody … no thought, no want, no do, no anything.

The Cs: If you did exactly that, you would reincarnate in a STO realm [a higher dimension].

LK-J: But [doesn't] being incarnated mean being in a body?

The Cs: No … the fourth-density STO [service-to-other being] is only partially physical [meaning more ethereal/astral]. A STO being does not consume nor possess…. Prime creator manifests in you but … who was secondary? Remember your legends are seen through a veil…. [T]here is much disinformation to wade through.

LK-J: [A]re the Orions these secondary creators?

From pp. 157–59: The Cs didn't directly answer this question here, but they later indicate that the Nordic race/the Orions are indeed the secondary creators of the humanoid species and that they mixed their genes with the Neanderthal genes to create the early humanoid species.

The Cs: Orion! This is your ancestral home and your eventual destination…. Orion is the most heavily populated region in your Milky Way Galaxy…. [It] extends across third- and fourth-density space. There are 3,444 inhabited worlds in this region…. There are primary houses, traveling stations and incubator laboratories in all second, third and fourth densities…. The Orion Federation created the Grays in five varieties as cybergenetic beings…. [T]he reptilians also inhabit planets in the Orion region in fourth density and are owned by the Orion STS beings as slaves.

LK-J: Are the Orion STS [beings] the infamous redheaded Nordic aliens?

The Cs: Yes! And all other humanoid combinations. The Nordic genes were mixed with the gene pool already available on Earth, known as Neanderthal (p. 175).

From pp. 157–59: According to the Cs, the biblical story of Cain and Abel symbolically represented the later reptilian (Sumerian/Anunnaki) takeover of Earth and of Earth's vibrational frequency which included DNA restrictions deliberately engineered by the reptilian geneticists. By adulterating human DNA the "predatory mind" of the egoistic STS reptilians was installed into the mind-body-spirit complex of early man, which twisted the natural order of cellular life on this planet and locked our planet into a holographic time loop, creating the illusion of the passage of time in a linear brain pattern, approximately 309,000 years ago. These changes made by the forces of darkness or STS reptilian races resulted in tremendous limitations in the perception of the early humanoid species. Perceiving only the third dimension was tantamount to "lowering a veil" over the consciousness of humanity, creating the perception of separation/division and introducing judgment, jealousy and the attitude of competition or brother against brother. The Cs commented that "the mark of Cain" means the jealousy knot on the spine, a physical residue of DNA restriction deliberately added by the reptilians.

LK-J: You mean ... the occipital ridge?

The Cs: Yes.... Spine had no ridge there ... jealousy emanates from there, you can even feel it.

LK-J: Do any of these emotions that we have talked about that were generated by DNA breakdown, were any of these related to what Carl Sagan discusses when he talks about the reptilian brain?

The Cs: [Yes.] In a roundabout way.

LK-J: How did they physically go about performing this act?

The Cs: DNA core is as yet (an) undiscovered enzyme relating to carbon. Light waves were used to cancel the first ten factors of DNA by burning them off. At that point a number of physical changes took place including the knot at the top of the spine.

LK-J: How did they effect this change...?

The Cs: Light wave alteration.... Light waves affect DNA.

LK-J: What was the origin of light waves?

The Cs: Our center ... our realm [sixth density].

LK-J: How did the reptilians use the light from this [sixth-density] realm?

The Cs: They used sophisticated technology to interrupt the light-fre-quency waves [emanating from sixth density].

LK-J: Well, was there a battle and you guys lost? Did another force ... defeat you and use the power of the light [frequencies] in order to alter us in different ways. Is this correct?

The Cs: Yes.... Now understand this. It is all part of natural grand cy-cle. We are at "front line" of universe's natural system of balance. That is where one rises to before reaching total union with "The One." Beings at sixth level [sixth density] ... STO and STS are both high-level thought forms "reflected at all levels of reality." It's all just lessons in the grand cycle.

Knight-Jadczyk continues her questions in *High Strangeness* (p. 233):

LK-J: The veil ... the perception of only one dimension.... Were these illusions programmed into us genetically through our DNA?

The Cs: Close. The alteration of human DNA by the forces of darkness ... resulted in numerous changes, including the imposition of the concept of monotheism [belief in one separate all-powerful entity], the perception of linear time and unidimensionality [awareness of only one dimension—the third].

Knight-Jadczyk comments:

> Every human being perceives according to their pro-
> gramming which is activated by their belief system. This
> is their state of awareness. They can only be aware of
> what they believe they can be aware of and all else be-
> comes either "invisible" or "anomalous" and disregard-
> ed or covered up by the survival program of the subcon-
> scious mind. (p. 233)

LK-J: [H]ow (were) these illusions enforced on us, how were they perceived by us?

The Cs: Temptation to limitation.

LK-J: So what you are saying to us is that the story of the temptation
in Eden was the story of humankind being led into this reality as a
result of being tempted. So, the eating of the fruit of the tree of the
knowledge of good and evil was...?

The Cs: ... giving in to temptation.... Free will could not be abridged if
you had not obliged [agreed to inhabit bodies to experience physical
sensations].

LK-J: Are human beings trapped in physical matter?

The Cs: (Yes) By choice ... to experience physical sensations. It was
group decision. Everything that exists in all realms of the universe
can experience existence in one of only two ways ... a long wave cycle or a short wave cycle. Going back to your question about "why"
humans are entrapped in physical existence, which is voluntary and
chosen ... is due to a desire to change from the long wave cycle

experience of completely ethereal or spiritual existence to the short wave cycle of ... physical existence. The difference is that a long wave cycle involves only very gradual change in evolution in a cyclic manner ... a short wave cycle involves a duality.... [T]his is the case with souls in physical bodies as is experienced on this Earth plane because the soul experiences an ethereal state for half the cycle and a physical state for the other half of the cycle (a diurnal time cycle of day and night, waking and sleeping consciousness). The necessity of forming the short wave cycle was brought about through ... the natural bounds of the universe when the "group mind of souls chose" to experience physicality as opposed to a completely ethereal existence.

The Cs conclude this discussion in *Debugging the Universe* by saying that the physical life experience of duality was seen to provide

> an increase in relative energy which speeds up the learning process of the souls and its two-dimensional interactive partners. In other words, flora and fauna and minerals, etc. All experience growth and movement towards reunion at a faster rate ... through this short wave (diurnal time cycle) of physical/ethereal transfer. (p. 164)

These patterns of growth are reflected in Knight-Jadczyk's comments in *High Strangeness:*

> The closest analogy to the view of reality presented by the Cassiopaeans is graphically explicated in the movie, The Matrix, wherein our reality is presented as a computer program/dream that "stores" human beings in "pods" so that they are batteries producing energy for some vast machine dominating the world. Certain programmed (archetypal patterns of) life scenarios of great emotional content are designed in order to produce the most "energy" for this machine. And it seems that pain

and suffering are the "richest" in terms of "juice" [for sustaining these hyperdimensional overlords). (p. 320)

Human beings exist to transduce cosmic energies of Creation via organic life. Our "higher selves" are the directors of this transducing of cosmic energies. (p. 331)

From *Debugging the Universe*:

[Consider] ... the idea of archetypes as slides through which the consciousness of seventh density projects itself into consciousness units ... (each vibrating at slightly different frequencies) ... and what we perceive as reality is nothing more than the myriad oscillations of these primeval, prismatically divided waveforms from seventh density (emanating as thought forms or concepts). It is implied in physics that a wave usually has a waver, so we may assume that our reality has a waver also. [Imagine] ... that man is an oscillation of the absolute and as such, has the potential of being augmented by other waveform expressions of energy and thus (by) expanding his own awareness ... [he can move into phase with the primal wave itself]. (pp. 306–07)

Put another way, you might say that the direction in which our energy flows is determined by our beliefs, activities and choices while in third density. To transcend the opposing STS forces seeking to "capture" the lower vibrational energies of human consciousness, using it to feed themselves and sustain their holographic creation, we must focus our energies on the higher-chakra frequencies of love, compassion, forgiveness and inclusion.

As described in *High Strangeness:*

Those whose intrinsic nature is toward Being (STO) follow the path of developing the ability to "see" and to choose alignment with the infinite potential of creation, thereby being conduits of Being as God chooses to manifest through them. They not only see that limitation is illusion, they consciously "act" … they utilize that knowledge to generate energy and light. (p. 334)

There are hyperdimensional realms beyond our normal human capacity to see, know, understand and be aware of due to our intentionally reduced perceptual capacities. However, we know of these realms from those who can see into these other dimensions: the shamans, remote viewers, psychics, yogins, saints, Masters, etc. In Knight-Jadczyk's *Almost Human*, she states:

The higher-density positive entities [STO beings] are [light generators], light beings. The higher-density negative [STS] beings are "light eaters" [they consume energy and light]. Love is light is knowledge. When they induce belief against what is objectively true, they have "eaten" the light—knowledge—of the person who has chosen blind belief over fact. When you believe a lie, you have allowed the eating of your energy of awareness. (p. 268)

In reference (*High Strangeness*) to the Cs' previous explanation that the Consortium is composed of groups of aliens and Earth's government, Knight-Jadczyk continues her questioning of the Cs (pp. 124–32):

LK-J: Bob Lazar [who worked at Area 51, a military base in Nevada] referred to the fact that aliens supposedly refer to humans as "containers." What does this mean?

The Cs: 94% of all population will be used.

LK-J: Used for what?

The Cs: Total consumption.

LK-J: What do you mean by consumption? Ingested?

The Cs: Consumed for ingredients.

LK-J: Why are humans consumed?

The Cs: They are used for parts.

LK-J: How can humans be used for parts?

The Cs: Re-prototype Vats exist. Missing persons go there and especially missing children.

LK-J: This is awful! I don't know how knowing this helps us.

The Cs: Must know—ease pain with meditation.

LK-J: Are the aliens using our emotional energies?

The Cs: Correct and bodies too. Each Earth year 10% more children are taken.

LK-J: What happens to souls? Is this physical only?

The Cs: Physical—souls are recycled.

LK-J: Who is responsible for this?

The Cs: Consortium.

LK-J: This is totally sick.

Cs: Sick is subjective.

LK-J: Why is this happening to us?

The Cs: Karma.

LK-J: What kind of karma could bring this?

The Cs: Atlantis.

LK-J: What did the Atlanteans do to bring this on us?

The Cs: Worshipped and served self to extreme.

LK-J: What can protect us?

The Cs: Knowledge, learn, meditate, read. Must know what consortium is doing.

LK-J: Why do we need to know these things?

The Cs: Very big effort on behalf of Orions and their human brethren [the consortium of the military/industrial complex on Earth] to create new race [New World Order] [to control Earth].

At this point I'm going to side-step for a moment and provide a bit of background information on Knight-Jadczyk, from her book *The Secret History of the World* (pp. 600–01). From the beginning of her experiment and during subsequent years, she maintained regular contact with the Cs throughout many personal life challenges, divorce, illnesses, a major auto accident, her research, remarriage, the authoring of her many books, the development of her blog site and various websites over many years' duration. Her work became well known in the public domain. So much so that she came to the attention of "the consortium." She was contacted twice by a member of the consortium who invited her and her physicist husband to become part of their global network supposedly addressing global issues and they offered them a generous financial funding package to boot. She declined because their offer would have required her and her husband to give up their goal of "waking people up to the hyper-dimensional nature of the global control system." In other words, the consortium wanted them to stop disseminating their research findings and the channeled information from the Cs to the public.

She states:

> I know of this individual [who is a member of this con-
> sortium] because of the research I did on game theo-
> ry. He was closely associated with Wheeler [a physicist
> who had worked on the Manhattan Project to develop
> the atomic bomb] and did studies on using game theory
> as a means of killing the most people with the least ex-
> penditure of energy as a means of reducing the planet's
> population significantly. (p. 601)

Now back to the dialogue between Knight-Jadczyk and the Cs in
this same book (pp. 586–87):

The Cs: Remember that the human (historical) cycle mirrors the cycles
of catastrophe, and human mass consciousness (and beliefs) play a
part.

LK-J: Can we accelerate the awakening? Is there a tool that enhances
free will?

The Cs: Yes, remember, you learn on an exponential curve. Once you
have become "tuned in." This means that you become increasingly
able to access the universal consciousness.

LK-J: So when a person is being ... controlled from outside, they are
hypnotized and controlled until they learn to stop it?

The Cs: Yes.

LK-J: So, in other words, knowledge and awareness makes you aware
that you have free will, and also makes you aware of what actions
actually are acts of free will.... When you know or suspect the difference between the lies, deception and truth ... you are in a position to be in control of your life?

The Cs: Yes ... once you have become ... "tuned in"... you become increasingly able to access the universal consciousness [the quantum field of awareness].

The learning, the process of discernment of the truth by accessing the universal field of consciousness, is extensively dealt with by the Cs via a discussion of gravity. In *High Strangeness* (pp. 235–37):

LK-J: Gravity seems to be a property of matter. Is this correct?

The Cs: And antimatter! Binder. Gravity binds all that is physical with all that is ethereal through unstable gravity waves!!!

LK-J: So they are a property or attribute of the existence of matter and the binder of matter ethereal?

The Cs: Sort of, but they are a property of antimatter too.

LK-J: So through unstable gravity waves, you can access etheric densities?

The Cs: Everything.... Gravity is the central ingredient of all existence. It is the binder of all creation. It is the "fuel" or life blood of absolutely everything that exists. Matter/anti-matter—one features atomic particle-based matter, the other (anti-matter) features pure energy in conscious form. Gravity is the balancing binder of it all ... the binder between matter and anti-matter... It is the foundational field from which all other fields emanate and it is the means by which the energy body is bound to the material body.

LK-J: So gravity is the unifying principle?

The Cs: Gravity is all there is.

LK-J: Do thoughts produce gravity waves?

The Cs: Yes.

LK-J: Is it possible ... that ... other beings draw this energy?

The Cs: Yes. And that in a general sense is what happens.... [F]or in-
stance] ... at the point of (sexual) orgasm ... that energy drains to
fourth density and STS beings there retrieve it [consume it].

Knight-Jadczyk concludes, and the Cs concur, that the generation
of gravity waves is really the collecting and dispersing of energies: giving
and being open (STO) is dispersing gravity and taking (STS) ... is collecting gravity or draining energy from the physical into the ether [the
astral—the fourth density or dimension].

From *Secret History of the World:*

> Our universe seems to be made up of matter/energy
> and of consciousness.... Matter/energy by itself doesn't
> even have a concept of "creation" or "organization." It
> is the consciousness that brings to life these concepts
> and by its interaction with matter pushes the universe
> towards chaos and decay or towards order and creation.
> If you are able to view the Universe as it views itself,
> objectively, without blinking, and with acceptance, you
> then become more "aligned" with the creative energy
> of the universe and your very consciousness becomes a
> transducer of order. Your energy of observation, given
> unconditionally, can bring order to chaos and can create
> out of infinite potential. Since humanity as a whole is an
> "organ" for transducing cosmic energies onto our planet,
> the suffering of humanity, the lies that humans believe,
> all have a profound effect on the planet. (pp. 602–05)

And in *Debugging the Universe:*

> For every mind that is unplugged and debugged, the po-
> tential effects on the universe are literally staggering. (p.
> 314)

In other words, embodied Souls have a choice in this dualistic holo-gram to align in a service-to-self (STS) orientation or in a service-to-others (STO) orientation. The intensity with which a being holds to the ego/personality's point of view and belief that its view of reality is real, objective and true, "it" being the sole arbitrator, controller of its person-al world, is the degree to which the STS (lower-vibrational-frequency) being is bound more tightly onto the karmic wheel of reincarnation, ignorant of the ever-so-subtle trap the ego/mind creates, and is held captive within.

In *High Strangeness:*

> The Wave Series [of books] include a historical analysis of the deception perpetrated upon mankind and propos-es ideas as to how to literally "change our universe" to another probable reality. We believe that this is the pur-pose of our contact with the Cassiopaeans—to strength-en, inform, educate, and assist us [in] gaining the knowl-edge that will set us free. (p. 213)

Paraphrasing Knight-Jadczyk, the Cassiopaeans defined the Wave as a macrocosmic quantum jump where our sector of space/time will momentarily collapse, before being reborn anew, which they call a phase transition. Our Earth will move from third density to fourth density. They also describe three different time cycles coming to a close at the same moment. According to the Cs, a 3,600-year cometary cloud cy-cle will bring destruction to parts of Earth from cometary bombard-ment and debris fields. There is a 309,000-year cycle, and a third cycle. The third will affect Earth in a 27-million-year orbital cycle of our Sun's "dark star" companion which will pass through the Oort cloud. This will enter our sector creating cometary debris clusters that will hit Earth and cause orbital disturbances in the planets of our solar system. In other words, a global cataclysmic change (pp. 325–26).

And in *Debugging the Universe:*

> The Cassiopaeans refer to [the Wave] as a state in which a person merges densities or traverses densities. It is the

merging of physical reality [third dimension] and ethe-real reality [fourth dimension] which involves thought form versus physicality. (p. 301)

From pp. 302–04:

LK-J: [W]hen The Wave comes, if [one has] reached the correct frequency vibration and has raised [themselves] up to the point that the Wave will take them, they will, at that point, move into fourth density, true?

The Cs: Close enough…. The Wave is transport mode. Many aliens will appear and be visible to us. The grand cycle is about to close presenting a unique opportunity.

LK-J: Does this mean that this is a unique opportunity to change the future?

The Cs: Future, past and present…. As we have told you, there are seven levels of density which involves, among other things, not only state of being, physically, spiritually, etherically and materially, but also, more importantly, state of awareness … state of awareness is the key element to all existence in creation. You … remember … that we have told you that this is, after all, a grand illusion…. So … if it is a grand illusion, what is more important, physical structure or state of awareness???? … Once you rise to a higher state of awareness, such things as physical limitation evaporate. And when they evaporate, vast distances, as you perceive them, become nonexistent. So just because you are unable to see and understand has absolutely no bearing whatsoever on what is or is not possible, except within your own level of density. And this is what almost no one on your level of density is able to understand. If you can understand it and convey it to them, you will be performing the greatest service that your kind has ever seen (pp. 318–19).

Deconstructing the Cassiopaean Paradigm

Belief that the Cassiopaeans are an insectoid race of sixth-dimensional beings whose job is genetic research, who live in the Cassiopaean star system on a planet called Carcosa.

Belief that they are part of the original group of creator gods from sixth density who genetically created the original humanoid species.

Belief that they are coming from one of Earth's future timelines, as "us" in the future, to communicate with Knight-Jadczyk and her group to specifically to warn the humanoid species of a plot to take over Earth.

Belief that the creator gods, in creating the various solar systems and galaxies, also created various life forms to inhabit these worlds, fell in love with their created forms and inhabited these forms to experience physical existence.

Belief that the original humanoid forms were created on the planet D'Ankhair in the constellation Scorpio and that these molecularized matter-based humanoid life forms caused the life force/Soul consciousness to concentrate and contract within these inhabited forms.

Belief that these actions by the creator gods caused a reaction within the higher hyperdimensional realms, causing the crystallization-solidification of dimensions one, two and three.

Belief that this crystallization created a separation between pure Soul consciousness and Souls embodied in various matter-based forms and created massive energy imbalances which created duality/polarity—a split between pure consciousness and the will/intention of separate consciousness units, creating the positive and negatives poles of the creation.

Belief that this split in consciousness developed into the self-perpetuating cycles of reincarnation entrapping all sentient beings in the lower-dimensional realms, thus causing Souls to be perpetually recycled from one bodily form to another till these consciousness units can evolve beyond the lower dimensions.

Belief that the humanoid species are members of a fragmented Soul group that was originally in union with the One—the Supreme Creator.

Belief that these originally molecularized humanoid forms were taken over and altered by three forces: the reptilians and cloned Grays, the Nephilim and the Orion/Nordic geneticists who intentionally manipulated humanoid DNA, leaving only two of the original twelve strands in place, separating the hemispheres of the brain, creating amnesia and lowering the overall frequency vibrations of the humanoid species in order to control and enslave.

Belief that the Orion/Nordic races originally created the Gray races in five varieties as cybergenetic beings to serve them.

Belief that the Nordic genes were mixed with all humanoid combinations of races evolving on Earth including the early Neanderthals.

Belief that the story of the fall of man in the garden is a distorted symbolic story depicting the temptation of the humanoid species to inhabit physical bodies by the reptilian, Gray and Nordic geneticists.

Belief that our planet is locked into a three-dimensional time/space hologram which was projected from higher consciousness units from seventh density, and that what humans falsely perceive as an objective three-dimensional world is in essence myriad oscillations of the primeval prismatically divided waveforms from seventh density.

Belief that this illusion is maintained through individual and collective mind/brains that project images onto the ether beyond the time/space dimension, creating repeating lifetimes that humans perceive as the space/time holographic three-dimensional "objective" world.

Belief that humans were genetically altered and engineered to transduce the cosmic energies of creation into organic matter-based life forms within the lower three-dimensional universes to serve and feed the STS hyperdimensional creator gods.

Belief that STO beings are light bearers and light generators and STS beings are light eaters who consume light and energy.

Belief that humanity has been trapped in this hyperdimensionally created world for 74,000 years, a world created and controlled by a group of hyperdimensional aliens known as the reptilians, the Grays and a group of Orion Nordic races.

Belief that these interdimensional races travel into and out of our time/space reality continually and have been doing so for thousands of years to control events in our world from their higher-dimensional realms.

Belief that the Earth-based consortium made up of members of the military, industrial, government complex (the new world order) and three negative alien races, the reptilians, the Grays and the Nordics have a contractual agreement whereby humans are being abducted for genetic experiments and eventually 94% of the populace will be allowed to be used for total consumption and the balance used as slaves.

Belief that the best way to counter this plan of a total takeover of humanity is for humanity to learn to differentiate between lies, deceptions and truth by using discernment and expanding our conscious awareness.

Belief that the collective consciousness of humanity when elevated to a higher frequency range through peaceful cooperation and compassionate care can move the populace into a higher frequency range beyond the third/fourth densities of illusion, deception and the repeating reincarnational cycles.

Belief that there is a cosmic wave moving into our sector of space/time that will create a "phase transition" moving Earth's planet from third density to fourth/fifth density.

Belief that this transit is due to the simultaneous closing of three different time cycles: a 3,600-year cometary cloud cycle, a 309,000-year cycle called "the wave" and a 26,900- or 27-million-year-orbital cycle of our Sun's dark star companion, which will pass through the Oort cloud and enter our sector of space, causing various alterations among the planets of our solar system.

Reference Keys: Cassiopaeans (web-a–e). Knight-Jadczyk (2003, 2005, 2008, 2009, 2011, 2012, 2013).

Chapter Seventeen

The Andromedan Worldview

THIS CREATION STORY is more akin to an intergalactic history lesson than to the more traditional Earth-bound mythic creation stories. Much of the history of planet Earth described by Robert Morning Sky, in one of the Sumerian/Babylonian versions of the creation story, fits right in with this worldview; but the Andromedans provide an even more in-depth, detailed perspective on the very ancient, hidden history of planet Earth and of our galactic origins. All of the information in this chapter was extracted and summarized from Alex Collier's book *Defending Sacred Ground*, and from his numerous personal public lectures, radio interviews and Youtube videos, which span more than twenty years.

Alex Collier is a contactee who has had thirty-two-plus years of ongoing intermittent contact with two Andromedans from the star system of Zenetae, a planet in the Andromedan star system in our galaxy, 623 million light years from Earth.

He first met the two Andromedan men who would become his teachers, Morenae and Vissaeus, when he was nine years old. While on a family picnic in a park in Woodstock, Michigan, Alex wandered off into the woods and as he was lying in the grass daydreaming, he was transported into an Andromedan mothership where these two men introduced themselves to him telepathically. They placed over his head some sort of electronic cap that emitted light and sound frequencies and showed him a computer screen on which played a series of visual images portraying a number of his past lives on other planetary bodies, including lives with these two men. It was quite emotional for nine-year-old Alex. He cried and became confused and upset while watching this panoramic viewing of his past lives. Morenae and Vissaeus told Alex he had promised in a past life that he would, in this life on Earth, become a disseminator of galactic history to the humanoid populace. Their shared mission, he was told, developed from their kinship as members of the same Soul group, represented throughout the galaxies, whose members enact creative life-imperatives that take shape differently in each context. Alex was given instruction about the way the mission was to unfold in the arena of Alex's life on Earth.

This first contact began his education by these two men about intergalactic history, Andromedan history, their race's social structure and their role as monitors and peacekeepers throughout interstellar space. Alex is quick to point out that he isn't the only contactee to whom this information has been given, but the other contactees, out of fear, declined to put this information out into the public arena. Alex himself has faced immense resistance and ridicule for making this information public and his life has been threatened more than once.

When Alex was returned to the park area from where he'd been taken, it was nighttime and he had no memory of where he'd been. As he made his way in the dark back to the picnic area, he saw bright floodlights, several police cars and his family standing around the area looking distressed. He ran straight over to his mother who grabbed him, hugged and kissed him, then abruptly slapped him for getting lost in the first place and scaring the family half to death. Alex didn't start remembering any of his contact experiences till he reached fourteen years of age, at which point the memories started surfacing.

The Andromedans told Alex that they are a very ancient, highly evolved race, living an average of 2,007 years. They are oxygen breathers who communicate telepathically through holographic thought forms. They are time travelers who holographically time travel by folding space/time. Because they communicate telepathically, their vocal cords are undeveloped. They stand between six and nine feet tall, have light-blue skin fading to white as they age. Some of them have elongated skull cases in the back of their heads. They are hairless and their pupils change color when they contemplate something. They also have an invisible spot in the center of their foreheads which flashes out different colors when they are communicating. They told Alex they have come to us from our future. Their race is approximately 4,300 to 4,500 years more technologically advanced than the humanoid race on Earth. The Andromedans said they are just one of many advanced galactic races capable of creating entire solar systems and of time travel. They highly value their children and their society is organized around educating their children to become adult members of a cooperative, peaceful, wise communal society.

They explained that there are four main types of planetary ecosystems in the multiverse, based on methane, ammonia, hydrogen and oxygen. The oxygen-breathing ecosystems are the most complex and require water for all their life forms. Earth is an oxygen-based ecosystem and is much rarer and more complex than the other three types of ecosystems. Being a respected elder race among the star nations, the Andromedans are involved in monitoring and negotiating between the two great orders of beings: the hydrogen-based races and the oxygen-based races in the galaxies. The Andromedan Council is composed of 143 different star nations and was formed to address problems and to keep peace among the various intergalactic star races.

According to the Andromedans, it was during Earth's Paleozoic Era—554–245 million years ago—that a dramatic explosion of diverse multicelled animals appeared on Earth. It was around this same time period that different extraterrestrial (ET) races in our galaxy began to develop space travel, began traveling outside of their own star systems and began discovering and communicating with other cultures and star races. Thus began the start of trade among these technologically advanced races. Per Andromedan history, many life forms on Earth were brought here by these intergalactic traders as Earth lies along a central galactic trade route. Originally Earth was in a different orbit closer to Mars and was an ice-covered planet. It was moved by ancient builder ET races that had the capacity to engineer entire solar systems to make them habitable for live organisms. These ancient builder races were able to terraform entire planetary bodies by moving moons around to alter a planet's rotation around their sun. They could even move entire planets closer to or farther from their suns to create environments favorable to microorganisms so that various plant and animal life forms could flourish. The builder ET races created the four main types of ecosystems—based on hydrogen, oxygen, methane and ammonia—all gases necessary for the introduction of microorganisms.

From approximately 245 million years ago to 65 million years ago, many planetary civilizations had full space-travel capacity and interplanetary trade was well established, increasing the need for natural resources and causing the exploration of different galaxies by these advanced sentient beings from different star or ET races. The most advanced of these colonizing ET races were the hydrogen-breathing Ciakar/Dracos from Alpha Draconis, the Orions from Sirius A and B and the oxygen-breathing Lyrans from the Lyra-Vega star system. As colonization became rampant, it required the development of interplanetary alliances: groupings of star races who set up rules and regulations for the colonization of planetary bodies in different galaxies and star systems. During this time period, various star races discovered an advanced means of space travel using already existing wormholes or stargates, which allowed these ET races to travel instantly to different galaxies.

It is believed by many ET races and by the Andromedans that these original wormholes were created by a group of Logoi or creator gods called the Paa Tal, who were the original creators and caretakers of this galaxy. The concept of wormholes was explained to Alex as "tubes of focused time" which were used by the Paa Tal and later on by the ancient builder ET races as an aid to ecosystem-building in the various galaxies and to transporting life forms from one galaxy to another. The Andromedans told Alex there were originally seventeen such wormholes created and used by the Paa Tal in our galaxy to carry life forms from one galactic ecosystem to another, of which only two are still operational due to the expansion over time of the different galaxies in the multiverse, causing wormholes to snap.

Of the four main types of ecosystems created by the ET builder races, the hydrogen-based ecosystem is by far the most abundant type of ecosystem in the multiverse. Our planet's ecosystem, being oxygen-based, occurs on only a very limited number of planets, per the Andromedans. They told Alex that each and every planetary body is sentient, as are all the life forms existing on every planetary body—as all were created from the consciousness or the intelligent energy of the Supreme Creator. The original humanoid race, per the Andromedans, came from another galaxy but first began evolving in this galaxy in the Lyran star system. They stated there are over 135 billion human beings living in the eight galaxies closest to ours and that our universe is a "21-trillion-year-old hologram."

During the Cainozoic Era extending from 65 million years ago to the present, mammalian life forms were transplanted onto three ecosystems in our solar system: Earth, Mars and Uranus. During this process, many ET races were visiting other planetary ecosystems through travel in huge motherships, carrying self-contained biospheres called "E-Dens"—fully transplantable biospheres containing all an ET race needs to exist on other planets with biospheres different from their home planets, including the capacity to grow whatever foodstuffs they need. These motherships are hundreds of miles long, complete spherical worlds unto themselves. Small scout ships, used for exploration, are also carried inside.

Per the Andromedans, the first E-Den on Earth was set down 899,701 years ago near the Arizona-New Mexico border by a group of Ciakar—Draco reptilian military officers. The Ciaker are a hydrogen-breathing group from the reptilian races. They tend to be very large and slower in movement than oxygen-breathing races due to their biorhythms and their biosystems being of a lower vibrational frequency. They cannot travel faster than the speed of light in space travel. According to the Andromedans, the oxygen-based races are capable of traveling up to four times the speed of light. The oxygen-breathing races are smaller in stature than the hydrogen-based races and function at a higher vibrational frequency. The oxygen-based galactic races are unusual in that all their member races are derived from a singular genetic line.

Another E-Den was established by the Orions, another reptilian race, in Euromani, China 763,132 years ago. Then 741,237 years ago the Capellans from Ursa Minor set down an E-Den at the base of Mount Yogan in southern Chile. Next the Vegans, also known as the Lyrans, from Vega established their first colony in North Africa 701,655 years ago along the Libyan-Nigerian border. The Cassiopaeans, a sentient insectoid race, came next, setting down a base 604,003 years ago in Algeria.

Then came the Nibiruans: Draco reptilians from Butese, who established an E-Den 585,133 years ago in Cairo, Egypt. Most of these galactic ET colonizers are hydrogen-based races, fascinated by the rarer oxygen-based life forms and ecosystems, which are the most complex and diverse of the form-types of ecosystems. Almost all of these ET races are master geneticists and all have the capacity to manipulate all life forms. Their aim in genetically manipulating oxygen life forms is to be able to adapt and complexify their hydrogen-based forms and the ecosystems on their home planets to become more adaptable to both types of ecosystems. Some ET races stay on Earth for a while then leave, never to return. Other races come and go, such as the Lyrans, the Orions from Sirius A, the Pleiadeans from Teygeta and Merope. The Ciakar-Draco came, colonized Earth and stayed, claiming Earth as part of their galactic empire.

More recently in our ancient Earth's pre-history, many different races joined together and founded a collective Earth colony in 71,933 BCE known as Lemuria on a continent located in the Pacific Ocean. In 31,107 BCE Lemuria was destroyed in a war between the collective founding races. During Lemuria's existence, Atlantis was founded in 57,600 BCE by another group of ET races including the Pleiadeans, Aldebarans, Antareans, Hayadeans, a group from Sagittarius, and the Andromedans, all oxygen-based races. Atlantis was built on a continent in the Atlantic Ocean not far from Portugal, but in 27,603 BCE Atlantis was destroyed due to the various races getting into conflicts with each other leading to wars in which they destroyed each other and the civilization they had jointly built up.

The Andromedans explained to Alex that all reptilian races—the Ciakar, Dracos, Orions, Sirians, Nibiruans, Anunnaki and a race they conquered and genetically manipulated to use as their minions and enforcers, known as the Dows (the Grays) from Zeta Reticuli—are originally all hydrogen-based races. The Ciaker/Draco/Orion/Anunnaki empire builders are considered to be the worst riffraff or criminal element among the various galaxies by all the other ET races. They have colonized, captured and enslaved not just Earth but twenty-one other planetary systems in our solar system, whose races are having the same problems Earth is having with these militant, marauding races of reptilians. These races believe themselves to be superior to all other races and are especially hostile to all oxygen-based races, treating them as inferior races whom they use as "a natural resource" much like humans breed and use cattle for human consumption. The reptilians use the oxygen-based races as their slaves and actually eat human flesh and feed off the "fear hormones" and fear energies produced by the oxygen-based races.

The Andromedans told Alex that the Orion and Sirius B reptilian ET races built the pyramids on Earth millions of years ago. They were built all over our planet and on other planets in our solar system as well. They are tetrahedonal geometrical frequency generators and were designed to create a specific electromagnetic and sound-frequency grid, which polarized and captured our entire solar system into a lower-frequency vibrational range. Holding Earth within this specific lower-frequency range prevented the oxygen-breathing races from being able to connect with their higher selves and their Oversouls, blocking the humanoid species from direct knowledge of our divine origins or recognition of our eternal unity with the Supreme Creator.

They also told Alex that there are 1,837 reptilians living inside our planet, 100–200 hundred miles beneath the surface, who have been living there for thousands of years, along with 18,000 Gray clones—both of which groups have bases on our Moon, on Mars and on one of the moons of Mars. They say the moons are all artificial satellites. There are also Orion and Sirius-B ET bases inside Earth. These regressive races all have technologies that are between 900 and 4,000 years ahead of human technologies.

The Andromedans, being time travelers, can move back and forth along Earth's timeline and see into our future. They determined that 357 years into Earth's future timeline there would be developing a significant negative vibrational shift in Earth's energy field due to the increasingly tyrannical actions of the regressive races controlling Earth and the other planets they have enslaved. They determined that if their Council members didn't intervene in Earth's timeline trajectory, tyranny would spread throughout Earth's solar system like a cancer and eventually plague all the benevolent star races residing outside our solar system in other galaxies. According to Alex, the Andromedan Council passed a directive to join forces with the 143 other benevolent star races represented in their intergalactic council. Their combined star fleets are here now in our galaxy and have entered our solar system, and negotiations are in process to remove these regressive ET races from our solar system and from the twenty-one other solar systems in our galaxy that are struggling under the same rampant tyrannical, criminal regimes that have taken over Earth.

According to Andromedan knowledge of Earth's ancient history, there have been at least three nuclear wars fought on Earth in the last 450,000 years, perpetrated on Earth's populace by the regressive reptilian ET races. During the last 5,600 years of Earth's recorded history there have been 15,400 wars instigated and perpetuated by the regressive ET races. There was discussion among the council members as to whether or not they should intervene in Earth's affairs. It was decided by a thin majority of star nations that because Earth beings have been manipulated and controlled by these regressive races for thousands of years, they deserve an opportunity to prove themselves capable of acting responsibly when not being suppressed and mind-controlled into killing each other in perpetual wars. Alex was told that the older more evolved ET races avoid having interactions with humans due to their extremely volatile and unpredictable emotional reactions and propensity to violence which alarm the calmer, wiser more evolved ET races.

The Andromedans told Alex that the humanoid species are considered to be genetic royalty by the other star races because humanoids carry twenty-two different extraterrestrial races' genetic codes in our DNA, generating twenty-two different genetic/body types. Some of our DNA came from the Paa Tal plasma light-beings, some of it came from primates, some of it came from the reptilians, and some of it from many of the earlier colonizing ET races. The Draco/Nibiruan/Anunnaki colonizers manipulated our ancestral DNA and intentionally reduced our brain capacity by placing a barrier in our brains through DNA manipulation to block memory of our Soul awareness. Every being on the planet is a Soul consciousness that is an energetic essence or force that is interdimensional and eternal and retains memory of the Soul's many lives. By altering human DNA, the energetic frequencies of the body and the brainwaves were slowed, altering the speed of thought and blocking our full Soul awareness. According to Morenae, in one of his many teaching sessions with Alex, the speed at which the human mind thinks is the speed at which humans perceive the speed of light. The speed of light is under the control of the brainwaves' frequencies.

In our three-dimensional hologram, the speed of light is equal to the collective thought frequencies of all the beings on this planet and in it. Thought can travel beyond the speed of light up to a billion light years in other higher-dimensional holograms. The cerebral generator in the brain is there to transform light speed to light years and this "condenses" the light power of the Soul, which is how the Andromedans travel and control their spaceships through their Soul/light/mind/brain frequencies.

The Draconian and Sirius B colonizers (both reptilian races) mated with the DNA-manipulated humanoid women, eventually creating a half-breed race which became known as the "blue bloods"—the "ruling elite families" on Earth who were left behind to rule Earth in the name of the Draco/Anunnaki/Sirian ET overlords and were given secret technology to enforce their rulership (the ark of the covenant being just one such item given to the Hebrew priesthood). Per the Andromedans, all religious beliefs promulgated on our planet were created by the reptilian races to control humanity and to keep humans in fear of reprisals from the capricious "gods" who unpredictably and regularly fought with and killed each other and frequently intentionally annihilated millions of human beings through nuclear wars, starvation, disease, religious inquisitions and outright torturing genocidal regimes headed by these reptilian psychopaths. As mentioned in the Sumerian/Babylonian creation story chapter, "sin" is a word/concept incorporated into our world religions by the reptilian races. The word "sin" is a pre-Sumerian Draco reptilian word meaning "genetic defect." The reptilian races view humans as genetically defective beasts—cattle, chattel to be used, eaten and/or abused as their personal property.

Earth has been colonized for the past 22 million years. The humanoids' existence as "genetic royalty" (with twenty-two "Soul signatures" in their DNA) was said by the Andromedans to reflect the fact that humans are descendants of the Paa Tal, creator gods who descended from the eleventh dimension to the third dimension to inhabit physical bodies, to experience space/time and physicality and to explore the concepts of free will and self-expression. Thus, humanoid DNA carries a specific chemical in the brain, excreted by the adrenal and pituitary glands, that carries this genetic coding in it.

According to Andromedan knowledge of intergalactic history, the Paa Tal descended from the eleventh to the third density through the planet Jupiter, which in fifth density is a sun and has hyperdimensional and hyperspatial properties. The Paa Tal, originally creator gods in non-physical plasma light bodies, were able, through mathematical and geometric holographic information transfer, to create each of the dimensions as holographic realities, with each dimension vibrating at a higher light/sound frequency than the ones below it, creating eleven different dimensions. Our three-dimensional world of so-called physical phenomena, the Andromedans explain, was created by the Paa Tal and is maintained by and dependent on human Soul consciousness (our brainwave generators) and on the higher-dimensional consciousness energies of the deities and angels to sustain it.

The Andromedans told Alex that the Paa Tal originally inhabited three-dimensional physical bodies that were green-skinned and had copper-based blood systems that made their original blood green like chlorophyll. Some had blood with a gold tint to it. All originally designed humanoid bodies also had copper-based blood systems and had fully functioning pituitary and thyroid glands. However, because of the Great Galactic Nuclear Wars between the Draco-Nibiruans and the Orion reptilian races, severe genetic damage was done to all the races in our solar system by radioactive fallout that filled the planetary atmospheres. It blanketed all planetary surfaces, which in turn caused atrophy of physical organs and damage to the original blood chemistry of the twenty-two types of terran (Earth-based) humanoid species. This contamination caused severe changes in the blood chemistry of all races stranded on the surface of the planet.

Blood types and skin colors changed over time. Humanoid skin tones went from green to red (Native Americans, Egyptians and Mayans) to yellow (Asians) to black (Africans) and to white (Caucasians). The white races were considered to be genetically defective and the weakest, since their altered blood chemistry caused severe anemia. Humanoid blood systems eventually became adapted to iron and became iron-based due to copper depletion from ambient radiation, and human blood became red. The copper depletion also caused reduced brain capacity, reduced nervous-system capacity and a reduced resistance to electromagnetic frequency variations.

According to Andromedan galactic history, the Paa Tal's original bodies were created from a combination of twenty-two different genetic DNA lines of ET races from all over the galaxies. Hidden Draconian records note the arrival of these Paa Tal creator gods in the lower dimensions. They are sometimes known as the Guardians, the Founders, the Gods of the First Time, etc., who manifested in physical bodies in the lower dimensions specifically to oppose and challenge the existing reptilian Draconian races and their negative systems of kingship, control and domination, and their assertion of ownership and enslavement of the conquered races.

Partly because the humanoid race is considered by the star ET races to be genetic royalty, with their Paa Tal ancestry of twenty-two lines of DNA, the star ETs agreed to intervene in our solar system's affairs and come to our aid. Aid is needed because the Draco and other regressive ET races with eons-old established underground and under-ocean bases have negotiated secret deals with Earth's dominant governments, controlled by the elite families. These regressive races agreed to exchange advanced technological and biological weaponry blueprints, to provide technical aid and to allow the corporate elite to mine gold in exchange for access to human adults and children.

The Andromedans told Alex that the reptilians are responsible for some 37,000 human children having disappeared, and every year the number of disappearances keeps increasing. They are using the children as a food source and are also draining brain fluids from these children after they are tormented into a terrified fear state so that a specific brain substance excreted from their adrenal and pituitary glands can be extracted. These specific excretions have a special genetic DNA coding in them which is what the reptilians are after. The reptilians can absorb these excretions but their bodies can't produce it. Our humanoid species carry this chemical in our brains due to the twenty-two different genetic lines within the human DNA that no other life form carries. These horrifically cruel and heinous crimes are justified by the regressive races who claim that because humans carry part-reptilian genetics in their DNA, humans are the property of the regressive races, who thus have every right to do what they do to the human populace on this and on other planetary bodies they have captured. The Grays, being a genetically cloned race originally used by the reptilians as their enforcers, are also involved in abducting humans and children and taking them to their underground bases or into their motherships for the purpose of extracting genetic materials in an attempt to create a hybrid race of Gray/humanoid ETs, which they hope to use to eventually replace humans.

Alex, after meeting with Morenae and Vissaeus for years, writing down, absorbing and publicly disseminating massive amounts of these galactic history lessons, asked Vissaeus one day, "What is to become of us?" Vissaeus's reply: Humans need to learn self-responsibility, to be responsible for their own choices and not turn over their Soul sovereignty to another so-called authority whether it be a government, a religious "authority" or an ET race masquerading as a "savior" of humanity. It is humanity's destiny to become the creator gods that we are descended from. We are to become galactic star beings and galactic teachers of other ET star races once we stand up and declare our freedom from this encroaching tyrannical element.

Vissaeus further explained that humanity is in the process of creating a new domain of knowing, a holographically structured society in which all information is available to everyone with no secrets or deceitfulness—an open society.

He explained that humanity's task is to call forth something that didn't exist before. An idea whose time has come. A new concept or idea that humanity needs to call forth and generate from nothing. Just as humans created the concept of "freedom and liberty" when Americans rebelled and began establishing the American colonies and wrote the Declaration of Independence to escape the religious and financial tyranny of the British ruling aristocracy. Americans called this concept into being from nothing, created the language to articulate it and then manifested it. Vissaeus then added, "We have called forth this drama so we can step into our power. We the people can change our world." The Andromedans gave Alex this important message to pass on to the human populace: "Your task on Earth at this time is to Wake Up! Step Up! And Declare your Sovereignty! Take back your planet from your enslavers. You are the saviors you have been waiting for."

And, according to the Andromedans, we are being helped at this time by massive cosmic changes happening not only in our galaxy but in all the spiritual dimensions above our third space/time dimension. These changes have been predicted by all the ancient worldwide preserved spiritual texts, each using different concepts and language to explain what these changes will encompass and how they will manifest in our reality.

The 26,000-year change cycle we are going through involves the creation of a new twelfth dimension above the eleventh. They explained that a new galaxy will be birthed in the Vega star system. We will have a seventeen-degree pole shift on Earth, and this will herald the beginning of the formation of a new twelfth dimension, which will purify and lift Earth above Earth's artificially blocked higher frequencies, pulling Earth into the higher fourth and fifth densities. The Andromedans asked Alex to remind humans that what appears to be time and motion from our perspective is, in reality, only the movement of consciousness upon a higher plane or dimension of awareness.

Deconstructing the Andromedan Paradigm

This cosmology is equally as complex and multidimensional a creation story as the Wingmakers', the Ra group/Elohim's and the Cassiopaeans' versions and bears many similarities to these other worldviews.

Belief that the "Isness" is the Supreme Creator—All That Is, originator of all that exists in potentiality, as infinite intelligent energy.

Belief that trillions of galaxies were formed by the Paa Tal creator gods emanating from the eleventh dimension downwards, creating all the dimensions below the eleventh through the creation of mathematical and geometric holographic forms; of which only the first through third dimensions manifest through condensed light and sound frequencies appearing as solidified matter.

Belief that all dimensions of the creation, the first through eleventh, are holographically projected structures imprinted into the ether.

Belief that the third-density hologram and third-density physical bodies cause humans to misperceive reality as a singular and solid space/time-based dimension, which is a perceptual illusion.

Belief that the Paa Tal (the plasma light-being creator gods) created the galaxies, and that other advanced builder ET races engineered various solar systems and created various life forms for these planetary bodies creating four different types of ecosystems: hydrogen-, oxygen-, methane- and ammonia-based.

Belief that these creator/colonizer terraforming ET races traveled through intergalactic wormholes to move from one area of the galaxy to another in "no time" to transport life forms to various planetary bodies.

Belief that the humanoid races on Earth are descendants of the original creator gods, the Paa Tal, and carry their genetic DNA, making them "genetic royalty."

Belief that that the original skin color of the twenty-two Earth-based humanoid species was green and their blood was originally green due to the original blood chemistry being copper-based—but became iron-based due to nuclear radiation on Earth causing blood chemistries to change over eons of time.

Belief that humans carry the combined DNA of the Paa Tal, the reptilians, and the originally created Earth-based ape species.

Belief that our universe is a 21-trillion-year-old hologram and there are 135 billion humanoid life forms living in holograms in the eight galaxies closest to ours.

Belief that Earth has been colonized off and on for the past 22 million years.

Belief that approximately 900,000 years ago, many advanced ET races began setting down E-Dens (self-contained biospheres) on Earth to explore Earth's ecosystem and to colonize Earth.

Belief that humans have been DNA-altered by many races over eons of time due to Earth being a rare oxygen-based ecosystem, with human DNA being highly prized by other ET races.

Belief that the reptilian races represent a major criminal element in the galaxies that have captured and enslaved many star races and use them as slaves and as a food source, manipulate their DNA and feed off humanoid fear-based hormonal secretions and biophotonic light emissions.

Belief that the ancient pyramids erected all over Earth and on other planets and moons were intentionally engineered to emit specific low-frequency electromagnetic waves to capture planets in a frequency net to prevent the higher spiritual frequencies from reaching our solar system, so that humans would be blocked from direct knowledge of their true divine origins.

Belief that humanity's true intergalactic origins and their ancient galactic history has been intentionally hidden to control and dominate Earth's populace.

Belief that the regressive reptilian races who have taken over Earth and twenty-one other planetary bodies in our solar system need to be removed to end the "reign of tyranny" they have imposed on many star races for millions of years.

Belief that the reptilian races have technologies that are 900–4,000 years ahead of human technologies.

Belief that being interdimensional time travelers, the Andromedans have a responsibility to connect with several humans on Earth related to their Soul group, to educate them about humanity's true origins and urge them to disseminate this information publicly.

Belief that the Andromedan Council composed of 143 star nations are actively intervening in planet Earth's affairs interdimensionally to prevent the tyrannical reptilian races from spreading their criminal activities throughout galactic civilizations in a future timeline.

Belief that the speed of thought determines the speed of light and that Andromedans are able to control their mind/brain/thought-wave frequencies, enabling them to travel many times the speed of light.

Belief that with these advanced technologies they can read the brainwave frequencies and therefore the thoughts and intentions of any species in any space/time dimension and know ahead of time what a single being or a collective of beings is thinking or planning to do before they do it.

Belief that they are aware of great cosmic movements currently taking place galactically that are altering all the dimensions of consciousness including the inner dimensions above our third dimension. They believe a twelfth dimension is forming, which is pulling all the dimensions below upwards into higher frequencies of light and sound waves.

Reference Keys: Andromeda (web). Collier (1996, 2002, web-a–b).

Chapter Eighteen

The Superstructure of the Cosmos

YOU'RE INVITED IN this chapter to step back several paces in order to gain a deeper, wider, more comprehensive view of the overarching structure of the cosmos, the superstructure underlying the processes of creation. Truly we live in a vast multiverse of many dimensions and planes of existence but at present we're confined to a tiny corner of it, this diurnally rotating, three-dimensional hologram known as terra firma or planet Earth. The intent here is to develop, in your mind's perceptual filter, the capacity to make finer and finer distinctions in perception so as to expand your knowledge base and your intuitive senses, allowing you to experience the free flow of ideas between different domains of knowing. This will facilitate your ability to move from the linear to the nonlinear and eventually into the transcendent domains, beyond the limiting polarized positionalities imposed by the split mind/brain maintained through the holographic space/time continuum.

Most of the linguistic explanations for how the multiverse came into being are vague approximations and inadequate as a means of describing the transcendent domains. As the creation proceeds it trickles down into the lower energetic subtle dimensions and terminates in the lower dimensions or planes—as this three-dimensional, seemingly matter-based, physical, objective plane of existence which limits, veils and blocks humanity's full perceptual capacities into a fraction of its true capabilities.

A few of the creation stories take place entirely or mostly within this three-dimensional hologram of planet Earth. Many of the creation stories in this book, however, include fantastic and extraordinary descriptions of higher, interdimensional and inner-dimensional planes filled with unusual and variegated sorts of beings (insectoids, Gray ETs, reptilians, Archons, blue-skinned Andromedans, etc.). These beings tell very tall tales indeed about human history, their perspectives on human history and their beliefs about how all species, humanoid and otherwise, came into existence. Recovered Sumerian cuneiform texts (the Seven Tablets of Creation) tell how the reptilians altered the humanoid species by mixing their DNA with human DNA and how they set up this entire three-dimensional hologram as an Anunnaki-designed inverted world—a body/mind/spirit control system.

The Anthroposophic version of the creation story for example is truly cosmic in its scope. Steiner had an uncanny extrasensory ability see into the structure of the cosmos, which he described in his many books and lectures. He described the creation as being undertaken by a hierarchy of divine spiritual, non-physical beings or sub-creator gods: beings in subtle energy bodies whom he described as "benign neutral functionaries" whose job is to interdimensionally oversee, aid and guide the development of planetary systems and the varied species living on and in these bodies.

As described in the Anthroposophic worldview, the Thrones, Cherubim and Seraphim existing in the higher realms, work directly with forces of cosmic movement, cosmic will and cosmic wisdom and intervene indirectly through the unconscious mind of humanity. Archangels or angelic forces Steiner depicts as loving, light-clad divine presences who oversee, aid and guide the Soul's evolutionary trajectory through the material and non-material dimensions or planes of creation. This brings to mind William Blake's quote: "Eternity is in love with the creations of time." Here Blake is poetically expressing the idea that non-corporeal eternal divine light beings inhabiting the higher planes, lovingly oversee and take great joy and delight in what humans, locked into this dimensional space/time hologram, can creatively bring forth into physical expression on the material plane in service to their expanding Soul comprehension.

The Elohim/Ra group explain their version in a somewhat similar way, saying in *The Law of One,* Book II:

> Our lenticular star system or galaxy contains 250 billion other suns like our own and was created by a single Logos or Creator God. Then other lesser sub-logoi or sub-creator gods were tasked with the further differentiation of intelligent energy into hierarchical structures of consciousness consisting of seven ... planes of existence. (p. 14)

A similar explanation of a benign celestial manifestation process is that expressed by the Anthroposophic view.

Other creation stories included in this book are told by interdimensional time travelers, who say they came to us from Earth's future timeline to give us their version of how the multiverse was created and by whom, how it got deviated in the space/time continuum, and what humanity needs to do to collectively correct this deviation. And finally, some of the creation stories are told by intergalactic races whose versions read more like intergalactic history lessons covering billions of years of intergalactic history, before planet Earth was ever accreted into a solid material body or terraformed.

Some worldviews include versions of an anthropomorphized creator god. A god made "in the image of man" rather than the other way around. For example, the conceptualized god of the Abrahamic traditions is characterized in parts of the Old Testament as having many human egoic traits—rage, jealousy, possessiveness, war mongering, need to control, vindictiveness and cunning. It's a common trait of human beings to imagine other sentient divine beings as being like them and having similar traits. It happens all the time in families with pets, where pets are imbued with humanlike traits ... oh, the dog's showing off for company or ... oh, the cat's jealous of the parrot, etc. In major motion pictures and in ancient and modern fairy tales too, animals—dragons, monkeys, fairies, ants, birds, mice, lions and swans, as well as inanimate objects—toys, spoons, shoes, cups, coins, brooms and celestial bodies, are animated or drawn giving them human-like traits, feelings and behaviors.

The intent in this chapter is to de-anthropomorphize concepts of god and to provide versions of the cosmic creational process that are more benign and neutral—unpolarized. Before the process of creation began there was no polarity, only Unity, One Supreme Creator, Prime Creator—the Immovable, pervasive, Infinite Intelligence of All That Is, Self-Existent, Omnipotent, Immanent and Omniscient. The Pure Essence of Prime Creator is Everywhere as Love and at the extreme unitary pole of the energies of creation there is only Love, Light and Bliss—All inclusive—All loving—All pervasive. When light and sound frequencies, the two primary aspects of God-into-Expression power, emanated from out of the infinite eternal essence of the Supreme Being, these manifested energies of light and sound created the light and shadow worlds—the positive and negative poles of creation, the spiraling dualistic energetic forces of creation.

Below is a de-anthropomorphized version of the creational process simply explained by Sri Yukteswar in his book *The Holy Science*:

> The Word Amen (Aum or the sound current) is the beginning of the Creation. The manifestation of Omnipotent Force (the Repulsion and its complementary expression ... the Attraction), is vibration, which appears as a peculiar Sound: the Word ... or Aum. In its different aspects Aum represents the idea of change [movement or vibration] which is Time, Kala, in the Ever-Unchangeable; and the idea of division, which is Space, Desa, in the Ever-Indivisible.... [From the two ideas—space and time—come four ideas] ... Word, Time, Space and the Atom ... or Anu.... These four ... are nothing but mere ideas.... The cause of creation is Anu or the Atoms [particles and waves].... They are en masse called Maya, the Darkness, as they keep the Spiritual Light out of comprehension; and each of them separately is called Avidya, the Ignorance, as it makes man ignorant [blind] even of his own Self.... [T]hese four ideas [thought forms] which give rise to all those confusions are mentioned in the Bible as so many beasts. Man, so long as he identifies

himself with his gross material body, holds a position far inferior to that of the primal fourfold Atom [vibration, time, space and atoms] and necessarily fails to comprehend ... [his true divine nature].... [Using the intellect (the ego/mind) of the material body] man is not able to comprehend the immaterial eternal essence.... Man cannot comprehend the divine reality unless he lifts himself above the unreal world of duality.... [Maya-Illusion], Avidya or Ignorance, being repulsion itself, cannot receive or comprehend the Spiritual Light, but reflects it. (pp. 24–26)

With the above explanatory framework in mind, it becomes much easier to comprehend the entire creational process as a benign celestial intergalactic energetic movement proceeding in orderly fashion from the highest plane of the galactic center spiraling outwards, divided by levels of conscious awareness till at some point the creational energies bifurcate into massive spiraling plasma-energy vortices of light and sound frequencies creating positive and negative poles of creation—think black holes and white holes whirling in interstellar space, creating innumerable galaxies and star systems in an infinitely expanding multiverse.

Sri Yukteswar, the Sant Mat Masters, Buddha and the Hindu Sages frequently refer to the polarized duality-based worlds as illusory/unreal, Maya/Darkness and Ignorance/Avidya. Sri Yukteswar referred in the above quote to "thought forms" giving rise to "confusion" which he said were mentioned in the Bible as "so many beasts." The Elohim/Ra group defined the concept of "free will/choice" as a thought-form projection, equivalent to "The Law of Confusion." Their statements imply that choice or duality creates the idea concept of a this and a that ... hence the distortion or split of a singular transcendent all-knowing consciousness into a bifurcation—a perceptual mental distortion or illusion—a blocking, binding and veiling of consciousness. In the *Law of One*, Book I, the Ra group states:

All thought is a distortion of consciousness. All finite energy is thought expressed in thought forms which create distortions in the consciousness of embodied beings living within the microcosm. (p. 79)

To expand on this concept of confusion- deception-distortion-illusion-maya- as so many "beasts" or "thought form projections," I quote from an article by John Lamb Lash from his website www.metahistory.org, posted October 2016, titled "The Great Deception – Part 2, Handling Supernatural Power":

> The mysterious power that produces the totality of framing structures in the Universe is called Mahamaya [which represents the divine power that makes the phenomenal universe recognizable to the senses].... The core of the Great Deception, the root delusion, the ultimate trick of Satan ... is to convince you that he DOES exist. The phantom [thought form] in your mind convinces you it is a real and objective entity, independent of you—that is the core of the GREAT DECEPTION. (web)

In essence Lamb is saying that the great deception is nothing but a psychic trap, nothing more than a thought form—a construct of the human mind. Thus humanity is trapped inside this virtual-reality game, this deceptive hologram of illusion, till we wake up to the fact that our "thought forms" are the basic building blocks that maintain the hologram. We are thus the unknowing, ignorant creators and maintainers of our own prison house—this three-dimensional hologram.

I propose that human beliefs as thought projections and emotional reactions produce electromagnetic frequencies in, around and through us, energetically extending from our bodies into our auric fields. They then extend into the field of the collective unconscious, the etheric and astral fields surrounding Earth. Then the sub-creator gods and sundry other negatively polarized parasitic entities existing in the etheric, astral and causal planes indirectly manipulate humanity and Earth's timeline by moving interdimensionally into and out of this three-dimensional space/time hologram. Here they indirectly manipulate situations that energetically sustain them and this three-dimensional holographic illusion through the manipulation and projection of human egoic thought forms and emotions into the collective unconscious mind of humanity to generate derision, chaos, suffering and destruction, all of which contributes to grist for the mill, the maintenance of the wheel of karma and the cycles of rebirth.

In order to comprehend such an appalling assertion, it is necessary to have a framework for understanding how this happens. Let us begin by using the concept of a holarchy. A holarchy is a hierarchical energetic structure where each level in the hierarchy is a whole and all wholes interpenetrate each other. At the macroscopic level of this superstructure are the galaxies spinning through the ether as vast spiraling energetic vortices, black and white holes, whirling plasma jets spewing out galaxies, star clusters and solar systems. All creational energy moves from a center point into a spiraling motion. For instance the spiraling motion of weather fronts swirling around the globe, the spiraling motion of tornadoes on land and whirlpools in the oceans, and the Coriolis force of the Earth's rotation where water spins in a clockwise direction above the equator and in a counterclockwise direction below the equator.

All of these are repeating fractal patterns at all levels of the superstructure. This equally applies to the microcosmic level of the superstructure of the cosmos. Even at the microscopic level this fractal pattern is repeated, as when electricity moves through a coil and creates a spiraling magnetic field around the coil. Consider the structure of the DNA which forms a double helix moving in a spiral motion. Even elementary particles spin around the nuclei of atoms in a chiral pattern where one-half of the particle is a perfect reflection of the other half.

This holarchic structure has been represented by all civilizations both ancient and modern through their art work, poetry, stone carvings and stories. Highly advanced technological civilizations tend to represent this holarchic structure through symbolic language and the use of geometric forms and mathematical formulas. Many early civilizations represented this holarchy through their creation stories utilizing anthropomorphized representations of the powerful forces of creation and naming them as so many gods and goddesses. It is these stories humanity is most familiar with.

In *Transcending the Speed of Light,* author Marc Seifer quotes Dane Rudhyar from his book *The Sun is Also a Star.* The following is Rudhyar's explanation for how this holarchy functions:

> Space during a period of cosmic manifestation actually represents the manner in which all the organized systems of activities operating in any region of the universe are interrelated and interacting. Space is not an empty container into which material substances are poured. It is the interrelatedness of all [bio-cosmic, intrastellar and galactic] activities ... operating at different levels of organization or planes of existence—the quality of their interactions and interdependence varies with each level. (p. 157)

Seifer continues:

> [E]ach person's mind ... [is] ... a microcosm of the universe. Just as DNA codes for the whole organism throughout every cell within it, the presence of the energy (light) from every star is also present in ... every sector in space and thus each spatial section ... code[s] for the whole. A map of the structure of the universe is present at every region in space (including the region that our brains occupy). The region of our minds, where this energy is reflected, is thus a form of counter-space, virtual space or inner realm that is potentially as vast as the outer world.... [S]tructured holographically, there are ... profound implications for such things as intergalactic information exchange and contact with higher beings. (p. 157)

Our holographically structured brains make us potentially capable of intergalactic travel, communication with interdimensional beings, and tapping into the information field of the ether. These capacities, when developed, give humanity access to the transcendent domains of knowing—knowing by direct perception. Rudhyar, again quoted by Seifer, states:

> The essential factor in this transformation of man's consciousness is the transmutation of the Solar "I" into the "Galactic We".... Everything not only is related to everything else but ... every entity, every mind interpenetrates every other entity ... as the consciousness of an individual begins to operate in the spiritual dimension[s] [man enters] the level ... of supermind. (p. 132)

To verify Rudhyar's concepts, below is an excerpt from a truly phenomenal new study published in *Frontiers in Computational* Neuroscience taken from the website messagetoeagle.com. The article written by staff writer Cynthia Kanzie states:

> A ground breaking discovery begins to reveal the brain's deepest architectural secrets and it's clear that our brain is even more advanced than we could ever imagine. Scientists have discovered a multi-dimensional universe in the [brain's] network. There are structures in the brain with up to eleven dimensions.... The superstring theory contends that there are ten dimensions... [This] has the potential to unlock one of the biggest mysteries of the universe ... how gravity and quantum physics fit together.... Researchers from the Blue Brain Project have used algebraic topology in a way that ... has never been used before in neuroscience. Neuroscientist Henry Markram, director of Blue Brain Project and professor at the EPFL [School of Computer and Communication Sciences] in Lausanne, Switzerland states, "There are tens of millions of these objects even in a small speck of the brain, up through seven dimensions. In some networks, we even found structures with up to eleven dimensions." This is where algebraic topology comes in; a branch of mathematics that can describe systems with any number of

dimensions. The mathematicians who brought algebraic topology to the study of brain networks in the Blue Brain Project were Kathryn Hess from EPFL and Rani Levi from Aberdeen University. "Algebraic topology is like a telescope and microscope [combined]. It can zoom into networks to find hidden structures [in the brain]," explains Hess. "The image[s] illustrate ... a universe of multi-dimensional structures and spaces [that can be seen in the neocortex]. Researchers ... report groups of neurons ... provide the missing link between neural structure and function." "The appearance of high-dimensional cavities when the brain is processing information means that the neurons in the network react to stimuli in an extremely organized manner," says Levi. "It is as if the brain reacts to a stimulus by building then razing a tower of multi-dimensional blocks, starting with rods (1D), then planks (2D), then cubes (3D) and then more complex geometries with 4D, 5D, etc. The progression of activity through the brain resembles a multi-dimensional sandcastle that materializes out of the sand and then disintegrates." [They conclude]: "The human brain is very complex, just like [a] supercomputer. We have not yet found a way to unlock all the brain's incredible capabilities...But if we have a multi-dimensional universe in our brain network, it means we could access higher dimensions! (web)

This truly amazing discovery, possible through the development of highly advanced imaging technology, gives credence to the concept of the multiverse being a construct of consciousness itself—consciousness being all-pervasive and interconnected at all levels of the creation. Comprehension of the interrelatedness of human consciousness at all levels of the creation can help move humanity toward a view of the cosmos that is not just out there but in here too—inside of us as information representations, thought-form constructs of the human mind.

Understanding how humanity's collective unconscious mind plays an integral part in the construction and maintenance of this three-dimensional hologram is of the utmost importance for each of us to grasp. We all must become consciously aware of and responsible for the perceptions, beliefs and conceptualizations we project as thoughts and emotional reactions into the collective unconscious thought field as they structure and define our relationship to ourselves, each other and the multiverse.

With that objective in mind let us re-examine the superstructure of the cosmic holarchy, noticing that at the top of the structure are de-anthropomorphized versions of the creational process, with the anthropomorphized versions proliferating lower down in the conceptual structure—with some of the names appearing at various levels of creator gods in more than one dimension.

THE SUPERSTRUCTURE OF THE HOLARCHY

ONE
THE SUPREME CREATOR, INTELLIGENT INFINITY, IMMOVABLE STILLNESS

TWO
MOVEMENT OF LIGHT WAVES AND SOUND FREQUENCIES
Vibrating quantum plasma strings emanating qualities of love, knowledge, discernment, truth and grace as intelligent finity combined with the movement and interplay of light waves (gluons, neutrinos, tachyons and photons) with sound frequencies creating rotating spiraling plasma vortices—massive toroidal energies forming the paired positive and negative cosmic energies of creation
Attracting and repelling forces of quantumly entangled electromagnetic frequency fields and gravitational force fields in the ether of the cosmos (**Void plane or the plenum**)

PAIRED COSMIC CREATOR FORCES
Supreme Creator – Soul Essences
Light Waves and Sound Frequencies –
Rotating Gravitational Force Fields

Masculine and Feminine Paired Forces of Creation
(Supercausal Plane)

Kal as Mind (waves) – Kali as Matter (particles) (Sant Mat Masters)

Aeon Christos – Aeon Sophia (Gnostic)

Krishna – Radha (Hindu)

Samantabhadra – Samantabhadri (Buddhist)

Jesus – Mary (Abrahamic)

Chaotic forces of Kishar – Ordering forces of Anshar (Sumerian/Babylonian)

Ra group / masculine forces of creation – Elohim / feminine forces of creation (Law of One)

Sun God/Jesus – Earth Goddess/Gaia (Anthroposophic)

THE MANY

MAHAMAYA: ANTHROPOMORPHIZED CREATOR, SUSTAINER, DESTROYER GODS
(CAUSAL, ASTRAL, ETHERIC AND PHYSICAL PLANES)

Cosmic beings—conscious intelligent energetic light beings and dark beings—with free will, desire and autonomy, tasked with further differentiation and maintenance of the multiverse existing within the lower holographic planes which they, as designers, create through the projection of thought forms (imaginary idea constructs), which then create geometric structures (holograms) for all created life forms, further creating, dividing, maintaining and destroying the lower worlds

Thrones, Principalities, Dominions, Seraphim, Cherubim and Archai, the Spirits of Personality

Father, Son, Holy Ghost, Archangels, Angels, Lucifer, Satan, Ahriman, Iblis

Christos, Sophia, Yaldabaoth, Archons

Brahma, Vishnu, Shiva, Vritra, Adityas, Danavas

Mahesvara, Mara, Asuras (demons), Devas (angels), Prajapatis

An (Anu), Ea (Enki), Baal (Enlil), Inanna (Ninhursag, Ninmah, Damkina), the Guardians, The Galactic Confederation, Council of Nine, Progenitors, the Life Planners, the Paa tal, the Andromedans, Wingmakers, Cassiopaeans, Mantids, Pleiadians, Lyrans

INTERDIMENSIONAL BEINGS IN THE LOWER PLANES
Some of whom are able to incarnate and/or assume temporary corporeal humanoid forms, cloned forms or hybrid forms made through mating with humanoids—either (STS) negatively polarized generators and maintainers of the illusory lower planes of duality/illusion, projecting negative thought forms through the collective unconscious mind of humanity, perpetrating the fear-based shadow worlds of darkness and chaos, or (STO) positively polarized interdimensional beings that project love/light energies into the lower realms through the collective unconscious of humanity, bringing forth ideas and acts of love, acceptance, compassion and unity to maintain balance and to elevate the consciousness of the collective mind of humanity

Upon close examination of the above holarchic superstructure, the ever-changing mental, emotional and physical chaotic states extant in the lower-dimensional space/time realms of polarity/duality become obvious due to their being located in the vicinity of the negative pole of the creation, the three-dimensional matter-based worlds. These ever-changing, moving, roiling electromagnetic energies of fear, confusion and chaos manifest at the physical level as ego-based strife, anxiety, loss, anger and trauma through perpetually induced destructive activities and events. Our hologram is maintained through the manipulation of humanity's thought-form projections and emotions via fear-based thoughts, fantasies and imaginings projected from the higher dimensions or hyperspace—the causal, astral and etheric planes. Since all points in time and space are connected through consciousness, the reptilians, the Orions, the Archons, the Grays and other negative entities moving through the etheric, astral and causal planes can and do influence us and indirectly manufacture our three-dimensional virtual realities (fictional ideas and thought-form projections of war, devastation, monsters, devils, and every depraved and scary thing imaginable) through the inner space of the unconscious collective human mind. Every thought the human mind can conceive of is a virtual-reality construct created by the consciousness of the egoic self. All objects/images/ideas in the multiverse are nothing but conjured realities—idea constructs, thought forms, or as Sri Yukteshwar called them, "so many beasts—all those confusions."

The Saints and Masters teach that once a Soul attains the supercausal plane, it is beyond the reach of the lesser rulers (the sub-creator gods) and is freed from the cycles of rebirth. The following is a quote from *Science of the Soul, Discourses of the Masters*:

> After creating human beings and other beings in the universe, Braham [ruler of the three worlds—physical, astral and causal] attached to each soul his agent in the shape of mind to confine the soul to his domain.... Matter and Mind so wholly engross the individual attention that one remains ignorant of [the way] the Royal Road leading to ... the pure spiritual region.... The way ... it findeth not but falleth into delusion again and again. (p. 99)

These sub-creator gods, hyperdimensional deities, descending from the supercausal plane, set up the holographic master game board and appointed themselves "master cosmic game keepers," the Lords of Karma. From their hyperdimensional perches they watch, control, judge and operate this system keeping Souls trapped in the karmic cycles of rebirth in the lower-dimensional holograms through the manipulation of the collective unconscious mind of humanity.

The Sufi Avatar Meher Baba, in *God Speaks*, writes:

> It is only in the God state that consciousness is free from samskaras [impressions left on the Soul as memories from former lives, which determine one's desires and actions in the present lifetime as karmic patterns].... Inert stone, which is the first and most rudimentary manifestation of partial consciousness, is, in this incomplete and partial state, too vague and unrefined to fulfill the purpose of creation which is to allow the Over-Soul to know Itself. Hence its finite identification with consciousness and its desire to be conscious of itself begins the illusory evolutionary movement into ever higher life forms or vehicles of expression till it ascends back into its original form in

the God state. It is only in human form that the latent potential for Self-Realization is present. (pp. 34–35)

The God state means God-realization, a return to the Soul's original state with full memory of its divine origin and a return to the planes or dimensions of pure bliss which stand above and beyond all duality in the pure spiritual planes at the positive pole of creation. Separation is a persistent illusion maintained only within the lower-dimensional holograms of deception. When unity consciousness prevails in the collective unconscious mind, the doors of perception will be opened for our individual and collective release from these lower-dimensional holographic virtual-reality worlds. The holograms will simply begin to dissolve away as our attention is withdrawn from them knowing them to be unreal, illusory thought-form projections, the imaginings of the collective unconsciousness of humanity.

Reference Keys: Blake (web). Hologram (web). Kanzie (web). L/L (1984). Lash (web-a–b). Meher (1973). Rudhyar (1975). Seifer (2008). Singh-MJ (2002). Steiner (web-b). Toroidal (web). Yukteswar (1984).

PART IV

Living In a Virtual-Reality Hologram

What the Bleep Is Going On?

That Depends on What You Believe!

The Dragon Mind

If perchance or by design in laying hands
upon the clay of life,
Thou hast fashioned for thyself a fierce
fire-breathing dragon,

Be not dismayed if the fire from its nostrils
doth singe thy flesh.

Inquire not the dragon's intent, but thine own.
For what blind unknowing mind would create
such a fierce and frightful creature......

And then ... adding further to the folly,
doth hourly breathe life into its veins.

Anonymous

Introduction to Part IV

IN PART III a macrocosmic view of the multiverse was mapped out using each of the creation stories to extract certain "universal concepts" to describe the origins of the creation and the history of the multiverse from various perspectives. In this section the microcosmic perspective will be added, giving readers a "bird's-eye view" of exactly how humanity's biomolecular body/brain/mind "bio-suit" was energetically and genetically designed and manipulated to collectively confine humanity within this three-dimensional holographic control system.

Unfortunately, the false belief systems humanity has been indoctrinated with and captured within since the beginning of programmed life on this planetary hologram, and the "predators' mind" embedded within our own, remain intact today. The intentionally collectively programmed beliefs of humanity hold our global civilizations, governmental structures, religious institutions and banking and monetary debt systems in place. All of which enslave humanity and serve to concentrate power among the planetary elite, the direct bloodline descendants of the reptilian Anunnaki colonizers and a faction of the higher-dimensional sub-creator gods who originally designed the holographic multidimensional worlds in the first place.

Our particular hologram was created through the manipulation of a vast sector of interstellar space wherein the sub-creator gods took a concave/convex light-reflecting plasma field creating geometric forms and molded them to form a gigantic lens in space/time which refracts light such that the world we see around us is simply captured, refracted, distorted photonic light and shadow, which in turn create the holographic images we perceive as the objectively solid three-dimensional world. To us the world appears magically real and solid. To the sub-creator gods, these holographic structures are tantamount to child's play! They created this programmed hologram and suspended it within the three-dimensional frequency range of space/time, as a staged learning sphere for Souls. Think of it as a galactic game-board for the creator gods, where we are the pieces they move around the game-board and they are the players, the forces of light battling the forces of darkness in the shadow worlds of the lower-dimensional holograms.

Chapter Nineteen focuses on the construction of the hologram and its human physical aspects. Chapter Twenty delves into the ways consciousness is manipulated across multiple dimensions.

Once we evolve to the point where we can perceive the unreality of the game and see through the illusory nature of the holograms, we'll be able to move beyond their confines.

Chapter Nineteen

The Construction of the Holographic Control System

BRUGH JOY, MD, referred to in Chapter Four, My Story, once said during a lecture, "We live in a school for gods in which we learn the consequences of thought in slow motion."

His statement reminds me of an experience I had many years ago during a class I was taking to become a certified medical hypnotist. The class instructor was demonstrating how to induce a hypnotic suggestion, and he was using the entire class as his subjects: he led us through a series of verbal suggestions structured of course in a particular way with specific vocal intonations, inferences and nonverbal cues—in other words, a group induction. He told us that in two minutes we would all get up from our chairs and try to lift them but they wouldn't budge because they would be glued to the floor. The class snickered and joked but then acted out this very scenario, myself included.

As I was bent over trying to lift my chair which wouldn't budge, I had the thought "This is ridiculous," and then my mind skipped back to the pre-induction knowledge that I lift and move objects around all the time, so of course I can lift this silly chair ... and immediately the chair lifted. As I stood looking around at my classmates, I was bemused by their antics in tugging, pulling and straining to lift their chairs while looking perplexed. Being acutely aware of my immediate experience juxtaposed with theirs, I was deeply struck by the power of spoken words, of modulated vocal expressions, bodily gestures, visual cues and verbal suggestions to suspend beliefs and/or implant false beliefs into the subconscious mind.

False beliefs are part of the "glue" that holds humanity hostage within this illusory three-dimensional world. The mind/brain interface observes the created world around us and, in the process of observing the external world, the meaning-making function of the split mind/brain projector transduces photonic light waves entering the eyes (the retinal cones) into the seemingly "objective" reality we observe and believe to be real. In Laura Knight-Jadczyk's book *High Strangeness*, she states:

> The mechanics of how such a holographic world operates was proposed by several physicists, one of which was J.A. Wheeler. He proposed ... that an observer watching the universe ... (actually) creates it in the process of observing it. (p. 318)

In other words, THE ACT OF OBSERVING THE PROJECTED WORLD OUTSIDE OF US IS ACTUALLY CREATING AND MAINTAINING THE HOLOGRAM. Each here-and-now moment of time being a nexus point of probabilities becoming actualities. In essence we are receivers/transducers of a projected reality generated from within our collective minds. The view of the world presented externally to us, the collective eye of human consciousness, is actually causing humanity to unknowingly maintain the hologram and the ongoing events in it. Knight-Jadzyk continues:

> As many physicists will tell you, all that really exists are "waveforms" and we are waveforms of reality, and our consciousness is something that "reads waves." We give form and structure to the waves we "read".... The view of the Cassiopaeans is that ... a paraphysical realm, another layer in the structure of space/time from which our own reality is projected (is) looping over and over again in endless variations ... with the hyperdimensional controllers acting from hyperdimensional space [the fourth, fifth and sixth dimensions] of which we have limited awareness and even less access.... Certain programmed life scenarios of great emotional content (are)

designed in order to produce the most "energy" for these ... [hyperdimensional controllers]. And it seems that pain and suffering are the "richest" in terms of "juice." (pp. 318–21)

What Knight-Jadzyk is saying here, unbelievable as it seems, is that the body/mind/brain bio-suit the Soul is contained within produces thoughts and emotions, energetic invisible electromagnetic "wave forms" in response to life events. Some positive and some negative depending on circumstances and our responses to them. Strong emotions emanating from the subtle emotional/energy body produce wave forms: large biophotonic light emissions and subtle electromagnetic sound frequencies that spread out into the third dimension (think of the concept of quantum entanglement) and bleed out into the fourth dimension where these energetic emissions are "eaten" or absorbed by the hyperdimensional controllers of our three-dimensional hologram.

Jay Alfred, author of *Brains and Realities*, in Chapter Seven "Deactivating the Brain," explains this same concept another way. He writes:

What exists out there, if we go by the findings of modern physics, is a superposed fluid reality—not the concrete reality generated by our biomolecular brain. This superposed state can be reached if no ... measurements are made by our sensory systems. This is extremely difficult to achieve in our decoherent biomolecular [split] brain which is fixated on this physical universe [the three-dimensional hologram].... Without an orientation to this three dimensional physical universe, the brain receives information from the next universe [the higher dimensions] via higher energy bodies. In a higher energy quantum-like universe, the wave function does not necessarily collapse. It continues to exist in a superposed state of void consciousness ... the absolute unitary state. In fact all elementary particles are in their absolute unitary state until observed in a particular context by a measuring instrument [the body/mind/brain]. (p. 58)

Beyond our brain-projected three-dimensional world is an ever-present, infinite quantum energetic field of fluid light and sound frequencies of varying densities corresponding to the seven planes of existence. Once the eternal Soul essence is born into a biological body, consciousness is confined within this atomic matter-based form and mistakenly perceives the world around it as an externalized objective matter-based reality through the biomolecular brain circuits. Alfred presents a view of the neurology that's involved:

> Neuroscientists have hypothesized seven fundamental cognitive operations in analyzing the operations of the brain as mind. These functions allow the mind to think, feel, experience, order and interpret events in the universe. (p. 56)

Basically these combined cognitive operations form a perceptual lens through which the mind makes sense of the world. Our split-brain binary perceptual system divides our perceived reality into pairs of opposites. Each perceptual split derives meanings from its contrasting opposite: light/dark, up/down, right/wrong, good/bad, past/future and self/other. David Icke has been explaining this perceptual anomaly to the reading public and to his conference attendees for decades. In his most recent book, *Phantom Self*, he describes our so-called solid objective world as a "giant computer simulation or a digital-holographic universe."

In his 2010 book, *Human Race, Get Off Your Knees*, Icke describes the human body as a receiver/transmitter of information connected, vibrationally and digitally, to the virtual-reality universe. The crucial element in transmitter/receiver technology is quartz crystal, and according to the work of Bruce Lipton, PhD, a cellular biologist, the membrane of every cell in the physical body is a liquid-crystal semiconductor. In Lipton's book *The Biology of Belief*, he explains that we have up to 75 trillion cells in our body, including our DNA which is also a crystalline structure. Its biomolecular structure is shaped in the form of a spiraling double helix that makes it a perfect receiver/transmitter, amplifying the frequencies of electromagnetic light that connect us into the virtual-reality hologram.

Quartz crystal has the ability to generate a fixed frequency and to convert vibrations into electromagnetic signals. The brain receives about 400 billion items of information every second. The body is a highly effective liquid-crystal conductor of electromagnetic signals as it is 70 percent water and has a salt/mineral content that enhances the electromagnetic transmission of visual images through the retina of the eyes into the visual cortex at the back of the brain—which then projects images as a three-dimensional hologram. The five senses decode the waveforms into electrical signals which the brain further decodes into the three-dimensional world we see as a projected digital pixilated construct.

In Richard L. Thompson's book *Maya: The World as Virtual Reality*, in Chapter One "Computers, Minds and Consciousness" (p. 23), he describes an interesting experiment. In this experiment, Silicon Graphics computers were used in the 1990s to demonstrate that subjects "placed in a high-quality, full-immersion, virtual-reality experiment will experience a three-dimensional simulated world that appears real to them." He goes on to describe experiments done with prosthetic eyes that have shown that it is possible for visual data to be perceived in a normal way, even though it enters the brain through unusual sensory channels:

> In the early 1970s Paul Bach-y-Rita developed a prosthetic eye using a low-resolution camera mounted on a blind person's glasses frame. The camera's signal generated a crude image in a 20x20 grid of tiny vibrators mounted on the person's belly or back.... It turned out that after a few hours of training, blind persons wearing this device could learn to read signs, identify objects and people's faces.... [T]actile information reaching the brain from nerves in the belly or back [was] ... used to create a conscious experience of vision. This suggests that detailed visual information from a virtual reality (a computer simulation) may give rise to normal visual perceptions in a subject, even if it is fed into the subject's brain through channels other than the optical nerves. (p. 24)

Technically speaking, one could unknowingly, or consciously and intentionally, deconstruct a pixilated, visually projected holographic image by reversing the entire process. Starting with the holographically projected image, looking directly and minutely into the image, you could see millions of tiny vibrating pixels that construct the images. Then observing further you could watch the pixels converting into vibrating electrical signals. Next they would dissolve from electrical vibrating particles into energetic wave forms, microscopic ghostlike vibrating light strings. Then these ethereal forms would disappear altogether and there would be nothing there—no visual image. This, amazingly, describes exactly the experience I had while on jury duty. If you remember, as I was sitting in the courtroom looking around, the solid walls began to visibly pixilate and vibrate. Millions of vibrating pixilated dots then morphed into etheric or transparent wave forms and then the walls disappeared altogether. You might call my experience "a transient malfunction of my brain/hologram interface" where I stepped outside of the virtual-reality three-dimensional illusion for a short time. Clearly, this feat wasn't consciously or intentionally induced. It happened quite accidentally while I was deeply engrossed in contemplating the ideas presented in Jane Roberts's book *The Nature of Personal Reality*. If humanity could gain conscious control of this deconstruction process, it would enable us to collectively dissolve this hologram of deception by moving beyond its confines.

Now to dive a little deeper into the body/mind/brain's structure by examining how the body/mind/brain produces the biochemical molecules of emotion, which are the energetic food sustaining our hyperdimensional overlords, along with our false belief systems of course. Excerpts from Knight-Jadczyk's *Debugging the Universe* set the stage:

> In 1984 breakthroughs in biochemistry enabled science to understand receptors (molecules) as a body-wide network of information; the biochemical basis of emotions.... Deoxyribonucleic acid also known as DNA is the fundamental molecule of life.... Each cell in the body contains multiple receptor molecules which constantly vibrate attaching and detaching from the surfaces of cells in response to chemical reactions. These receptors

function as sensing molecules at the cellular level just as our five senses act as sensory organs at the macro level in relationship to our external environment. Receptors are the first components of emotion... [A]ll receptors are proteins.... [P]roteins bind with ligands.... [L]igands are chemical keys ... which when attached to proteins ... create a chain reaction of biochemical events ... at the cellular level ... which translate to large changes in behavior, physical activity even mood.... The ligand receptor system['s] primary function [is] ... to move through extra-cellular space ... the blood and cerebrospinal fluid ... stimulating complex and fundamental changes in the cells....

Peptides are produced not just in the brain but all over the body and are composed of proteins, prime substances of photonic light.... They convey information to the cells of the body. They exist in the cortex of the brain and in the limbic system or emotional brain.... (pp. 207–21)

Candace Pert, in her book *Molecules of Emotion,* quoted by Knight-Jadczyk, states:

Emotional states or moods are produced by the various neuropeptide ligands, and what we experience as an emotion or a feeling is also a mechanism for activating a particular neuronal circuit—simultaneously throughout the brain and body—which generates a behavior involving the whole creature.... (p. 45)

Knight-Jadczyk continues by saying:

Emotions constantly regulate what we experience as reality. Research suggests that the nervous system scans the outer world for material that it is prepared to find by virtue of its already laid circuits, its internal patterns of past experiences including early imprinting in infancy. The superior colliculus in the midbrain ... controls the muscles that direct the eyeball and controls which images are permitted to fall on the retina. This means that an emotional center of the brain literally controls what we see [and how we interpret the events we see]. (p. 223)

There are three layers of the human brain representing different stages of evolution. The brain stem was the earliest to develop and is called the reptilian brain. No doubt humanity inherited many reptilian traits due to their genetic manipulations, adding some of their DNA to our ancient ape-species DNA. Remember in the Andromedan galactic history story, they referred to the reptilian races as the riff-raff, the criminal element in our galaxy, dumped here from another galaxy eons ago! The limbic system of the brain came second and is called the mammalian brain. The last or most recent system to develop evolutionarily speaking is the cerebral cortex, the forebrain, the seat of reason also known as the neomammalian brain. It is in the frontal lobes through the process of thinking, reasoning, awareness and the use of willpower that the emotional and physiological responses to experience are retained in the neural networks. The higher qualities of empathy, love, compassion, unselfishness and service-to-others behaviors are developed in the neocortex or forebrain.

The lower vibrational frequencies or "survival responses" are generated from the oldest and most primitive portion of the brain, the brain stem, often called the R-complex or the reptilian complex. This "reptilian complex" was described by Carl Sagan in his original 1977 book, *The Dragons of Eden: Speculations on the Evolution of Human Intelligence*. The reptilian brain or R-complex is the most primitive area of the brain and is where the most animalistic, instinctual, primal, predatory responses come from. Such traits as aggression, cold-blooded killing, torture, ritualistic behaviors, compulsions, addictions, rigidity, hierarchical status, obsessions, sexual aggression, pathological jealousy, warlike competition and desire for dominance, power and control. All these behaviors are primitive survival/fear-based emotional responses. The activation of any of these intense primitive emotional responses can cause the R-complex (the survival instincts) to override the more rational functioning of the more recently developed prefrontal cortex and can result in unpredictable, chaotic, aggressive, murderous behaviors. Remember that the Andromedans mentioned that they avoid the human species as much as possible due to our generally unpredictable, often violent intense emotional reactions, which the Andromedan race finds alarming and incomprehensible.

Jay Alfred, in further describing how the body/mind/brain interface works, states in *Brains and Realities*:

> The parietal lobes are associated with the orientation of the body in space and processing information about time and space.... The left superior parietal lobe creates the perception of the physical body's boundaries.... Blocked off from neuronal activity, the parietal lobe cannot create a sensation of a boundary between the physical body and the outside world, which may explain the meditator's sense of oneness with the universe, say Newberg and d'Aquili [neuroscientists from the University of Pennsylvania School of Medicine who presented results of their findings in their book, *The Mystical Mind: Probing the Biology of Religious Experiences*]. (pp. 53–54)

In other words, when neuronal activity is suspended in the parietal lobes, the neuroscientists discovered that a person either in deep meditation or a drug-induced blockage perceives themselves as endless, everywhere present and intimately connected with All That Is, having the sensation of infinity and timelessness that feels absolutely real to that person. With this understanding of how the brain/mind creates the sense perception of a separate self, it becomes clear that our perception of ourselves as separate beings arises as a byproduct of the brain/mind's spatial and temporal perception located in the parietal and frontal lobes of the brain. Hence THE PERSONAL "I," THE SEPARATE SELF OF THE EGO, ARISES AS A BYPRODUCT OF SPATIAL AND TEMPORAL PERCEPTION GENERATED IN THE PARIETAL AND FRONTAL LOBES OF THE BRAIN, which in turn creates the space/time matrix, the illusory brain-projected three-dimensional holo-gram.

Knight-Jadczyk concludes her discussion of how the mind operates in *Debugging the Universe:*

> The mind is not material yet it has an interface system with the body and this is the neurochemical network. The mind of the body is the Predator's mind, connected to strings like a marionette with the strings in the hands of the fourth density puppet masters—the Control System. (p. 224)

To repeat Knight-Jadczyk's statement, "THE MIND OF THE BODY IS THE PREDATOR'S MIND." This is the "FOREIGN IN-STALLATION" that was so insightfully referred to by the Yaqui sha-man Don Juan Matus, while instructing his student Carlos Castaneda in the ways of the "real but invisible world" and in the "deceitful ways of the predators" which he sometimes refers to in his books as "the flyers." Here are some excerpts of Don Juan's quotes from Castaneda's book *The Active Side of Infinity*, from the chapter on "Inorganic Awareness":

> There exists in the universe a perennial force, which the sorcerers of ancient Mexico called the dark sea of aware-ness ... responsible not only for the awareness of organ-isms, but for the awareness of entities that don't have an organism.... [T]he old shamans discovered that the en-tire universe is composed of twin forces ... at the same time opposed and complementary to each other.... [O]ur world is a twin world ... populated by beings that have awareness but not an organism: ... inorganic beings. [F]or this reason, the old shamans called them inorganic beings.... [T]wo types of awareness coexist without ever impinging on each other because each type is entire-ly different from the other.... [T]he universe at large is crammed to the brim with worlds of awareness, organic and inorganic. (pp. 189–90)

He concludes by explaining to his student Carlos that all cognition is a "closed interpretation system" that puts limits and sets parameters to possibility. In other words our cognitive faculties, our so-called objective thinking mind, is "their mind"—which imprisons us within a closed system of cognition/perception that is not real, that is projected and maintained by us collectively as the virtual-reality world.

This same message has been given to humanity by the ancient sages of Hinduism and Buddhism, except that they call it maya/illusion instead of a digital, holographically created universe.

Similar to the shamanic and Eastern explanations for this phenomenon is the Gnostic worldview described in Chapter Eleven. In their texts they describe two different forms of Archons. One form they describe as a large amoeba-like unicellular organism inhabiting interstellar space, functioning like a form of electrical capacitor that constantly absorbs energy. These organisms are called by some shamans "sky fish." NASA and a few independent astronomy buffs with the necessary advanced photo equipment have taken infrared photos of these creatures in space and have posted the images on the internet. Don Juan calls an earthly interdimensional version of the second type of Archon "flyers." The shamans and the ancient Gnostics both describe them as interdimensional energetic intelligences that can take on various forms: a predatory cybernetic group of shapeshifters with a hive intelligence; mind parasites, technologically skilled at mimicry and replication.

The Gnostic texts state that Yaldabaoth, the fallen demented reptilian demiurge, and these Archontic beings, existed long before our particular planetary system was ever formed. As their story goes, you'll recall that they conspired to deviate the Aeonic creator god Sophia's original design blueprint for the divine Anthropos: the organic, living, divinely intelligent light beings (Souls), carriers of the life-force/essence of God within them, which were being formed within the Pleroma, the plasmasphere of fullness, the subatomic realm from which the galaxies were formed. Yaldabaoth and the Archons, watching the Aeon Sophia's miraculous creation from the Kenoma—a lower-vibrational realm of darkness, chaos and nothingness in interstellar space—became jealous and envious, knowing that they lacked this divine essence of living light which had been encoded into the Anthropos template. They captured the divine Anthropos blueprint containing the essences (the Souls), disconnected them from Source and locked them into simulated worlds by deviating their original divine DNA template, blocking their pure conscious awareness, separating them from unity with the Supreme Creator and placing them into lower-dimensional holograms.

As described previously, humans are of two minds: higher intuitive intelligent awareness, which is the direct knowing awareness of the Soul, the true Self of unity consciousness, and "their mind": a lower-vibrating, dense, negating, separating, judging ego/mind, the split-brain consciousness of the body/mind bio-suit that was superimposed upon the original Anthropos template, thus creating the original split of unity consciousness into duality consciousness locked into a body. The lower mind includes the constructed ego/mind/intellect of the personality self, operative from the top of the causal plane through all planes below it. This is the "false or illusory self" described in the sacred Vedic and Buddhist texts and in the teachings of the Saints and Masters, the same "mind parasites" described by the Gnostics in their sacred texts, and the same "foreign installation" or "predator's mind" described by Don Juan Matus to Carlos Castaneda.

Referring back to Don Juan's concept of "the flyers"—the dark forces—there are hyperdimensional realms beyond our capacity to see or be aware of due to humanity's blocked perceptual capacities. However, we know of the existence of these realms from those who have developed the capacity to see into them—the shamans, remote viewers, psychics, yogins, avatars, saints and masters. There exists a hierarchy of higher-density beings or deities (light beings) that are divided or split by their intentions into two categories. The Abrahamic religions refer to them as angels and demons. The Elohim/Ra group refers to them as service to self (STS) or service to other (STO) beings, Hindu religions refer to these deities as Adityas and Danavas. The positive STO beings (angels) are light beings, solar deities, bearers of light and light emitters. The negative STS beings (demons) are the dark Archontic forces, the "predatory light eaters."

Don Juan further explains to Castaneda that shamans can see humanity's subtle-energy bodies:

He explained that sorcerers see infant human beings as strange luminous balls of energy, covered from the top to the bottom with a glowing coat, something like a plastic cover that is adjusted tightly over their cocoon of energy. He said that that coat of awareness was what the predators consumed, and that when a human being reached adulthood, all that was left of that glowing coat of awareness was a narrow fringe that went from the ground to the top of the toes.... That fringe permitted mankind to continue living but only barely.... [T]his narrow fringe of awareness was the epicenter of self-reflection, where man was irremediably caught. By playing on our self-reflection, which is the only point of awareness left to us, the predators create flares of awareness that they proceed to consume in a ruthless predatory fashion, and in this manner they keep us alive in order for them to be fed with the energetic flare of our pseudo-concerns. (pp. 220–21)

He goes on to explain that humanity's narrow range of awareness is centered on the mental and emotional processes of self-referencing (egocentrism—the only point of awareness left to humans), which is the reason humanity is unknowingly trapped. By confining humanity within this narrow frequency range of self-referencing awareness, and by manipulating humans into producing stress, anxiety, anger and fear-based reactions, the mind predators manipulate humans into producing "flares of energy" [photonic light] which they consume. (Beyond this structural setup, specific techniques of manipulation will be expanded upon in Chapter 20.)

Don Juan continues by declaring:

Man the magical [divine] being he was originally designed to be, is no longer magical.... [H]e is an average piece of meat.... [I]f the mind predators don't eat our glowing coat of awareness for a while ... it'll keep on growing.... Shamans discovered that through mental disciplines and silencing all thought, they could keep the predators' mind at bay long enough for their glowing coat of awareness to grow back to its original volume. In this way the "foreign installation" would flee, allowing the practitioner of these maneuvers the total certainty of the mind's "foreign origin"; and, furthermore, with regular practice of these maneuvers, the predators' mind would eventually flee permanently. In this way the shamans were able to vanquish the mind of the predator. They were able to see, to know, and to refuse to honor agreements which they never consciously agreed to participate in ... such as consenting to having their glowing coats of awareness consumed by these predatory beings. (pp. 221–25)

The saints, avatars and shamans from various traditions, each using their own style of linguistic expression, jointly express the same concept; i.e., that all embodied souls have been captured within the lower-dimensional holograms, and our energies of consciousness are being used to maintain them. Through the Soul/essence consciousness encapsulated within the mind/body/spirit bio-suit, the constructed ego/self energetically and unknowingly projects each embodied being's personal emotions, feelings, most intimate thoughts, experiences and beliefs into the energetic quantum information field, perpetuating this vast intricate control system—this energetic, chaotic, virtual-reality whirlpool of constant motion and emotional turmoil—where humans are the prey and the ego/mind is the predator. How clever and devious of those sub-creator gods to have devised such a complex, intimate and hidden control system projecting the entire planetary solar system around us in three-dimensional living color, light and sound. Then, adding further to our entrapment, implanting their predatory minds inside our own. Thus we are of two minds—the lower one of which perpetuates the illusion of our collective confinement within this one tiny holographic portion of the vast multiverse.

Remember in the Elohim/Ra group's creation story, the Elohim described themselves as the "creator gods" of the physical universe from tenth density (a very high, subtle-vibrational-frequency realm) who are immortal/eternal as they live beyond the space/time continuum. They stated their function was to interface with Earth, coordinate Sun and star systems, and work with life forms throughout various densities representing different levels of consciousness defined by vibrational frequencies. They said they created the initial templates for life in space through the projection of anchor points and the spinning of energy through them creating rudimentary holograms of congealed light. Then, to solidify the light forms projected into these holograms, they created interlocking holograms. I think their explanation resonates with the scientific explanation below of the formation of the universe.

Quantum plasma, an expression of intelligent energy, makes up 99.99 percent of the observable universe. Plasma has the ability to self-organize and shift massive electrical fields that generate intergalactic environmental changes over interstellar distances. These vast cosmic plasma fields are carriers of photonic light energy in the form of electricity that generates huge arcing plasma filaments. When electrical currents pass through these plasma filaments, the interaction causes them to spiral around each other, creating strings of filaments known as "Birkeland currents" (named after a Norwegian physicist and researcher). These currents create massive rotating energetic torsion fields—some of which are light years across. Doesn't this scientific description of the intergalactic creational process remind you of the activities described by the Elohim/Ra creator gods and of the Gnostics' description of the activities of the twelve paired Aeonic creator gods?

These electrically charged, massively circulating cosmic plasma fields are the energetic precursors at the subatomic level of all forms of matter. They birth all particalized matter forms—the galaxies, the Sun, the stars, all planetary bodies—and they animate all biological organisms through rotating electromagnetic currents. This includes the massive macrocosmic interstellar energy fields of star nurseries birthing stars and the microcosmic processes that operate through all sentient life forms, including the humanoid species.

David Talbott and Wallace Thornhill, in their book *Thunderbolts of the Gods*, quoted in *Remember Who You Are* by David Icke, state:

From the smallest particle to the largest galactic formation, a web of electrical circuitry connects and unites
all of nature, organizing galaxies, energizing stars, giving birth to planets and, on our own world, controlling
weather and animating biological organisms. There are
no isolated islands in an electric universe. (p. 63)

This electrical emanation of the universe connects everything
through a tapestry of interconnected electrical plasma waveforms, torsion fields, mathematical and geometric algorithms and electromagnetic fractal, holographic templates which form galaxies, planets, stars, the
subtle dimensions and all physically and interdimensionally manifested
species, humanoid or otherwise. The human body also emits plasma
waves (Birkeland currents) which form subtle electrical toroidal fields
around the body such that when two humans are in close proximity,
their fields link automatically and unconsciously. With conscious awareness and intention, individual consciousness can be extended into the
quantum consciousness field and be in instant communication with any
life form anywhere in the multiverse. The geo-electromagnetic field of
Earth and the bio-electromagnetic field of the body are intimately interconnected and are in constant communication at the subtlest levels,
which the Heart Math Institute has been able to measure with highly
sensitive technical measuring instruments implanted at various sites on
the planet.

The human brain/heart's electrical activity mimics the electrical
activity of the planet. The human aura emits electromagnetic currents
running through the energetic nadis and meridians, through the central
nervous system and throughout the energetic chakra system of the etheric body. The physical and subtle bodies are electrical receiver/transmit-
ters. The magnetosphere that surrounds the Earth could be described as
a plasmasphere, a bubble or electromagnetic net. This holographically
projected three-dimensional electromagnetic net of illusion has effectively disconnected us from the conscious awareness of our eternal Soul
Self and our connectedness to pure consciousness/intelligent energy
which is present everywhere in the multiverse. It is the medium we live
in, albeit unconsciously and unknowingly. Within our space/time ho-

logram, a "veil" was drawn down over the consciousness of humanity, as described in the Elohim/Ra group's creation story and as "the illusion of separation or maya" described in the teachings of the Saints and Masters. This net of illusion is projected from within the human body/mind/brain's visual cortex outward 360 degrees and is what creates and maintains the illusion of our seemingly solid three-dimensional world.

Essentially, the Elohim/Ra narrative tells of a group of divine light beings, sub-creator gods, who created the templates for all life forms from within the galactic center and set them in motion throughout the intergalactic plasmasphere. Originally the design and intent of the sub-creator gods (also called Aeons/pleromic light beings) were for humanity—the divine Anthropos—to live in a paradisiacal unified light realm. The original Anthropos design template included the "divine intelligence" of the Supreme Creator expressed through an organically light-encoded living form containing the life/essence of the Supreme Creator.

Much later on in the creational evolvement of the multiverse, numerous technologically advanced intergalactic races evolved prior to the creation of the humanoid species. These races include the Lyrans, Pleiadians, Vegans, Andromedans, Cassiopaeans, Orions, Arcturians and others. All of whom made genetic alterations in the humanoid DNA over eons of evolutionary cycles. Each of these races have their own version of the intergalactic creation story. Many of the more evolved intergalactic races refer to planet Earth as a "living library," meaning a living genetic pool of twenty-two different races, containing the original DNA template set in motion by the sub-creator gods (the Aeons) within the Milky Way Galaxy. At some point in the evolutionary trajectory of the multiverse the humanoid species was deviated. The lower, analytical, thinking mind coupled with the egotistical/personality self is the "false self" which attached itself to us and through which we have been deceived into believing is our own self instead of the Soul, the One True Self, the God Self we truly are, as described in all the sacred texts and in the teachings of the Saints and Masters.

Remember the first *Matrix* movie where Morpheus tells Neo:

> The matrix is everywhere. It is all around us, even now
> in this very room. You can see it when you look out your

window, or you turn on your television. You can feel it
when you go to work, when you go to church, when you
pay your taxes. It is the world that has been pulled over
your eyes to blind you from the truth. What truth? That
you are a slave, you were born into bondage ... born into
a prison you cannot smell, or taste or touch. A prison for
your mind. (web)

Here is the TRUTH cleverly wrapped in the cloak of fiction. Art
forms can express deep symbolic ideals and truths, and can package
these concepts—incomprehensible to the ego/mind—in creative ways
that can bypass the conscious mind, the lower analytical ego/mind. Of
course, their "mind within us" would promptly reject such a concept as
impossible or ridiculous just as the ego/mind (their mind within us) has
been programmed to do: reject the real and cling to the unreal.

This three-dimensional virtual-reality world constitutes a "Master
Game" whom the opposing factions of creator gods devised for their
own amusement and creative play, which they claim they did benignly to
ostensibly "speed the evolutionary trajectory of the humanoid species."
Humans are, as Rudolf Steiner so aptly stated, "the religion of the gods."
The sub-creator gods described in a number of creation stories worship
us because we are the living puppets that populate and energetically perpetuate their designed holographic Master Game. Even though the cards
have been stacked against us and the game has been rigged, as we wake
up we will collectively join together and begin dissolving this hologram
of deception by transcending the ego/mind, the false, limited, illusory
self. By beginning this inner sacred journey of the heart, reconnecting
with our true eternal Soul Self, we can transcend the lower holograms
of deception.

Robert S. de Ropp, a biochemist and author of *The Master Game:
Pathways to Higher Consciousness*, writes:

Seek above all for a game worth playing. Such is the ad-
vice of the oracle to modern man. Having found the
game, play it with intensity—play as if your life and
sanity depended on it. (They do depend on it.) ... The

Master Game is played entirely in the inner world, a vast and complex territory about which men know very little. The name of the game is true awakening, full development of the powers latent in man. The game can only be played by people whose observations of themselves and others have led them to a certain conclusion, namely, that man's ordinary state of consciousness, his so-called waking state, is not the highest level of consciousness of which he is capable. In fact, this state is so far from real awakening that it could appropriately be called a form of somnambulism, a condition of "waking sleep." Once a person has reached this conclusion ... a new appetite develops within him, the hunger for real awakening, for full consciousness. He realizes that he sees, hears and knows only a tiny fraction of what he could see, hear and know, that he lives in the poorest, shabbiest of the rooms in his inner dwelling, but that he could enter other rooms, beautiful and filled with treasures, the windows of which look out on eternity and infinity. (pp. 11, 21)

All these negative deities or forces—Yahweh, Lucifer and the fallen angels, Yaldabaoth and the Archons, Kal/Kali (the Negative Power and their sons, Brahma, Vishnu and Shiva), the Danavas, the Hindu Serpent Demon/gods and the Buddhist Mara—call them what you will—are thought-form projections, representations of the negating forces of creation, energetic forces that attempt to dupe and block humanity from evolving beyond the lower-dimensional inner planes of the astral and causal. All these lower dimensions are under the control of these negative forces or sub-creator gods. To use the Sant Mat Masters' terminology, the creator god Kal (the Negative Power) and his subordinate creator-god/sons—Brahma, Vishnu and Shiva (the Lords of Karma)—are the administrators, rulers and controllers of these lower-dimensional realms which are their exclusive domain.

When we die and leave the body, we are taught through the world's religions to believe we are either going to heaven or hell, or will have to reincarnate due to our karmas or will be merging forever into the eternal light of God's heavenly light realm at the time of the resurrection of all Souls. If you are a materialist, you believe you will simply cease to exist at death. All are false beliefs masquerading as truth! Only those who can traverse the inner dimensions know this. Those inorganic, shapeshifting, Archontic, cybernetic administrators meet us, greet us and welcome us as soon as we leave the physical body and enter the astral plane. Masquerading as angelic light beings, our heavenly guides, our guardians or the agents of Satan, depending on our beliefs, direct us through a "life review" in the astral realms. This is another reason to develop an inner life through meditation so that with inner practice, at death one may pass beyond the astral plane, beyond these control systems.

All human lives and actions are holographically recorded in the etheric quantum information field containing the space/time records of all activity of each and every individuated Soul within the three lower-dimensional physical, astral and causal worlds. These records are selectively played back to us by the cybernetic administrators of these worlds, operating under their overlords known as the Lords of Karma. With a focus on humanity's failures and shortcomings, feelings of unworthiness, sinfulness, etc., these feelings are gently and surreptitiously used to elicit shame and guilt feelings and the need for reconciliation/reparation/correction. Then the disembodied Souls are gently but firmly bidden to agree to another supposedly freely chosen incarnation in one of their three-dimensional virtual-reality worlds. Our beliefs, such as believing we are unworthy, entrap us as we try again and again in lifetime after lifetime to become "worthy" of God's love, to become perfect beings "earning through our efforts" the right to ascend into the heavenly spiritual realms by being good, loving and caring beings while embodied. Of course with all memories of past-life experiences and previously learned life lessons erased, we are locked onto the ever-revolving wheel of reincarnation within this space/time holographic virtual world. We are born repeatedly, kind of like *Groundhog Day*, into repetitive lives preprogrammed with yet more pain, suffering, loss and confusion within these illusory holograms of deception.

Quite the Virtual-Reality Master Game, eh! And all for the entertainment, amusement and power accrual of a contingent of negative creator gods—those "fallen ones" who in their desire to create got trapped by their desire to possess their creations and themselves fell (or were banished) into the lower dimensions they created and control. They devolved into self-serving demiurges desiring to supplant the Supreme Creator and be worshipped as God themselves. Thus they created the self-perpetuating mind-controlled space/time holograms of deception, domination and control. We are living in their deviated creation and we need to wake up and see the Master Game for what it is so we can learn methods for transcending it. This message has been repeatedly told to us by the Saints and Masters of all ages and preserved in their sacred texts.

In the lower dimensions of consciousness, the Soul is effectively blocked through the ego/mind (the predator's mind in us) from evolving beyond these lower dimensions due to the false beliefs programmed and imprinted through the body/mind and the memory erasure that occurs between each incarnation to ensure we don't develop or retain the critical knowledge or the capacity to discern the truth of our situation. We are programmed to accept what we are taught from birth. Thus the negative powers control us not only in embodied physical life but through our before-and-after lives as well. By redirecting us back into the lower dimensions—the physical, astral and causal realms—again and again, under the cause/effect karmic laws and the consequences of our actions while incarnated, Souls are essentially blocked from remembering our true eternal, divine nature.

If humanity were able to have direct knowledge and full memory of its divine origins, its divine Essence, and be reconnected with the Soul Self within, we would then be able to transcend the reincarnational trap of the lower dimensions and would no longer be under the control of these negative creator gods—who would lose their stolen, subverted energy, their power supply of enslaved Souls who unknowingly perpetuate their insane, greedy, cruel, destructive, usurious virtual worlds through our every thought and action. Our perceived suffering, through false perceptions and beliefs imprinted in the brain/mind and via DNA transfer at conception, is the energetic juice, the photonic light energy that sustains these negative sub-creator gods.

So far, they've done an outstanding job of deceiving humanity and of installing their demiurgic tendencies into the humanoid DNA template as the egoic mind. In the Sant Mat Masters' version of the creation story, Kabir told his initiate Dharam Das that Kal, the Negative Power, was expelled from the pure spiritual realms of eternity and confined to the lower physical, astral and causal regions for his negative, deceitful actions and for his greed and desire to control all creation. Kabir told his initiate during their dialogues in *The Ocean of Love* that "The Negative Power rules by encapsulating and controlling the lower regions thereby standing opposite to infinity/eternity and opposite to the Godhead."

Reference Keys: Alfred (2006). Castaneda (1998). de Ropp (1968). Groundhog (web). Icke (2012, 2016). Kabir (1982). Knight-Jadczyk (2008, 2012). L/L (1984). Lash (2006). Lipton (2005). Matrix (web). Newberg (1999). Pert (1997). Roberts (1982). Sagan (1986). Steiner (web-c). Talbott (2005). Thompson (2003). Thunderbolts (web).

Chapter Twenty

Interdimensional Manipulation of Consciousness

AS DESCRIBED IN the previous chapter, we live within a very narrow frequency band of perception. The outer five senses turn waveform information into electromagnetic frequencies that act as "frequency fences" forming and limiting our perceptions to the three-dimensional hologram. Once we develop an understanding of expanded states of awareness, knowing they do exist, we can then begin developing the capacity to access the higher dimensions and perceive beyond this hologram of deception. This chapter includes numerous accounts of human experiences in other dimensions. The goal here is to expand your possibility parameters in reading about reports of experiences that stretch the mind's ability to embrace and include possibilities beyond the ordinary.

Since every part of the hologram contains a miniature version of the whole within it, the Soul encased in the physical body is a "moveable hologram" and contains the entire multiverse within its consciousness. The electrical activity in the brain actually mimics the electrical activity in the multiverse. We are in the universe and the entire universe is in us. All dimensions of form-life were created out of pure consciousness. Everything is conscious because all there is is consciousness in all its infinite manifestations and forms, be they subtle-energetic etheric light forms or matter-based forms.

Different dimensions of consciousness resonate at different electromagnetic frequencies or vibrational rates even though they all interpenetrate each other like radio waves. Numerous names and descriptions of these dimensions or planes of existence have been described in Part I and in the various creation stories, in sacred religious texts, esoteric writings, the teachings of the Masters, and indigenous shamanic traditions. There are minor differences and disparities in the terminologies used to describe the various dimensions. These dimensions of consciousness vary in frequency and in density, with the physical plane of existence representing the slowest of frequencies and the densest of energies appearing as congealed matter. The terms "dimensions" and "planes" have slightly different meanings: the dimensions are subtle gradients of consciousness existing within each plane or sphere of existence.

Vibrational rates can be considered to exist within mathematically and geometrically precise, narrow bands of frequencies. Each frequency band extends outward multidirectionally to its boundary, and at the boundary point there are overlapping frequencies somewhat like radio frequencies that bleed into each other. This is one way of expressing boundary divisions between different levels or dimensions of conscious awareness. Dimensions can be conceptualized as moving from the slower, denser, opaque, compacted vibrations of physical matter to ever more refined gradations of higher, lighter, faster, transparent frequency vibrations of the purely spiritual realms. The Saints and Masters describe them as levels or planes of existence having different admixtures or gradations of pure spirit/pure consciousness intermixed with varying degrees of subtle etheric energy, with the densest level being physical matter where conscious awareness slowly develops. For a full explanation of the this model of the universe and its division into planes as taught by the Sant Mat Masters, please refer to Chapter Four in *The Path of the Masters* titled "The Creation and Order of the Universe."

All of the planes/dimensions are enfolded within the construct of the multiverse. To understand from a more scientific perspective, consider David Bohm's explanation in *Wholeness and the Implicate Order*, Chapter Seven "The Enfolding-Unfolding Universe and Consciousness":

> In the implicate order the totality of existence is enfolded within each region of space/time. So, whatever part, element, or aspect we may abstract in thought (or unfold), this still enfolds the whole and is therefore intrinsically

related to the totality from which it has been abstracted. Thus wholeness permeates all that is ... and both cosmos and consciousness is a single unbroken totality of movement. (pp. 218–19)

Holding in consciousness the concept of "interdimensional," we can proceed to the material in this chapter which focuses on the testimony of numerous individuals in various settings, giving documented examples of the numerous and nefarious ways humanity has been and continues to be manipulated and deceived by various types of interdimensional beings from beyond our three-dimensional world.

The ancient Gnostics were fully aware of the Archons and the reptilian races and wrote of them around 100 BCE. Fast forward to the 1990s when Carlos Castaneda—briefly mentioned in Chapter Nineteen's discussion of the structure of the hologram—encounters certain inorganic alien beings while in the company of Don Juan. Moving more deeply into interdimensional manipulation of consciousness: Castaneda doesn't believe that such beings could even exist and is horrified when the shaman begins to educate him about their presence and shows him how to see them. The shaman explains:

We have a predator that came from the depths of the cosmos and took over the rule of our lives. Human beings are its prisoners. The predator is our lord and master. It has rendered us docile, helpless. If we want to protest, it suppresses our protest. If we want to act independently, it demands that we don't do so.... [T]he predators have given us our systems of beliefs, our ideas of good and evil, our social mores. They are the ones who set up our hopes and expectations, our dreams of success or failure. They have given us covetousness, greed and cowardice. It is the predators who make us complacent, routinary and egomaniacal. (pp. 218–20)

As described in the previous chapter, shamans call this alien mind "THE FOREIGN INSTALLATION" which exists in every embodied human being. The true authentic mind of humanity is part of divine cosmic intelligence, the consciousness of the Supreme Creator that pervades all dimensions. But due to the intrusion of the Archontic predators and the meddling of the intergalactic races with humanoid DNA, the mind/brain was deviated, hijacked and infiltrated by these inorganic lower-consciousness imitators. The Gnostics warned humanity in their writings that the Archons had invaded the human psyche mentally, psychologically, emotionally and astrally. According to the Gnostics, these Archontic beings are shapeshifters, able to move about interdimensionally to confront, control and frighten humans both physically and astrally.

Don Juan, after explaining all this to Castaneda, shows him ways and means of discerning their presence and gives him some strategies to guard against this alien intrusion. Don Juan tells Castaneda: sorcerers of ancient times "found out that if they taxed the flyers mind with 'inner silence,' the foreign installation would flee, giving to any one of the practitioners involved in this maneuver the total certainty of the mind's foreign origin..." (p. 225).

In other words, the realization that another's collective mind is operating in our minds only becomes fully understandable once the "foreign installation" has been exposed and expelled from within. Only then can we come to realize, know and accept that the original authentic higher divine mind of the soul is not the same as the lower deviated ego/mind that we have erroneously been duped into believing belongs to us and is exclusively ours alone. This is the true message the Gnostics were trying to give to humanity back in 100 BCE through their sacred written texts and the teachings of their Phosters or Masters. Their texts were burned and the Gnostics were brutally murdered to repress these so-called "heretical" teachings. The main aim and effect of Archontic intrusion is to block humanity from its original pure Soul awareness, stop its divine evolutionary trajectory and keep the Soul locked into the lower holograms of deceptive illusion.

Remember in the Sant Mat Masters' creation story, Kabir gives similar information to his initiate Dharam Das, though he uses different terminology to explain this deceitful setup of Kal—the Negative Power—who Kabir says created and controls the physical, astral and causal planes of existence by encapsulating the lower regions of space/time in matter. Kabir told his initiate that Kal is the individualized mind in each embodied Soul and that Kal created duality/polarity, the ego/mind and all mental concepts and beliefs as thought forms projected from the lower mind, which, by their opposing nature, create divisiveness among humanity and among religious and scientific communities, generating ongoing arguments, wars and killing over opposing conceptualizations and beliefs.

Each and every visual symbolic image, our language, our collective beliefs, all create divisive thought structures within the three-dimensional hologram. All structured beliefs held in the mind of humanity are designed to maintain the illusion of separation. These thought forms and emotions are invisibly projected beyond one's supposedly private inner space into the ether, the datasphere, the quantum information field of the collective consciousness. There, the thought forms take on a separate, sometimes wavering and fuzzy, sometimes clear and perfectly formed, existence as wave forms in space/time. This thinking/projection process further reinforces the concept of the self/other dichotomy where every object is seen as a thing separate from the self, reinforcing the false belief in our separateness from All That Is and from other evolving dimensions of consciousness in the etheric, astral, causal and supercausal levels of consciousness.

Again, all these phenomena occur within multiple interpenetrating dimensions—making it possible for maneuvers in subtle realms to affect the actions, thoughts, and feelings of those inhabiting the denser realms. Amplifying our awareness of the interpermeability of these dimensions can help make us more aware of the consequences of our thoughts and actions. Two writers who've been especially helpful on this topic are Graham Hancock and Michael Talbot.

Hancock and his wife, Santha Faiia, authors of *Heaven's Mirror*, state:

> [O]ur world is not real at all but rather a sinister sort of virtual reality game in which we are all players, a complex and cunning illusion capable of confusing even the most thorough empirical tests—a mass hallucination capable of extraordinary depth and power designed to distract

souls from the straight and narrow path of awakening which leads to immortal life. (pp. 144–45)

Talbot in *The Holographic Universe* goes into great depth in explaining out-of-body experiences as holographic phenomena. He states:

[I]n a holographic universe, location is itself an illusion. Things and objects possess no definite location as everything is ultimately nonlocal, including consciousness. Basically we are at heart a vibrational pattern consisting of many interacting and resonating frequencies not contained in the brain, but in a photographic quantum energy field that both permeates and surrounds the physical body. (pp. 234–36)

Sri Aurobindo, the Indian mystic whose many books on the nature of consciousness are quoted in several chapters here, stated in *On Yoga* (excerpted from Talbot's *The Holographic Universe*):

...to plumb the subtler, implicate regions of the psyche requires a shift of attention. He discovered, through meditation, a vast inner territory: "a realm beyond space and time composed of a multicolored infinity of vibrations peopled by nonphysical beings so far in advance of human consciousness that they make us look like children.... These beings can take on any form at will and in their truest form these beings appear as pure vibration. (pp. 262–64)

Others have entered these same vast inner regions through the use of entheogens or psychoactive agents such as ayahuasca, peyote or psilocybin mushrooms, which have been in use throughout history and are used in mystical or shamanic contexts to enhance healing, transcendence, and revelation and to open the inner vision. These inner regions have been well traveled by shamans from every culture and civilization in the world. They utilized entheogens in their sacred practices to open gateways into the inner dimensions of consciousness and have brought back many corroborating accounts of the existence of interdimensional realms and the manipulation of human consciousness by the inhabitants of these realms.

For example, Talbot in *The Holographic Universe* describes in detail anthropologist Michael Harner's experience of entering these inner realms under the influence of ayahuasca. The following is an excerpted version of his experiences:

> In 1960 the American Museum of Natural History sent Harner on a year-long expedition [to the Peruvian Amazon] to study the Conibo, and while there, he asked the Amazonian natives to tell him about their beliefs. They told him that if he really wanted to learn, he had to take a shamanic sacred drink made from a hallucinogenic plant known as *ayahuasca*, "the soul vine." He agreed, and after drinking the bitter concoction had an out-of-body experience in which he traveled a level of reality populated by what appeared to be the gods and devils of the Conibo's mythology. He saw demons with grinning crocodilian heads. He watched as an "energy-essence" rose up out of his chest and floated toward a dragon-headed ship manned by Egyptian-style figures with blue-jay heads.... But the most dramatic experience he had during his spirit journey was an encounter with a group of winged, dragonlike beings that emerged from his spine. After they had crawled out of his body, they "projected" a visual scene in front of him in which they showed him what they said was the "true" history of the Earth. (p. 267)

They telepathically explained to him that they were responsible for both the origin and evolution of life on the planet and showed him magnificent panoramic images of hundreds of millions of years of evolutionary activity in a vivid colorful display that was unimaginable. They told him they resided not only in humans but in all life and had created the multitude of living forms that populate the Earth to provide themselves with "a hiding place" from some undisclosed enemy in outer space. They also stated that "humans were but their receptacles and servants."

After his vision ended and he recovered normal consciousness, he sought out a blind elder, a respected shaman in the village, and questioned him about the dragon-like beings and their claim that they were the true masters of the Earth. The shaman smiled with amusement and said, "Oh, they're always saying that. But they are only the Masters of Outer Darkness" (p. 267).

Talbot provides many other examples and direct quotes from individuals who had out-of-body experiences or who had traversed the inner planes. Here is a quote from George Russell, a well-known turn-of-the-century Irish seer who reported seeing many "beings of light" during his journeys to the inner worlds, reported in *The Fairy-Faith in Celtic Countries* by W. Y. Evans-Wentz (excerpted from *The Holographic Universe*):

> There was at first a dazzle of light.... [T]hen I saw that this came from the heart of a tall figure with a body apparently shaped out of half transparent or opalescent air and throughout the body ran a radiant, electrical fire, to which the heart seemed the center. Around the head of this being and through its waving luminous hair, which was blown all about the body like living strands of gold, there appeared flaming wing-like auras. From the being itself, light seemed to stream outwards in every direction; and the effect left on me after the vision was one of extraordinary lightness, joyousness ... ecstasy. (p. 273)

Talbot makes a point of asking us to consider the possibility that what we have been reading about and viewing for centuries as quaint folklore and mythology, including biblical accounts of visitations by gods or by archangels, are actually sophisticated accounts of the cartography of the inner dimensions and the multitude of beings both malevolent and benevolent that reside within these various inner dimensions.

Shamans from such diverse cultures as the Kung! bushmen of the Kalahari desert, the Australian Aborigines, the Inuit of the Canadian Artic and the Conibo Indians of Peru have rich and ancient traditions validating their conviction that the supernatural or interdimensional "spirit world" does exist. Not only does it exist but they understand and accept that these dimensions are senior to the physical dimension and have a profound influence on our three-dimensional world. The means used to enter these other dimensions vary from tribe to tribe and continent to continent. The various means are universal, though, and remain the same across cultures and centuries: drumming, chanting, dance, trance, meditation, ritual isolation, silence, fasting and/or ingesting entheogens.

Hancock, in his quest to understand this worldwide phenomenon of interdimensional travel and encounters with supernatural beings set out to do research for his book *Supernatural*, first published in England in 2005. To do research for the book, he stayed with various Amazonian shamans and ingested the entheogens psilocybin, ayahuasca and ibogaine. His experiences included having personal encounters with the identical beings that the shamans encountered under the influence of entheogens. As a result of his experiments, he came to the conclusion that interdimensional beings do exist around us and within us. They are aware of us and take an active interest in humanity but exist at a different electromagnetic-frequency wavelength, beyond the normal range of human sensory awareness, and therefore are invisible. They become visible when humans either spontaneously enter into altered states of consciousness or enter these states through the ingestion of chemical substances.

In researching the materials included in *Supernatural*, Hancock also worked very closely with well-known psychiatrist Rick Straussman, MD of the University of New Mexico, who published the first federally funded human hallucinogen research in the US in twenty years. Dr. Straussman's project involved eleven years of closely monitored studies in which dimethyltryptamine (DMT), the primary psychoactive alkaloid in the ayahuasca brew, was given in purified form by injection to volunteers who then reported their experiences. These subjects' experiences were later documented and included in Straussman's 2001 book, *DMT: The Spirit Molecule: A Doctor's Revolutionary Research into the Biology of Near-Death and Mystical Experiences*. The results of his study were extraordinarily unusual and caused Straussman to consider the possibility that

DMT was able to chemically alter the receiver wavelength of the brain's neurons, by tuning attention in to a different electromagnetic channel or frequency band, allowing a person to see into the interdimensional realms and to connect with these unseen worlds and communicate with their residents—which are not normally accessible.

Hancock disclosed in *Supernatural* some amazingly close parallels between the experiences of ancient and modern shamans, some but not all under the influence of entheogens, the experiences of modern alien abductees, and the experiences of Straussman's subjects under the influence of DMT—all of whom had encounters with the very same interdimensional beings and described very similar visual and sensory experiences. There are gory and graphic details of different forms of torture, of magical surgery, and of implantation of crystals into the bodies and heads of the shamans, abductees, and Straussman's subjects. Each told stories of experiences of dismemberments, piercings, extractions of brains, organs, eyes, etc., and of sometimes interdimensional sexual relations with different beings. Many of these shamanic experiences are depicted in ancient preserved shamanic cave art paintings from around the world, some of which were visually reproduced in *Supernatural*. Hancock also reproduced accounts of documented historical ethnographic studies of hunter-gatherer societies from all over the world going back centuries. Unfortunately, the ancient cave artwork and the preserved verbal accounts of these interdimensional encounters have been summarily dismissed and discounted by modern anthropologists as "primitive mythology."

In a series of three national polls conducted by the Roper Organization in 1991, it was established that approximately one out of every five adult Americans has, at one time or another in their lives, had unusual experiences such as waking up paralyzed with the sense of a strange figure or presence in the room. In addition, one in eight have experienced a period of one hour or more of lost time, one in ten have felt the experience of flying through the air, one in twelve have seen unusual lights or balls of light and one in twelve have discovered puzzling scars on his or her body without remembering how or where they got them.

Commonly shared experiences known to be associated with alien abductions have been documented in thousands of hours of interviews with abductees often conducted under hypnosis by the late John Mack, a professor of psychiatry at Harvard; John Carpenter, a therapist from Springfield, Missouri; David Jacobs, an associate professor of history at Temple University; and the late Budd Hopkins, a New York-based author, researcher and counselor with specialized knowledge of the abduction phenomena. Based on test samples from 6,000 respondents, it was determined that one out of every fifty adult Americans may have had abduction experiences either as an adult or child. There are consistent reports by abductees of having had unusual, terrifying and painful experiences during the time of their abduction(s). These experiences are often humiliating and traumatizing due to the abductees being paralyzed, controlled by the "alien or interdimensional beings" and subjected to incomprehensibly painful medical procedures and/or forced sexual encounters.

Take for example the famous case of Betty and Barney Hill who stated that they were abducted by small humanoid aliens from their car and teleported into a UFO in 1961. They described the following in *Supernatural*:

> "[The aliens had] rather odd shaped heads, with a large cranium, diminishing in size as it got toward the chin. And the eyes continued around to the sides of their heads.... The texture of the skin was grayish, almost metallic looking.... I didn't notice any hair.... I didn't notice any proboscis, there just seemed to be two slits that represented the nostrils." Betty related that she was separated from her spouse and subjected to a medical examination by these beings during which a long needle was inserted into her navel causing her agonizing pain. (p. 111)

Another abductee described in *Supernatural* (p. 114), Sandy Larson, stated she was taken up into a UFO from where she was able "to see the Earth from space through the end of a luminous tunnel." She reported she was subjected to "radical surgery in which beings removed her brain and set it down beside her." An abductee named Carlos told Dr. Mack that he "had been floated up into a spacecraft and placed on a table that looked like a block of crystal. A female alien being instructed the reptilian-faced, insectile-bodied, robot-like entities to perform an operation on him. The operation was excruciatingly painful and involved the use of crystals."

Another well-known case is that of Travis Walton, a logger. While returning home after a day of work with six co-workers driving a truck at dusk, they all observed a light in the trees rising over a bluff. The light turned out to be a UFO that hovered over the dirt road they were on. They stopped to observe. Travis exited the truck to get a closer look at UFO and while standing the middle of the dirt road was hit by a beam of light coming from the bottom of the UFO. This happened on the night of November 5, 1975, in Snowflake, Arizona. Travis was knocked unconscious and his buddies fled the scene in a panic. When they returned they could find no trace of Travis. It was reported to local law enforcement and initially the six co-workers were accused of killing Travis. Then Travis mysteriously re-appeared five days later in a town near the location where he had been abducted. He told family and friends of his abduction experience and later wrote a book about his experience titled *Fire in The Sky, the Walton Experience*. He described seeing a couple of alien beings similar to those described by Betty Hill, but these aliens had eyes with eyelids that opened and closed. He later remembered that he had awakened in a panic and run through the ship till he was intercepted by a tall male in some sort of space suit with a helmet who led him to another area where he was placed on a table, surrounded by several beings, and given some sort of anesthesia. He then woke up on the side of the dirt road not far from where he had been originally abducted five days earlier, with no initial recollection of what had transpired over the five-day period of his absence. In this instance, he was not painfully probed as in many other cases in so far as he could recollect, he but was traumatized by the experience.

These and numerous other accounts of abductees share eerily similar patterns of experience. What is uncanny is that their descriptions match closely the ethnographic accounts of shamans having hallucinatory or interdimensional experiences. For example, as reported in *Supernatural* (pp. 84–86), a Kazak, Kirgiz shaman from Siberia told ethnographers, "I have five spirits in heaven who cut me with forty knives, prick me with forty nails." Another account by an Arunta shaman in Australia says that "a spirit throws an invisible lance at him which pierces his neck from behind, passes through his tongue, making therein a large hole, and then comes out through his mouth," and a Warramunga shaman in Australia reports that "a snake is put in their heads and their noses are pierced by a magical object."

Hancock describes in *Supernatural* one of his own experiences, while under the influence of ayahuasca, as strange and terrifying:

> I begin to see snakes, coiling and writhing. Nausea increases and the visionary experiences ratchet up a notch and become more sinister. I have the sense of gazing through a tunnel with serpents coiled at the side of it close to my eyes, threatening to fall on me. I throw up, then the serpents morph into Chinese dragons with beards and long serpentine bodies. It's as though a Chinese painting has come to life. Then I feel something sinister and I see the gray heart-shaped face of an alien with a strange harsh expression and I see space ships, flying saucers all around with this commanding, unpleasant alien presence observing me. I am afraid if I allow the vision to continue I'm going to be taken up into those metal ships. I don't want to be taken up and I open my eyes to stop what I am seeing but the images continue....
> (pp. 50–64)

Here are several accounts given by some of Straussman's subjects while under the influence of medically supervised injected DMT doses, all carefully documented in his book *DMT, The Spirit Molecule* and reported in Hancock's *Supernatural*. Many volunteers reported seeing the inner workings of machines and the insides of computer boards. Here is Sara's account:

> I always knew we weren't alone in the universe. I thought that the only way to encounter them is with bright lights

and flying saucers in outer space. It never occurred to me to actually encounter them in our own inner space. I thought the only things we could encounter were things in our personal sphere of archetypes and mythology. I expected spirit guides and angels, not alien life forms.... I saw some equipment or something ... it looked like machinery. (p. 249)

Here is Lucas's report after a high-dose DMT session:

There is nothing that can prepare you for this. There is a sound, a bzzz. It started getting louder and louder and faster and faster. I was coming on and coming on and then POW! There was a space station below me and to my right. There were at least two presences, one on either side of me, guiding me to a platform. I was also aware of many entities inside the space station—automations, android-like creatures.... They were doing some kind of routine technological work and paid no attention to me. In a state of overwhelmed confusion, I opened my eyes. (p. 251)

Here is an account by a subject named Aaron:

There was no turning back. After a moment or two I became aware of something happening to my left. I saw a psychedelic, Day-Glo-colored space that approximated a room whose walls and floor had no clear separations or edges. It was throbbing and pulsing electrically. Rising in front of me was a podium-like table. It seemed that some presence was dealing, serving something to me. I wanted to know what it was and "sensed" the reply that I had no business there. The presence was not hostile, just somewhat annoyed and brusque. (p. 252)

And another account by Dimitri:

WHAM! I felt like I was in an alien laboratory…a sort of landing bay or recovery area. There were beings…. They had a space ready for me. They weren't as surprised as I was…. There was one main creature, and he seemed to be behind it all, overseeing everything. The others were orderlies, or dis-orderlies. They activated a sexual circuit, and I was flushed with an amazing orgasmic energy…. When I was coming out, I couldn't help but think, aliens. (p. 253)

Here are a few of the experiences of Rex who told Straussman:

When I was first going under there were these insect creatures all around me. They were clearly trying to break through. I was fighting letting go of who I am or was. The more I fought, the more demonic they became, probing in to my psyche and being. I finally started letting go of all parts of myself, as I could no longer keep so much of me together…. They were interested in emotion. As I was holding onto my last thought, that God equals love, they said, "Even here? Even here? " I said, "yes, of course." [In another session]: They are still there, I was making love to them. They feasted as they made love to me. I don't know if they were male or female, but it was extremely alien, not necessarily unpleasant. The thought came to me with certainty that they were manipulating my DNA, changing its structure … and then it started fading. They didn't want me to go. (pp. 255–56)

Eli, another subject, reported that he saw:

…like threads of words or DNA or something. They're all around here. They're everywhere…. When I looked around it seemed like meaning or symbols were there. Some kind of core of reality where all meaning is stored. I burst into its main chamber. (p. 268)

And one more example of such encounters in *Supernatural*, taken from Straussman's *DMT, The Spirit Molecule*, is the report of a female subject during a 1950s trial conducted by a Hungarian medical doctor named Stephen Szara who gave DMT to a large number of subjects in clinical trials to assess its possible value as a psychiatric drug. On April 30, 1956, female patient KZ reported (p. 259) under the influence of DMT that "her heart had been removed." She went on to describe seeing "strange creatures, dwarfs or something, they were black and moved about." She announced that she "was flying as if I were floating between Earth and sky." There are many more reports in this book too numerous to mention here.

Hancock's conclusion after his extensive research is that parallel and multiple dimensions do exist but they vibrate at different electromagnetic frequencies and are thus invisible except when we enter these frequency bands or inner dimensions in altered states of consciousness. Dr. Straussman also concluded that ingestion of DMT allows us to access different levels of reality that are permeating and suffusing our own but are normally invisible to us. In discussing the results of his research on DMT with Hancock, who interviewed him in *Supernatural* (Appendix II), Straussman commented that he was very "puzzled" by the consistent comments made by his many subjects that "they were expected" by the alien beings they encountered in their travels to these other dimensions.

This is not so puzzling if you remember what Don Juan Matus explained to Carlos about the "alien mind being a foreign installation which exists in every human mind." Please take this assertion deeply under consideration and ask yourself, "What if this is true?" What if our three-dimensional world is nothing remotely resembling what we've been programmed to believe? What if our oh-so-treasured and private sense of our individual self as an inviolate self-contained body/mind/ego/ personality were a total sham ... a technologically designed, holographic multidimensional projection created and controlled by intellectually superior technologically advanced non-corporeal beings—alien-Archontic-mind parasites? What if we have been deceived, manipulated, lied to, and used for eons by these Archontic-shapeshifting beings who watch us and control us from these inner dimensions?

Initially this concept was so repugnant to me and so far-fetched, that I had trouble holding onto the concept long enough to assimilate it and write about it. It seemed so diabolical a concept that my (their) ego/mind kept rejecting the idea even as I was engaged in researching and writing about it. Connecting all the dots while I did research for the book actually gave me a massive migraine headache on a number of occasions. Perhaps your (their) mind is now backpedaling just as quickly as did mine initially, going into "yeah-buts," "now-wait-a-minutes," and endless intellectual forays down labyrinthine passageways that all ended in cul de sacs of confusion and denial. Your mind may be rationalizing all this information right now. You may even be thinking to yourself: what an insane, crazy idea … or … all those ayahuasca-using individuals were simply "hallucinating" on drugs. But what about all those abductees who were clearly not on any drugs during the times of their abductions, whose thousands upon thousands of documented testimonies match almost exactly the experiences of Dr. Straussman's subjects? Hmm!

Finding the commonalities in biochemistry and multiple accounts of the ways "reality" is created and "managed" can provide evidence for this phenomenon. To use the DMT example, Dimethyltryptamine is an endogenous (produced or synthesized within the organism) psychoactive chemical naturally produced and secreted by the human pineal gland. It is the active ingredient in ayahuasca and comes from a family of hallucinogenic molecules called tryptamines that have a role in information storage in the neural networks and in genetic material … available to consciousness under certain conditions. Tryptamine comes from the parent molecule tryptophan, a key amino acid through which DNA replicates and constructs itself.

Swiss anthropologist Jeremy Narby, author of *The Cosmic Serpent: DNA and the Origins of Knowledge*, hypothesized that human DNA was intelligently designed and "minded" as an information-storage device. He proposed that the double-helix structure of DNA is an ancient high-level biotechnically created structure containing over 100 trillion times as much information by volume as our most-sophisticated modern computers. He also states in his book that he believes our DNA was developed off-planet and arrived on Earth some four billion years ago. Narby further proposes that our DNA code may conceal "intelligent messages" for us emanating from whichever "clever entities" invented the DNA code technology in the first place. It seems (and ancient Sumerian archaeological clay tablets do record this process of DNA manipulation) that the fingerprints of the Anunnaki colonizers and other extraterrestrial races are all over our DNA codons.

In these accounts, the genetic tinkering took place over eons of time, during Earth's prehistory, and they designed many versions of humanoids before perfecting a version that was initially a partly physical and partly etheric ape-humanoid body-form—which eventually evolved to become the fully physical three-dimensional form of Homo Sapiens Sapiens we inhabit today. Remember from Part III that the Wingmakers stated that the DNA of three different races was used in varying combinations to produce the traits and qualities desired in the ape-humanoid forms which these races planned to use as slaves on Earth and later on back on their home planets. The serpent race, per the Wingmakers, are a reptilian race of beings distinct from the Anunnaki but closely related to them genetically. This serpent race were known to be "life carriers." They were, like the Anunnaki, interdimensional beings able to initiate the formation and evolution of planetary bodies in various galaxies by seeding these planetary bodies with life forms somewhat similar to the concept of directed panspermia, a concept proposed by Francis Crick as a possible means by which our planet may have been originally terraformed. He came to this conclusion after an analysis of meteoric material that revealed the presence of 74 amino acids of which 55 had no known counterpart on Earth. Crick concluded that our pre-biotic chemistry has a possibly extraterrestrial origin and that there most likely exists a mechanism for the delivery of this ubiquitous DNA material intergalactically.

Studies of the brain structure have revealed some surprising facts about the pineal gland. Referenced in David Wilcock's book *The Source Field Investigations,* in an article titled "The Mind's Eye" from USC's *Health & Medicine Journal*, Dr. Richard Cox writes: "Under the skin in the skull of a lizard lies a light-responsive 'third eye' which is the evolutionary equivalent of the bone encased hormone-secreting pineal gland in the human brain" (p. 56). Julie Ann Miller in an article in *Science News* writes, "A reptile's pineal gland has the same shape and tissue as a normal eye and there is a direct biological connection between the pineal gland and the retina of the eye as both are primarily responsible for the body's recognition and processing of external light" (p. 57).

And in a 1986 paper by A. F. Weichmann in the science journal *Experimental Eye Research*, he states:

> [S]everal relationships exist between the pineal gland and retina ... although the mammalian pineal gland is considered to be only indirectly photosensitive, the presence of proteins in the pineal which are normally involved in photo-transduction (light sensing) raises the possibility that direct photic events may occur in the mammalian pineal gland. (p. 57)

Straussman's subjects often reported numerous visual effects such as complex swirling colors and patterns, complicated and beautiful geometric scenes, spinning colors, visions of alien creatures, machinery, tunnels, stairways, ducts, spinning discs, shiny metallic surfaces, shooting lights, etc. These visual effects are also consistently reported by UFO abductees at various points during their experiences in addition to encountering exactly the same types of alien beings that the DMT volunteers had encountered: aliens who consistently treated both the DMT volunteers and the abductees essentially as specimens to be examined and controlled. In many instances, the aliens conducted "painful and traumatic" intrusive medical procedures on both the DMT subjects and on the abductees. Dr. Straussman strongly advocates for the hypothesis that, when tuned to the "right receiver wavelength"—by DMT ingestion or the secretion of the right amounts of endogenous DMT into the pineal gland—the brain is fully able to perceive other dimensional realities normally invisible to us.

Interdimensional contact is becoming a more and more commonly reported experience—and not just by abductees. Many individuals have developed the capacity to move about interdimensionally in an altered state of consciousness and to see into the dimensions. By delving deeper into the mounting evidence of these states, plausible explanations can be found for the increasingly common phenomena of interdimensional contact and alien abductions: there is evidence of this having been happening since our early ancestral cave dwellers appeared and began evolving on this planetary body. Why has this phenomenon been increasing over the past eight decades and what is the purpose? For one explanation I turn to well-known author and researcher Jacques Vallee, author of ten or so books on the topic of alien abduction and flying-saucer sightings. In his most recent book *Wonders in the Sky: Unexplained Aerial Objects from Antiquity to Modern Times*, co-authored with Chris Aubeck, he provides chronological documentation of some 500 reports of these events beginning in antiquity up through 1879.

His research verifies that this phenomenon has been with us since the dawn of recorded history. Vallee is a well-respected astrophysicist who worked at the Stanford Research Institute, as well as a leading paranormal researcher. In one of his earliest published and most famous books, *Messengers of Deception: UFO Contact and Cults*, he states, quoted in Knight-Jadczyk's *High Strangeness*:

> I believe there is a system around us that transcends time as it transcends space. The system may well be able to locate itself in outer space, but its manifestations are not spacecraft in the ordinary "nuts and bolts" sense. The UFOs are physical manifestations that cannot be understood apart from their psychic and symbolic reality. What we see in effect here is not an alien invasion. It is a control system which acts on humans and uses humans. (p. 81)

After extensive research of her own on the topic of alien abduction and UFOs, Knight-Jadczyk comes to a conclusion similar to Vallee's that there is indeed an alien presence on and around our planet, it's real and it's being covered up. She says (*High Strangeness*, p. 87), "It appears that these beings can plunder our world, our lives and our minds at will." In her hours and hours of sessions with the Cassiopaeans (Chapter Sixteen), she asked many questions about how these abductions happen. The following are technical explanations of the techniques of interdimensional manipulation given to her by the Cs (*High Strangeness*, pp. 153–54).

The Cs describe the densities in a way very similar to the Elohim/ Ra group and the Saints and Masters. They tell her that the ether is composed entirely of consciousness and it is the foundation and essence of all created realities. Matter and consciousness are so intertwined and merged that without the one the other could not exist. The higher densities are ethereal realms and the three lower densities are material. The fourth density, they explain, is an intermediate or transitional density (the astral realm) because it is a level of consciousness that is still somewhat material but less so than third density. When you traverse densities there is a merging of the physical and ethereal realms which involve thought forms versus physical forms. The Cs explain that time is a nonexistent artificial illusory creation only for the point of learning, and once a being advances beyond third density, it is no longer needed. It is from fourth density that most abductions take place, so it is important to have a clear understanding of the densities; otherwise, humanity will have no comprehension of what is taking place in trans-density interactions and will be baffled by them.

The Cs continue:

> You are not normally removed as a physical three-dimensional being from one locator to another ... the time frame is ... frozen... [W]hat this means is that your perception of time in your three-dimensional body ceases to pass during this period of time ... called "zero time"....
> The soul imprint occupying that particular host body is removed forcibly, transported to another locator and re-molecularized as a separate physical entity/body for purpose of examination, implantation. The soul imprint is used for the purpose of duplication process. It is then demolecularized and the soul imprint is replaced back into the original body at the original locator (the time/space reference points in the third dimension).... [T]his is not a physical three-dimensional experience in its entirety. All first-, second- and third-density beings possess a soul imprint.... [T]hat is what is extracted. From the soul imprint, a duplicate copy or clone, if you will, which appears on fourth density can then be studied and the original soul imprint is then replaced into the original

body from whatever density it was taken from.... [C]omplete duplication for purposes of examination, alteration of sensate and implanting; need not be done in third density ... can be done completely in fourth density.... Life force is never removed. The soul is extracted ... using a type of technology (transdimensional atomic remolecularization) to extract the soul imprint of a person.... To control their subjects they use ... technologies ... which can cause extreme physical reactions, disorientation ... and can implant screen memories to manipulate space/time.... On occasion the fourth-density beings doing the abduction can astrally make a mistake in time-referencing points of third-density illusion. On rare occasions the ... subject ... can actually find themselves replaced in a wrong third-density time frame ... and can find themselves several hours, days, weeks or even sadly years, prior to the beginning of the event ... which could of course cause insanity. (pp. 154–58)

In another source, *The Law of One* Book III, the Ra group also explains to Don Elkins a similar abduction tactic used by the Orion ET groups:

The Orion group uses the physical examination as a means of terrifying the individual and causing it to feel the feeling of an advanced second-density being such as a laboratory animal. The sexual experiences of same are a sub-type of this experience. The intent is to demonstrate the control of the Orion entities over the Terran inhabitant.... [T]he thought-form experiences are subjective and, for the most part, do not occur in this density. (p. 21)

Returning to Knight-Jadczyk's account, she asks the Cs to explain who or what the gray aliens are and how they function. Here are summaries of their explanations (from *High Strangeness*):

They are cybernetic probes and decoys created by the reptilian races to study humanoid brains and bodies. They use reflective remolecularization imaging via energy focused through the gazing process done by the gray clones during the abduction process. Behind their eyes is a camera-like technology system which can induce thought paralysis, read the thoughts of the abductee, and send telepathic messages. Implants are used to monitor and control the abductees' sensory system. The gynecological and reproductive exams are used to extract life-force energy from the lower-energy chakra centers. They are interested in sexual energy because it feeds them in fourth density. Most humanoid orgasmic energy drains to fourth density. (pp. 154–56)

Screen memories are frequently implanted to block memory of the procedures used during the abductions to take life-force energy from the abductees. When tissue samples are taken from the abductees these tissue samples are used for cloning purposes. The gray aliens want to eventually switch physical realities, meaning they plan to move from fourth-density reality and enter into the cloned bodies themselves so that they can live in third density on the planet. In cases of alien beings abducting humans and subjecting them to cruel and tortuous deaths, the purpose of these acts is to induce extreme fear and terror which causes their physical bodies to produce certain hormonal products, which fuel the energy needs and provide a form of nourishment for these interdimensional entities. (pp. 156–58)

They can nourish themselves both through etheric energy means and physical means. Physical means can include drinking blood and blood byproducts which they absorb through their pores. Both the reptilian beings and the Grays do this. Even though the Grays were artificially created, they mimic the nourishment functions of the reptilians. Through interaction with the souls of the reptilians, the Grays function as projections mentally and psychically of the reptilians. The Grays operate like fourth-dimensional probes for the reptilians. Both must absorb negative energy because they are examples of fourth-density STS (service-to-self) predatory beings which live off of the energy extracted from second- and third-density beings. Their race is dying and this is why they are so desperately trying to take as much energy as possible from humans. Their intention has been the same for the past 74,000 years of Earth time. They freely move back and forth from a "still state of time/space" which is beyond Earth's space/time dimension and from there they manipulate and control events and people on Earth. When a reptilian looks at a human they can read their minds. They know and understand precisely how the separation of the three minds—conscious, subconscious and unconscious—operates in humanity. (pp. 159–66)

A further clarification is warranted here to explain how interdimensional manipulation of our consciousness functions throughout the holographic system. Just as quantum computers can "trap atoms" to initiate a wave motion between them in a silicon crystal, the holographic universe we perceive visually is like a fluid medium. In our preprogrammed interactions with our virtual-reality world we operate through these mind/body computers projecting energetic signatures or information into the holographic field called "personalities." Personality archetypes are like personality software programmed into our body/mind/ spirit complex computer, which confines us to a specific range of electromagnetic fields of expression also known as "archetypal personality patterns." These patterns are consistent within every culture and civilization as studied and established by Carl Jung, the Swiss psychiatrist. He identified some seventy basic archetypal patterns that all humanoid species express across all societies and all races.

For an explanation of the nature of archetypal mind, and how it functions within the holographic system, refer back to the Ra channeled material. Book Four of *The Law of One* series is primarily about the archetypal mind. In this book Ra states, "The archetypal mind IS the mind of the logos." Remember a logos is a sub-creator god. He further states:

> The creation, of which your logos is a part, is a protean entity which grows and learns upon a macrocosmic scale. The logos is not a part of time.... [A]ll that is learned from experience (in time) by the body/mind/spirit complex ... is therefore the harvest of that Logos...." [A protean entity is like Proteus, a sea god, very changeable, readily taking on different shapes and forms]. The logos created seven levels of progression for spiritual evolution through seven densities.... [A]ll of these concept complexes exist within the roots of the mind and it is from this resource that their guiding influence and leading motives may be traced. (pp. 18, 25)

To translate, he is saying that our body/mind/spirit complex computer has been programmed to operate through specific predetermined sets of energetic signatures called "archetypal personality patterns" and they operate or play out as certain predetermined life experiences through the body/mind/spirit complex in the hologram in each lifetime. All the experiences humanity collectively gains in each lifetime (through the archetypal mind) feed and maintain the mind of the logos (the sub-creator gods of the physical, astral and causal planes).

Also in Book Four, Don Elkins, the physicist, asks Ra, "Did this logos ... plan for this ... and know all about it prior to its plan?" Ra's response: "This is exquisitely correct" (p. 17).

We exist simultaneously in multiple dimensions through the waking conscious mind, the dreaming subconscious mind, and the sleeping unconscious mind, also known as the universal mind of unity consciousness, which overlap and represent different ways of perceiving, knowing, experiencing and understanding our inner and outer worlds. We can perceive ourselves as being individual beings, yet we are all connected at the level of the Soul. Hence the teachings of the Saints and Masters who repeatedly tell humanity, "We are all one." The patterns and expressions of the individualized personality are held within the larger, universally programmed patterns of the unconscious, the universal/archetypal mind, also the quantum field where we are literally all one unity consciousness.

So at the quantum level the Saints and Masters' teachings are true when they say that what you do to another, you do to yourself, because at the deepest level of consciousness there is only One consciousness.

Reference Keys: Bohm (2002). Castaneda (1998). Hancock (1999, 2007). Jacobs (1993, 1995). Johnson (1997). Knight-Jadczyk (2001, 2008). L/L (1984). Lash (web-d). Mack (2000). Narby (1998). "Panspermia" (web). Straussman (2001). Talbot (1991). Vallee (1969, 1979, 2010). Walton (1997). Wilcock (2011).

PART V

Evolving Higher Dimensions of Consciousness:

How Do We Get from Here to There?

That Depends on What You Do!

Since everything is but an apparition,
Perfect in being what it is,
Having nothing to do with good or bad,
Acceptance or rejection,
One may well burst out in laughter.

Tibetan Buddhist Teacher Long Chen Pa

Introduction to Part V

NOW THAT YOU'VE become familiar with just a few of the innumerable explanations of how we all arrived here, and what our ultimate destination is, I'm going to shift the focus toward an explanation of "The Divine Experiment" and how it manifests and operates on all levels of the creation—to create a context for the journey inward to the higher dimensions of awareness.

Think of the creation stories as linguistic "maps" representing a gigantic shopping-mall directory. But instead of a mall map, imagine a map showing a top-down view of the multiverse, with an arrow pointing to planet Earth saying "You are here." Now imagine zooming out and looking down upon this gigantic map of our entire galaxy, with the major zodiacal constellations clustered around the periphery of the Pole Star/axis moving in a slow circular movement—the precession of the equinoxes rotating the celestial clockworks.

Now zoom this visual image out till you can see our entire Milky Way Galaxy and the billions of other galaxies in the multiverse. Now find the exit point in the center of the Milky Way indicating the entry point into the galactic core or the Great Central Sun, the center from which the Supreme Creator emanated all that appears to be manifested as the creation—all of which are in truth nothing but "imaginal thought forms." We emerged originally as a singular divine group Soul essence or Oversoul existing in unity consciousness. We then began a journey into the multiverse of imaginal thought forms, descending down through the inner light-filled planes and the pure spiritual thought-form planes, and eventually devolving into or manifesting into the spirit/matter mixed worlds as various embodied forms. The lower-dimensional worlds are made of Soul consciousness mixed with energy atoms, forming externally seen thought forms made of what appears to be solid matter but which is in reality a three-dimensionally projected, congealed thought form made of light and sound waves. We emanated from out of the galactic core as pluriforms of the Supreme Creator—pure conscious intelligent energy beings—and this is where we are to return in completing our journey back to Source.

Chapter Twenty-One

The Pathway Home to Source

PREPARING AN INTERDIMENSIONAL pathway for the Soul to traverse from here inside the hologram back to its true home in Source is the ultimate purpose of a meditation practice. The journey is lengthy and fraught with seemingly insurmountable obstacles. We are "living pieces on a multidimensional cosmic game board" designed by the sub-creator gods. If we knew the game, all the plays and how to win, it would be "game over."

So for now within this space/time hologram, we are engaged in playing or acting out a microcosmic imaginal thought-form game. It's all a phantasmagorical multidimensional cosmic movie intricately designed for our Soul's ever-expanding awareness. Once we realize the truth of our being—that we are living eternal Souls, the essence of the God Self, and as such are co-creators with the Supreme Creator—we can engage in the return journey. This realization will eventually free us of the need for physical embodiment, allowing us to manifest in whatever light-body form we choose and to function on whichever higher dimension we choose to inhabit.

The many obstacles to Self-realization and God-realization have been described in the previously enumerated creation stories. A couple of examples of such obstacles were described in the Gnostic text "Hypostasis of the Archons: The Reality of the Rulers," which was written some time during the third century CE, and in texts from the *Nag Hammadi Library*. The Gnostics wrote extensively of the battle between the Children of Light and the Rulers (the Archontic forces) of Darkness. The Gnostics believed that the Soul on its return journey back to Source was required to pass beyond Yaldabaoth's (Kal's, Lucifer's, Iblis's) matter-created universes in order to return to the Pleroma, the Galactic Center, by passing through a Milky Way Galaxy star gate. They believed that each of the seven star gates, wormholes or gateways to the inner dimensions, corresponded to the seven chakra centers in the body. These gateways, they believed, were guarded and access blocked by the Archontic forces (the mind parasites). Souls, after having consciously reconnected with their light bodies through their activated chakra energy centers, and desiring to ascend back through the inner realms to Source, were required to give a password to the Archons (the guardians of the gates) allowing the Souls to pass through each of the inner portals or gateways to each of the inner dimensions or planes. The Gnostics also believed that the Souls, in their light bodies, needed to be guided through these inner planes by a spiritual guide, a "phoster or light bearer," "a knower of the way," a Living Master, Saint or Guru—which coincides with the teachings of Sant Mat.

These seven inner planes described by the Gnostics are the same inner dimensions or planes described in the teachings of the Masters and Saints, in the Elohim/Ra group materials, by prophets of the Old Testament and by others as the physical, etheric, astral, causal, supercausal, void, and pure eternal planes of Truth. The Sumerians and the Egyptians were well acquainted with these inner planes. Laurence Gardner, in *Genesis of the Grail Kings*, points out that the Plane of Sharon was referred to frequently in the *Egyptian Book of the Dead* texts as the Plane of the Orbit of Light or the Plane of Knowing. The Sant Mat Masters refer to this plane as the Plane of Truth. Reaching this plane requires an opened third eye, an opened crown chakra, an inner guide and the activation of the subtlest and purest form of light body.

In the book *Discourses on Sant Mat*, Saint Kabir says:

> The gate to liberation is one-tenth the size of a mustard seed, but the mind is like an elephant and it is difficult for it to pass through.... [W]ith a true Master ... the narrow passage to liberation is widened and one can freely come and go without difficulty. (p. 21)

Reference to this same inner process was mentioned by the Master Jesus when he said (Matthew 19:24), "It is easier for a camel to pass through the eye of a needle than for a rich man to enter the kingdom of heaven."

It's interesting to note the similarities among so many ancient texts describing the dimensions of the gods, the inner planes, the realms of the immortals and the methods and means of reaching them. According to mythologist William Henry in *Starwalkers and the Dimension of the Blessed:*

> In ... the second century AD, a group of Christian Gnostics described the sphere of Earth being surrounded by a twelve-angled pyramid [a dodecahedron].... [T]hese twelve angles are described as "eyes," "pipes" ... "holes" or "halls" in the Earth. These it appears are the ... halls leading to the Dimension of the Blessed. (p. 166)

> The opening chapters of the *Egyptian Book of the Dead* are called the coming forth by day and the entrance into [the] mythical hidden place [of] Amenta.... Amenta is divided into twelve domains. Amenta in twelve sections with twelve gates represented heaven in twelve divisions, i.e. the twelve signs of the solar zodiac. These are twelve gates in the night that the pharaoh's barque travels. In Hindu Puranic symbolism the geography of the world with Meru at its center is represented as a twelve-petalled lotus. (p. 164)

Henry makes further connections to the inner dimensions by pointing out that in the *Egyptian Book of the Dead* many references are made to serpents or dragons. The Egyptian word *Duat* means the divine netherworld also known as Amenta, the inner dream world or the "astral world" encircling Earth, depicted in Egyptian symbolism as a great snake or dragon encircling the Earth's outer rim. Henry states, "[T]he dragon is a universally used ancient symbol of cosmic consciousness and 'Riding the Dragon' signifies awakened cosmic consciousness and access to the

Dimension of the Blessed" (p. 118). Ancient paintings of the Buddhist Padmasambhava show him riding through the air on a dragon, likewise for the ancient painted and sculpted images of the Hindu god Shiva.

Remember in the Sant Mat creation story, Shiva is described by Saint Kabir as a destroyer god, son of Kal and Kali who with his two brothers, Brahma and Vishnu, are the Lords of the Causal Realm, the Lords of Karma; controllers of the cycles of death and rebirth of the Souls in the lower dimensions. This visual symbolism of the dragon was used by the ancient Egyptian, Chinese and South American cultures and was depicted in their preserved artworks showing how the higher-dimensional creator gods moved throughout the cosmos—the inner dimensions—the etheric, astral and causal planes.

In one of the versions of the Sumerian/Babylonian creation story, Tiamat is described as a great serpent goddess or dragon whose body was violently split in half creating the primordial seas, the life-giving waters of creation. In the Sant Mat creation story, Kal is described as swallowing Kali, the great mother of all creation, carrying the seed essence of God whom he then spit out, and together they created all the lower dimensions. In one of the many Hindu versions of the creation story, it is said that our multiverse came into manifestation through emanations or vibrations coming from the galactic core out of which flew a great mother goddess described as a great mother bird hatching a giant cosmic egg.

Henry continues:

> The Cosmic Egg is a female symbol for the universal womb or the matrix of space-time. When this egg cracked open, all life appeared. Cosmic energy or seed essence [is] the seed from which all life ... sprang into existence and fanned out in waves ... which resemble whirling galaxies. (p. 119)

This description sounds very similar to the Gnostic creation story describing how Sophia—the divine feminine creator Aeon—gave birth, from out of the Pleroma, to whirling pleromic nebular clouds of all-pervasive love/light filling the depths and heights of the cosmic waters, creating the first emanations of infinite potential, energetic thought forms, as whirling galactic light vortices later forming into interstellar star clusters and rotating galaxies. According to Carl Woebcke, author of *The Illustrated Astrology Textbook*:

> The Galactic Center or Core is also called the Great Central Sun. Our sun being but one of a collection of about two hundred billion stars known collectively as the Milky Way. The Galactic Center, around which the Milky Way revolves, completes its cycle once every quarter billion years. The Great Central Sun emits the highest vibrations of love. The sun of our solar system acts as a step-down transformer of the Galactic Center's radiating energy of love. (web)

The Theosophists believed that...

> the Seven Stars of the Pleiades transmit the spiritual energy of seven rays from the Galactic Logos to the seven stars of Ursa Major ... then to Sirius. From there, the energies are sent through the Sun to the ... Earth and ... to the human race.... Sirius is a binary star system ... the brightest star system in the night sky and can be seen from almost anywhere on Earth's surface. It is around 25 times more luminous than the Sun and its color is bluish white. It was known as "Tir" by the Egyptians. (web)

Returning to the visual of the map of the cosmos, with the arrow pointing to Earth, saying "You are here," this is where we are to begin the return journey. This is, however, an INNER journey, NOT an outer one involving advanced technology, spacecraft, time travel, parallel universes or any other scientific/technological/artificial intelligence, electromagnetic neural-net transmitter interface or any other matter-based means of interdimensional space travel. All of these are imaginal thought forms that the hyperdimensional controllers, the creator/sustainer/destroyer gods, are continually projecting into the collective mind. By introducing these "new ideas" to humanity they "bring their agendas into manifestation" through the manipulation of the imaginal thought forms of the collective unconscious mind of humanity.

How can we evolve back into our former levels of cosmic consciousness? The ascension process involves traversing back up the devolutionary pathway that all Souls originally followed when emanating and dispersing throughout the multiverse. Within our physical form lies a hidden blueprint, the energetic chakra system, a conduit inside the body which when activated through meditation and the help of a competent inner guide can provide the Soul an inner-dimensional pathway to follow, allowing the Soul to begin its return journey to Source. The pathway home to Source is inside each embodied Soul but lies dormant till awakened. The inner-dimensional gateway is at the third-eye center, and the means of consciously transcending the duality matrix of the mind is through meditation and the guidance of a competent Master or Saint.

Becoming aware of the inner pathways back up the stair-steps of creation merits our attention and engenders a question. How did we get into this predicament in the first place? Studying the creation stories from multiple perspectives can provide us with some possible answers and a deeper awareness of hidden truths intentionally obscured from humanity's conscious awareness. I propose, based on the various versions of how we all came to be, that it all started a long, long time ago in a galaxy far, far away! The sub-creator gods, pleromic light deities, were given the power and authority by Supreme Creator to create the multiverse imbuing it with the Love, Light and Life-Force Essence of the Supreme Creator. Having never done such a thing, the pleromic light deities were given a conceptual blueprint to follow by the Supreme Creator. Following this blueprint, the deities "imagined" the multiverse into existence by projecting their subtle thought forms through intergalactic-sized light and sound waves. These imaginal thought-form waves moved throughout the quantum plasmasphere: the still, unmoving ocean of pure conscious infinite intelligent energy. Thus was created, out of the immovable stillness of infinity, "motion." Through the projection of their thought-form waves the anu (atom) was created. This massive movement of energy formed swirling, whirling galaxies formed of pleromic light and sound waves. In the Vedic texts these light waves are called Jot and the sound waves are called Aum or Nam. The Christians call this divine creative power the Logos or Word of God. Out of these light and sound waves, vast shimmering galactic spirals took shape, forming exquisite geometric, holographic forms floating like multicolored jewels in interstellar space. A contingent of these intelligent deities, sub-creator gods of pure pleromic light, were given the task of further differentiating and refining the creation. They were tasked with creating stars, solar systems, planetary bodies and innumerable, beautiful, intricately designed living life forms, all imbued with the Love, Light and Life Essence of the Supreme Creator.

And ... this is about where the "divergence" or "glitch" in the divine experiment or creational process occurred. There was an unforeseen anomaly, an aberration in the subtle thought-form projections of some of these sub-creator gods. It was a divergent thought form called "DESIRE," which occurred when some of the sub-creator gods began observing their creations. In the act of observing their created living thought forms, they admired them and became enamored of them. They saw that their created forms were beautiful, illumined, alive and desirable. They yearned to "possess" them, to inhabit these beautiful forms so as to experience first-hand the sensory awareness they had imbued into these life forms. Their desire to possess and to inhabit these living life forms pulled them toward the objects or thought forms of their desire through what are called "vrittis" (Sanskrit): whirlpools or fluctuations of consciousness in the form of energetic thought forms propelled by desire.

So, from the singular unified field of infinite Love, Light and Life, a divergent force came into being: the force of "desire" which bound these creator deities to their created thought-form objects. Thus the subject/object split manifested within a finite portion of the infinite realm of pure conscious divine intelligence. The deities became bound by their desire to possess their living thought-form projections. This anomalous division or split of consciousness into the self/other dichotomy replicated itself in the design templates of all the lower planes or dimensions of the creation below the fifth plane, the pure light/truth realms. Remember, there are loosely seven planes of the creation. So approximately from the supercausal plane downward, these subtle thought-form projections called "desire" replicated themselves into the energetic thought-field fabric or ether of the lower dimensions. The body/mind/spirits of all subtle and matter-based conscious living thought forms carry this imprint of desire/will which is embedded through the sensorium (the five senses) of all living life forms.

In animals—second-dimensional life forms—this desire manifests as primitive instinct: the impulse or will to live, the instinct to survive, grow and thrive through movement, through the ingestion of matter-based food substances for sustenance, through excretion and through reproduction of the species. In third-dimensional humanoid life forms, this instinct, this will/desire to live, to move, to have, to be and to do, is transmuted into invisible/energetic thought forms of "desire" and "emotion" as the species evolves. In humans, desire manifests as an energetic "attraction" which the body/mind/spirit holds toward the object of its desire—which can be either a thought-form/idea or a seemingly solid matter-based object. The body's mind/brain projects thought forms as objects of desire external to its self in the ether of inner space. The split mind/brain makes a perceptual distinction between self/other which is in reality one thing: holographic thought forms are continually being projected by the mind into the ether. One type is visible to the outer eyes, named as congealed seen objects in three-dimensional solid form. Another type is invisible to the eyes but expressed and comprehended as mental ideas and concepts expressed in symbolic verbal language. Mental thoughts are projected into the etheric or quantum field as conceptual/abstract thought-form symbols, perceived by us as internal and private but shared indirectly through language. The third type is our projected emotions, our feelings, invisible to the outer eyes but present and felt as moving energies, impressions, sensory feelings, attractions and revulsions swirling in and around the subtle energy fields of all embodied beings. The unique impressions and expressions of each egoic self can be read by clairvoyants, by clairsentients and by interdimensional beings as the unique frequency signature of an individual embodied being.

Desire creates an energetic movement, a feeling, an energetic vortex, an attraction (a quantum entanglement) between the person and their thought-form projections—the objects of desire. Every image projected from the mind creates electromagnetic lines of force or energy connecting the mind with its thought forms. In *The Path of the Masters,* the Masters and Saints teach:

> [T]he "evil" [error of the ignorant, unconsciously auto-
> matically projected impulses and thoughts of the mind]
> lies not in the concept or idea of will/desire per se, but
> in the nature of what is desired. The "evil" [binding] lies
> in the direction of the pull of the attention toward that
> which is desired. (p. 387)

Base desires drag and bind the embodied Soul into the lower, dens-
er, oppressive, negative dimensions or planes of existence. Detaching oneself from base desires allows the Soul to be pulled upwards into the higher, freer, more expansive love- and light-filled higher dimensions. Attention and desire are the energetic means by which the energetic Soul moves through the quantum information field. When the egoic person-ality self desires an object external to itself—a conceptual idea, quality or value—a living energetic thought form is projected, tying or "binding" the egoic self to the three-dimensionally projected thought-form idea or object through attachment. By identifying with the projected object as I, Me or Mine, a binding line of energetic force is made between the egocentric personality self and the object of its desire.

To explain it another way, here is a quote from Massimo Citro, MD, author of *The Basic Code of the Universe.* He cogently explains the world as a virtual reality by stating:

> Matter does not exist. It is an idea. Reality is a complex
> system of frequencies that the neuronal networks trans-
> late into feelings and internal images. It is subjective and
> virtual.... The universe is nothing but a mental creation
> of everything, because in reality everything is mind....
> Virtual reality is determined; true reality, however, mani-
> fests itself on the other side of things. (pp. 240, 244)

In other words, this virtual-reality hologram we are living in is the manifestation of objects produced by the mind.

According to the teachings of the Saints and Masters, detachment from the normal objects of desire unbinds the mind. To love or hate anything, or to desire to possess or control another being, object or concept, creates attachment, which binds and enslaves. Detachment or detached love, honoring all sentient life forms, is a higher, nobler form of love than that which desires and demands to possess, to own or to control. Desire to have, possess or own leads to identification with the object of one's desire and thereby to bondage and enslavement through the projected thought forms of the mind.

Each of the creation stories utilizes the same universal, mythical, symbolic language of archetypal imagery (thought forms) to convey complex concepts. All follow a similar archetypal thought-form template. The hero's journey also known as the Soul's journey is depicted as a movement through all of the created thought-form worlds. Archetypal concepts are storied or placed into a linearly expressed framework because that is how the split mind/brain perceives. From humanity's perspective, everything has a beginning, a middle and an end—a past, a present and a future in space/time. Within the structure of our three-dimensional space/time hologram, the mind/brain has been structured to perceive in this limited linear way. The stories of the creation and the stories we tell the world about who we believe ourselves to be follow this same pattern.

The Soul's journey is framed as a departure, leaving home/Source and encountering a cosmic adventure by entering into unknown territories, intergalactic light-realm universes, strange inexplicable confusing interdimensional alien worlds, and even dark eerie astral underworlds of terror, darkness and despair. All of which are mere imaginal thought forms we imbue with life. During this adventure into the created thought-form multiverse, the Soul encounters many strange objects and beings—some benevolent, divine and beautiful, others malevolent, ugly and predatory. World cultures and religions are resplendent with sculpted carvings and paintings depicting multitudes of such chimerical demonic and angelic beings. Many of these beings are represented as threshold guardians, some humanoid, some angelic, some demonic and some as animalistic chimerical fierce-looking creatures who guard the entryways of ancient stone temple complexes on Earth. These guardians are stone-sculpted images representing inner-dimensional beings or deities.

The star gates described previously are energetic entryways into the inner dimensions of the etheric, astral, causal, supercausal, void and Truth planes. The inner-dimensional guides can be loving and helpful or they can be deceitful and act as guards blocking the Soul's entry into these threshold realms via these star-gate pathways leading to the inner dimensions. In the higher planes of existence, the superluminal realms, consciousness moves at faster-than-light speeds and all information is perceived and known instantly. This entire process is universally represented as an archetypal journey: the Departure, the Adventure and the Return.

Spiritually speaking, the return represents the Soul's accumulation of the highest transcendent levels of knowledge and its eventual return to a state of pure conscious awareness of the Truth of the totality of existence of All That Is. This knowledge of Truth enables the Soul to return (with the guidance and protection of an inner guide) to the place from which it began, becoming once again One with the One in full conscious awareness of its God-Self as All That Is. We're all Soul sojourners circumambulating the multiverse. The hero's journey is a metaphor for the Soul's journey into creation and back to Source, the infinite motionless cause and origin of all that moves upon the face of the waters of creation. In each and every being the seed essence of the God-Self-resides as the dormant, as yet unawakened Soul essence. Once the Soul Self awakens, it yearns for reunion with Source. Once this yearning in the heart is awakened, the Soul begins its journey back to Source, to reunite with the One. In reuniting with Source, the Soul then comes to know and realizes its True Self as the Essence of God and knows that God has returned to God.

Repeating what was said previously, "We get from here to there through meditation." Why meditation? To still the ever-oscillating whirling thought forms produced by the predator's mind in us, this foreign installation which is continually impressing into the human collective unconscious negative, fearful, anxious, divisive and opposing thought forms sowing deceit, chaos and fear in the three-dimensional hologram we call the world. The Saints and Masters call the collective unconscious mind of humanity the "treacherous, tumultuous ocean of consciousness." This energetic ocean of mind-generated thought forms tosses the embodied Soul to and fro in a tumultuous sea of uncertainty, change, impermanence, loss, confusion and chaos.

Hmmm ... chaos.... Isn't that the outer realm of darkness, called the Kenoma in the Gnostic creation story, from which the Archontic mind parasites originated and from whence they attached themselves to the descending Anthropos, the divine seed essence, the Soul? The Saints and Masters teach that "the mind" attached itself to the Soul in its descent downward from the supercausal plane to the causal plane. The mind, say the Masters, is the agent of Kal, the foreign installation which enshrouds the Soul in the lower dimensions of duality. It is only when Soul reaches the supercausal plane that the "secret agent provocateur"— the foreign installation, the egoic mind—is shed, allowing the radiance of the unencumbered Soul to shine in its pristine light body, said by Saint Kabir in *The Ocean of Love: The Anurag Sagur of Kabir* to "shine with the brilliance of 16,000 suns" (p. 109).

Hopefully by now you've gained some glimmer of the direness of the depth of the Soul's predicament, its entrapment in this treacherous multidimensional game initiated and perpetrated by the sub-creator gods, the Lords of Karma, the desire-possessed, service-to-self deities. So long as humanity remains blinded by the dualistic perceptual deception of the ego/mind; the embodied Soul will remain trapped within the reincarnational cycles unknowingly controlled and ruled by the Archonitc mind parasites and the Lords of Karma, the creator/sustainer/destroyer gods who rule this feudal system of enslavement, recycling the Souls on the karmic wheel of life-death-rebirth.

Volumes have been written in the Vedas, and in Buddhist and Tibetan texts, about the Law of Karma and how it works. The following is a very, very condensed version of how this system operates to entrap the Soul. Remember that Maya represents illusion/imagination/unreality. All created worlds are illusory, therefore unreal, as they were created through the "imagination," the thought-form waves of the creator deities. We are mini-gods, Soul fragments of the Supreme Creator whose Light Essence photonic light waves have been captured and used by the creator/sustainer/destroyer deities to create all holographic life forms in the lower dimensions. This includes energetically congealed matter-based forms and thought forms, energetic light and sound frequency waves emitted by all body/mind/spirit forms. We have the same creative capacity as the creator gods. When we imagine something, we create a subtle thought form and through these subtle thought forms we create the world we inhabit. Duplicating their patterns of imaginal thought-form creation, we create and then fall in love with our creations, become attached to them and desire to possess or own them. This is in essence how the body/mind/brain bio-suit operates to enslave the Soul. The mind/brain projects a thought form or sensation of desire into the ether or quantum field, which attaches the ego/mind to these objects through lines of force (electromagnetic/photonic light streams) projected energetically from the egoic self to the objects of its desire in the ether or quantum field—thus drawing particular life experiences to the egoically constructed and confused personality self, consistent with its beliefs and past karmic impressions.

This system, explained in depth in *Dancing with Siva: Hinduism's Contemporary Catechism,* operates as an inevitable, automatic, unconscious consequence of embodied life. The ego self, the personality or false self, grows and develops and becomes "the doer" of actions in the world (known in Sanskrit as the "ahamkara," the "I-maker"). Karma means "action," so every action binds the Soul by creating an impression in the mind/memory (the neural networks). These accumulated impressions are called "samskaras" which accompany the Soul from lifetime to lifetime. From these collected impressions emanate desires, cravings and longings that live in the body/mind/spirit's subtle-energy body through the sensorium, the five senses. These desires and longings called "vasanas" are like swarms of locusts or mind parasites (the Archontic forces) which impel the ego/mind to action. The ego/mind follows its streams of thought-desires, seeking enjoyment and avoiding pain. From the enjoyment of objects, further desires arise as cravings or longings to repeat the experience which are called "trishna." These cravings build attachments to the objects of desire. The ego retains memories of experiences of pleasure and of pain. The ego seeks objects of pleasure and attempts to avoid objects bringing pain. These whirls of thought forms create movement, which maintains the dualistic swing of thought projections generating actions, which rotate the karmic wheel of cause/effect, which perpetually churns the ocean of consciousness.

This perpetual movement of thought forms through the ego/mind creates a frequency oscillation, a swinging between the dualistic poles of thought forms of desire/avoidance, pleasure/pain, gaining/losing, loving/hating, peace/war, creation/destruction, living/dying, good/evil, forgiveness/revenge, etc. To still the mind through meditation is tantamount to stopping (for brief periods of time) the constant motion of the whirling thought forms that are rotating the cause/effect karmic wheel. To still or silence the mind means to refrain from feeding the "mind parasites"—the Archons, the secret-agent provocateurs. This foreign installation feeds off of our lower negative energetic thought forms. All of our desires, our cravings, vanities, worries, anger, lust and fear-based thought forms generate acts of violence, war and chaos in the world. Lower thought forms are described by the Masters and Saints as "the five enemies of man; passions that manifest as five destructive impulses projected by the ego/mind: lust, anger, greed, attachment and vanity" (*Path of the Masters*, pp. 276–77).

If you've ever visited a World Heritage Site or a National Park you'll likely have seen signs posted asking that visitors refrain from feeding the wildlife: the bears, geese, deer, squirrels, fish, seals, penguins, birds, monkeys, etc. Understanding the destructive nature of the mind parasites and the chaos they perpetuate in our dimensional holograms, it would be eminently more effective and useful to post signage all over the world, reminding embodied Souls everywhere (visitors to planet Earth) to refrain from feeding the Archons, the mind parasites, who feed off of our negative, low-vibrational thought forms and emotions, creating chaos, confusion, destruction and fear in the world. It's the negative thought-form projections as emotions and actions that fuel the energetic downward rotation of the three lower chakra centers: survival/fear, reproduction/sex and desire/power/greed—all of which produce low-frequency photonic light frequencies, the food of the Archons.

Once the embodied Soul evolves to the point where it sees the game and makes a conscious aware choice to act as a loving presence in the world, this opens and spins the chakra energies upward instead of downward, opening the heart-chakra energies and generating the upward flow of "prana," the life-force energies of the Soul essence, which generate higher, more-expansive vibrational light and sound frequencies. To have feelings of loving compassion for all sentient beings raises the overall vibrational frequency of the Soul, and one gradually ceases to be a "food source" for the dense lower-plane mind parasites; and eventually one moves beyond the machinations and manipulations of the hyperdimensional overlords of the lower planes or dimensions of consciousness.

These hyperdimensional enforcers of Karmic Law, the creator/sustainer/destroyer gods—the Lords of Karma—operate in a machine-like manner as impartial unfeeling judges. They enforce the Laws, which form the holographic structures of the lower dimensions of creation, without mercy and without deviation. The Soul must struggle to disentangle itself from these containers, these veils, which act as blocks to the Soul's ability to know the truth of its divine origins.

The Saints and Masters teach that "to be no more under the Law" means to be freed from the Karmic Laws operative in the lower planes of consciousness up to the supercausal plane of the multiverse. In the higher dimensions of consciousness, the Supreme Creator's will prevails, which is the law of love, mercy, grace and forgiveness. These qualities are emanated by the Sons of God, the embodied Living Masters, the Saints, the Godmen, the Divine Intercessors, the Emissaries of God. These perfected Souls take birth into the lower dimensions of consciousness (the form worlds) solely for the purpose of awakening and freeing the entrapped Souls and guiding them back to Source, to reunite with the Supreme Creator.

As the Masters and Saints describe in *Philosophy of the Masters*, volume V:

> The knowledge of the Master(s) is the "eternal light of the heart." This knowledge is ... behind the veil of the mind, and it is found in the ... Royal Vein inside every human being.... This knowledge leads to the release from birth and death and no one but the Master(s) possess it.... Its development is a matter of practice, and its secrets can only be had from one who has himself practiced it. (pp. 23–24)

Continuing in the *Philosophy of the Masters*, volume V, it is explained that the bright light rays which emanate from the astral form of the Saints are described as the "dust of their feet." This "dust" is also described as the melody of Nam [the inner sound current also emanating from their astral bodies] which dismantles the deceptive illusions of the mind and takes the soul beyond action and space/time and breaks the powers of the five senses, eventually freeing the Soul of the illusion of separation and of suffering (pp. 48–50).

Sant Mat means the teachings of the Saints. Their teachings comprise a complete body of knowledge, both a theory and a practice—a science of the Soul—that provides an infallible method of achieving spiritual progress, of entering the pathway leading the Soul back to Source, to the Supreme Creator. This meditation practice purifies the mind and draws the consciousness upwards, allowing the Soul to rise through the inner spiritual dimensions above and beyond the physical, astral and causal planes. The Living Masters guide the lost and bound Souls onto this pathway which has been described in numerous books. It is said, in *Discourses on Sant Mat:*

> This gift, given to the initiates of the Living Masters, is so holy that in all the world there is no relation so close and so sacred as that between Master and pupil. (p. xxiii)

Here is a quote from Master Sant Baljit Singh, from a talk given at Pimpalner, India on February 5, 2008, quoted from *Know Thyself as Soul: 2014 India Report*:

> We need to recognize our true selves and see that we are a form of Light.... [T]o experience the inner Light, we first need to follow the teachings of the Master, and then we can enter within and see ourselves as Light.... The Light emanates from Naam and spreads throughout the creation. (p. 18)

And another quote from a talk given by Him at Nawan Nagar, India on November 14, 2010, quoted from the same magazine:

God is one, and so we should not think there is anyone except Him. He is omnipresent and prevalent in the
entire creation, including within each living organism.
When we realize our higher self, then we will experience
Him within us and within all other living beings. (p. 18)

Here is a beautiful summation which is from *The Upanishads,* translated by Eknath Easwaran:

Bright but hidden, the Self dwells in the heart.
Everything that moves, breathes, opens, and closes
lives in the Self. He is the source of love
and may be known through love but not through
thought. He is the goal of life. Attain this goal!

The shining Self dwells hidden in the heart.
Everything in the cosmos, great and small,
lives in the Self. He is the source of life,
Truth beyond the transience of this world.
He is the goal of life. Attain this goal! (p. 113)

Reference Keys: Citro (2011). Discourses (1963). Easwaran (1999). Galactic (web). Gardner (web). Henry (2007). Johnson (1997). Kabir (1984).
Philosophy (1967). Singh-SB (2008). "Sirius" (web). Subramuniyaswami
(1993). "Theosophy" (web). Woebcke (web).

Chapter Twenty-Two

And the Truth Is …

———————————

OUT OF THE One came the manyness of the creation. All That Is is an emanation of the Supreme Creator. The love/light/life-force essence, as light and sound currents emanating from the creator, created All That Is. The light with its shadow or darkness created the positive and negative poles of the creation. These positive and negative energies of the creative forces in the multiverse whirl, rotate and move around each other in a plasmic dance of creation. The dance or movement of light and sound currents becomes "Jagat" (Sanskrit) for "moving thing." This moving thing is pure intelligent aware consciousness in the constant motion of creation, maintenance, and destruction or dissolution of moving things in the form of waves or particles. Consciousness projects thought forms out of itself as moving streams of light and shadow.

The multiverse is molded of these living streams of light and shadow which form the scaffolding upon which all creation is built. Creation is nothing but thought-form projections. We are all thought forms projected from the pure intelligent consciousness of God who created All That Is. As individuated Souls, as God droplets we are carriers of the love/light/life force essence of God within us as embodied living Souls. We, humanity, are co-creators with God because we share His creative capacities. Through His projected light and sound frequencies He created the multiverse. With our projected thought forms we create and maintain this hologram we live inside of. The minds of all embodied Souls—the mind/intellect of everyone—perpetually generates and projects thought forms. These thought forms radiate into the quantum light field (the ether) as living moving images made up of dualistic concepts such as love/hate, desire/indifference, hope/despair, war/peace, etc. All thought projections at this dimensional level are split into self/other as subject/object thought forms (an illusion of the hologram).

We are all imagining an illusive world into existence through the projection of our thought-form ideas into the ether, the collective unconscious which forms the cosmic moving picture screen of the collective consciousness of all beings (embodied or not), each operating from its particular dimensional level of awareness.

To quote Paramahansa Yogananda (*Autobiography of a Yogi*):

> He (God) sends His beams of Light through the films of successive ages and pictures are thrown on the backdrop of space. Just as cinematic images appear to be real but are only combinations of light and shadow, so is the universal variety a delusive seeming…. The countless forms of life are naught but figures in a cosmic motion picture. Temporarily [through] man's five sense perceptions the transitory scenes are cast on the screen of human consciousness by the infinite creative beam … issuing from the single white light of a Cosmic Source…. God is staging super-colossal entertainment for His children making them actors as well as audiences in His [cosmic] theater. (p. 319)

This cosmic theater is nothing but the play of light and dark images upon a cosmic motion picture screen—a moving screen of ideas, images and concepts projected by humanity onto the universal screen of consciousness. Yogananda continues:

> Creation is light and shadow both, else no picture [outpicturing of thought-form projections] is possible…. The good and evil of Maya [duality-illusion] must ever alternate in supremacy…. One's values are profoundly changed when he is finally convinced that creation is

only a vast motion picture [a moving thing of illusion] and that not in it but beyond it … lies [one's] eternal home. (pp. 319–20)

At this point you may be wondering: where is "beyond it"? Well, according to the Masters and Saints, our eternal and true home is beyond the causal plane, beyond the supercausal plane, beyond the void plane, and in the pure spiritual plane of Truth, the fifth plane of pure consciousness. This plane is pure consciousness shorn of the mind. It is a pure light realm of eternal perfect knowledge, peace and bliss. The planes above this are where Soul began its journey into the cosmic dream worlds. The mind (the agent of deception) is the creator of the cosmic dualistic swing of light and dark forces through thought-form projections. Mind is shed once it passes beyond the top of the causal or mental plane. Beyond the causal plane the Soul is freed from the entanglement/enchantment/enmeshment of the mind and its thought-form projections. The Soul is at last freed from the limits of its meandering multidimensional explorations of the cosmic dream world and is freed from the binding Karmic Laws operative in the lower dimensions. Karmic Law operates mechanically and automatically in the lower dimensions as cause-effect activity. These dimensions were created and are controlled by the creator/sustainer/destroyer gods or deities through the holographic mind matrix. A great deception, a delusion of consciousness, has been perpetrated upon the living Souls by the sub-creator gods, the negative forces of the creation.

Remember the Buddha said, "With our thoughts we create the world." What have we created? Just look around you! All that we see on screens (screens built by human hands) reflecting around us everywhere—on our movie screens, our TVs, on our iPhones, on painted billboards and in spoken word images through radio broadcasts aimed at us 24/7 by the control matrix: all are projected thought forms of negativity in every form: war, killing, terror, fear, grief, hatred, abuse, greed—all projections and manipulations of the ego/minds of humanity.

These cosmic scary movies are now being extended and projected off-planet to include happenings not just on our planet, in our solar system, but out into entire intergalactic worlds. The same old Master

Game (the forces of light against the forces of darkness) just extended out into an intergalactic playing field. And what is the theme? Same as always: right/wrong, evil/good, wars, winning/losing, destruction, chaos, conquest, division, blame, shame, guilt and punishment. Wake Up Humanity! Are you ready to withdraw you attention, your light essence and your consciousness from this diabolically sick "Master of the Universe Game" being played out through us?

Each and every creation story detailed herein is a variation on a cosmic theme. Think of Russian nested Matryoshka dolls. Except that instead of nested dolls they are nested stories or plays, within plays, within plays, all of which are nothing more than the "play of consciousness." My consciousness has projected a stream of thought forms into your consciousness as ideas, concepts and theoretical suppositions laid out as word symbols in the form of this book you are reading. My writing this book and your reading it have projected upon the screen of your mind some very radical and challenging ideas. Intentionally so, to awaken your curiosity and wonderment. To guide you into questioning your beliefs because they form the bedrock of your life and generate consequences which extend beyond just this lifetime. Whatever you believe, you make real in your personal world and in our collectively constructed reality hologram.

According to Yogananda:

> Old Testament prophets called *maya* by the name of Satan (lit., in Hebrew, "the adversary").... Satan or *Maya* is the Cosmic Magician who produces multiplicity of forms to hide the One Formless Verity. In God's plan and play *(lila)*, the sole function of Satan or *Maya* is to attempt to divert man from spirit to matter, from Reality to unreality.... Maya is "from the beginning" because of its structural inherence in the phenomenal worlds [that known or perceived by the senses]. These are ever in transitional flux [movement] as antithesis [opposition] to the Divine Immutability [the unchanging eternal Truth]. (p. 322)

The Cosmic Magicians cleverly installed an adversary in our midst. But it was hidden in the last place on Earth we would ever think to look: inside our own ego/selves. The adversary is the mind and it lives inside each of us.

Yogananda continues, saying:

> Desires [as thought-form projections and feelings] are the chain(s) that bind man to the reincarnational wheel.... The substance of a dream is held in materialization by the subconscious thought of the dreamer. When the cohesive thought of the dreamer is withdrawn in wakefulness, the dream and its elements dissolve. When he [humanity] awakens in cosmic consciousness, he effortlessly dematerializes [dissolves] the illusions [thought forms] of the cosmic dream universe. (pp. 360–61)

The Soul embodied through the body/mind/intellect emanates the essence of life, the eternal Soul light of the consciousness of the Supreme Creator. The mind of the body constantly projects thought forms in the waking state, the dream state and the unconscious state. These thought forms radiate into the ether or quantum thought field as the constant movement of photonic light mixed with matter (shadow) which produces the illusion of the holographic world we see moving all around us in three-dimensional living color.

Thought-form projections manifest in the third dimension as matter, or congealed light forms, through human attention/observation. To use a metaphor from metallurgy, consider the concept of making an "alloy." This process involves taking a pure substance such as gold and mixing it with a debased or inferior metal such as copper. The resulting mixture is called an alloy, in this case rose gold. Taking this concept into the realm of spirit, think of the Soul essence as having been placed into the container of the body/mind/intellect creating a matter-based alloy. The Soul's light essence mixed with the matter of the bodily form creates an alloy, a "debased" substance. In chemistry the word "ligare" means to bind chemically. In religion, the word "ligare" means to bind symbolically through the use of thought-form concepts and beliefs. In considering what is bound to what, the word "alien" means something foreign—unnatural—other. Something opposed to the natural order. The negative pole of creation (this three-dimensional hologram) is opposed to the natural order of the universe. It is opposite to the positive pole of the creation. It is "debased," thus matter mixed with spirit creates illusion, deception, misperception and confusion, through the ego/mind of the body.

In legal terminology, the word "aliunde" means from another place—a law from some other source, not deriving from the original source. The Law of the Supreme Creator is the Law of Love, Mercy, Grace and Forgiveness derived from Original Source, the Supreme Creator. Karmic Law is "aliunde": a law derived not from Original Source, but a law created and imposed on humanity from the causal plane of consciousness by the Lords of Karma, the creator/sustainer/destroyer gods or deities. They created this Karmic system of imprisonment through the use of "metempsychosis," which means to contain the Soul in a body and then move the Soul from body to body (also known as transmigration of the Soul). These matter-based forms, our body/minds, have captured and deluded the Soul into believing itself to be the body/mind/ego self.

The mind (the foreign installation) is the "not self" that projects and maintains the illusory hologram in place. Soul essence is the subject, the "I am" of pure consciousness. All else is "other"—objects, ideas, concepts, images, feelings projected by the mind into existence as thought-form holograms. From below the fifth plane, all of these descending dimensions or planes of consciousness are composed of nothing but consciousness existing as different subtle forms of deities, conscious aware beings possessing differing degrees of awareness and projecting differing types of imagery or thought-form projections from their particular dimension or plane of existence. All planes of existence are filled with variegated life forms, each projecting its unique thought forms into the ether, the quantum field of each plane of existence of consciousness. It's ALL the projection of consciousness as a multidimensional cosmic movie. All beings, whether in formed-matter bodies or in pure-light bodies, project thought-form images onto the cosmic movie screen, which is composed of nothing but consciousness. Pure conscious awareness IS ALL THAT IS, as the Masters and Saints keep explaining to sleeping humanity.

To wake up means to wake up "in the dream" while living in the body, in the hologram, and know it all as a projection of consciousness—a multidimensional cosmic movie—the play of light and shadow thought forms. This concept of a movie being projected through the mind reminds me of an amazing drawing made by a nine-year-old-child I was working with as a psychotherapist years ago. I've never forgotten the drawing she made for me during our therapy sessions together. The drawing was of a two-story house with flames pouring from all the windows. The front door was hanging open and askew. There were bombs falling from several airplanes in the sky, exploding all around the house. Shards of metal debris were falling onto the ground and onto the roof of the house. There were no people in her drawing. It was an image of utter destruction and devastation. The caption she printed at the bottom of the drawing said, "Stop the world, I want to get off!"

How profoundly she had captured her experience of feeling trapped in this three-dimensional hologram filled with projected images of fear, death, destruction and danger everywhere. So how do we "stop the world"? We do so by taking time out every day to engage in a meditation practice to "stop our minds" from outpicturing and projecting negative thought-form images into the quantum field of the collective consciousness of humanity. Meditation builds the neocortex of the brain and re-wires it neuronally, allowing the locked-down Soul essence to reconnect with its higher energy centers through the energetic chakra system in the heart, third-eye and crown chakras. This reconnection through daily meditation opens and expands the higher-electromagnetic-frequency energy centers and generates an energetic opening, an awakening and a turning upward—thus drawing and spinning upward the light and sound frequencies of the Soul into the higher energy centers. This process awakens the divine blueprint (original DNA template) of the Anthropos, the true Soul self-locked into the body/ego/mind. This is an inner alchemical process, the turning of a base metal into gold: a metaphor for the awakening and purification process of removing base impurities covering the Soul essence.

The base impurities (alloys) are all the false beliefs, all the negative thought-form projections and fear-based emotions pouring from the ego/self into the collective unconscious of humanity. This includes all the judgments, the self/other dichotomies, the dualistic outpicturing of thought-form concepts of right doing and wrong doing, all the negative feelings, the hurting, the blaming and the shaming. All of these thought-form projections maintain our three-dimensional hologram. DOING is manifesting. This is what the ego/self, the mind, DOES through the projection of its desires and emotions followed by its actions. The mind creates, through the five outer senses, thought forms perceived as physical objects in the dimensional hologram. The five inner senses produce inner images, ideas and feelings, projected by the ego/mind into its inner emotional space (astral body). These thought-form projections do not just go into what we consider to be our own personal, private inner space, but are actually projected into the collective quantum consciousness field.

BEING is emanating. To emanate means to issue forth, to come from a source. The emanation is the thing emitted. The Soul's essence emits "light frequencies." It is a light-generator—a carrier of light. Simply by being present and aware, it shines its light of conscious awareness wherever it IS. This is what the life-force essence of the Soul IS—a form of pure light. It is "the glowing coat of awareness" described by Don Juan Matus to Carlos Castaneda, discussed in Part IV. Every waking moment of our lives, we are generating emotions and thought forms which manifest as light and sound frequencies.

Meditating is the process of "undoing" all our thought-form projections and emotional projections. Meditating is a vibrational energetic frequency-alignment process. A process of recalibrating ourselves to the Soul essence—the True Self. When the overall vibrational frequency of the Soul is calibrated to the higher, faster frequencies of the dimensions of love/light, this velocity of frequency can catapult the Soul essence beyond the illusory lower dimensions of duality and into the higher planes of unity consciousness. It's an inside job!

Beyond all beliefs, all duality and all thought-form projections, lies the Truth, the One True Reality from which we all emanated as God droplets, as Light Bearers in light bodies. The demiurgic deities, the lower-level creator gods, captured our Soul essences, our light-emitting essences, and use them to maintain the physical, astral and causal planes or holograms of existence. This is the "Master Game" we are destined to transcend. But only when we are ready, of course. Are you ready yet? If you're not ready, that's fine, because the True reality stands outside of and beyond space/time. The True Reality exists in the timeless planes of eternity and infinity.

The sole and sacred function of the Living Masters and Saints is to take on a physical form (embody) into this hologram of deception and to search for and find those Souls who are ready to exit. Then to extract them from the Master game of deception. "Ready" means the embodied Soul has evolved to the point of being able to discern the truth of its predicament. The embodied Soul develops a longing, a yearning to escape and to go home, so to speak. Remember in Chapter Two of Part II, when I was waiting to meet the Living Master for the first time in his physical form? Standing in line, I couldn't fathom what I would say to him, so I decided that whatever I said would just be a spontaneous expression in the moment. When finally I sat down face to face with Him, the words I blurted out were, "I want to go home faster, Master!" That was my Soul speaking, not my mind. My mind was clueless. It was my Soul essence, my True Self expressing Its desire to exit the game and go home.

The Living Masters emanate from their being the highest vibrations of pure love/light, which awakens and cleans the Soul, removing the debased elements covering the Soul essence. They have the power and the means of releasing the Soul from this delusional system through an initiation/meditation process which awakens the Soul from its slumber of ages. This is why the Living Saints and Masters throughout Earth's history have been so venerated, worshipped, loved and honored.

It has truly been my deepest desire and my sincerest intent, in writing this book, to open a pathway beyond your minds, dear readers, and into your hearts, where the Soul essence of each resides. May your hearts swell with the desire to awaken from the dream, to reconnect your Soul with the Supreme Creator and to join together with all Souls in unity consciousness resonating in the love/light/life of the Soul's true Essence. With clear intent and compassion may we act in concert to dissolve the terrible holograms of deception by stilling all thought-form projections and emanating feelings of love, beauty, peace and forgiveness, and by engaging in daily acts of kindness and compassion.

As living Souls, we hold the power of co-creation within us. What is our collective intention? How about we all engage in daily meditation, clean the mirror of our hearts, and allow the light of the True Self, the Soul, to shine its light into this dark shadowy hologram and transmute it into light?

Included below are some inspiring quotations from several treasured sources.

From Mumtaz Ali in *The Jewel in the Lotus: Deeper Aspects of Hinduism*:

> The blissful supreme is right here—so simple and so clear.... You may live in this world and do your duties, earn your livelihood, and yet remember to keep in touch with your true Self, the spark from the great fire, the drop from the great ocean, by meditating regularly, so that, in the spotless and clear mirror of your heart, Divinity's reflection glows. From your heart, then, will the serene rays of the spirit proceed and fill other hearts with bliss. (p. 2)

A quote by Sant Baljit Singh in *Know Thyself as Soul* Magazine, 2016 Issue 3, taken from a talk given at Nagpur, India:

> Meditation is the only process which can subdue the mind and thus enlightenment can be achieved. Meditation protects one from being carried away by the powerful clutches of Maya (illusion). When your mind turns inward, then the impressions and strong oscillations of your mind will settle down. Thoughts are not real and can be compared to the waves of the ocean. When you begin to realize the subtle aspects of Maya, then you will naturally become aware of the absolute higher truth. (p. 5)

From David Hawkins in *Transcending the Levels of Consciousness*:

The energy field of Love is innately gratifying in and of its own quality. It is discovered that Love is available everywhere and that lovingness results in the return of love. Although love may start out as conditional, with spiritual intention it becomes a way of life and a way of relating to life in all its expressions. As Love progresses, it seeks no return or gain for it is self-rewarding by virtue of its completeness since it has no needs. The capacity for Love grows so that the more one loves, the more one can love, and there is no end point or limitation. In addition, it is discovered that to be loving is also to be lovable. (p. 248)

From the beloved classic *The Prophet*, by Kahlil Gibran:

Love gives naught but itself and takes naught from itself.
Love possesses not nor would it be possessed;
For love is sufficient unto love.
When you love you should not say, "God is in my heart,"
but rather, "I am in the heart of God."
And think not you can direct the course of love, for love,
if it finds you worthy, directs your course.
Love has no other desire but to fulfil itself.
But if you love and must needs have desires, let these be
your desires:
To melt and be like a running brook that sings its melody
to the night.
To know the pain of too much tenderness.
To be wounded by your own understanding of love;
And to bleed willingly and joyfully.
To wake at dawn with a winged heart and give thanks for
another day of loving;
To rest at the noon hour and meditate love's ecstasy;
To return home at eventide with gratitude;
And then to sleep with a prayer for the beloved in your
heart and a song of praise upon your lips. (pp. 14–15)

And lastly, an excerpt from a beautiful poem written by Paramahansa Yogananda, entitled "Samadhi":

> Vanished the veils of light and shade....
> Perished these false shadows on the screen of duality....
> Each particle of universal dust ...
> I swallowed all, transmuted all....
> From joy I came, for joy I live, in sacred joy I melt.
> Ocean of mind, I drink all creation's waves.
> Four veils of solid, liquid, vapor, light,
> Lift aright.
> I, in everything, enter the Great Myself.
> Gone forever: fitful, flickering shadows of mortal memory;
> Spotless is my mental sky—below, ahead, and high above;
> Eternity and I, one united ray.
> A tiny bubble of laughter, I
> Am become the Sea of Mirth Itself. (pp. 170–71)

I've dedicated this book to my beloved Masters—those divinely incarnated Godmen, those Knowers of the Way back to Source. I've taken you all on a circuitous tour through marvels of architectural wonders—towering thought-form structures of familiar and foreign belief systems. All of which were designed to stretch the possibility parameters of your minds.

I've intentionally woven the teachings of the Sant Mat Masters throughout the text to seed ideas into your consciousness and to provide thought arrows pointing to specific methods and means of exiting this illusionary mind-hologram.

The window to the heart, where the Soul essence dwells, can be opened by those perfect Masters who hold the keys to this process of awakening. Of all the things that have come to me in this lifetime, the most treasured and precious of all are the unconditional love, grace and company of a Living Saint.

In conclusion, I would be remiss in not providing readers with information about how to connect with a Sant Mat Master, if you are so inclined. Information about meditation on the inner light and sound are available at www.santmat.net.

I wish you Godspeed—a term used to request God's blessing on an endeavor, usually a long journey or a risky venture—as the journey is long and This Embodied Life is short!

Reference Keys: Ali (2011). Gibran (1986). Hawkins (2006b). Singh-SB (2016). Yogananda (2003).

Chapter-Key References

This Embodied Life: **Introduction**
Rumi, Jalaluddin (web-a). Accessed April 1, 2017. http://www.go-odreads.com/author/quotes/875661.Rumi.

Part I: Beliefs, Contexts and Domains of Knowing
Kumara, Tiara (2016). *Morphogenesis & The Skill Sets of Evolution: Evolutionary Teachings for Accelerated Spiritual Development and Humanitarian Service.* CreateSpace Independent Publishing Platform.
Mouravieff, Boris (2014). *Gnosis,* Vol 1. Accessed April 2, 2017. http://issu.com/deconstructingconsciousness/ docs/gnosis_book_1.

Chapter One: The Linear Domain of Beliefs
Goswami, Amit, PhD (1993). *The Self Aware Universe: How Consciousness Creates the Material World.* G.P. Putnam's Sons.
Hawkins, David R., MD PhD (2004). Audio. *Transcending the Mind.* Veritas Publishing.
———— (2006a). *Discovery of the Presence of God.* Veritas Publishing.
———— (2011). *Dissolving the Ego, Realizing the Self.* Hay House, Inc.
Patanjali (2003). *The Yoga Sutras of Patanjali:* A New Translation with Commentary by Chip Hartranft. Shambhala Publications Inc.
Rhinehart, Luke (1976). The Book of est. Holt, Rinehart and Winston of Canada, Limited.
Talbot, Michael (1991). *The Holographic Universe.* Harper Collins Publishers.
Weiner, Eric (2008). *The Geography of Bliss.* Twelve Hachette Book Group.
Wilber, Ken (2000). *Integral Psychology.* Boston: Shambhala Publications, Inc.

Chapter Two: The Nonlinear Domain of Context
Aurobindo, Sri (1990). "The Release from the Ego." In *The Synthesis of Yoga.* Lotus Press. Accessed April 2, 2017. http://www.surasa.net/aurobindo/synthesis/part-2.html#ch09.

Erhard, Werner (1982). *The End of Starvation: Creating an Idea Whose Time Has Come*. The Hunger Project.

Fuller, Buckminster (web). Accessed April 1, 2017. http://www.goodreads.com/authorquotes/11515303.R/ buckminster_fuller.

Hawkins, David R., MD, PhD (2003). *I: Reality and Subjectivity*. Veritas Publishing.

————— (2006b). *Transcending the Levels of Consciousness: The Stairway to Enlightenment*. Veritas Publishing.

————— (2011). *Dissolving the Ego: Realizing the Self*. Hay House, Inc.

Millay, Jean, ed. (2010). *Radiant Minds* (update of *Silver Threads* 1993: Targ, Radin, et al.). Millay.

Steiner, Rudolf (web-d). Accessed April 2, 2017. http://www.en.wikiquote.org.

Tesla, Nikola (web). Accessed March 31, 2015. http://www.themindunleashed.com.

Chapter Three: The Transcendent Domains

Aurobindo, Sri (1990). "The Release from the Ego." In *The Synthesis of Yoga*. Lotus Press. Accessed April 2, 2017. http://www.surasa.net/aurobindo/synthesis/part-2.html#ch09.

Brihadaranyaka Upanishad, I.iv.10 (web). Accessed June 17, 2017. http://www.metaphysicalmusing.com.

Gibran, Khalil (1986). *The Prophet*. Fifty-seventh printing. Pocket edition. Alfred A. Knopf, Inc.

Hawkins, David R., MD, PhD (2002). Audio. *The Way to God: Radical Subjectivity: The I of Self*. Veritas Publishing.

Joye, Shelli R. (2012). "The Trinitarian Psychophysics of Saccidananda in Sri Aurobindo's Philosophy of the Upanishads." California Institute of Integral Studies Department of Philosophy & Religion. Spring issue. http://www.academia.edu/3717823/The_Trinitarian_Psychophysics_of_Sri_ Aurobindo.

Rumi, Jalaluddin (web-b). Accessed April 1, 2017. http://www.higherexistence.com.

Part II: Entering the Hologram

Swetlishoff, Marlene (web). Accessed August 14, 2013. http://www.therainbowscribe.com.

Chapter Four: My Story

Goddard, Harald (web). Accessed April 1, 2017. http://www.books. google.com/The_Practical_Well-Being_Programme. Taylor & Francis.

Haisch, Bernhard (web). Accessed April 1, 2017. "Brilliant Disguise: Light, Matter and the Zero-Point Field." http://enthea.org/ library/brilliant-disguise-light-matter-and-the-zero-point-field/.

Meher Baba (1995). *Discourses by Meher Baba*. Ahmednagar: Avatar Meher Baba Perpetual Public Charitable Trust. Third Printing.

PANDAS (web). Accessed April 1, 2017. http://www.pandasnetwork. org/understanding-pandaspans/what-is-pandas/.

Rhinehart, Luke (1976). *The Book of est*. Holt, Rinehart and Winston of Canada, Limited.

Roberts, Jane (1982). *The Nature of Personal Reality*. Bantam Books.

Shankara, Adi (1970). *The Crest Jewel of Discrimination*. Reprint. Mumbai: Bharatiya Vidya Bhavan.

Yogananda, Paramahansa (2003). *Autobiography of a Yogi*. Self-Realization Fellowship.

Chapter Five: Meetings with the Living Master

Aurobindo, Sri (2010). *The Life Divine*. Pondicherry: Sri Aurobindo Ashram.

Hawkins, David R., MD PhD (2001). *The Eye of the I from Which Nothing is Hidden*. Veritas Publishing.

——— (2008). *Reality, Spirituality and Modern Man*. Ontario: Axial Publishing Co.

Johnson, Julian, MD (1997). *The Path of the Masters*. 16th edition. Beas, India: Radha Soami Satsang.

Leeming, David (2002). *Myth, A Biography of Belief*. Oxford University Press.

Meher Baba (1995). *Discourses by Mehar Baba*. Ahmednagar: Avatar Meher Baba Perpetual Public Charitable Trust. Third Printing.

Singh, Sant Kirpal (1988). *Spiritual Elixir*. Second edition. Ruhani Satsang Books.

Singh, Sant Thakar (2005). *The Secret of Life*. Florida: Edition Naam.

Part III: Twelve Creation Stories

Hawkins, David R., MD PhD (2004). *The Highest Level of Enlightenment.* Audio Book. Nightingale-Conant.

Vonnegut, Kurt (1998). *Cat's Cradle.* Dell Publishing.

Chapter Six: Scientific Materialism Worldview

Chiao, Raymond Y. (web). Accessed April 2, 2017. http://www.scientificamerican.com/article/what-is-known-about-tachy/.

Davies, Paul and John Gribbin (2007). "The Death of Materialism." In *The Matter Myth.* Simon & Schuster.

Horgan, John (1996). *The End of Science: Facing the Limits of Knowledge in the Twilight of the Scientific Age.* Basic Books.

Kaku, Michio (web). Accessed April 1, 2017. http://www.cnsnews.com/news/article/barbara-hollingsworth/string-theory-co-founder-sub-atomic-particles-are-evidence-0.

Lipton, Bruce (2005). *The Biology of Belief: Unleashing the Power of Consciousness, Matter and Miracles.* Mountain of Love/Elite Books.

Materialism (web). Accessed April 1, 2017. http://www.dictionary.com/browse/materialism?s=t.

National Geographic (web). "Origins of the Universe." Accessed April 1, 2017. http://www.nationalgeographic.com/ science/space/universe/origins-of-the-universe.

Chapter Seven: The Abrahamic Worldview

"Abrahamic Religions": Wikipedia contributors (web). Accessed April 1, 2017. http://www.en.wikipedia.org/wiki/ Abrahamic_religions.

"Ancient Hebrew": Wikipedia contributors (web). Accessed April 1, 2017. www.en.wikipedia.org/wiki/Ancient_Hebrew_ writings.

Bartlett's (web). Accessed April 1, 2017. http://www.bartleby.com/essay/The-Beginning-of-Life-in-the-Book-P3JE86USVJ.

"Biblical Canon": Wikipedia contributors (web). Accessed April 1, 2017. http://www.en.wikipedia.org/wiki/Biblical_canon.

"Biblical Cosmology": Wikipedia contributors (web). Accessed April 1, 2017. http://www./en.wikipedia.org/wiki/Biblical_ cosmology.

"Bible Version Debate": Wikipedia contributors (web). Accessed April 1, 2017. http://en.wikipedia.org/wiki/ Bible_version_debate.

English Bible History (web). Accessed April 1, 2017. http://www. Timeline of How we got the English Bible.org, http://www. christiananswers.net/q-eden/edn-ordercreation.html, and www. greatsite.com/timeline-english-bible-history/. Accessed April 1, 2017.

Genesis 1 & 2 (web). Accessed April 1, 2017. http://www.servantofje-suschrist.com/kjv1611/genesis/chapter_01.html and http://www.kingjamesbibleonline.org/Genesis-Chapter-1/Chapter-2 (Standard version).

"Genesis Creation Narrative": Wikipedia contributors (web). Accessed April 1, 2017. http://www.en.wikipedia.org/wiki/Genesis creation narrative.

The Holy Bible, King James Version (1940s). Trade Paperback. Cleveland and New York: The World Publishing Company.

"Islamic Mythology": Wikipedia contributors (web). Accessed April 1, 2017. http://www.en.wikipedia.org/wiki/Islamic_mythology.

The Oral Law—Talmud & Mishna (web). Accessed April 1, 2017. http://www.JewishVirtualLibrary.org. Accessed April 2, 2017.

"Talmud": Wikipedia contributors (web). Accessed April 1, 2017. http://www.en.wikipedia.org/wiki/Talmud.

"Ten Commandments": Wikipedia contributors (web). Accessed April 1, 2017. http://www.jewfaq.org/10.htm (Older Hebrew version of the Ten Things versus King James version of the Ten Commandments).

Chapter Eight: The Sumerian/Babylonian Worldview

Alford, Alan F. (1999). *Gods of the New Millennium: Scientific Proof of Flesh & Blood Gods.* Hodder & Stoughton.

———— 2000. *When the Gods Came Down: The Catastrophic Roots of Religion Revealed.* Hodder & Stoughton.

Alien (web-a). Accessed April 1, 2017. http://www.bibliotecapleyades. net/esp_autor_zeitlin.htm#Chronicles_of_The_Gírkù.

———— (web-b). Accessed April 1, 2017. http://www.bibliotecapleyades.net/vida_alien/esp_vida_alien_18h.htm.

———— (web-c). Accessed April 1, 2017. http://www.bibliotecapleyades.net/vida_alien/ esp_vida_alien_63.htm.

———— (web-d). Accessed April 1, 2017. http://www.bibliotecap-leyades.net/vida_alien/secret_darkstars/images/gen21E.jpg. Accessed

———— (2000). *When the Gods Came Down: The Catastrophic Roots of Religion Revealed*. Hodder & Stoughton.

Babylonian (web-a). "The Babylonian Legends of the Creation" [Page 10 of 36]. Accessed April 1, 2017. http://www.aolib.com/reader_9914_9.htm, Aolib.com.

———— (web-b). *The Babylonian Legends of the Creation*. Accessed April 1 2017. http://sacred-texts.com/ane/blc/ index.htm.

Boulay, R. A. (2003). *Flying Serpents and Dragons*. The Book Tree. Accessed April 2, 2017. http://www.sacred-texts.com.

Brandenburg, John (1999). *Dead Mars, Dying Earth*. Element Books.

———— (2011). *Life and Death on Mars: The New Mars Synthesis*. Adventures Unlimited Press.

Budge, E. A. Wallis (1921). *The Babylonian Legends of Creation*. Accessed April 2, 2017. http://www.Aolib.com.

Clark, Gerald R. (2013). *The Anunnaki of Nibiru: Mankind's Forgotten Creators, Enslavers, Saviors and Hidden Architects of the New World Order*. Gerald R. Clark, publisher.

Dalley, Stephanie, trans. (2000). "Myths from Mesopotamia: Creation, the Flood, Gilgamesh and Others," from the first tablet from the *Atrahasis*, Old Babylon version pp. 9–10, *Oxford World Classics*. Oxford University Press.

Farrell, Joseph P. (2005). *The Giza Death Star Destroyed: The Ancient War for Future Science*. Adventures Unlimited Press.

———— (2007). *The Cosmic War: Interplanetary Warfare, Modern Physics and Ancient Texts*. Adventures Unlimited Press.

———— (2011a). *Genes, Giants, Monsters and Men: The Surviving Elites of the Cosmic War and Their Hidden Agenda*. Feral House.

———— with Scott D. de Hart (2011b). *The Grid of the Gods: The Aftermath of the Cosmic War and the Physics of the Pyramid Peoples*. Adventures Unlimited Press.

Gateways to Babylon (web). Accessed June 7, 2017. http://www.gatewaystobabylon.com/essays/ essaysenki.world.html.

Gibil (web). Accessed April 2, 2017. http://www.theancientaliens.com/ nuclear-weapons.

Hardy, Chris H., PhD (2014). *DNA of the Gods: The Anunnaki Creation of Eve and the Alien Battle for Humanity*. Bear & Co.

King, L. W. (web). "Annals of the Kings of Assyria." Accessed April 2, 2017. https://catalog.hathitrust.org/Record/ 000852548.

Knight, Christopher and Alan Butler (2006). *Who Built the Moon?* Walker.

Kramer, Samuel Noah (1945). "A Sumerian Paradise Myth." *Bulletin of the American Schools of Oriental Research*. Supplementary Studies, 1.

———— (1956). *History Begins in Sumer*. Doubleday.

———— (1961). *Sumerian Mythology*. First edition. University of Pennsylvania Press.

———— (1971). *The Sumerians: Their History, Culture and Character*. University of Chicago Press.

———— (1989). *Myths of Enki, the Crafty God*. Oxford University Press.

Langdon, Stephen (1915). *The Sumerian Epic of Paradise, the Flood and the Fall of Man*. Philadelphia: University Museum.

Marciniak, Barbara (1994). *Earth: The Pleiadian Keys to the Living Library*. Bear & Company.

"Me (mythology)": Wikipedia contributors (web). Accessed April 2, 2017. http://www.en.wikipedia.org/wiki/ Me_(mythology).

Morning Sky, Robert (1996). *The Terra Papers – Hidden History of Planet Earth*. Accessed April 1, 2017. http://www.rdgable.files.wordpress.com/2011/09/the_terra_papers_ parts_1_and_2.pdf.

Mummy (web). Accessed April 1, 2017. http://www.disclose.tv/news/ Extraterrestrial_Mummy_Found_in_Egypt/86067.

Mutwa, Credo (2003). *Zulu Shaman: Dreams, Prophesies and Mysteries (Songs of the Stars)*. Destiny Books.

O'Brien, Christian (1999). *The Genius of the Few*. Dianthus *Publishing*.

Parks, Anton (2007). *Adam Genesis*. Novelle Terre.

———— (2013a). *The Secret of the Dark Stars*. Pahana Books.

———— (2013b). *Eden: The Truth about Our Origins*. Pahana Books.

———— (web-a). Accessed April 1, 2017. http://www.antonparks.com/ AntonParks_First_interview.pdf.

———— (web-b). Accessed April 1, 2017. http://www.antonparks.com/ main.php?lang=en&page=eden#.

———— (web-c). Accessed April 1, 2017. http://www.karmopolis.be/ pipeline/ anton_parks.htm.

———— (web-d). Accessed April 1, 2017. http://www.karmapolis.be/ pipeline/anton_parks2_2.htm.

———— (web-e). Accessed April 1, 2017. http://www.Open Seti.org.

Penre, Wes (web). Accessed April 1, 2017. http://www.wespenre.com/ site-index.htm.

Project Gutenberg (web). *The Babylonian Legends of Creation.* Ebook. Accessed April 1, 2017. http://www.gutenberg.org/files/ 9914/9914-h/9914-h.htm. British Museum.

Rosenberg, David (2006). *Abraham: The First Historical Biography.* Basic Books.

Scranton, Laird (2010). *The Cosmological Origins of Myth and Symbol: From the Dogon and Ancient Egypt to India, Tibet and China.* Inner Traditions.

Sitchin, Zecharia (1990). *Genesis Revisited.* Avon Books.

———— (1998). *The Cosmic Code: Book VI of the Earth Chronicles.* Harper Collins.

———— (2001). *The Lost Book of Enki: Memoirs and Prophecies of an Extraterrestrial God.* Bear & Co.

Smith, George (web). Accessed April 2, 2017. https://en.wikipedia. org/wiki/George_Smith_(Assyriologist).

Stephany, Timothy J. (2013). *Enuma Elish: The Babylonian Creation Epic.* Create Space Independent Publishing.

Tellinger, Michael (2012). *Slave Species of the Gods: The Secret History of the Anunnaki and Their Mission on Earth.* Bear & Co.

Chapter Nine: The Hindu Worldview

Aurobindo, Sri. (1995). *Secret of the Vedas.* Lotus Press.

Prabhupada, Swami A. C Bhaktivedanta, Trans. (2011). *The Srimad-Bhagavatam Canto Two, Chapter Ten.* First e-book edition. Bhaktivedanta Book Trust.

Bishop, Peter and Michael Darton, eds. (1988). *The Encyclopedia of World Faiths: An Illustrated Survey of the World's Living Religions.* Facts on File Publications.

Brown, W. Norman (web). "The Creation Myth of the Rig Veda."
    In *Journal of the American Oriental Society*, vol. 62, No. 2 (1942)
    pp 85–98. Accessed April 2, 2017. http://www.jstor.org/sta-
    ble/594460?seq=1#page_ scan_tab_contents.

Chatterji, J. C. (1992). *The Wisdom of the Vedas*. Quest Books.

Hinduism (web-a). Accessed April 3, 2017. http://www.himalayanacad-
    emy.com/ readlearn/basics/fourteen-questions.

———— (web-b). Accessed April 3, 2017. http://www.hinduwebsite.
    com.

"Hinduism": Wikipedia contributors (web). Accessed April 2, 2017.
    http://www.simple.wikipedia.org/wiki/Hinduism.

Meredith, Susan and Clare Hickman (2010). *The Usborne Encyclopedia of
    World Religions*. Facts on File Publications.

Pattanaik, Devdutt (2003). *Indian Mythology, Tales, Symbols and Rituals form
    the Heart of the Subcontinent*. Inner Traditions.

Chapter Ten: The Buddhist Worldview

Bishop, Peter and Michael Darton, eds. (1988) *The Encyclopedia of World
    Faiths: An Illustrated Survey of the World's Living Religions*. Facts on
    File Publications.

Bodhi, Bhikku, ed. (2005). *In the Buddha's Words: an Anthology of Discours-
    es from the Pali Canon*. Wisdom Publications.

Buddha (web-a). Accessed April 2, 2017. http://www.khamkoo.com/
    uploads/9/0/0/4/9004485/life_of_the_buddha.pdf.

———— (web-b). Accessed April 2, 2017. http://www.pacificbuddha.
    org/wp-content/uploads/2014/01/In-the-Buddhas-Words.pdf.

Buddhism (web-a). Accessed April 2, 2017. https://books.google.
    com/books?id=enUKAQAAMAAJ&printsec= frontcover&-
    source=gbs_ge_summary_r&cad=0#v=onepage&q&f=false.

———— (web-b). Accessed April 1, 2017. http://www.buddhanet.net/
    budsas/ebud/whatbudbelieve/297.htlm.

———— (web-c). Accessed April 2, 2017. http://www.khandro.net/
    buddhism_paths_tibetan.htm.

———— (web-d). Accessed April 2, 2017. http://www.religioustoler-
    ance.org/buddhism.htm.

———— (web-e). Accessed April 2, 2017. http://www.sacred-texts. com/journals/mon/abudgen.htm.

———— (web-f). Accessed April 2, 2017. http://www.thoughtco.com/ buddhism-4133165. Accessed

Edmunds, Albert J., trans. (1904). "A Buddhist Genesis." In *The Monist, A Quarterly Magazine Devoted to the Philosophy of Science*, Volume XIV. Wisdom Quarterly. Accessed April 2, 2017. http://www. jstor.org/stable/27899497?seq= 1#page_scan_tab_contents-A.

Gunasekara, Dr. Victor A. (web). "Basic Buddhism, A Modern Introduction to the Buddha's Teaching." Accessed April 2, 2017. http://www.budsas.org/ebud/ebdha104.htm.

Nanamoli, Bhikku (web). "The Life of Buddha." *American Buddhist Journal.* Accessed April 2, 2017. http://www.About.com Buddhism.

"Pali": Wikipedia contributors (web). "The Tripitaka or Pali Canon," the First Buddhist Scripture and Early Buddhist History; The First Five Centuries. Accessed April 2, 2017. http://www. en.wikipedia.org/wiki/ P%C4%81li_Canon.

Robinson, R. H. and W. L. Johnson (1997). *The Buddhist Religion: A Historical Introduction*. Wadsworth Publishing Co.

Sadakata, Akira and Hajime Nakamura (1997). *Buddhist Cosmology Philosophy and Origins*. Kosei Publishing Co.

Walshe, Maurice, ed., trans. (1987). *The Long Discourses of the Buddha* (Introduction). Wisdom Publications.

"Zen": Wikipedia contributors (web). Accessed April 2, 2017.http:// www.en.wikipedia.org/wiki/Zen.

Chapter Eleven: The Gnostic Worldview

Barnstone, Willis and Marvin Meyer, eds. (2003). *The Gnostic Bible, Gnostic Texts of Mystical Wisdom from the Ancient and Medieval Worlds*. Translations of Pagan, Jewish, Christian, Sethian, Hermetic, Mandaean, Manichaean Islamic and Cathar texts. Boston: Shambala. Accessed April 2, 2017. http://www.classicalastrologer. files.wordpress.com/ 2012/12/the_gnostic_bible.pdf.

Behr, John, ed. (2015). *Irenaeus of Lyons: Identifying Christianity*. Reprint. Oxford University Press.

Doresse, Jean (1970). *The Secret Books of the Egyptian Gnostics; an Introduction to the Gnostic Coptic Manuscripts*. New York: AMS Press.

Hoeller, Stephan A., Gnostic Bishop (web). "The Origins of the Gnostic Movement," "The Gnostic Theory of Alien Intrusion," "Alien Dreaming," "The Enigma of the Archons," "How we are Deviated, Motives and Methods of the Archons," "A Gnostic Catechism," "The Gnosis Archive," "The Genesis Factor." Accessed April 2, 2017. http://www.gnosis.org/gnintro.htm.

Irenaeus of Lyons (web). *Against Heresies*. Book I. The Gnostic Society Library. Accessed April 2, 2017. http://www.gnosis.org/library/advh1.htm#1-8-5.

Lash, John Lamb (2006). *Not in His Image*. Chelsea Green Publishing.
——— (web-b). Accessed April 2, 2017. "Origins of the Gnostic Movement," "The Gnostic Story of Alien Intrusion," "The Archon Files," "The Enigma of the Archons," "How We Are Deviated, Motives and Methods of the Archon." http://www.metahistory.org/sitemap.php#gnostique.

Layton, Bentley, trans. (web). From *The Nag Hammadi Library*: "The Hypostatis of the Archons: The Reality of the Rulers." Accessed April 2, 2017. http://www.gnosis.org/naghamm/hypostas.html.

Nag Hammadi Library (web). Accessed April 2, 2017. http://www.bibliotecapleyades.net/nag_hammadi/contents.htm.

Reimer, Carol A. (2013). *Sophia and the Archons*. Rosebud Publications.

Chapter Twelve: The Elohim/Ra Group Worldview

Free, Wynne (web). *The Creator Gods of the Physical Universe Want to Talk to You* (2014), pp. 1–44. Channeled messages from the Elohim, available in audio and transcription formats: How the Universe was Created, 6-03-2013. How the Universe was Created, 1-6-14. Ra'An Talks About Building Humanity, 10-17-2011. Ra'An Tells Us About the Origins of Humanity, 9-12-11. Where Do Atoms and Molecules Come From? 10-24-2011. Ra Materials Made Simple, 2-16-2013. About Crop Circles, 3-20-2013. Wynn and Carla Explore the Law of One and Easter, 3-31-2013. Accessed April 2, 2017. http://www.thespiritchannel.net-Intelligent-Infinity and http://www.intelligent-infinity.com.

———— with David Wilcock (2004). *The Reincarnation of Edgar Cayce.* Berkeley: Frog, Ltd.

L/L Research – Don Elkins, Carla Ruekert and James Allen McCarty (1984). *The Law of One*, Books I-IV. Whitford Press, division of Schiffer Publishing, Ltd.

———— (web). Channeled sessions. Accessed April 2, 2017. http://www.llresearch.org and http://www.lawofone.info.

Chapter Thirteen: The Anthroposophic Worldview

Shepherd, Arthur P. (1990). *Rudolf Steiner: Scientist of the Invisible.* Reprint. Inner Traditions.

Steiner, Rudolf (1959). *Cosmic Memory: A Prehistory of Earth and Man.* Rudolf Steiner Publications, Inc.

———— (1994). *How to Know Higher Worlds: A Modern Path of Initiation.* Anthroposphic Press: Classics in Anthroposophy. Accessed April 1, 2017. http://www.books.google.com.

———— (2008). *An Esoteric Cosmology; Evolution, Christ and Modern Spirituality.* Steiner Books.

———— (2015). *Outline of Occult Science.* Reprint: out-of-print English edition of the Gunn translation. CreateSpace Independent Publishing.

———— (web-a). Accessed April 1, 2017. http://goodreads.com/author/quote/2593.Rudolph_Steiner?page:2.

———— (web-b). Accessed April 1, 2017. "Three Streams in the Evolution of Mankind." Lecture Series 184 (1918). http://wn.rsarchive.org/lectures.

Chapter Fourteen: The Sant Mat Masters Worldview

Kabir (1984). *The Ocean of Love: The Anurag Sagur of Kabir.* Translated by Raj Kumar Bagga, Partap Singh and Kent Bicknell. Second edition. Sanbornton, NH: Sant Bani Ashram.

Philosophy of the Masters (1967). vols. I–V. First edition. Beas, India: Radha Soami Satsang.

Sar Bachan (1955). *The Teachings of Soamiji Maharaj.* Beas, India: Radha Soami Satsang.

Singh, Maharaj Sawan (1963). *Discourses on Sant Mat.* Beas, India: Radha Soami Satsang.

Singh, Sant Kirpal (1967). *Godman*. Delhi: Ruhani Satsang.
———— (1976). *The Teachings of Kirpal Singh*. vols. 1–3. Manchester, NH: Sant Bani Press.

Chapter Fifteen: The Wingmakers Worldview

Childress, David Hatcher, ed. (2007). *The Time Travel Handbook*. Adventures Unlimited Press.
Mahu, James (1998). *The Ancient Arrow Project*. Ebook. Wingmakers LLC. Accessed April 2, 2017. http://www.wingmakers.com.
———— (2008). Project Camelot Interview. Accessed April 2, 2017. http://www.projectcamelotportal.com.
———— (2009). Conscious Media Interview. Accessed April 2, 2017. http://www.wingmakers.com.
Neruda, Dr. Jamisson (1998). The Fifth Interview (pdf). Accessed April 2, 2017. http://www.wingmakers.com.
Wingmakers (web-a). Accessed April 2, 2017. http://www.wingmakers.com.
———— (web-b). Accessed April 2, 2017. http://www.lyricus.org.
———— (web-c). Accessed April 2, 2017. http://www.eventtemples.org.
———— (web-d). Accessed April 2, 2017. http://www.spiritstate.com.
———— (web-e). Accessed April 2, 2017. http://www.sovereignintegrl. blogspot.com.

Chapter Sixteen: The Cassiopaean Worldview

Cassiopaeans (web-a). Accessed April 2, 2017. http:// www.cassiopaea.com.
———— (web-b). Accessed April 2, 2017. http://www.cassiopaea.org/forum/.
———— (web-c). Accessed April 2, 2017. http://www.cassiopaea.org.
———— (web-d). Accessed April 2, 2017. http://www.cassiopaea.org/cass/index.html.
———— (web-e). Accessed April 2, 2017. http://www.quantumfuture.net/.
Knight-Jadczyk, Laura (2003, 2011). *Petty Tyrants and Facing the Unknown, Navigating the Traps and Diversions of Life in the Matrix*. Vols. 5 & 6. Red Pill Press.

———— (2004). *High Strangeness, Hyperdimensions and the Process of Alien Abduction*. Red Pill Press.

———— (2005). *The Secret History of the World and How to Get Out Alive*. Red Hill Press.

———— (2009). *Almost Human*. Book Seven of The Wave Series. Red Pill Press.

———— (2012). *Debugging the Universe: The Hero's Journey*. Red Pill Press.

———— (2013). *Comets and the Horns of Moses*. Red Pill Press.

Chapter Seventeen: The Andromedan Worldview

Andromeda (web). Accessed April 2, 2017. http://www.bibliotecapleyades.net/esp_andromedacom.htm.

Collier, Alex (1996). *Defending Sacred Ground: The Andromedan Compendium*. Leading Edge International Group.

———— (web-a). Archive of public talks, radio and Youtube interviews, including a transcript of "A History of the Galaxy." Accessed April 2, 2017. http://www.alexcollier.org.

———— (web-b). Interview with Art Bell on Coast to Coast. Accessed April 1, 2017. http://www.youtube.be/UoFLLOqZnc. 2016 Update 8/13/2016.

Chapter Eighteen: The Superstructure of the Cosmos

Blake, William (web). Accessed June 28, 2017. http://www.wikiquote.org/wiki/William_Blake.

Hologram (web). Accessed April 2, 2017. https://uwaterloo.ca/physics-astronomy/news/study-reveals-evidence-universe-hologram.

Kanzie, Cynthia (web). Accessed June 20, 2017. "Cliques of Neurons Bound into Cavities Provide Missing Link between Structure and Functions." *Frontiers in Computational Neuroscience* (2017) DO; 10.3389/fncom.2017-00048, from www.messagetoeagle.com.

L/L Research – Don Elkins, Carla Ruekert and James Allen McCarty (1984). *The Law of One*, Books I-IV. Whitford Press, division of Schiffer Publishing, Ltd.

Lash, John Lamb (web-a). Accessed April 2, 2017. http://www.metahistory.org.

———— (web-b). Accessed April 2, 2017. http://www.metahistory.org/
Telestics/GreatDeception3.php, Part 2, "Handling Supernatural
Power," October 16, 2016.

Meher Baba (1973). *God Speaks: The Theme of Creation and Its Purpose.*
Second edition. Sufism Reoriented.

Rudhyar, Dane (1975). *The Sun is Also a Star.* Dutton.

Seifer, Marc, PhD (2008). *Transcending the Speed of Light: Consciousness,
Quantum Physics, and the Fifth Dimension.* Inner Traditions.

Singh, Maharaj Jagat (2002). *The Science of the Soul, Discourses of the Masters.* Beas, India: Rhada Soami Satsang.

Steiner, Rudolf (web-b). Accessed April 2, 2017. "Three Streams in
the Evolution of Mankind." Lecture Series 184 (1918). http://
www.wn.rsarchive.org/Lectures/GA184/English/RSP1965/
ThrStr_index.html.

Toroidal (web). Accessed April 2, 2017. http://www.cosmometry.net/
the-torus-dynamic-flow-process.

Yukteswar, Swami Sri (1984). *The Holy Science.* Los Angeles: Self-Realization Fellowship.

Part IV: Living in a Virtual-Reality Hologram

Chapter Nineteen: The Construction of the Holographic Control System

Alfred, Jay (2006). *Brains and Realities.* Trafford Publishing.

Castaneda, Carlos (1998). *The Active Side of Infinity.* Laugan Productions.

de Ropp, Robert S. (1968). *The Master Game.* Dell Publishing.

Groundhog Day (web). Accessed April 1, 2017. http://www.imdb.com/
title/tt0107048/.

Icke, David (2012). *Remember Who You Are, Remember Where You Are and
Where You Come From.* David Icke Books.

———— (2016). *Phantom Self.* David Icke Books.

Kabir (1984). *The Ocean of Love: The Anurag Sagur of Kabir.* Translated
by Raj Kumar Bagga, Partap Singh and Kent Bicknell. Second
edition. Sanbornton, NH: Sant Bani Ashram.

Knight-Jadczyk, Laura (2008). *High Strangeness: Hyperdimensions and the
Process of Alien Abduction.* Red Pill Press.

————— (2012). *Debugging the Universe: The Hero's Journey.* Red Pill Press.

L/L Research – Don Elkins, Carla Ruekert and James Allen McCarty (1984). *The Law of One.* Book I. Whitford Press, division of Schiffer Publishing, Ltd.

Lash, John Lamb (2006). *Not in His Image.* Chelsea Green Publishing.

Lipton, Bruce (2005). *The Biology of Belief: Unleashing the Power of Consciousness, Matter and Miracles.* Mountain of Love/Elite Books.

Matrix (web). Accessed April 1, 2017. http://www.imdb.com/title/tt0133093/.

Newberg, Andrew, and d'Aquili, Eugene (1999). *The Mystical Mind: Probing the Biology of Religious Experience.* Fortress Press.

Pert, Candace (1997). *Molecules of Emotion: The Science behind Mind-Body Medicine.* Touchstone.

Roberts, Jane (1982). *The Nature of Personal Reality.* Bantam Books.

Sagan, Carl (1986). *The Dragons of Eden: Speculations on the Evolution of Human Intelligence.* Ballantine Books, reprint.

Steiner, Rudolf (web-c). Accessed April 1, 2017. https://rudolfsteinerquotes.wordpress.com/2015/09/30/man-ideal-of-the-gods/.

Talbott, David, and Wallace Thornhill (2005). *Thunderbolts of the Gods.* Mikamar Publishing.

Thompson, Richard L. (2003). *Maya: The World as Virtual Reality.* Institute for Vaishnava Studies.

Thunderbolts (web). Accessed April 1, 2017. http://www.thunderboltsproject.com.

Chapter Twenty: Interdimensional Manipulation of Consciousness

Bohm, David (2002). *Wholeness and the Implicate Order.* Routledge Classics.

Castaneda, Carlos (1998) *The Active Side of Infinity.* Laugan Productions.

Hancock, Graham (2007). *Supernatural: Meetings with the Ancient Teachers of Mankind.* The Disinformation Company Ltd.

————— and Santha Faiia (1999). *Heaven's Mirror: Quest for the Lost Civilization.* Three Rivers Press.

Jacobs, David (1993). *Secret Life: Firsthand Documented Accounts of UFO Abductions.* Simon & Schuster.

————— (1995). *Abduction: Human Encounters with Aliens.* Simon & Schuster.

Johnson, Julian, MD (1997). *The Path of the Masters.* 16th edition. Beas, India: Radha Soami Satsang.

Knight-Jadczyk, Laura (2001). *Debugging the Universe*. Red Pill Press.
———— (2008). *High Strangeness: Hyperdimensions and the Process of Alien Abduction*. Red Pill Press.
L/L Research – Don Elkins, Carla Ruekert and James Allen McCarty (1984). *The Law of One*. Books I–IV. Schiffer.
Lash, John, and Lydia Dzumardjin (web-d). Accessed April 3, 3017. "Beyond the Tyranny of Beliefs-The Topic of Topics, Gnostic Parallels in the Writings of Carlos Castaneda." http://www.Metahistory.org.
Mack, John (2000). *Passport to the Cosmos: Human Transformation and Alien Encounters*. Thorsons.
Narby, Jeremy (1998). *The Cosmic Serpent: DNA and the Origins of Knowledge*. London: Victor Gollancz.
"Panspermia": Wikipedia contributors (web). Accessed August 5, 2017. http://en.wikipedia.org/wiki/Panspermia.
Straussman, Rick, MD (2001). *DMT: The Spirit Molecule: A Doctor's Revolutionary Research into The Biology of Near-Death and Mystical Experiences*. Park Street Press.
Talbot, Michael (1991). *The Holographic Universe*. Harper Collins Publishers.
Vallee, Jacques (1969). *On UFO's, Folklore and Parallel Worlds*. Contemporary Books.
———— (1979). *Messengers of Deception: UFO Contacts and Cults*. Ronin Publishing.
———— and Chris Aubeck (2010). *Wonders in the Sky: Unexplained Arial Objects from Antiquity to Modern Times*. TarcherPerigee.
Walton, Travis (1997). *Fire in the Sky: the Walton Experience*. Da Capo Press.
Wilcock, David (2011). *The Source Field Investigations*. The Penguin Group.

Part V: Evolving Higher Dimensions of Consciousness

Long Chen Pa (web). Accessed April 2, 2017. http://quotes.justdharma.com/everything-is-but-an-apparition.

Chapter Twenty-One: The Pathway Home to Source

Citro, Massimo, MD (2011). *The Basic Code of the Universe: The Science of the Invisible in Physics, Medicine and Spirituality.* Park Street Press, a division of Inner Traditions International.

Discourses on Sant Mat. (1963). Beas, India: Radha Soami Satsang.

Easwaran, Eknath (1999). *The Upanishads: A Classic of Indian Spirituality.* Nilgiri Press.

Galactic Center (web). Accessed. April 2, 2017. https://www.myastrol-ogybook.com/galactic-center-great-central-sun.htm.

Gardner, Laurence (web). Accessed April 2, 2017. Lecture: "Genesis of the Grail Kings." https://www.bibliotecapleyades.net/biblianazar/esp_biblianazar_21.htm.

Henry, William (2007). *Starwalkers and the Dimension of the Blessed.* Adventures Unlimited Press.

Johnson, Julian, MD (1997). *The Path of the Masters.* 16th edition. Beas, India: Radha Soami Satsang.

Kabir (1984). *The Ocean of Love: The Anurag Sagur of Kabir,* Second Edition. Sanbornton, New Hampshire: Sant Bani Ashram.

Philosophy of the Masters. (1967). Volume V. First edition. Beas, India: Radha Soami Satsang.

Singh, Sant Baljit (2014). *Know Thyself as Soul: India Report.* Florida: Edition Naam.

"Sirius": Wikipedia contributors (web). Accessed April 2, 2017. https://en.wikipedia.org/wiki/sirius.

Subramuniyaswami, Satguru Sivaya (1993). *Dancing with Siva: Hinduism's Contemporary Catechism.* Fourth edition. India/USA: Himalayan Academy.

"Theosophy": Wikipedia contributors (web). Accessed April 2, 2017. https://en.wikipedia.org/ wiki/theosophy.

Woebcke, Carl (web). Accessed. April 2, 2017. *Illustrated Astrology Textbook.* http://www.myastrologybook.com/galactic-center-great-central-sun.htm:

Chapter Twenty-Two: And the Truth Is...

Ali, Sri Mumtaz (2011). *The Jewel in the Lotus: Deeper Aspects of Hinduism.* Fourth edition. Magenta Press.

Gibran, Kahlil (1986). *The Prophet*. Fifty-seventh printing. Pocket edition. Alfred A. Knopf, Inc.

Hawkins, David R., MD, PhD (2006b). *Transcending the Levels of Consciousness: The Stairway to Enlightenment*. Veritas Publishing.

Singh, Sant Baljit (2016). *Know Thyself as Soul* Magazine. Issue 3. Florida: Edition Naam.

Yogananda, Paramahansa (2003). *Autobiography of a Yogi*. Self Realization Fellowship.

Consolidated References

Alford, Alan F. 1999. *Gods of the New Millennium: Scientific Proof of Flesh & Blood Gods.* Hodder & Stoughton.

———— 2000. *When the Gods Came Down: The Catastrophic Roots of Religion Revealed.* Hodder & Stoughton.

Alfred, Jay. 2006. *Brains and Realities.* Trafford Publishing.

Ali, Sri Mumtaz. 2011. *The Jewel in the Lotus: Deeper Aspects of Hinduism.* Fourth edition. Magenta Press.

Alien. web-a. Accessed April 1, 2017. http://www.bibliotecapleyades. net/esp_autor_zeitlin.htm#Chronicles_of_The_Gírkù.

————. web-b. Accessed April 1, 2017. http://www.bibliotecapleyades. net/vida_alien/esp_vida_alien_18h.htm.

————. web-c. Accessed April 1, 2017. http://www.bibliotecapleyades. net/vida_alien/ esp_vida_alien_63.htm.

————. web-d. Accessed April 1, 2017. http://www.bibliotecapleyades. net/vida_alien/secret_darkstars/images/gen21E.jpg. Accessed

Andromeda. Accessed April 2, 2017. http://www.bibliotecapleyades. net/esp_andromedacom.htm.

Aurobindo, Sri. 1990. "The Release from the Ego." In *The Synthesis of Yoga.* Lotus Press. Accessed April 2, 2017. http://www.surasa. net/aurobindo/syn thesis/part-2.html#ch09.

————. 1995. *Secret of the Vedas.* Lotus Press.

————. 2010. *The Life Divine.* Pondicherry: Sri Aurobindo Ashram.

Babylonian. web-a. "The Babylonian Legends of the Creation" [Page 10 of 36]. Accessed April 1, 2017. http://www.aolib.com/reader_9914_9.htm, Aolib.com.

————. web-b. *The Babylonian Legends of the Creation.* Accessed April 1 2017. http://sacred-texts.com/ane/blc/ index.htm.

Barnstone, Willis and Marvin Meyer, eds. 2003. *The Gnostic Bible, Gnostic Texts of Mystical Wisdom from the Ancient and Medieval Worlds.* Translations of Pagan, Jewish, Christian, Sethian, Hermetic, Mandaean, Manichaean Islamic and Cathar texts. Boston:

Shambala. Accessed April 2, 2017. http://www.classicalastrolo-ger. files.wordpress.com/ 2012/12/the_gnostic_bible.pdf.

Bartlett's. Accessed April 1, 2017. http://www.bartleby.com/essay/ The-Beginning-of-Life-in-the-Book-P3JE86USVJ.

Behr, John, ed. 2015. *Irenaeus of Lyons: Identifying Christianity.* Reprint. Oxford University Press.

Bishop, Peter and Michael Darton, eds. 1988) *The Encyclopedia of World Faiths: An Illustrated Survey of the World's Living Religions.* Facts on File Publications.

Blake, William. Accessed June 28, 2017. http://www.wikiquote.org/ wiki/William_Blake.

Bodhi, Bhikku, ed. 2005. *In the Buddha's Words: an Anthology of Discourses from the Pali Canon.* Wisdom Publications.

Bohm, David. 2002. *Wholeness and the Implicate Order.* Routledge Classics.

Boulay, R. A. 2003. *Flying Serpents and Dragons.* The Book Tree. Accessed April 2, 2017. http://www.sacred-texts.com.

Brandenburg, John. 1999. *Dead Mars, Dying Earth.* Element Books.

———. 2011. *Life and Death on Mars: The New Mars Synthesis.* Adventures Unlimited Press.

Brihadarayaka Upanishad, Liv. 10. Accessed June 17, 2017. http://meta-physicalmusing.com.

Brown, W. Norman. "The Creation Myth of the Rig Veda." *Journal of the American Oriental Society*, Vol. 62, No. 2. 1942) pp. 85–98. Accessed April 2, 2017. http://www.jstor.org/stable/594460?se-q=1#page_ scan_tab_contents.

Buddha. web-a. Accessed April 2, 2017. http://www.khamkoo.com/ uploads/9/0/0/4/9004485/life_of_the_buddha.pdf.

———. web-b. Accessed April 2, 2017. http://www.pacificbuddha. org/wp-content/uploads/2014/01/In-the-Buddhas-Words.pdf. Accessed April 2, 2017.

Buddhism. web-a. Accessed April 2, 2017. https://books.google. com/books?id=enUKAQAAMAAJ&printsec= frontcover&-source=gbs_ge_summary_r&cad=0#v=onepage&q&f=false.

———. web-b. Accessed April 1, 2017. http://www.buddhanet.net/ budsas/ebud/whatbudbelieve/297.htlm.

———. web-c. Accessed April 1, 2017. http://www.khandro.net/buddhism_paths_tibetan.htm.

———. web-d. Accessed April 2, 2017. http://www.religioustolerance.org/buddhism.htm.

———. web-e. Accessed April 2, 2017. http://www.sacred-texts.com/journals/mon/abudgen.htm.

———. web-f. Accessed April 2, 2017. http://www.thoughtco.com/buddhism-4133165. Accessed

Budge, E. A. Wallis. 1921. *The Babylonian Legends of Creation.* Accessed April 2, 2017. http://www.Aolib.com.

Cassiopaeans. web-a. Accessed April 2, 2017. http://www.cassiopaea.com.

———. web-b. Accessed April 2, 2017. http://www.cassiopaea.org/forum/.

———. web-c. Accessed April 2, 2017. http://www.cassiopaea.org.

———. web-d. Accessed April 2, 2017. http://www.cassiopaea.org/cass/index.html.

———. web-e. Accessed April 2, 2017. http://www.quantumfuture.net/.

Castaneda, Carlos. 1998. *The Active Side of Infinity.* Laugan Productions.

Chatterji, J. C. 1992. *The Wisdom of the Vedas.* Quest Books.

Chiao, Raymond Y. Accessed April 2, 2017. http://www.scientificamerican.com/article/what-is-known-about-tachy/.

Childress, David Hatcher, ed. 2007. *The Time Travel Handbook.* Adventures Unlimited Press.

Citro, Massimo, MD. 2011. *The Basic Code of the Universe: The Science of the Invisible in Physics, Medicine and Spirituality.* Park Street Press, a division of Inner Traditions International.

Clark, Gerald R. 2013. *The Anunnaki of Nibiru: Mankind's Forgotten Creators, Enslavers, Saviors and Hidden Architects of the New World Order.* Gerald R. Clark.

Collier, Alex. 1996. *Defending Sacred Ground: The Andromedan Compendium.* Leading Edge International Group.

———. web-a. Archive of public talks, radio and Youtube interviews, including a transcript of "A History of the Galaxy." Accessed April 2, 2017. http://www.alexcollier.org.

———. web-b. Interview with Art Bell on Coast to Coast. Accessed April 1, 2017. http://www.youtube.be/UoFLLOqZnc. 2016 Update 8/13/2016.

Dalley, Stephanie, trans. 2000. "Myths from Mesopotamia: Creation, the Flood, Gilgamesh and Others," from the first tablet from the *Atrahasis*, Old Babylon version pp. 9–10, *Oxford World Classics*. Oxford University Press.

Davies, Paul and John Gribbin. 2007. "The Death of Materialism." In *The Matter Myth*. Simon & Schuster.

de Ropp, Robert S. 1968. *The Master Game*. Dell Publishing.

Dennis, Kingsley L. 2012. *The Struggle For Your Mind; Conscious Evolution and the Battle to Control How We Think*. Inner Traditions.

Discourses on Sant Mat. 1963. Beas, India: Radha Soami Satsang.

Doresse, Jean. 1970. *The Secret Books of the Egyptian Gnostics; an Introduction to the Gnostic Coptic Manuscripts*. New York: AMS Press.

Easwaran, Eknath. 1999. *The Upanishads: A Classic of Indian Spirituality*. Nilgiri Press.

Edmunds, Albert J., trans. 1904. "A Buddhist Genesis." In *The Monist, A Quarterly Magazine Devoted to the Philosophy of Science*, Volume XIV. Wisdom Quarterly. Accessed April 2, 2017. http://www.jstor.org/stable/27899497?seq=1#page_scan_tab_contents-A.

English Bible History. Accessed April 1, 2017. http://www.Timeline of How we got the English Bible.org, http://www.christiananswers.net/q-eden/edn-ordercreation.html, and www.greatsite.com/timeline-english-bible-history/. Accessed April 1, 2017.

Erhard, Werner. 1982. *The End of Starvation: Creating an Idea Whose Time Has Come*. The Hunger Project.

Farrell, Joseph P. 2005. *The Giza Death Star Destroyed: The Ancient War for Future Science*. Adventures Unlimited Press.

———. 2007. *The Cosmic War: Interplanetary Warfare, Modern Physics and Ancient Texts*. Adventures Unlimited Press.

———. 2011a. *Genes, Giants, Monsters and Men: The Surviving Elites of the Cosmic War and Their Hidden Agenda*. Feral House.

——— with Scott D. de Hart. 2011b. *The Grid of the Gods: The Aftermath of the Cosmic War and the Physics of the Pyramid Peoples*. Adventures Unlimited Press.

Free, Wynne (web). *The Creator Gods of the Physical Universe Want to Talk to You* (2014), pp. 1–44. Channeled messages from the Elohim, available in audio and transcription formats: How the Universe was Created, 6-03-2013. How the Universe was Created, 1-6-14. Ra'An Talks About Building Humanity, 10-17-2011. Ra'An Tells Us About the Origins of Humanity, 9-12-11.. Where Do Atoms and Molecules Come From? 10-24-2011. Ra Materials Made Simple, 2-16-2013. About Crop Circles, 3-20-2013. Wynn and Carla Explore the Law of One and Easter, 3-31-2013. Accessed April 2, 2017. http://www.thespiritchannel.net-Intelligent-Infinity and http://www.intelligent-infinity.com.

———— with David Wilcock. 2004. *The Reincarnation of Edgar Cayce*. Berkeley: Frog, Ltd.

Fuller, Buckminster. Accessed April 1, 2017. http://www.goodreads.com/authorquotes/11515303.R/buckminster_fuller.

Galactic Center. Accessed April 2, 2017. https://www.myastrology-book.com/galactic-center-great-central-sun.htm.

Gardner, Laurence. Accessed April 2, 2017. "Genesis of the Grail Kings." https://www.bibliotecapleyades.net/biblianazar/esp_biblianazar_21.htm.

Gateways to Babylon. Accessed June 7, 2017. http://www.gatewaystobabylon.com/essays/ essaysenki.world.html.

Genesis 1 & 2. Accessed April 1, 2017. http://www.servantofjesuschrist.com/kjv1611/genesis/chapter_01.html and http://www.kingjamesbibleonline.org/Genesis-Chapter-1/Chapter-2. Standard version.

Gibil. Accessed April 2, 2017. http://www.theancientaliens.com/nuclear-weapons.

Gibran, Khalil. 1986. *The Prophet*. Fifty-seventh printing. Pocket edition. Alfred A. Knopf, Inc.

Goddard, Harald. Accessed April 1, 2017. http://www.books.google.com/The_Practical_Well-Being_Programme. Taylor & Francis.

Goswami, Amit, PhD. 1993. *The Self Aware Universe: How Consciousness Creates the Material World*. G.P. Putnam's Sons.

Groundhog Day. Accessed April 1, 2017. http://www.imdb.com/title/tt0107048/.

Gunasekara, Dr. Victor A. "Basic Buddhism, A Modern Introduction to the Buddha's Teaching." Accessed April 2, 2017. http://www.budsas.org/ebud/ebdha104.htm.

Haisch, Bernhard. Accessed April 1, 2017. "Brilliant Disguise: Light, Matter and the Zero-Point Field." http://enthea.org/library/brilliant-disguise-light-matter-and-the-zero-point-field/.

Hancock, Graham. 2007. *Supernatural: Meetings with the Ancient Teachers of Mankind*. The Disinformation Company Ltd.

———— and Santha Faiia. 1999. *Heaven's Mirror: Quest for the Lost* Civilization. Three Rivers Press.

Hardy, Chris H., PhD. 2014. *DNA of the Gods: The Anunnaki Creation of Eve and the Alien Battle for Humanity*. Bear & Co.

Hawkins, David R., MD PhD. 2001. *The Eye of the I from Which Nothing is Hidden*. Veritas Publishing.

————. 2002. Audio. *The Way to God: Radical Subjectivity: The I of Self*. Veritas Publishing.

————. 2003. *I: Reality and Subjectivity*. Veritas Publishing.

————. 2004. Audio. *The Highest Level of Enlightenment*. Nightingale-Conant.

————. 2004. Audio. *Transcending the Mind*. Veritas Publishing.

————. 2006a. *Discovery of the Presence of God*. Veritas Publishing.

————. 2006b. *Transcending the Levels of Consciousness: The Stairway to Enlightenment*. Veritas Publishing.

————. 2008. *Reality, Spirituality and Modern Man*. Ontario: Axial Publishing Co.

————. 2011. *Dissolving the Ego, Realizing the Self*. Hay House, Inc.

Henry, William. 2007. *Starwalkers and the Dimension of the Blessed*. Adventures Unlimited Press.

Hinduism. web-a. Accessed April 3, 2017. http://www.himalayanacademy.com/ readlearn/basics/fourteen-questions.

————. web-b. Accessed April 3, 2017. http://www.hinduwebsite.com.

"Hinduism": Wikipedia contributors (web). Accessed April 2, 2017. http://www.simple.wikipedia.org/wiki/Hinduism.

Hoeller, Stephan A., Gnostic Bishop. "The Origins of the Gnostic Movement," "The Gnostic Theory of Alien Intrusion," "Alien Dreaming," "The Enigma of the Archons," "How we are

Deviated, Motives and Methods of the Archons," "A Gnostic Catechism," "The Gnosis Archive," "The Genesis Factor." Accessed April 2, 2017. http://www.gnosis.org/gnintro.htm.

Hologram. Accessed April 2, 2017. https://uwaterloo.ca/physics-astronomy/news/study-reveals-evidence-universe-hologram.

Horgan, John. 1996. *The End of Science: Facing the Limits of Knowledge in the Twilight of the Scientific Age.* Basic Books.

Holy Bible, King James Version, The. 1940s. Trade Paperback. Cleveland and New York: The World Publishing Company.

Icke, David. 2012. *Remember Who You Are, Remember Where You Are and Where You Come From.* David Icke Books.

————. 2016. *Phantom Self.* David Icke Books.

Irenaeus of Lyons. *Against Heresies.* Book I. The Gnostic Society Library. Accessed April 2, 2017. http://www.gnosis.org/ library/ advh1.htm#1-8-5.

Jacobs, David. 1993. *Secret Life: Firsthand Documented Accounts of UFO Abductions.* Simon & Schuster.

————. 1995. *Abduction: Human Encounters with Aliens.* Simon & Schuster.

Johnson, Julian, MD (1997). *The Path of the Masters.* 16th edition. Beas, India: Radha Soami Satsang.

Joye, Shelli R. 2012. "The Trinitarian Psychophysics of Saccidananda in Sri Aurobindo's Philosophy of the Upanishads." California Institute of Integral Studies Department of Philosophy & Religion. Spring issue. http://www.academia.edu/3717823/ The_Trinitarian_Psychophysics_of_Sri_ Aurobindo.

Kabir. 1984. *The Ocean of Love: The Anurag Sagur of Kabir.* Translated by Raj Kumar Bagga, Partap Singh and Kent Bicknell. Second edition. Sanbornton, NH: Sant Bani Ashram.

Kaku, Michio. Accessed April 1, 2017. http://www.cnsnews.com/ news/article/barbara-hollingsworth/string-theory-co-founder-sub-atomic-particles-are-evidence-0.

Kanzie, Cynthia. Accessed June 20, 2017. "Cliques of Neurons Bound into Cavities Provide Missing Link between Structure and Functions." *Frontiers in Computational Neuroscience.* 2017) DO; 10.3389/fncom.2017-00048, from http://www.messagetoeagle.com.

King, L. W. "Annals of the Kings of Assyria." Accessed April 2, 2017. https://catalog.hathitrust.org/Record/ 000852548.

Knight, Christopher and Alan Butler. 2006. *Who Built the Moon?* Walker.

Knight-Jadczyk, Laura. 2001. *Debugging the Universe.* Red Pill Press.

————. 2003, 2011. *Petty Tyrants and Facing the Unknown, Navigating the Traps and Diversions of Life in the Matrix.* vols. 5 & 6. Red Pill Press.

————. 2004. *High Strangeness, Hyperdimensions & the Process of Alien Abduction.* Red Pill Press.

————. 2005. *The Secret History of the World and How to Get Out Alive.* Red Hill Press.

————. 2008. *High Strangeness: Hyperdimensions and the Process of Alien Abduction.* Red Pill Press.

————. 2009. *Almost Human.* Book Seven of The Wave Series. Red Pill Press.

————. 2012. *Debugging the Universe: The Hero's Journey.* Red Pill Press.

————. 2013. *Comets and the Horns of Moses.* Red Pill Press.

Kramer, Samuel Noah. 1945. "A Sumerian Paradise Myth." *Bulletin of the American Schools of Oriental Research.* Supplementary Studies, 1.

————. 1956. *History Begins in Sumer.* Doubleday.

————. 1961. Sumerian Mythology. First edition. University of Pennsylvania Press.

————. 1971. *The Sumerians: Their History, Culture and Character.* University of Chicago Press.

————. 1989. *Myths of Enki, The Crafty God.* Oxford University Press.

Kumara, Tiara. 2016. *Morphogenesis & The Skill Sets of Evolution: Evolutionary Teachings for Accelerated Spiritual Development and Humanitarian Service.* CreateSpace Independent Publishing Platform.

L/L Research – Don Elkins, Carla Ruekert and James Allen McCarty. 1984. *The Law of One,* Books I–IV. Whitford Press, division of Schiffer Publishing, Ltd.

————. Channeled sessions. Accessed April 2, 2017. http://www.llresearch.org and http://www.lawofone.info.

Langdon, Stephen. 1915. *The Sumerian Epic of Paradise, the Flood and the Fall of Man.* Philadelphia: University Museum.

Lash, John Lamb. 2006. *Not in His Image*. Chelsea Green Publishing.

———. web-a. Accessed April 2, 2017. http://www.metahistory.org.

———. web-b. Accessed April 2, 2017. http://www.metahistory.org/ Telestics/ GreatDeception3.php, Part 2, "Handling Supernatural Power," October 16, 2016.

———. web-c. Accessed April 2, 2017. "Origins of the Gnostic Movement," "The Gnostic Story of Alien Intrusion," "The Archon Files," "The Enigma of the Archons," "How We Are Deviated, Motives and Methods of the Archon." http://www.metahistory.org/ sitemap.php#gnostique.

——— and Lydia Dzumardjin. web-d. Accessed April 3, 3017. "Beyond the Tyranny of Beliefs-The Topic of Topics, Gnostic Parallels in the Writings of Carlos Castaneda." http://www. Metahistory.org.

Layton, Bentley, trans. From *The Nag Hammadi Library*: "The Hypostasis of the Archons: The Reality of the Rulers." Accessed April 2, 2017. http://www.gnosis.org/naghamm/hypostas.html.

Leeming, David. 2002. *Myth, A Biography of Belief*. Oxford University Press.

Lipton, Bruce. 2005. *The Biology of Belief: Unleashing the Power of Consciousness, Matter and Miracles*. Mountain of Love/Elite Books.

Long Chen Pa. Accessed April 2, 2017. http://quotes.justdharma.com/ everything-is-but-an-apparition.

Mack, John. 2000. *Passport to the Cosmos: Human Transformation and Alien Encounters*. Thorsons.

Mahu, James. 1998. *The Ancient Arrow Project*. Ebook. Wingmakers LLC. Accessed April 2, 2017. http://www.wingmakers.com.

———. 2008. Project Camelot Interview. Accessed April 2, 2017. http://www.projectcamelotportal.com.

———. 2009. Conscious Media Interview. Accessed April 2, 2017. http://www.wingmakers.com.

Marciniak, Barbara. 1994. *Earth: The Pleiadian Keys to the Living Library*. Bear & Company.

Materialism. Accessed April 1, 2017. http://www.dictionary.com/ browse/materialism?s=t.

Matrix. Accessed April 1, 2017. http://www.imdb.com/title/ tt0133093/.

Meher Baba. 1973. *God Speaks: The Theme of Creation and Its Purpose*. Second edition. Sufism Reoriented.

———. 1995. *Discourses by Meher Baba*. Ahmednagar: Avatar Meher Baba Perpetual Public Charitable Trust. Third Printing.

Meredith, Susan and Clare Hickman. 2010. *The Usborne Encyclopedia of World Religions*. Facts on File Publications.

Millay, Jean, ed. (2010). *Radiant Minds* (update of *Silver Threads* 1993: Targ, Radin, et. al.). Millay.

Morning Sky, Robert (1996). *The Terra Papers – Hidden History of Planet Earth*. Accessed April 1, 2017. http://www.rdgable.files.wordpress.com/2011/09/the_terra_papers_ parts_1_and_2.pdf.

Mouravieff, Boris. 2014. *Gnosis*, Vol 1. Accessed April 2, 2017. http://issu.com/deconstructingconsciousness/ docs/gnosis_book_1.

Mummy. Accessed April 1, 2017. http://www.disclose.tv/news/Extra-terrestrial_Mummy_Found_in_Egypt/86067.

Mutwa, Credo. 2003. *Zulu Shaman: Dreams, Prophesies and Mysteries. Songs of the Stars*. Destiny Books.

Nag Hammadi Library. Accessed April 2, 2017. http://www.bibliotecapleyades.net/nag_hammadi/contents.htm.

Nanamoli, Bhikku. "The Life of Buddha." *American Buddhist Journal*. Accessed April 2, 2017. http://www.About.com Buddhism.

Narby, Jeremy. 1998. *The Cosmic Serpent: DNA and the Origins of Knowledge*. London: Victor Gollancz.

National Geographic. "Origins of the Universe." Accessed April 1, 2017. http://www.nationalgeographic.com/ science/space/universe/origins-of-the-universe.

Neruda, Dr. Jamisson. 1998. The Fifth Interview. pdf. Accessed April 2, 2017. http://www.wingmakers.com.

Newberg, Andrew, and d'Aquili, Eugene. 1999. *The Mystical Mind: Probing the Biology of Religious Experience*. Fortress Press.

O'Brien, Christian. 1999. *The Genius of the Few*. Dianthus Publishing.

Oral Law—Talmud & Mishna, The. Accessed April 1, 2017. http://www.JewishVirtualLibrary.org. Accessed April 2, 2017.

PANDAS. Accessed April 1, 2017. http://www.pandasnetwork.org/understanding-pandaspans/what-is-pandas/.

Parks, Anton. 2007. *Adam Genesis*. Novelle Terre.

————. 2013a. *The Secret of the Dark Stars.* Pahana Books.

————. 2013b. *Eden: The Truth about Our Origins.* Pahana Books.

————. web-a. Accessed April 1, 2017. http://www.antonparks.com/ AntonParks_First_interview.pdf.

————. web-b. Accessed April 1, 2017. http://www.antonparks.com/ main.php?lang=en&page=eden#.

————. web-c. Accessed April 1, 2017. http://www.karmopolis.be/ pipeline/ anton_parks.htm.

————. web-d. Accessed April 1, 2017. http://www.karmapolis.be/ pipeline/anton_parks2_2.htm.

————. web-e. Accessed April 1, 2017. http://www.Open Seti.org.

Patanjali. 2003. *The Yoga Sutras of Patanjali:* A New Translation with Commentary by Chip Hartranft. Shambhala Publications Inc.

Pattanaik, Devdutt. 2003. *Indian Mythology, Tales, Symbols and Rituals form the Heart of the Subcontinent.* Inner Traditions.

Penre, Wes. Accessed April 1, 2017. http://www.wespenre.com/site-index.htm.

Pert, Candace. 1997. *Molecules of Emotion: The Science behind Mind-Body Medicine.* Touchstone.

Philosophy of the Masters. 1967. vols. I–V. First edition. Beas, India: Radha Soami Satsang.

Prabhupada, Swami A. C Bhaktivedanta, trans. 2011. *The Srimad-Bhagavatam* Canto Two, Chapter Ten. First e-book edition. Bhaktivedanta Book Trust.

Project Gutenberg. *The Babylonian Legends of Creation.* Ebook. Accessed April 1, 2017. http://www.gutenberg.org/files/ 9914/9914-h/9914-h.htm. British Museum.

Reimer, Carol A. 2013. *Sophia and the Archons.* Rosebud Publications.

Rhinehart, Luke. 1976. *The Book of est.* Holt, Rinehart and Winston of Canada, Limited.

Roberts, Jane. 1982. *The Nature of Personal Reality.* Bantam Books.

Robinson, R. H. and W. L. Johnson. 1997. *The Buddhist Religion: A Historical Introduction.* Wadsworth Publishing Co.

Rosenberg, David. 2006. *Abraham: The First Historical Biography.* Basic Books.

Rudhyar, Dane. 1975. *The Sun is Also a Star.* Dutton.

Rumi, Jalaluddin. web-a. Accessed April 1, 2017. http://www.go-odreads.com/author/quotes/875661.Rumi.

———. web-b. Accessed April 1, 2017. http://www.higherexistence.com.

Sadakata, Akira and Hajime Nakamura. 1997. *Buddhist Cosmology Philosophy and Origins*. Kosei Publishing Co.

Sagan, Carl. 1986. *The Dragons of Eden: Speculations on the Evolution of Human Intelligence*. Ballantine Books, reprint.

Sar Bachan. 1955. *The Teachings of Soamiji Maharaj*. Beas, India: Radha Soami Satsang.

Scranton, Laird. 2010. *The Cosmological Origins of Myth and Symbol: From the Dogon and Ancient Egypt to India, Tibet and China*. Inner Traditions.

Seifer, Marc, PhD. 2008. *Transcending the Speed of Light: Consciousness, Quantum Physics, and the Fifth Dimension*. Inner Traditions.

Shankara, Adi. 1970. *The Crest Jewel of Discrimination*. Reprint. Mumbai: Bharatiya Vidya Bhavan.

Shepherd, Arthur P. 1990. *Rudolf Steiner: Scientist of the Invisible*. Reprint. Inner Traditions.

Singh, Maharaj Jagat. 2002. *The Science of the Soul, Discourses of the Masters*. Beas, India: Rhada Soami Satsang.

Singh, Maharaj Sawan. 1963. *Discourses on Sant Mat*. Beas, India: Radha Soami Satsang.

Singh, Sant Baljit. 2014. *Know Thyself as Soul: India Report*. Florida: Edition Naam.

———. 2016. *Know Thyself as Soul:* Magazine. Issue 3. Florida: Edition Naam.

Singh, Sant Kirpal. 1967. *Godman*. Delhi: Ruhani Satsang.

———. 1976. *The Teachings of Kirpal Singh*. vols. 1–3. Manchester, NH: Sant Bani Press.

———. 1988. *Spiritual Elixir*. Second edition. Ruhani Satsang Books.

Singh, Sant Thakar. 2005. *The Secret of Life*. Florida: Edition Naam.

Sitchin, Zecharia. 1990. *Genesis Revisited*. Avon Books.

———. 1998. *The Cosmic Code: Book VI of the Earth Chronicles*. Harper Collins.

———. 2001. *The Lost Book of Enki: Memoirs and Prophecies of an Extraterrestrial God*. Bear & Co.

Smith, George. Accessed April 2, 2017. https://en.wikipedia.org/wiki/George_Smith_(Assyriologist.

Steiner, Rudolf. 1959. *Cosmic Memory: A Prehistory of Earth and Man.* Rudolf Steiner Publications, Inc.

———. 1994. *How to Know Higher Worlds: A Modern Path of Initiation.* Anthroposphic Press: Classics in Anthroposophy. Accessed April 1, 2017. http://www.books.google.com.

———. 2008. *An Esoteric Cosmology; Evolution, Christ and Modern Spirituality.* Steiner Books.

———. 2015. *Outline* of *Occult Science.* Reprint: out-of-print English edition of the Gunn translation. CreateSpace Independent Publishing.

———. web-a. Accessed April 1, 2017. http://goodreads.com/author/quote/2593.Rudolph_Steiner?page:2.

———. web-b. Accessed April 1, 2017. "Three Streams in the Evolution of Mankind." Lecture Series 184. 1918. http://wn.rsarchive.org/lectures/GA184/English/RSP1965/ThrStr_index.html.

———. web-c. Accessed April 1, 2017. https://rudolfsteinerquotes.wordpress.com/ 2015/09/30/man-ideal-of-the-gods/.

———. web-d. Accessed April 2, 2017. http://www.en.wikiquote.org.

Stephany, Timothy J. 2013. *Enuma Elish: The Babylonian Creation Epic.* Create Space Independent Publishing.

Straussman, Rick, MD. 2001. *DMT: The Spirit Molecule: A Doctor's Revolutionary Research into The Biology of Near-Death and Mystical Experiences.* Park Street Press.

Subramuniyaswami, Satguru Sivaya (1993). *Dancing with Siva: Hinduism's Contemporary Catechism.* Fourth edition. India/USA: Himalayan Academy.

Swetlishoff, Marlene. Accessed August 14, 2013. http://www.therainbowscribe.com.

Talbot, Michael. 1991. *The Holographic Universe.* Harper Collins Publishers.

Talbott, David, and Wallace Thornhill. 2005. *Thunderbolts of the Gods.* Mikamar Publishing.

Tellinger, Michael. 2012. *Slave Species of the Gods: The Secret History of the Anunnaki and Their Mission on Earth.* Bear & Co.

Tesla, Nikola. Accessed March 31, 2015. http://www.themindunleashed.com.

Thompson, Richard L. 2003. *Maya: The World as Virtual Reality*. Institute for Vaishnava Studies.

Thunderbolts. Accessed April 1, 2017. http://www.thunderboltsproject.com.

Toroidal. Accessed April 2, 2017. http://www.cosmometry.net/the-torus-dynamic-flow-process.

Vallee, Jacques. 1969. *On UFO's, Folklore and Parallel Worlds*. Contemporary Books.

————. 1979. *Messengers of Deception: UFO Contacts and Cults*. Ronin Publishing.

———— and Chris Aubeck. 2010. *Wonders in the Sky: Unexplained Arial Objects from Antiquity to Modern Times*. TarcherPerigee.

Vonnegut, Kurt. 1998. *Cat's Cradle*. Dell Publishing.

Walshe, Maurice, ed., trans. 1987. *The Long Discourses of the Buddha*. Introduction. Wisdom Publications.

Walton, Travis. 1997. *Fire in the Sky: the Walton Experience*. Da Capo Press.

Weiner, Eric. 2008. *The Geography of Bliss*. Twelve Hachette Book Group.

Wikipedia contributors. "Abrahamic Religions." Accessed April 1, 2017. http://www.en.wikipedia.org/wiki/ Abrahamic_religions.

————. "Ancient Hebrew." Accessed April 1, 2017. http://www.en.wikipedia.org/wiki/Ancient_Hebrew_ writings.

————. "Bible Version Debate." Accessed April 1, 2017. http:// en.wikipedia.org/wiki/ Bible_version_debate.

————. "Biblical Canon." Accessed April 1, 2017. http://www.en.wikipedia.org/wiki/Biblical_canon.

————. "Biblical Cosmology." Accessed April 1, 2017. http://www./ en.wikipedia.org/wiki/Biblical_ cosmology.

————. "Genesis Creation Narrative." Accessed April 1, 2017. http:// www.en.wikipedia.org/wiki/Genesis creation narrative.

————. "Hinduism." Accessed April 2, 2017. http://www.simple.wikipedia.org/wiki/Hinduism.

————. "Islamic Mythology." Accessed April 1, 2017. http://www.en.wikipedia.org/wiki/Islamic_mythology.

————. "Me. mythology." Accessed April 2, 2017. http://www. en.wikipedia.org/wiki/ Me_(mythology.

————. Pali: "The Tripitaka or Pali Canon," the First Buddhist Scripture and Early Buddhist History; The First Five Centuries. Accessed April 2, 2017. http://www.en.wikipedia.org/wiki/ P%C4%81li_Canon.

————. "Panspermia." Accessed August 5, 2017. http://en.wikipedia. org/wiki/Panspermia.

————. "Sirius." Accessed April 2, 2017. https://en.wikipedia.org/ wiki/Sirius.

————. "Talmud." Accessed April 1, 2017. http://www.en.wikipedia. org/wiki/Talmud.

————. "Ten Commandments." Accessed April 1, 2017.www.jewfaq. org/10.htm. Older Hebrew version of the Ten Things versus King James version of the Ten Commandments.

————. "Theosophy." Accessed April 2, 2017. https://en.wikipedia. org/ wiki/Theosophy.

————. "Zen." Accessed April 2, 2017.http://www.en.wikipedia.org/ wiki/Zen.

Wilber, Ken. 2000. *Integral Psychology*. Boston: Shambhala Publications, Inc.

Wilcock, David. 2011. *The Source Field Investigations*. The Penguin Group.

Wingmakers. web-a. Accessed April 2, 2017. http://www.wingmakers. com.

————. web-b. Accessed April 2, 2017. http://www.lyricus.org.

————. web-c. Accessed April 2, 2017. http://www.eventtemples.org.

————. web-d. Accessed April 2, 2017. http://www.spiritstate.com.

————. web-e. Accessed April 2, 2017. http://www.sovereignintegrl. blogspot.com.

Woebcke, Carl. Accessed April 2, 2017. *Illustrated Astrology Textbook*. http://www.myastrologybook.com/galactic-center-great-central-sun.htm.

Yogananda, Paramahansa. 2003. *Autobiography of a Yogi*. Self-Realization Fellowship.

Yukteswar, Swami Sri. 1984. *The Holy Science*. Los Angeles: Self-Realization Fellowship.

About the Author

Domonic Kay earned a Master's Degree in counseling psychology and worked as a licensed psychotherapist in various clinical and administrative positions for twenty-six years. Trained in a number of energy therapy skills, she achieved quality results treating complex trauma, her clinical specialty.

She's been a lifelong student of cosmology and esoteric spiritual teachings. Her meeting with a Living Master in 1984 initiated a deep exploration into the truth about the human predicament. In 2008 Domonic began extensive research in preparation for authoring this book. After retiring in 2010, she devoted full time to the book's completion and published *This Embodied Life* in 2018. Her book implores readers to question everything we've been taught about reality and challenges readers by offering up a cornucopia of ideas and theories regarding humanity's true origins. *This Embodied Life* exposes the hidden underpinnings of this tangled web of deceit and reveals how the world's religions have been complicit in hiding this truth.

Domonic has many hobbies but takes special delight in teaching Soul Collaging workshops. She currently resides in Northern Arizona and enjoys the beautiful high vistas and sacred red rocks of Sedona, Arizona.

Made in the USA
Middletown, DE
04 December 2018